I pray that you may have the power to comprehend, with all the saints, what is the breadth and length and height and depth, and to know the love of Christ that surpasses knowledge, so that you may be filled with all the fullness of God.

EPHESIANS 3:18-19

The Power to Comprehend with All the Saints

THE FORMATION AND PRACTICE OF A PASTOR-THEOLOGIAN

Edited by

Wallace M. Alston Jr. & Cynthia A. Jarvis

William B. Eerdmans Publishing Company
Grand Rapids, Michigan / Cambridge, U.K.

Published 2009 by
Wm. B. Eerdmans Publishing Co.
2140 Oak Industrial Drive N.E., Grand Rapids, Michigan 49505 /
P.O. Box 163, Cambridge CB3 9PU U.K.

Printed in the United States of America

15 14 13 12 11 10 09 7 6 5 4 3 2 1

Library of Congress Cataloging-in-Publication Data

The power to comprehend with all the saints: the formation and practice of a pastor-theologian / edited by Wallace M. Alston Jr. & Cynthia A. Jarvis.
p. cm.
Includes bibliographical references.
ISBN 978-0-8028-6472-7 (pbk.: alk. paper)
1. Pastoral theology. I. Alston, Wallace M., 1934- II. Jarvis, Cynthia A.

BV4017.P65 2009
253 — dc22

2009023112

www.eerdmans.com

To

Craig Dykstra

and

Christopher Coble

and

the Lilly Endowment, Inc.

Contents

Preface

The prayer of the apostle writing to the Christian community in Ephesus was that its members "would have the power to comprehend with all the saints what is the breadth and length and height and depth and to know the love of Christ that passes knowledge." The essays in this volume were written by pastors of churches, a few of whom have moved to other forms of ministry since writing their essays, but all of whom consider themselves to be pastors in current service. Unlike other discussions of the nature and purpose of the ministry, this volume is concerned to bring the pastoral voice into conversation with both the academy and the church in an effort to gain a comprehensive perspective on how a theologically substantive ministry comes into being and what difference a theological orientation to the vocation makes in pastoral practice.

The contributors also are pastors who participated in the Pastor-Theologian Program of the Center of Theological Inquiry in Princeton, New Jersey. The Pastor-Theologian Program, funded in large part by the Lilly Endowment, Inc. from 1996 to 2005, sought to define the ordained ministry as a theological vocation, and theology as the servant of the church. The presupposition underlying the Pastor-Theologian Program was that the crisis faced by the contemporary American church is neither organizational nor programmatic but theological in nature. The crisis *of* the church is simply the public face of the crisis *in* the church, which is essentially a crisis of faith.

Grants from various foundations have supported studies by social scientists of the phenomenology of this crisis. These studies have been useful and suggestive as to the dimensions and proportions of the problem, but they have seldom touched the heart of the matter. The heart of the matter is the loss of the church's identity as a theological community, occasioned by the distance at which the church often lives from the source and sources of its faith and life.

The church is often assisted but never renewed by management skills, goal-setting processes, and strategic planning. The renewal of the church is not a human contrivance. It is accomplished by the power of the Holy Spirit and thus is perceived by the faithful as a gift of God. If history is any indication, the gift of renewal is most frequently given and experienced when the church places itself within the realm of possibility, namely, in the context of those means of grace by which the Spirit is known to work. The means of grace that historically have been the vehicles of renewal are the Bible, worship, theology, fellowship, witness, and service. Thus the church faithfully waits for the gift of renewal when it brings its mind as well as its heart to the tasks of preaching, teaching, pastoral care, church administration, and public witness.

The Separation of Theology and Church

A significant part of the current crisis in the church is the hiatus between mind and heart, between academic theology as an intellectual discipline and ecclesial theology as a confessional stance. The achievement of a high level of competence in the exposition, explication, and application of the Christian tradition requires the discipline of rational analysis, including the mastery of languages, texts, ideas, cultures, and extensive bibliographies. It also requires the maintenance of a certain critical distance from the subject of its inquiry in order to distinguish the more from the less true. The bridging of the gap between the academic study of theology and the confessional theology of the church, between the critical distance that rational analysis requires and the profound commitment that Christian witness implies, is not easy and is accomplished only with great skill. It is with this skill, its origin and deployment, that these essays are concerned.

Furthermore, there is a tendency on the part of many theological seminaries, especially those that live in the shadow of secular graduate education, to become institutions for the advanced study of religion. Seminary faculties are increasingly educated in graduate schools of secular universities and are often called to teaching positions without the basic theological degree (M.Div.) or any disciplined study of the theological tradition in which they are to teach. Seminary teachers frequently write not for the church, but for other professionals in the guild. The primary purpose of the theological seminary, particularly of a denominational seminary, which should be to prepare people to be theologians for the church, is undercut by the hegemony of the guild, the priority of which is understandably not that of maintaining the identity of the Christian church.

As a consequence of these circumstances, there has been a sharp decline in the ministry in congregations of the pastor-theologian. The movement from seminary faculty to the ministry of a congregation, and conversely from congregation to classroom, has all but ceased. Pastor-scholars are rarely included on seminary faculties. This brand of professionalism has resulted in that which once was not the case, namely, a profound separation in the life of the church between serious theological work and congregational life. This separation also gives focus to the essays that follow.

The Trivialization of the Church

One of the legacies of the Lutheran and Reformed traditions is the subordination of questions of polity and program to convictions concerning the essence of the church. Continental Protestantism, contrary to popular opinion, began not with the question, "How can I find the gracious God?" or "What is the meaning of my life?" but with questions concerning the nature of the church, such as "What is the essence of the true church?" and "What are the marks by which it may be recognized?" Questions about polity and confessional boundaries were secondary to the conviction that the church is the people of God, constituted by the Word of God. Other ecclesiologies approach the essence of the church in other ways, e.g., the Roman Catholic, Anglican, and representatives of the Anabaptist tradition. But in one way or another, each would confess that the church, unique among all other social constructs, is a profoundly theological reality.

The Protestant Reformers also had a clear understanding of the ordained minister as theologian for the church. None would have suggested that the ordained ministry is essential to the church, only the Word of God heard in faith and obeyed in love. But they knew that the minister fulfilled an indispensable function for the well-being of the church. The task of the minister was understood to be the theological task of the exposition, explication, and application of the Word of God in preaching, teaching, pastoral care, and church administration. The expectation was that, through such service, God would renew the church and transform society. Other ecclesiologies would confess that the ordained ministry is essential to the existence of the church. But again, all would agree that the minister's task is not primarily organizational or institutional, but theological in nature.

A striking fact about the church in our time is that where ministers pursue their calling as church theologians the church lives . . . and where they do not, the church tends to be trivialized and languishes. One might well document the fact that the crisis in the church parallels the loss of theological identity by the church and the shift in its understanding of the minister from that of theologian to that of chief executive officer. Hence the recovery of a substantive doctrine of the ordained ministry as a theological vocation, as well as a strategy for the formation and support of the pastor as theologian, are crucial for the revitalization of contemporary Christian communities.

We hope that these essays will be instructive and provocative for men and women considering and preparing for the Christian ministry, as well as for pastors in current service whose ministry is an enacted prayer for the power to comprehend with all the saints.

WALLACE M. ALSTON JR.
and
CYNTHIA A. JARVIS

The Formation of a Pastor-Theologian

The Genesis of Theological Existence

Wallace M. Alston Jr.

A discussion of the genesis of theological existence is always in danger of giving credit where credit is not due unless it speaks the last word first. The last word, when all is said and done, is that the genesis of theological existence is beyond our human capacities adequately to analyze or fully to document. To be sure, there are influential factors that play their own particular part in the formation of theological consciousness, and the contributors to this volume have sought to explore many of them from the vantage point of their own experience. But even if they should amount to more in importance than the sum of their parts, they remain inadequate to explain how and why theology engages certain people, claims them, and extends to them an irresistible invitation to lifelong commitment. Thus the last word that must now be spoken first is that theological existence is inexplicable apart from the initiative of the living God. Theological existence is a gift of God. God alone makes a pastor a theologian.

Christian existence, of course, is theological existence in its most general sense. What we are talking about here is not a quality of life reserved for ministers. God invites all people to live a theological existence, to love God with the whole heart, mind, and soul, and the neighbor as the self. All people are beckoned, though never bludgeoned, to view all of life . . . personal, social, economic, political, and ecclesial . . . in the light of Jesus Christ, and to live accordingly. The difference that being Christian makes is that the Christian has been given a point of view, a theological perspective on life in this world, that frees one to reflect on a multiplicity of circumstances, favorable and unfavorable, from the standpoint of the promises of God, and empowers one to live without loss of balance or poise in the face of whatever life has in store.

The invitation to theological existence issued to all people, however, encounters some with enormous energy and urgency. God enters into their innermost souls, minds, hearts, and wills, lays upon them an irresistible claim, and hovers over their decisions and actions until the day they die. These whom God so calls and claims are not better than anyone else, not smarter or wiser or closer to God. In fact, being acutely aware of what they ought to be by virtue of this call and claim, many of these people know better than most how far short they fall and how great is the hypocrisy that even their best intentions and accomplishments betray. Nevertheless, to them this invitation to theological existence is extended to a lifelong commitment to the church and its ministry, and by them it is perceived to be a summons so compelling as to be irresistible, so attractive as to be delightful.

Karl Barth described "the existentials of evangelical theology" in terms of a movement or process of development, the elements of which are wonder, concern, commitment, and faith.[1] Although Barth's typology is not identical to my own, I am indebted to his discussion for my own construction of how God awakens a person to theological existence. How does theological existence come to be? How is it that God makes a pastor a theologian? It would be impossible for me to pursue an answer to that question without reference to my own experience. On the basis of my experience, I venture to suggest that the formation of a theological existence involves six elements or occasions: an awareness of mystery, the acknowledgment of claim, a summons to understand, the freedom to commit, the experience of delight, and the desire to confess.[2]

An Awareness of Mystery

Human life is encompassed by mystery. No aspect of human life can account for itself, even after all causes and consequences have been assessed. "All

1. Karl Barth, *Evangelical Theology* (Grand Rapids: Eerdmans, 1963), pp. 63-105.

2. Other formative occasions are suggested in essays by Anita Warner and Robert Ballance in this volume.

known existence points beyond itself."[3] Reason cannot dispel the mystery. No cause is ever a complete or adequate explanation of an event. Events do have a history, to be sure, but a perceived cause can be only one of a myriad of possibilities that might have been actualized. Linear living, therefore, is infused by mystery.

The understanding of ourselves is even more elusive. The self is a creature of nature, subject to its limits and laws, but the self is nevertheless able to transcend itself and perceive an address from beyond itself in terms of a "Must," a "May," and an "Ought." Furthermore, the moral constitution of human being is fraught with mystery. The existence of evil in us is almost as enigmatic as the desire to do good. "So I find it to be a law that when I want to do good, evil lies close at hand" (Rom. 7:21).

Finally, the mystery we have met in life overcomes us in death. The mystery that awaits us beyond death is but the antiphonal response to the mystery that anticipated our birth. Why were we born? For what purpose are we in life? What is beyond the limits of birth and death? "Deep calls unto deep," said the psalmist, "at the thunder of thy cataracts" (Ps. 42:7, KJV).

The awareness of mystery is the harbinger of the presence of the triune God, the initial onset of God, Father, Son, and Holy Spirit, into the consciousness of the creature. This awareness often occurs to us in the early years. It meets us as the apperception of presence beyond all natural knowing, of belonging beyond all earthly kinship, of "something out there" or "in here" to which we are accountable. "All my own earliest memories have in them such an element of encounter," said John Baillie. "I cannot remember a time when my life seemed to be my own to do with as I pleased. From the very beginning its centre was not itself or in me, but outside itself and me. I was, of course, in the first instance, under the authority of the elder members of the household. . . . Yet my earliest memories clearly contain the knowledge that these elders did but transmit and administer an authority of which they were not themselves the ultimate source."[4]

Likewise, I cannot recall a time when I first became aware of mystery. I do recall that, even as a young child, I had an undefined sense of living "in the presence of." Perhaps it appeared to me first in a vague sense of expectation. I think I knew in my earliest years that my life was not my own, that my

3. Reinhold Niebuhr, *Discerning the Signs of the Times* (New York: Charles Scribner's Sons, 1946), p. 154.

4. John Baillie, *Invitation to Pilgrimage* (Oxford: Oxford University Press, 1942), p. 45.

life had been given me, and that I was responsible for what I did with it. Perhaps I knew it first in the experience of vulnerability and incapacity. I recall early on the feeling of not being up to it, of being fragile, ill-equipped, and prone to failure. Perhaps it was the paradox of chronic homesickness which I experienced both in and away from home, coupled with the compelling desire to rebel against everything about my home except the love I knew was there. The awareness of mystery was particularly acute when first I came face to face with death, the death of my grandparents and that of my cousin, Bobby, who was my childhood soulmate. My version of the ancient question, "Why is there something and not nothing?" took the form of asking why I was, what it meant that Bobby was not and I was, and what it might feel like not to be. As I recall, it was when I tried to think my own death and found it impossible to do that I said my first unscripted prayer.[5]

But mystery is not child's play, nor can an awareness of mystery simply be explained by one's upbringing. There is no doubting the fact that my awareness of mystery came to me from my parents. With Baillie, I always understood them to be under the same constraint that they were intent upon transmitting to me.[6] Furthermore, I did not doubt that, if I traced the generations back to their beginning, the constraint would be there as well. Had I grown up in another kind of home, with parents whose religious orientation was quite different, my memories would certainly be very different. I might have been the child of another religion or of no religion at all. Yet I believe that even these very different memories would bear some genealogical resemblance to the experiences I have described. I have difficulty in conceiving of any form of human existence that is not in some way or other, at one time or another, awakened to an awareness of mystery.

However that may be, there is no theological existence apart from an awareness of mystery. The loss of a sense of mystery in the life of the church is largely responsible for the marginalization of the church in contemporary life. Nothing is more tragic than the pastor whose awareness of mystery has been dulled by routine or lost over time. The awareness of mystery is that which holds the door of pastoral practice open for miracle and leaves the

5. Robert W. Jenson, *On Thinking the Human* (Grand Rapids: Eerdmans, 2003), pp. 14-15. "To think your own death, celebrate the Vigil of Easter. Or of course its archetype, Passover. Or say Kaddish, which notably laments the dead only by way of praise of God. . . . I do not believe death can be thought, in the first person, or any other way than as Christian theology, or indeed as Christian liturgy and devotion" (p. 15).

6. Baillie, *Invitation,* p. 46.

pastor astonished in its presence. This astonishment, according to Barth, "stands at the beginning of every theological perception, inquiry, and thought, in fact at the root of every theological word."[7]

The Christian faith resolves the mystery of life by the mystery of God. The Christian faith is trust in the trustworthiness of God as revealed in Jesus Christ. "It believes that God has made Himself known. It believes that He has spoken through the prophets and finally in His Son. It accepts the revelation in Christ as the ultimate clue to the mystery of the relation of God's nature and purpose in the world, particularly the mystery of His justice to His mercy. But these clues to the mystery do not eliminate the periphery of mystery. God remains 'deus absconditus.'"[8] Mystery is thus the gracious guise of the presence of the triune God.

The Acknowledgment of Claim

Mystery is both personal and persistent. Like a great lover that will not be denied, it will not leave us alone. It hangs around, so to speak, brooding over our existence as yet uncreated and unordered by the Word, eliciting from us a response. It may be rejected, repressed, or postponed for a time, but it will not finally be denied. It leaves one restless and unsatisfied until it is joined in struggle or conversation. The great mystics have taught us to admire the mystery of God, and that is a necessary corrective to our rigid rationalisms.

Anselm of Canterbury was well aware of the beauty of God and of the sensuality of theology. "O God of truth," he prayed, "I ask that I may receive, that my 'joy may be full.' Meanwhile, let my heart meditate upon it, let my tongue speak of it. Let my heart love it, let my tongue discourse upon it. Let my soul hunger for it, let my flesh thirst for it, let my whole substance desire it, until I enter 'into the joy' of my 'Lord,' who is the triune and one God,

7. Barth, *Evangelical Theology*, p. 64.

8. Niebuhr, *Discerning the Signs*, pp. 154-55. "The rites of the Church frequently excel the more rationalized forms of the Protestant faith by their poetic expression of mystery. There is, for instance, an advantage in chanting rather than saying a creed. The musical and poetic forms of the creed emphasize the salient affirmation of faith which the creed contains, and slightly derogate the exact details of symbolism through which the basic affirmation is expressed. That is the virtue of the liturgical and sacramental Church, which is hardened into a pitiless fundamentalism when every 'i' is dotted and every 't' crossed in the soberly recited credo" (p. 157).

'blessed forever. Amen.'"[9] But theological reflection on the identity and character of mystery cannot end in fascination, admiration, or desire. If mystery is in fact the onset of the triune God in human experience, it confronts, grasps, and engages a person and lays upon that person its claim. Theological existence begins to take human shape and form with the acknowledgment of this claim. To be a theologian is to be drawn into the content of theology by the one with whom theology has to do. To be a theologian is to experience the claim: "Tua res agitur," this matter concerns you![10]

The one who acknowledges this claim is immediately subject to question. Karl Barth tells of the once famous Professor Tholuck of Halle, who would visit the rooms of his students and ask, "Brother, how are things in your heart?" How are things with you, "not with your ears, not with your head, not with your forensic ability, not with your industriousness," but with your heart?[11] When God lays claim to a person, the claim is often perceived in terms of the evangelical question about the state of one's soul. How goes it with your soul? How does your faith fare? Are you really where you ought to be, doing what you ought to be doing, or are you trying to evade this one who has drawn near to you with a claim upon your life? The question put to every theologian, pastor or teacher, young or old, over and over again by the one of whom theology speaks is, "How are things in your heart?"

To be a Christian theologian, however, involves still more than personal claim. It involves a shared existence in a community of faith and practice. A theological existence, which begins with an awareness of mystery, acquires its specifically Christian identity in a eucharistic community created by the Word of God. Cyprian, in the third century, must have been thinking of the genesis of theological existence when he said of the church, "of her womb we are born, by her milk we are nourished, by her breath we are quickened."[12] John Calvin, in the sixteenth century, was thinking similar thoughts when he identified "the external means or aids by which God invites us into the society of Christ and holds us therein"[13] with the church,

9. "An Address (Proslogion)," *The Library of Christian Classics (LCC),* vol. 10 (Philadelphia: Westminster Press, 1956), p. 93.

10. Barth, *Evangelical Theology,* p. 76.

11. Barth, *Evangelical Theology,* p. 83.

12. Cyprian, "The Unity of the Catholic Church," *LCC,* vol. 5 (Philadelphia: Westminster Press, 1960), p. 127.

13. John Calvin, *Institutes of the Christian Religion,* Book IV (Philadelphia: Westminster Press, 1960), p. 1011.

"into whose bosom God is pleased to gather his sons, not only that they may be nourished by her help and ministry as long as they are infants and children, but also that they may be guided by her motherly care until they mature and at last reach the goal of faith."[14]

The Summons to Understand

Anselm is best known for his classic statement of the dialectic between faith and reason. His attitude toward the relation of faith and reason is indicated by the title of his major work on the subject, "Proslogion — Faith in Search of Understanding."[15] Anselm, who is sometimes accused of conceding more than he ought to reason, goes to great lengths to identify himself as a theologian by refusing to subject the assurance of faith to the judgment of reason. Anselm's search for understanding has to do with the content of faith, not the other way around. His point is that faith in the God of revelation cannot rest in itself, but must seek to understand itself through the work of reason. "I am not trying, O Lord, to penetrate thy loftiness, for I cannot begin to match my understanding with it, but I desire in some measure to understand thy truth, which my heart believes and loves. For I do not seek to understand in order to believe, but I believe in order to understand."[16]

For Anselm, I suppose, and for me to be sure, faith's search for understanding is no casual affair. It is something that faith must do if it is to be obedient to God. It has about it the character of a command. Theological existence involves a summons to knowledge because one senses that he is known, to "re-search" because one finds himself searched, to thinking and reflection because she becomes aware that someone is thinking of her, to speech because she hears someone speaking to her long before she can utter a coherent sentence in reply.[17]

Why is that so? How are we to understand the compelling summons of theological existence to understand? One explanation has to do with the nature of God. It follows from the conviction that God is Truth, the origin and source of all truth, upon whom all partial truths are dependent, and to

14. Calvin, *Institutes,* p. 1012.
15. *LCC,* vol. 10, pp. 69-93.
16. "Proslogion," *LCC,* vol. 10, p. 73.
17. Barth, *Evangelical Theology,* p. 76.

whom all truths finally lead. This means that if God is to be known and served, God must be known and served with the life of the mind as well as with the heart and the will. A faith that fails to claim the mind for the service of God is dangerous and unreliable. The service of God through the life of the mind is indispensable to any other form of service that may be rendered to God.

A second explanation has to do with the nature of human being as intelligent being. Human being is thinking being. The Creator has equipped the human creature with the capacity to objectify and transcend reality, including time, space, the natural world, and the self, and to reflect on the possibilities inherent in real time and space for significance and purpose, pleasure and pain. The mere fact that a human being is "intelligens" means that the Christian of all people is summoned to discern what is conceivable by humankind about God and to articulate it with reasonable clarity. Contemporary men and women who are not only highly intelligent and well educated but who make use of their intellectual capacities in daily life are unlikely to commit themselves to a faith that they do not understand.

Third, there is the intriguing, exhilarating, even sensuous character of the subject itself, which flirts with our minds until we are overwhelmed with wonder, love, and praise. "How precious to me are thy thoughts, O God! How vast is the sum of them!" exclaimed the psalmist (Ps. 139:17). There is something utterly captivating about the Word of God that moves in on our existence at such depths that we are effectually called,[18] as it were, to greater intimacy through a deeper understanding of the one who speaks.

Finally, the summons to understand receives its sense of urgency from the historical context of the recipient of a theological existence. Each particular moment in history has its own distinctive possibilities and problems. Questions arise on the boundaries between the known with which we are comfortable and the unknown of which we are afraid. They move in on our existence in these boundary situations where the known lacks the power to assure us that everything will be all right. They catch us off guard when our foundations are shaken by such things as sickness, death, tragedy, guilt, suffering, and war. Faith is summoned to understanding "both be-

18. "The Westminster Confession of Faith," Chapter XII, *The Book of Confessions*, Presbyterian Church (U.S.A.). The particular phrase I have in mind is "and effectually drawing them to Jesus Christ; yet so as they come most freely, being made willing by his grace."

cause God is always greater than our ideas of God, and because the public world that faith inhabits confronts it with challenges and contradictions that cannot be ignored."[19]

The Freedom to Commit

Theological existence structures the whole of life when one is free to commit. Commitment is not an act of the will. Commitment is beyond the power of the will to effect. One must be set free from a myriad of constraints, inhibitions, and apprehensions if one is to commit oneself to another. The freedom to commit must be given by the one to whom commitment is proffered. It has been said that there is no greater joy than that of freely doing the will of one who loves you. To be free is to do what is expected of us, but more, it is freely to choose what one has been chosen to do. The theologian is one who knows that he or she has been chosen and thereby set free for a particular kind of perception, inquiry, thought, and speech, not for the sake of self, but for the sake of others. Theological existence thus invites one to move beyond the awareness of mystery, the search for understanding, and the acquisition of knowledge, yet without leaving any of the three behind, to a level of commitment best described as "the conviction of things not seen" (Heb. 11:1).

Conviction is related to belief, but the two are not identical. The Greek word which is regularly translated "conviction," is actually closer to the English word "proof," which in this context connotes something that is certain to be true. The familiar verse from Hebrews, therefore, amounts to a definition of what faith does, not of what faith is. What faith does is to give to things future, which as yet are only hoped for, the reality of present existence. It irresistibly convinces us of the realty of things unseen by bringing us personally and contemporaneously into their presence.

Conviction, in one sense, is a human act whereby one responds in faith to the onset of God with the words, "I believe." It is the decision of one who has been brought personally and contemporaneously into the eschatological reality of God's presence and governance to orient and to direct one's life to these things as yet unseen, and to treat them as present fact. On the other

19. Daniel L. Migliore, *Faith Seeking Understanding* (Grand Rapids: Eerdmans, 1991), p. 3.

hand, the movement of a person from an awareness of mystery to conviction has never been viewed merely as a human act. Rather it has always been the testimony of the community of faith that the experience of conviction is testimony to the presence and activity of the Holy Spirit in a person's life — that conviction is not the product of the will, but the gift of the Spirit.

However that may be, there is no theological existence without conviction. Apart from conviction theology is little more than idle speculation. Theology, like other intellectual disciplines, has to do with the question of truth. But unlike other disciplines, one of the means by which theology pursues the question of truth is conviction. Conviction, in the final analysis, is trust in the trustworthiness of that which has been revealed, but it is not diffused trust in which the personal, moral, and intellectual capacities of a person are excluded. It is trust that has been given the assurance of reality by being drawn contemporaneously into the presence of things unseen.

The Experience of Delight

Conviction is to faith as faith is to delight. Faith is the midwife that delivers conviction into the hands of delight. Faith is the "condition sine qua non" of theological existence, without which no one can become a Christian, much less a Christian theologian. "Faith is the special event that is constitutive for both Christian and theological existence."[20] What happens in the event of faith is that God sets a person free from all constraint, to believe in God's Word and to trust God's promise of love for the world, the people of God, and also the pastor-theologian. In short, faith is "a sober as well as a brave appropriation of a firm and certain promise."[21]

The manner in which one experiences faith varies, of course, but in one form or another faith incites in one the experience of delight. To delight is to take pleasure in the object of one's delight. The psalmist calls the person blessed whose "*delight* is in the law of the Lord" (1:2). In another instance, the psalmist speaks of the pleasure he takes in all testimony to God's will and way on earth. "In the way of thy testimonies I *delight* as much as in all riches. . . . I will *delight* in thy statutes; I will not forget thy word . . . for I find my *delight* in thy commandments, which I love. . . . If thy law had not been

20. Barth, *Evangelical Theology,* p. 100.
21. Barth, *Evangelical Theology,* p. 102.

my *delight*, I should have perished in my affliction" (119:14, 16, 47, 92). Likewise, the Apostle Paul says, "For I *delight* in the law of God, in my inmost self . . ." (Rom. 7:22). The freedom to trust and believe in spite of the odds issues not only in comfort and empowerment, but also in delight.

Theological existence is sheer delight. Theology makes people happy. It is a pleasure to read, write, think, and speak of the things pertaining to God if in doing so we perceive that we are doing what we are expected to do. Theology is fun, more fun even than watching the New York Giants play football, if we perceive it to be our choice to do what we were chosen to do. Theology, according to Karl Barth, is a happy science. "Why are there so many really woeful theologians who go around with faces that are eternally troubled or even embittered, always in a rush to bring forward their critical reservations and negations? . . . A theologian may and should be a pleased or satisfied (person), if not always on the surface then all the same deep within."[22] There is no greater joy or satisfaction that a pastor can know than that of being a pastor-theologian. It is the pastor's delight to be pleased and satisfied to think, read, write, and speak of God to and among a people with whom he or she has been entrusted.

The Desire to Confess

The public confession of faith, whether from the pulpit or the pew, be it in a classroom or by a hospital bed or beside an open grave, is an essential moment in theological existence. When one confesses one speaks out before other people and with other people the thoughts and convictions of one's heart and mind. Confession makes outward what is inward. In confession one takes a stand on the most important questions of life, reveals one's commitments, declares what one believes to be true, identifies one's ultimate loyalty, and defies every contrary claim on one's life. A confession of faith is the seal and courage of theological existence.

In one sense, the confession of faith is an intensely personal expression of theological existence. It is evidence of the maturation of theological apperception from a vague and undefined awareness of mystery to conviction and faith concerning the presence and activity of the triune God "pro me." One is brought to the point of confession, not by one's own volition or

22. Barth, *Evangelical Theology*, p. 94.

agency, but by the inner testimony of the Holy Spirit. One is not motivated to confess by fear, neither fear for the state of one's soul nor the fear of rejection by the world, but by the joy of one who is unashamed to say aloud what is perceived to be true. George A. Buttrick, in an unpublished sermon, once characterized confession as the sharing of a joy.

In another sense, however, Christian confession is a communal occasion whereby one publicly appropriates for oneself the faith-consensus of the community. Martin Luther is said to have told the story of a peasant who was asked by a stranger what he believed. "What the church believes," the man replied. Luther commented that the man could not possibly have been saved. Luther was right in the sense that just as no one can do someone else's dying, so one cannot believe in another's stead. But Luther was wrong if he is understood to suggest that one must begin "de novo" in matters of faith in each new generation. Confession for the Christian is an ecclesial act whereby one identifies with the history of belief often called the "apostolic tradition."

When the church ordains a person to pastoral ministry, the church has every right to know where the person stands in relation to the faith-consensus of the Christian community. The church needs assurance that the person to be ordained is not the purveyor of private opinion or personal religious idiosyncrasies, but that he or she freely identifies with the historic faith of the church. That does not mean that there is no room in confession for honest doubt, serious reservation, or outright rejection of church dogma. In the language of the Reformed tradition, one may "declare scruples," which means that one takes exception, reserves the right to interpret, or rejects a particular point of doctrine that is judged to be "adiaphora." But one whom the church ordains to be a trustee of "the faith once delivered" should be expected to claim in principle and in essence what the church has claimed to be true.

The corollary of the assumption that confession is an ecclesial as well as a private act is the assumption that the pastoral ministry is not a pro-fession but a con-fession. Theological education bent on training religious professionals rather than educating pastor-theologians demeans the church and undercuts its witness. Pastoral ministry is a confession of that which is unseen yet inwardly believed. The pastor is called of God and ordained by the church to the ministry of structuring that which is unseen yet believed as a part of the structured world of systems and institutions. By means of preaching, teaching, pastoral care, and church administration, the pastor seeks to bring "the kingdom not of this world" (John 18:36) to partial visibility in this world through the parabolic witness of the church. The assumption on which the church's ordination to pastoral ministry rests is that the pastor will understand and undertake this ministry as a theological vocation.

In conclusion, it must be noted and frankly admitted that there are many other and better things that might be said about the genesis of theological existence. What has been said here is not intended as a program or chronology of how theological existence comes to be. The elements that constitute theological existence may well vary from person to person. The order of their appearing may be quite different from that which has been portrayed in this essay. It does appear to me, however, that whenever and wherever theological existence structures and motivates a human life, these six formative moments are likely to be present in one guise or other: an awareness of mystery, the acknowledgment of claim, the summons to understand, the freedom to commit, the experience of delight, and the desire to confess.

The profound scholar, Venerable Bede (672/3-735), was well aware of the fact that theological existence is impossible to maintain apart from prayer, and with his prayer this essay ends.

> I pray thee, good Jesus, that as thou hast graciously granted me to drink in with delight the words of thy knowledge, so wouldst thou mercifully grant me someday to reach thee, the fount of all wisdom, and to appear forever before thy face. Amen.[23]

23. *LCC,* vol. 9, p. 401.

The Bible and Theological Formation: On Becoming a Theologian of the Cross

V. F. (Bud) Thompson

> *We have only our wits, some suggestions offered by the host of witnesses that surround us, and the promise that the spirit of truth will lead us into the truth. Our enterprise is more like sailing than like building cathedrals. We don't have control over the elements — just enough to navigate in the face of surprising shifts of wind and changed water conditions. Some would perhaps hope for more stability but for sailors bedrock is where sunken ships lie.*
>
> Donald Juel[1]

The questions before the authors of this volume are questions having to do with who and what contributes to the theological formation, appetite, and existence of Christian ministers. Why do some ministers of the gospel seem to have a more conscious, deeper, and more vital theological existence than others? Why are some more theologically articulate? Why do some bring to the pastorate a more discerning theological imagination? In the course of even the most casual discussions among pastors, it becomes apparent that theological formation is shaped by influences as varied as our lives — family, worshiping community, significant events, undergraduate and seminary ed-

1. "Your Word Is Truth," *Lutheran Quarterly* 10, no. 2 (Summer 1996): 131.

ucation, as well as mentors and the great host of theologians who have gone before and who stand alongside.

I could not adequately account for my own experience if I did not begin with the Bible. While the silence of the Bible in the church has been widely rehearsed,[2] the ecumenical theological study with other pastor-theologians in which I have been engaged for the past ten years has convinced me that my experience is not unique. The Bible has been crucial to the theological formation of most of us who identify ourselves as pastor-theologians. We stand with those in the historic tradition of the church, from Augustine to Bonhoeffer to our contemporaries, whose deep engagement with the Bible has gone hand in glove with their theological vitality.[3]

This is not to say that in each new generation of faith the encounter with the Bible automatically issues in theological vitality. The animating promise of the Bible as it has been heard in one generation can become a life-denying, deadly force of oppression in the next generation. Leander Keck has suggested that the cultivation of an engagement with the Bible is analogous to the lifelong relationships within a multigenerational, extended family.

> Like most extended families, the Bible is not an easy book to live with. Nonetheless, it is only by living with it that we can be influenced by it and can appropriate its ways of thinking and its vocabulary so that we know ourselves as part of the same family. . . . To live with the Bible does not necessarily blind us to its limits or its role in oppressions. . . .[4]

While recognition of the Bible's limits and role in oppressions has been the occasion for some to abandon the Bible in favor of a gentler and kinder religious text, Keck sees promise in plumbing the depths of the lived experi-

2. See James D. Smart, *The Strange Silence of the Bible in the Church: A Study in Hermeneutics* (Philadelphia: Westminster Press, 1970). More recently Leander Keck's "The Premodern Bible in the Postmodern World," *Interpretation* 50, no. 2 (1996): 130-41. And more recently still, Stephen Prothero, *What Every American Needs to Know and Doesn't* (San Francisco: Harper, 2007).

3. This volume, in its focus on theological formation from the standpoint of the experience and thought of significant pastor-theologians, attests to the vital place of the Bible as the text of faith. Both theological formation and pastoral practice arise from and are shaped in critical conversation with the Bible, as well as with those with whom we read it. See especially the essays by Brant C. Copeland, James L. Haddix, V. Bruce Rigdon, and Kenneth H. Carter Jr. in this volume.

4. Keck, "The Premodern Bible in the Postmodern World," p. 135.

ence of the Bible to learn "what is important, life-giving, and emancipating in it . . . [but if the promise is to be realized] nothing can replace reading the text again and again, questioning and being questioned, objecting and being objected to, discovering and being discovered."[5] If the church fails to cultivate in its ministers affectionate regard for the Bible as well as the facility to read it appreciably and respectfully in the service of the life of faith, the church will continue to suffer the loss of its identity, mission, and integrity.

My own infatuation with the Bible began in childhood. Later, in my seminary years, the historical-critical method opened up new and more sophisticated ways of reading and appreciating the promise of the Bible. But it was in the early days of pastoral service to the church that my engagement with the Bible was intensified, and it remains unabated to the present day. I remember clearly my first day of pastoral service to the church. On that day I felt that I had been personally called into question by the fiery deaths of a mother and daughter of the parish: What in God's name is to be said and, of equal importance, who am I to say it?

The question has never gone away. It is always there, not just at bedside in the hospital, not only at graveside, but every Sunday: What word in the name of God is to be spoken into the rough and tumble of the congregation's moral, political, and existential life, there being so much experienced — public and private — that is contrary to the church's confession of faith? What is to be said and who am I to say it?

As any minister of the gospel knows, it is not at all a question unique to one minister's experience. The question has a long history reaching back to the oldest recollections and reflections of God's people. It is a question that has been held in common by ministers of God's Word in all times and places, from the great ones of the Bible — Sarah, Moses, Deborah, Nathan, Isaiah, Jeremiah, Peter, Mary, and Paul — to present-day preachers. But in addition to acknowledging the question, the Bible contains the promise of what has been spoken and heard as the life-giving Word of God in Christ.

Yet in the experience of many people today, the promise of the Bible seems to be spent, leaving behind a religiosity that squeezes the life out of creation, like a toxin that poisons everything.[6] If that experience is in any

5. Keck, "The Premodern Bible in the Postmodern World," p. 135.

6. Consider the recent rash of anti-God books: *God Is Not Great: How Religion Poisons Everything* by Christopher Hitchens; *The God Delusion* by Richard Dawkins; *Letter to a Christian Nation* by Sam Harris; *Atheist Universe* by David Mills; *God: The Failed Hypothesis* by Victor Stenger; *The End of Faith* by Daniel Dennett.

sense the case, perhaps it only gives new life to Paul's analysis of the problem as it existed among believers in ancient Corinth. According to Paul, the problem had to do with the distinction between "killing letter" and "life-giving Spirit." His discussion of this distinction takes us to the heart of the matter, illuminating the cruciform way in which the encounter with the Bible animates and shapes the theological existence of believers in general and pastor-theologians in particular. Being an avid sailor, nautical metaphors come to mind when considering the relevance of Paul's insights to our subject, beginning with our lack of control over the forces of nature. Acknowledging our lack of control over the elements — having just enough wit to navigate in the face of surprising shifts of wind and changed water conditions — the present contribution to this volume seeks to examine the place of the Bible in the formation of Christian pastors. We cast off, therefore, from the standpoint of Paul's contention that the ministry of the church rises or falls with the proclamation of the gospel, not of letter but of Spirit, for the letter kills but the Spirit gives life (2 Cor. 3:4-6).

Getting Under Way

Gilbert Meilaender has pointed out that "much of what we learn . . . comes from gradually working our way into a tradition of thought and learning from predecessors within it, especially those who are acknowledged masters."[7] Thus the aim here is to begin thinking through the implication of Paul's understanding of Christian ministry for the theological formation of pastors from the standpoint of the Augustinian-Lutheran tradition, the tradition that informs my own formation.

More than one interpreter[8] of 2 Corinthians has already pointed out that, in order to define and defend his apostolic service to the church, Paul in this letter has taken up the antithetical distinction between letter and Spirit. It is a distinction that, in another context, he had used more generally to illuminate the nature of Christian identity and existence (see, e.g., Rom. 2:27-29;

7. Gilbert Meilaender, *Augustinian Reflections on the Christian Life* (Grand Rapids: Eerdmans, 2006), p. 167. See also Cindy Jarvis's paper in this volume. This same point is made in the extremely helpful volume, *The Art of Reading Scripture,* ed. Ellen Davis and Richard Hays (Grand Rapids: Eerdmans, 2003), p. xvi.

8. The impressive list of modern interpreters who read the passage in this way would include Bultmann, Käsemann, Barrett, Roetzel, Matera, Lambrecht, etc.

7:6). As Käsemann has put it, "the antithesis . . . is now [in the Corinthian context] no longer applied to Christians in general [as in the Romans context], but to the apostle in particular, as the bearer of the gospel."[9] In either context the point of the distinction is that speech in the name of God may kill or make alive. Even the profoundest hope and consolation can be spoken in such a way as to kill. This occurs when unconditional promises of God are turned into conditional promises for which humanity qualifies by fulfilling performative requisites.

Think of the difference to the ear of doubt. On the one hand, "All you have to do is believe," no matter how well intended, is nonetheless a killing word if it only turns doubt inward in remorse and despair over what has not been possible. Over against that, imagine greeting doubt with the good news: "Yes, you are guilty as charged in your unbelief, along with other great and shameful sins. But the astonishing news is that the Lord has a great affection for doubters and other sinners for whom Christ gave himself all the way to death and back! He has commissioned me, minister of the good news, to declare to you here and now that he is for you, doubts and all, no ifs, ands, or buts."

This is what Luther was driving at in the Reformation revolution with respect to God talk. The distinction between law and gospel aims to identify the proper work of the Christian ministry, namely, to speak the unconditional promise of God.

> This is made clear by the Apostle in his letter to the Romans (3[:21]): "But now the righteousness of God has been manifested apart from the law." St. Augustine interprets this in his book, *The Spirit and the Letter (De Spiritu et Littera):* "Without the law, that is, without its support." In Rom. 5[:20] the Apostle states, "Law intervened, to increase the trespass," and in Rom. 7[:9] he adds, "But when the commandment came, sin revived." For this reason he calls the law a law of death and a law of sin in Rom. 8[:2]. Indeed, in 2 Cor. 3[:6] he says, "the written code kills," which St. Augustine throughout his book, *The Spirit and the Letter,* understands as applying to every law, even the holiest law of God.[10]

9. Ernst Käsemann, *Perspectives on Paul* (Philadelphia: Fortress Press, 1971), p. 148.

10. *Luther's Works,* American Edition, ed. Theodore Tappert (Philadelphia: Fortress Press, 1967), vol. 31, pp. 42-43, quoted in Gerhard Forde, *On Being a Theologian of the Cross* (Grand Rapids: Eerdmans, 1997), pp. 24-25.

To sharpen the point, it is not just that humanity fails to achieve salvation by way of the law's demands; it is that God never intended salvation to be a human accomplishment in the first place. The law is not the God-given means by which humans are to achieve salvation. Rather, by the law God defeats the human effort to attain salvation. In the words of Rudolf Bultmann: "the Law leads into sin the man who has forsaken his creaturely relation to God and wants to procure life for and by himself: it does this in order thereby to bring him back again to the right relation to God,"[11] as well as to the neighbor. The restoration of humanity to a life-giving relation with the Creator is not completed by the law. The restoration is complete only when humanity embraces by faith the promise of God to justify our existence in Christ. Only in that way is the human being free to live a truly human existence, caring for creation and the neighbor with whom we are given to share it. The art of human existence is learning to eschew any other foundation on which to base one's ultimate justification, in whatever form, living solely by faith in the promise of God. The good of human works is not to justify the self, but to serve the well-being of the neighbor, as the law makes clear. We are commanded to love God with the whole heart, mind, and soul, and the neighbor as the self. At heart the distinction between letter and spirit refers to the way in which God acts upon us through the Word of scripture. In this sense the distinction, as Gerhard Sauter puts it, is about God's freedom in his judgment. It implies that every word of scripture can kill or make alive. It is not so much a distinction regarding the content of scripture. It is rather an observation about the way that God uses the spoken word where and when he pleases. It is about what the Word actually does to the hearer. In this sense the distinction does not belong to the pastor-theologian. As Sauter observes, "No one can have the authority to state that one text is God's word of judgment and another is God's word of grace. Law is God's sentence of judgment and gospel is God's sentence of salvation. Both may come upon us in the same word. . . . We can neither determine nor codetermine how or when a text will be law or gospel. What we can 'know,' however, is that God is judge and savior."[12]

The purpose of theology, consequently, is to prepare and drive the ministry of the church to the execution or the proclamation of the Word of

11. Rudolf Bultmann, *Theology of the New Testament,* trans. Kendrick Grobel (New York: Charles Scribner's Sons, 1955), vol. 1, p. 265.

12. Gerhard Sauter, "The Art of Reading the Bible: An Art for Everyone?" *The Princeton Seminary Bulletin* 28, no. 2 (2007): 208.

God according to these two uses, or toward these two ends: to extinguish the ambition to stand before God on the basis of good works, or as Bultmann has it, to defeat "the self-powered striving to undergird"[13] one's own existence independent of God in the first place; and in the second place, to raise up believers who live by faith in the justifying promise of God and by love in the neighbor. In this ministry, writes Paul, proclaimer and proclamation become one: "My speech and my proclamation were not with plausible words of wisdom, but with a demonstration of the Spirit and of power, so that your faith might rest not on human wisdom but on the power of God. . . . Not that we are competent of ourselves to claim anything as coming from us; our competence is from God, who has made us competent to be ministers of a new testament, not of letter but of spirit; for the letter kills, but the Spirit gives life" (1 Cor. 2:4-5; 2 Cor. 3:5-6). Or as Paul put it even more bluntly, "I have been crucified with Christ; and it is no longer I who live, but it is Christ who lives in me" (Gal. 2:20).

Hoisting Sail

Keeping in mind the twofold purpose of theology — (1) to extinguish the ambition to stand before God on the basis of good works and (2) to raise up believers to live by faith in God and by love in the neighbor — we turn on the basis of 2 Corinthians 3:4-6 to consider more pointedly the implication for the formation of the pastor-theologian. Hoisting sail with only our wits to navigate, pastor-theologians who are formed in the Pauline understanding of the ministry soon appreciate that, on every page of scripture, they face the killing letter and the life-giving Spirit. From this standpoint, according to Paul's argument, the crucial question is not merely whether ministers along with the rest of humanity will have a theological existence, whether they will be formed in one or another theological orientation to life and God. Rather as Paul intimates, it is a question of whether our theological formation and imagination will lead to a ministry of life or death. As one of my teachers used to admonish us in our student days, "Becoming a theologian is not a matter to be taken lightly. We [along with the communities we serve] can be blessed by it if we 'get it right,' as well as cursed by it if we don't."[14]

"Getting it right," as Paul argues, is not, ironically, our theological

13. Sauter, "The Art of Reading the Bible," vol. 1, p. 264.

14. Gerhard Forde, *On Being a Theologian of the Cross*, p. 11.

achievement. Rather "getting it right" is something that God does to and for us. What God does to and for us always appears in the shape of cruciform existence, namely, in a life that dies to self-justification and lives by the promise of God's justification. Again, as Paul had put it to the Christian congregation in Galatia: "I have been crucified with Christ; and it is no longer I who live, but it is Christ who lives in me" (2:20). Augustine also said as much to Pelagius, "To this same healing medicine, mystically shown forth in Christ's passion and resurrection, the apostle points in his next words. 'Know ye not that as many of us as were baptized in Christ Jesus were baptized into his death? Therefore we are buried with him by baptism into death, that like as Christ rose from the dead through the glory of the Father, even so we also should walk in newness of life.'"[15] Likewise Luther proclaimed to the congregation of believers in Wittenberg: "The cross alone is our theology." The cross is the shape of the pastor-theologian who is consequential for the proclamation of the gospel of Jesus Christ.

"Getting it right," in other words, involves a radical discontinuity in the life of the theologian, a discontinuity so radical that the only language appropriate to its description is the language of the cross. We die to the old self and its efforts to get it right in order that the new self may arise to God by faith in his promise and to the neighbor by love.

Setting the Course

A distinction needs to be made before we enter further upon these deep waters. The cross is not being talked about here merely as a symbol for voluntary sacrifice of which one may boast. That understanding is frequently the theological tack of Christian piety. Sooner or later such an understanding is bound to turn into self-righteous paternalism or self-righteous contempt toward the very ones whom the minister is called to serve. There are dangers on either side of the way of the cross: on the one side, despair and resignation; on the other side, pride and cynicism. The cross does not name the pious achievement of which the believer may boast, but names the experience from which the crucified cannot self-regenerate, from which the only promise of life is the promise of forgiveness.

Considered from the standpoint of the wisdom of the world, God in

15. *Augustine: Later Works*, "The Spirit and the Letter," ed. John Burnaby (Philadelphia: Westminster Press, 1955), p. 201.

Christ offers no promise for the advancement of human spiritual ambitions, no promise to transform the world into somebody or other's idea of political utopia, heaven on earth. Christ is of no use to our vision of the kingdom come. So in the end he is wasted — rejected, mocked, abused, betrayed, denied, abandoned — wasted. We do it over and over again. "You must get this thought through your head," Luther implores the Wittenberg congregation, "you are the one who is torturing Christ. . . . Therefore beware, lest you do as those perverse people who torture their hearts with their sins and strive to do the impossible, namely, get rid of their sins by running from one good work or penance to another."[16] That is what reading the Bible in its literal sense does to us. The letter kills.

If we consider the distinction between letter and Spirit in our own time and in language more seductive to our postmodern sensibilities, we find ourselves facing the crisis of death and life as we ask "What in God's name am I to say?" The distinction in our time may be imagined in terms of two archetypical myths, each of which shapes human existence and self-understanding in radically different ways.

If myth is, as Gerd Theissen contends, "the initial attempt of reason *(logos)* to understand the world and assign human beings a place in it,"[17] then the crucial question for our project, regardless of who influences our interest and appetites for theology, is to consider which story grips and shapes the theological imagination, for the two stories make for very different theological understandings and pastoral practices.

Since the ancient days of the Greeks, the most common overarching story we tell about ourselves, albeit in countless variations, is the story that Paul Ricoeur has called the "myth of the exiled soul."[18] This is the story which, for the most part, possesses and informs the philosophical and theological imagination of the West. The distinctive feature of the story, according to Ricoeur,

> is that it divides man into "soul" and "body" . . . and then on that basis it proceeds to tell how the "soul," divine in its origin, became human —

16. LW 42:10.

17. *The Bible and Contemporary Culture,* trans. David E. Green (Minneapolis: Fortress Press, 2007), p. 2.

18. Quoted in Gerhard Forde, *On Being a Theologian of the Cross,* p. 5; from Paul Ricoeur, *The Symbolism of Evil,* trans. Emerson Buchanan (New York: Harper & Row, 1967), pp. 279ff.

> how the "body," a stranger to the soul and bad in many ways, falls to the lot of the soul — how mixture of the soul and the body is the event that inaugurates the humanity of man and makes man the place of forgetting, the place where the primordial difference between soul and body is abolished. Divine as to this soul, earthly as to his body, man is the forgetting of the difference; and myth tells how that happened.[19]

The soul, exiled from its true existence, languishes within the limitations imposed by its bodily captivity.

Not all is lost, however; the soul's plight is not hopeless. Hope flickers, even if dimly. The soul knows that it is meant for a higher existence, if only the flickering flame can be rekindled to the full brightness of its glorious potential. The promise of the soul's restoration to its original glory comes afoot the rescuing sage. Ricoeur explains: "the myth of the exiled soul is *par excellence* the principle and promise of 'knowledge,' of 'gnosis,'" by which the soul is restored to its true and glorious destiny.[20]

A theological imagination formed by the story of the exiled soul will see and treat the world of experience accordingly. The story, one might say, provides a material hermeneutic that informs and shapes theology's operation. For example, consider how the theological imagination shaped by the myth of the exiled soul reads Genesis 3. In the beginning Adam and Eve, created in the goodness of pure humanity, occupy paradise in harmony with God, one another, self, and all creation. But seduced by the tempter they fall from the glory of their nobility into sin and disobedience; the soul falls captive to the depravity of illegitimate material pursuits, driven by greed, lust, and intolerance.

Given that understanding of the human predicament, theology is bound to imagine that its purpose — embodied in the minister as spiritual director or moral compass — is to instruct the soul along the path of upward spiritual mobility to glory. The minister is to inspire the soul to adopt the necessary industry and perseverance, open-mindedness and commitment to justice, to reach the goal, however exactly glory is defined. There is even a place for the cross in the glory story. Assuming that enlightened humanity under its own steam will fall short of the glory, it will be necessary, as Gerhard Forde explains, that reparation "be made, grace restored, and purg-

19. Ricoeur, *The Symbolism of Evil,* pp. 279-80.

20. Ricoeur, *The Symbolism of Evil,* p. 304.

ing carried out so that return to glory is possible. The cross [is] quite neatly assimilated into the story as the reparation that makes the return possible."[21]

Coming About

When it comes time to turn a sailing vessel to a new downwind tack the helmsman alerts the crew with the command, "Prepare to come about" or simply, "Ready about." That time has now come in the course of our reflection on the theological formation of ministers. We turn more pointedly toward the second purpose of theology: namely, to the Spirit's use of God's word to raise up believers who live by faith in the justifying promise of God and by love in the neighbor.

If the letter kills, then it is only that the Spirit might give life. If "in his suffering Christ makes our sin known, then through his resurrection he justifies us and delivers us from all sin, if we believe this."[22] When the resurrection of Christ is proclaimed "for you," as Luther continues his meditation on the suffering of Christ, the believer is given permission to pass beyond the cross to see that "the friendly heart of Christ beats with such love for you that it impels him to bear with pain your conscience and your sin. . . . We know God aright when we grasp him not in his might or wisdom (for then he proves terrifying),[23] but in his kindness and love. Then faith and confidence are able to exist, and then man is truly born anew in God."[24] It is in this sense that Paul declares, "There is no distinction. They are *now* justified by his grace as a gift through the redemption that is in Christ Jesus" (3:24). Just so the way is opened to a new way that was not there before.

Or to pick up in our day where Ricoeur left off, for theologians of the cross, the cross cannot be fit into another story. The cross is its own story. The cross fits the theologian into the story of God's costly grace. That is what Luther meant, "The cross alone is our theology." There is no escape. The let-

21. Forde, *On Being a Theologian of the Cross,* p. 6.

22. LW 42:12.

23. When theology imagines that the aim is to grasp God in his wisdom and might, it issues, Luther contended, either in self-righteous pride and presumption so characteristic of the American religious right or in the anti-theistic polemic which as recent publication trends indicate, characterizes a growing segment of the western intellectual elite. See note 6 for a brief list of recent publications.

24. LW 42:13.

ter kills. The Spirit makes alive. The believer is liberated from the quest for self-glorification to live — by faith in the promise of Christ and by love in the neighbor — a down-to-earth ordinary life.

For the pastor-theologian, the cross opens the Bible so that we who must wonder "What in God's name is to be said" may see the human predicament for what it is. The greatest danger posed to the well-being of the creation is not that humans are tempted to fall into an existence beneath their intended dignity. That is always of course a temptation, but it is an obvious temptation against which humanity, whether Christian or not, has its guard up. The world has no shortage of moralists, Christian or otherwise, to keep humanity alert against the temptation to make less of itself. The danger that poses the more devastating threat is the temptation to believe that merely being human is not enough. The temptation is to imagine we might virtuously transcend our creaturely bounds, take our destiny into our own hands, and begin lording our self-righteous vision over others. In other words, we imagine that the Lord God is fortunate to have such enlightened theologians to represent him to the world. Self-righteous presumption is the sin that crucifies Jesus, as the New Testament makes so painfully clear. By the time we realize our sin it is too late to self-rescue from calamity. The cross is the end of the glory story. As Luther contends in the Heidelberg Disputation, "The thirst for glory is not sated; it is extinguished."[25] If there is to be a resurrection to life for humanity, then it comes only at the mercy of the forgiveness of the risen Jesus. Only that can do it.

Of course the theologian of glory will find no good news in a message like that. The theologian of glory will take deep offense, and that is understandable. The cross strikes at the very core of the quest for glory. The whole point of human existence according to the theology of glory is to pursue the heroic, upward path to the higher existence. The theologian of glory is bound to ask: What's left of life if the goal of glory is taken away? And that of course is the point. According to the story of the cross, nothing is left of the old existence. Ashes to ashes, dust to dust. Just so, we have come about, sailing beyond the bedrock where sunken ships lie, toward the distant shore and the city whose builder and founder is God!

25. LW 42:13.

Running Before the Wind

We who have been given just enough to navigate in the face of surprising shifts of wind and changed water conditions must consider whether or not we are up to speaking the Word of the Lord entrusted to us for the Nineveh of our day. That will of course always remain to be seen. But at least this much may be said: theologians of the cross, disabused of a pious but false resolution of broken and fragmented reality, suffer revulsion at all easy words designed to smooth over the roughness of life, as though somehow the purpose of theology were to explain and justify God in order to make God attractive to people. Theologians of the cross, according to Vitor Westhelle, enter upon the subject matter of faith from within the experience of a sustained *tentatio,* what Luther referred to as *Anfectung:* "a theology being done by those afflicted, assailed, oppressed, and on trial."[26] Theology of the cross will permit no daffodils to be hung on the cross by way of pretty theological systems. Hope lies not in explanations but in the promise of God. Like the music of Johann Sebastian Bach, theologians of the cross may stare the darkness squarely in the face, calling it what it is in the promise of hope arising.

Therefore when facing concerns related to the common order, theologians of the cross, in keeping with the Pauline distinction between killing letter and life-giving Spirit, neither shriek pious platitudes, nor shrink into a mere ministry of presence in the face of existential crisis and affliction. In solidarity with the neighbor who suffers, they proclaim the cross as the song of hope. In the interest of listening with both ears, they are careful to discern when the time is a time to speak or to refrain from speaking. Theologians of the cross will neither decree pious political solutions, nor retreat into a political quietism in the midst of the ambiguities of temporal existence, but will dare, as Luther advised, to sin boldly in service of the neighbor and the neighborhood.

On the basis of Paul's understanding of the ministry, the pastor-theologian is compelled to enter into the rough and tumble of public debate and political action when the temporal well-being of the creation is at stake. The pastor-theologian enters the political life of the community as a sober realist, seeking to make pedestrian, down-to-earth, persuasive arguments for

26. Vitor Westhelle, *The Scandalous God: The Use and Abuse of the Cross* (Minneapolis: Fortress Press, 2006), p. 36.

that which is in the public interest. We do not claim special knowledge from above that should be privileged as the revealed truth to bring in the kingdom — neither progressives nor conservatives, neither traditionalists nor revisionists, neither evangelicals nor liberals have been given this knowledge. In this sense, Luther advised, Christians live as though God does not exist. We live by ordinary reason and sight, caring for the creation and those with whom we are given to share it. We are free to live as though God does not exist because, as Luther also contends, we believe in the God on whose promises everything depends.

Finally, our confidence lies in the promise of God in Christ which speaks a hope against all hope and so faces "the terrible void . . . of a God that, according to our perception, cannot be but the One who is against God. In Luther's words: 'to flee from and find refuge in God against God.' Such is the impossibility that makes theology possible."[27] As Paul puts it, "For if we have been united with him in a death like his, we will certainly be united with him in a resurrection like his" (Gal. 6:5). This is not merely a personal hope; it is the cosmic hope for "a new heaven and a new earth." Theologians of the cross find themselves in solidarity with the broken world precisely at those points where it would be easy to give up and retreat into an evangelical cocoon or personal spiritual nirvana. But there is no refuge, for the letter kills. The cross blocks the flight into otherworldly, simplistic, soothing, reductionist pietisms — whether existential or political — that aim to escape the accusation and/or the hiddenness of God. Theologians of the cross, led by the Spirit who gives life, are directed back to the world as it is with hope, living simultaneously as if everything depends on God and as if there were no God.

The letter kills; the Spirit gives life. That there is a future for humanity on this side of the cross of Christ can only mean that we receive it passively as a new life, calling to mind the God who bent down to form "man from the dust of the ground, and breathed into his nostrils the breath of life; and the man became a living being" (Gen. 2:7). As the minister of the gospel declares to the penitent, "Upon your confession and in obedience to our Lord's command I declare to you the entire forgiveness of all your sin." An attack on the sinner's attempt to justify the self by good works, the cross brings to an end the old being under the law and brings forth the new being in Christ. Against the darkness of our mythic self-delusion, the Word of God explodes like a

27. Westhelle, *The Scandalous God*, p. 59.

great flash of light. The absolution lights up our true reality, mercifully enacts the message of the Bible to us, casts us "on that creative love of God, which makes the object of its love out of the nothing to which the sinner has been reduced."[28]

The pastor-theologian whose life arises from an encounter with the Bible as the story of the cross, whose life arises from the ashes of confession and absolution, is in the same breath granted a new theological orientation to life. Instead of attempting to see through earthly appearances to the hidden counsels of God, one sees reality for what it is through suffering and the cross. There is no secret path to glory, no creative theological maneuvering to save humanity. In the promise of the resurrection which comes afoot the absolution, theologians of the cross dare to name the trials and troubles, the failure and the guilt, the disappointment and grief, the joy and success what they are — the end of glory, the end of law, works, self-justification, the end of all that falsely promised to save us from the cruciform of confession and absolution, and the beginning of faith in the promise of God.

Blow, Spirit, Blow

Given that the theological existence of pastors formed in this way by the Bible is more like sailing than building a cathedral, one is aware that today, on more than one front, the theology of the cross is regarded with suspicion and opposition. Among the questions that challenge this approach to theology are the following: Does the cruciform shape of theology glorify suffering and equate Christian mission with masochism? Does the church's emphasis on the cross perpetuate violence? Does a theology of the cross encourage political quietism by construing salvation primarily in existential terms? Does the cross exacerbate the oppression and victimization of those most vulnerable? Is a theology of the cross too negative to be of positive value? Is a theology of the cross so offensive to modern sensibility that it is simply untenable? When for example the cross appears contemporaneously to be a "case of divine child abuse,"[29] one might well wonder if it isn't time substantively to object.

28. Forde, *On Being a Theologian of the Cross,* p. 12.

29. See Joanne Carlson and Carole R. Bohn, eds., *Christianity, Patriarchy, and Abuse: A Feminist Critique* (Cleveland: Pilgrim Press, 1989).

These are serious questions that deserve sustained attention. Theologians of the cross have no choice but to enter sympathetically into conversation and solidarity with those who raise them. While such sustained engagement is not possible in the context of this essay, we have attempted to navigate these deep waters and to go some distance in explaining why for us, for whom the cross is our theology, there is no other way. We can do no other, as Luther confessed when he was required to answer for his theology. There was and is nothing heroic about his answer or about our answer. Rather, as he explained from his deathbed, "we are beggars"[30] with no hope, no boast, no justification, no basis for entering into theology and the life of faith, apart from Christ crucified. For in the event of Christ crucified we are justified to proclaim that there is nothing — no matter how ugly or unacceptable — outside the realm of God's redemption. Indeed, the cross declares that God's love for God's broken and rebellious creation runs so deep that God is even willing to bear the denial of God for the sake of restoring our life together in the promise of becoming what so far we have failed to be.

The thirst for glory is understandable. We read the Bible, so to speak, with dust in our mouths. We would like to believe that there is something we can do to redeem ourselves, to write a different ending to the story, as did the scribes who, in later manuscripts of Mark, appended a happy ending to the Jesus story, an ending that would rescue the story. But as Frank Kermode rightly observes, neither violence nor interpretive cunning has served to bring in the kingdom.[31]

Dust to dust, ashes to ashes. When there is no promise in self-regeneration, how is theology to answer the "massive experience of guilt and sorrow, of responsibility and irresponsibility in the aporias of politics, economics, and scientific ethics, which oppress us and confront us daily with the reality of evil"?[32] If this massive experience marks the end of an old life in theology, then it also marks the beginning of faith, a new way of theologically being finally free of the self and free for the neighbor by faith in God's promise. Theological life that is anchored in the cross of Christ is a life lived for the other in the promise of the resurrected Jesus, the Alpha and Omega of our theology. To be sure, as Donald Juel points out, lest we fall into theo-

30. LW 54:475.

31. See Kermode's *Genesis of Secrecy* (Cambridge, MA: Harvard University Press, 1979) for an extended discussion of the promise and peril of interpretation.

32. Oswald Bayer, "With Luther in the Present," *Lutheran Quarterly,* 21, no. 1 (Spring 2007): 10.

logical presumption or triumphalism, "We do not 'have' Jesus even at the end of the story, and there is no guarantee that we can wrest a promise from him or lock him safely away by hermeneutical tricks. . . . But perhaps that is just where the promise resides. 'There you will see him, as he told you.' Jesus has promised an encounter with him against which there is no assured defense. God will be put off neither by our failures . . . nor by our most sophisticated interpretive schemes. And if this 'good news about Jesus Christ' is God's work within the intimate realm of human speech, there is reason to hope that our defenses will finally prove insufficient and that we will not have the last word."[33] There, where theology reaches its limit and gives way to speaking the promise of Jesus, the old way comes to an end and a new way of being a theologian, a theologian of the promise, is begun.

33. Donald H. Juel, *A Master of Surprise: Mark Interpreted* (Minneapolis: Fortress, 1994), p. 121.

Raising Pastor-Theologians: Let the Children Say It First

Brant S. Copeland

Vignette #1

On January 4, 2004, I received an email letter from a college student in the congregation. In part, it read:

> Your congregation has nurtured me for the past 18 years. In the early years they taught me lessons and fed me Graham crackers and apple juice while my parents worshiped in the great big sanctuary. Later, they taught me to sing and I put on my red and white robe, stood in front of what seemed to be thousands of people, and led them in worship. I played hangman with a pew buddy named Julia as I half-listened to your splendid sermons. As a middle-schooler the youth group strengthened both my faith and my friendships with youth and adults.
>
> At your church I clanged obnoxious bells in a cold back room and climbed in the steeple to see a bell of a completely different sort. In high school the church choir, potlucks, youth group, and mission trips fed my spirit and welcomed my contributions. With your church's help I participated in a delegation to South Africa, five Montreat Youth Conferences and countless Worship and Music Conferences, two national planning teams, two Youth Triennia, served as the Presbyterian Youth Connection Co-Moderator, attended four General Assemblies, and spent two summers working on Montreat Summer Staff. All this was done with wor-

> ship and sacrament at the center of your congregation's life. I am forever indebted to the congregation of Old First Church.
>
> For over two years now I have mainly attended worship with the student congregation of St. Olaf College. I've worshiped there but intentionally have not sought out membership in the congregation. Instead, I've kept my membership at Old First. It is thinking of that congregation, resting on my faith, and planning for my future vocation that I'd like to become an Inquirer into Ministry of the Word and Sacrament in the Presbyterian Church (U.S.A.). I understand that I should do this through Florida Presbytery with the sponsorship of your session. With your blessing, I would like to begin this process. . . .[1]

The goal of this volume is to identify those elements in congregational life that contribute to the formation of pastor-theologians. It seems clear from this young man's letter that he is aware from an early age that his Christian identity was being formed through the worship and work of his home congregation. He speaks of worship and mission in a congregation that "fed my spirit and welcomed my contributions." He even displays a grudging appreciation for "obnoxious bells" — clearly not his first choice of liturgical instrument.

In this young man's case, it appears that whatever it is his congregation did to nurture Christian vocation in general and ministerial vocation in particular *worked.* While the Holy Spirit can use any experience — positive or negative — to form pastor-theologians, it seems this young man's positive experiences in his home church had a great deal to do with his decision to prepare for pastoral ministry. And, judging from this early bit of correspondence, he is well on his way toward becoming a pastor-theologian.

In the Reformed understanding of pastoral ministry, the notion of *call* is central.[2] John Calvin and Reformed confessions speak of two parts of a call to ministry: the internal or secret call that a person feels deep within the heart, and the external call that is received from the church. While all Christians are called in baptism to serve God in Jesus Christ, some are called to particular service as ministers of Word and Sacrament. The efforts that congregations make to bring up all children in "the nurture and admonition of the Lord" not only strengthen *Christian* vocation,

1. Personal correspondence: Adam J. Copeland to Brant S. Copeland, January 4, 2004.
2. See the essay by W. Rush Otey III in this volume.

but also *ministerial* vocation. Christian nurture is, first and foremost, a *theological* enterprise.

There is, of course, no infallible formula for producing pastor-theologians. Sometimes pastor-theologians are formed despite their experience growing up in congregations. The best congregations can do is to give careful attention to the theological implications of congregational practice. For good or ill, congregations teach the faith in everything they do. Too often the theology congregations *espouse* is not the theology they *practice.*

How do congregations raise up disciples like Adam, the writer of this letter? No program or formula is guaranteed, but congregations must begin with corporate worship. No educational program or outreach ministry nurtures people in faith more effectively than theologically informed worship on the Lord's Day. At the same time, nothing a congregation does has more potential to distort the gospel than worship on the Lord's Day. Worship is the central and essential act of the gathered community. Congregations that get worship "right" are the congregations most likely to produce theologically acute disciples and even the occasional pastor-theologian.

Children in the Assembly

Who comprises the Christian *assembly,* the community that gathers round what Gordon Lathrop calls "bath, book, and table"?[3] If congregations follow the example of scripture, the practice of the early church, and the theological logic of infant baptism, the answer must be "both adults and children." The scriptural evidence for the presence of children in the assembly, though far from ample, is more than adequate. The lack of frequent references to children in Acts and the Epistles is to be expected for the simple reason that their presence was assumed.

At Pentecost Peter proclaims the *kerygma,* the promise which "is for you, for your children, and for all who are far away, everyone whom the Lord our God calls to him."[4] Although there is no scholarly consensus on the matter, many interpreters agree that the "households" of adult converts mentioned in Acts included both slaves and children.[5] Luke reports that young

3. Gordon W. Lathrop, *Holy Things: A Liturgical Theology* (Minneapolis: Fortress Press, 1993).

4. Acts 2:39 NRSV.

5. For a full discussion, see O. M. Bakke, *When Children Became People: The Birth of*

Eutychus was present at the late-night meeting in Troas where Paul was the featured speaker — present, that is, until he fell asleep and tumbled out of an upper-floor window.[6] Paul breaks off his talk long enough to minister to the boy, then promptly takes up where he left off. If Paul is surprised to find a child in the assembly, Luke does not say so.

And why should Paul be surprised? In the Jewish world, children's presence and participation were normative for temple and synagogue. Children also had a prominent role in pagan worship in the Greco-Roman world. Christians from both Jewish and pagan backgrounds "would have found it perfectly natural that children would carry out functions in their liturgy."[7] Children continued to be present and active in the Christian assembly well into the fourth century, serving as singers in choirs of both boys and girls, and taking specific roles in the liturgy.

In his study of children in the early church, O. M. Bakke reports that, "When the *Apostolic Constitutions* regulate the intercessory prayer for catechumens, we are told that when the deacons mention the individuals by name, the congregation is to reply with the *Kyrie eleison.* The text continues, 'Let the children say it first *(et ante cunctos pueri).*'"[8] John Chrysostom (347-407) made a special link between children and prayers imploring God's mercy, and recommended that they should function as intercessors.[9] Bakke concludes:

> From the mid-third century, and perhaps from the New Testament period onward, children received the sacraments; in a wide geographic area, they were baptized and took part in the Eucharist. This implies that they were regarded as subjects with needs of their own and with the capacity to receive the same spiritual gifts as adults. The fact that they received baptism and communion also shows that they were perceived as full members of the community.
>
> Children's active participation went further, however. The sources tell us that they played an active part in hymn-singing, that they were

---

Childhood in Early Christianity, trans. Brian McNeil (Minneapolis: Augsburg Press, 2005), pp. 224-30.

6. Acts 20:7-12 NRSV.

7. Bakke, *When Children Became People,* p. 256.

8. *Apostolic Constitutions* 8.6, as cited in Bakke, *When Children Became People,* p. 255.

9. Bakke, *When Children Became People,* p. 255.

cantors, and they had a special responsibility in praying the *Kyrie eleison.* They also read scriptural texts in the liturgy. In other words, they were visibly present and made their own contribution to worship.[10]

As lay participation in the liturgy declined in the Middle Ages, so did the participation of children. However, numerous Reformed confessions and catechisms affirm the theological basis for children's presence and participation in worship. Children belong in worship because, by grace, they are full members of the New Covenant. Their presence is consistent with (I would say mandated by) the same theological rationale that justifies infant baptism. That rationale is expressed over and over in documents of the Reformed tradition. The *Heidelberg Catechism* of 1563 is just one example:

> **Question 74:** Are infants also to be baptized?
> **Answer:** Yes, because they, as well as their parents, are included in the covenant and belong to the people of God. Since both redemption from sin through the blood of Christ and the gift of faith from the Holy Spirit are promised to these children no less than to their parents, infants are also by baptism, as a sign of the covenant, to be incorporated into the Christian church and distinguished from the children of unbelievers. This was done in the Old Covenant by circumcision. In the New Covenant baptism has been instituted to take its place.[11]

The Directory for Worship, part of the Constitution of the Presbyterian Church (U.S.A.), provides presbyters with practical guidelines for living out this theological principle:

> Children bring special gifts to worship and grow in the faith through their regular inclusion and participation in the worship of the congregation. Those responsible for planning and leading the participation of children in worship should consider the children's level of understanding and ability to respond, and should avoid both excessive formality and condescension. The session should ensure that regular programs of

10. Bakke, *When Children Became People,* p. 259.

11. *The Book of Confessions* (Louisville: Office of the General Assembly Presbyterian Church [U.S.A.], 1999), par. 4.074.

> the church do not prevent children's full participation with the whole congregation in worship, in Word and Sacrament, on the Lord's Day.[12]

Churches that exclude children from Lord's Day worship, whether by scheduling educational programs at the same time as worship, or by organizing "children's worship" in lieu of worship with adults, must provide a *theological* rationale for these practices. However well intentioned or consumer-friendly, these programmatic conflicts constitute a form of liturgical apartheid which, in my opinion, is inconsistent with scripture, the practice of the early church, and the theology of the church.[13]

Forms of Children's Participation in the Assembly

It is entirely possible for congregations to welcome and include children in Lord's Day worship without condescension, which Marva Dawn terms "dumbing down."[14] Children as young as four or five years, depending on their developmental maturity, can serve as ushers, greeters, and singers in choirs. As they begin to master the written word, they can serve as readers of scripture. Careful preparation, of course, is required for these tasks, as should be the case for all leaders of worship, regardless of age.

Vignette #2

> Daniel, who has Down syndrome, is serving as usher for the first time. With great dignity he walks forward with the offering plate, passes it to

12. *The Book of Order* (Louisville: Office of the General Assembly Presbyterian Church [U.S.A.], 1999), par. W-3.1004.

13. In recent years several churches have adopted "worship education" based on an approach championed by Sonja M. Stewart and Jerome W. Berryman in *Young Children in Worship* (Louisville: Westminster/John Knox Press, 1989). Curricula based on Stewart and Berryman's ideas employ storytelling and sensorimotor activities in a "worship center" apart from the worshiping congregation. However effective these curricula might be in fostering worshipful habits and attitudes in children, the very fact that they take children away from the corporate worship of the assembly makes them theologically inadequate. Children learn to worship *by worshiping within the assembly.* Participation precedes cognition.

14. Cf. Marva Dawn, *Reaching Out without Dumbing Down: A Theology of Worship for the Turn-of-the-Century Culture* (Grand Rapids: Eerdmans, 1995).

the worshipers on the front pew, and waits for it to be passed back so that he can pass the plate to the second pew. When the plate is returned, Daniel is surprised to find it empty. With appropriate indignation, he passes the plate again to the same pew.

The offering plate does not return empty the second time.

Even before they can read, children can learn to say or sing regular parts of the liturgy, such as the *Kyrie eleison,* Apostles' and Nicene Creeds, Lord's Prayer, *Sursum corda, Sanctus,* Memorial Acclamation, and Great Amen. They can join in responses for litanies. When the Intercessions or Prayers of the People are offered by the leader as a series of brief petitions (rather than the "Long Prayer" or "Pastoral Prayer"), children can join the congregational response to each petition, saying, for instance, "Hear our prayer."

Rather than spend weeks rehearsing an anthem to perform for the congregation, children's choirs can be incorporated into the adult choir, a practice encouraged by the Choristers' Guild of America. In the congregation I serve, choristers in first through fifth grade sing with the adult choir twice a month. It is not unusual for these children to sing texts in Latin or German set by ancient, classical, and modern composers. Repertoire for children's choirs need not be cute or maudlin. Least of all should it be entertaining for adults.

Most children have an innate enthusiasm for participation in the Lord's Supper. At their own developmental level, they are capable of "discerning the body, which is Christ."[15] Even children who are still in the concrete operational stage of development, lacking abstract thinking, know what it feels like to be included in the family meal of the people of God, just as they feel keenly their exclusion from that meal. Children practice *fiducia* (trust) as in time they acquire the abstract language of *fides* (belief). The Eucharist communicates Christ's presence in multivalent dimensions — many of which are accessible to children. ". . . it is to such as these that the kingdom of God belongs."[16]

Although the church in John Calvin's Geneva did not admit children to the Table until they had memorized the propositional truths contained in his catechism, Calvin's understanding of the real presence of Christ in the sacrament has profound implications for contemporary eucharistic practice. Calvin asserted that the truth of God can be experienced in the Lord's Sup-

15. 1 Corinthians 11:29.
16. Mark 10:14.

per. The nature of divine truth in the context of the Supper is not propositional, but experiential. Christ is spiritually present to the believer through the experience of eating and drinking. In discussing the mystery of Christ's real presence in the Supper, Calvin writes:

> Now, if anyone should ask me how this takes place, I shall not be ashamed to confess that it is a secret too lofty for either my mind to comprehend or my words to declare. And to speak more plainly, *I rather experience than understand it.* Therefore I here embrace, without controversy the truth of God in which I may safely rest. He declares his flesh the food of my soul, his blood its drink [John 6:53-56]. I offer my soul to him to be fed with such food. In his Sacred Supper he bids me take, eat, and drink his body and blood under the symbols of bread and wine. I do not doubt that he himself truly presents them, and that I receive them.[17]

Vignette #3

> As an elder is serving Communion to the people who are coming to the Table, she tears off a piece of bread from the loaf and gives it to seven-year-old James, saying, "The body of Christ, given for you." The boy's eyes widen. He looks at the bread that has been placed in his open hand. In worship education classes James has been taught to respond, "Amen." Instead he says, "Wow!"
>
> "*I rather experience than understand it.*"

Children tend to respond well to those portions of worship that call for kinesthetic participation — standing, singing, kneeling, walking forward for Communion, eating, drinking, and "lifting holy hands" to God in prayer. Even when they are simply sitting with the congregation, they can attend to what is being said or sung by worship leaders.

Vignette #4

> Richard, the father of Noah, age 6, is at his wits' end. Even though he and Noah have reviewed the appropriate protocol to be observed dur-

17. John Calvin, *Institutes of the Christian Religion,* IV (1559) (italics added).

ing less active parts of the liturgy, as the first lesson is being read, Noah slips *under* the pew. He remains there while the reader narrates the call of Samuel.

Noah knows this story well. He has just studied it, as the church school curriculum follows the lectionary for the Lord's Day. Richard, however, is not listening to the reader very closely. He's wondering how to extract his son from under the pew without disturbing other worshipers. As the reader nears the end of the lection, Richard hears a voice from below:

"Dad, listen to this next part! Samuel thinks it's Eli, but it's really God!"

When adults see young children drawing pictures during the reading of scripture or the preaching of the sermon, they assume children are not paying attention. In fact, young children are masters of multi-tasking. Even the six-year-old who is lying under the pew might very well be attending to the word of God.

Congregations do not need to dumb down liturgy in order to include children. Neither do they need to interrupt the liturgy with a children's sermon or time with children. Children are fully capable of overhearing the gospel in the language of grown-ups. When the language of worship is rich in biblical allusion and the words are chosen carefully, children acquire the vocabulary of faith even as they are in a process of appropriating its meaning. In other words, *participation precedes cognition.*

Raising Children to Participate in the Assembly

The hymnal is the theological primer of the assembly. Most Christians get their working theology as much from the hymns they sing as from the sermons they hear. When Christians are confronted with tragedy and heartache, they do not tend to quote sermons. They quote hymns. A pastor who strives to be a theologian should give careful attention to the theological content of congregational song.

Hymnody is all the more critical for children. What people sing as children stays with them all their lives. Adam, the college senior who applied to become an Inquirer in ministry, wrote in the introduction to a college paper about the importance of sound words set to worthy music:

I cannot keep from singing. Church music, especially hymnody, has always been part of my life. Among the earliest songs I learned were songs of faith like "Jesus Loves Me" and "Jesus Loves the Little Children." I can still remember Sunday afternoon rehearsals of the church Carol Choir that I joined as a kindergartener. The choristers did not learn pedantic children's pieces intended to endear us to the congregation when we led them in worship. Rather, we sang texts imbued with solid theology to simple tunes fit for children's voices. One of my early favorites was the hymn "God of the Sparrow." I can still remember Mrs. Whitaker teaching us the hymn on a cheap keyboard in the upstairs classroom of the church education building. She taught us how to sing Jaroslav Vajda's text with clear diction, a text that as Don Saliers suggests "is a bold and surprising list of images of God, with a corresponding list of questions we must ask."[18] Imagine twenty children aged five to nine clad in bright red vestments with white cottas singing boldly in the front of the sanctuary:

God of the sparrow God of the whale
God of the swirling stars
How does the creature say Awe
How does the creature say Praise

And then several verses later:

God of the ages God of the hand
God of the loving heart
How do your children say Joy
How do your children say Home[19]

Vignette #5

Several years ago, I presided at the funeral for a woman who had committed suicide. As I was leading the graveside committal service, the woman's older sister spontaneously broke out in song.

Jesus Christ is risen today, Alleluia!
Our triumphant holy day, Alleluia!

18. Don E. Saliers, *Worship Come to Its Senses* (Nashville: Abingdon Press, 1996), p. 31.
19. *Presbyterian Hymnal,* no. 272.

She stopped abruptly. The mourners around the grave looked embarrassed. Unable to bear the unfinished word, I sang the rest of the stanza:

Who did once upon the cross, Alleluia!
Suffer to redeem our loss, Alleluia!

After the benediction, the sister sought me out in order to apologize. "I just felt moved to sing that song. I'm not sure why. I haven't heard it since I was little. I used to love that song, but the church I go to now only sings praise choruses — not hymns. I knew it was the right song to sing, but I just couldn't remember the words."

Recognizing the importance of hymnody for forming children in the faith, First Presbyterian Church of Tallahassee gives kindergarteners in the congregation their own copy of the *Presbyterian Hymnal.* In addition, the Christian Education Council has prepared a handbook for parents entitled *Cornerstones.* This guide identifies stages in children's faith development and suggests biblical passages, creeds, prayers, and hymns that children should know as they grow in the faith. *Cornerstones* also has sample Bible and hymn studies for families to use at home. Accompanying *Cornerstones* is a cassette tape of service music used in the liturgy. Here is an abbreviated version of the approach taken by the writers of *Cornerstones:*[20]

Birth Through Age Five

Children in this age grouping are in a stage of faith development called **Experiential**. In this stage children experience the whole world, including their faith, through their five senses. They experience God when they are with people who love God. Important issues revolve around love, caring, and acceptance, and the main issue is **trust**.

Bible Passages

At this age, reading a passage over and over is a way to make children familiar with a text. Although you will not be able to do in-depth study with a

20. *Cornerstones,* unpublished resource produced by First Presbyterian Church, Tallahassee, Florida.

child of this age, do not discount the value of exposing your child to scripture early in life. The church school teachers of our class for two-year-olds can tell you how much their students do pick up from weekly lessons. Our emphasis here is on both repetition and use. Rather than always bringing your child to the Bible, also bring the Bible to the situation. Repetition occurs in various situations and not just at planned learning times.

Psalms	Psalm 100:1-3
	Psalm 122:1
	Psalm 104:1
Old Testament	Genesis 1:1
	Genesis 1:1-5
New Testament	Luke 2:1-20 (story of Jesus' birth)
	Matthew 22:36-40
	Ephesians 4:32

Hymns

#304 Jesus Loves Me
#150 Come, Christians, Join to Sing (v. 1)
#299 Amen, Amen (refrain only)
#338 Kum Ba Yah
#267 All Things Bright and Beautiful (refrain only)[21]

Corporate Worship with Your Family

- Begin to familiarize your child with the Lord's Prayer by praying it together.
- Bring your child to the sanctuary to explore when there is not a worship service.
- Ask the minister or director of Christian education to meet you at the sanctuary to give you and your child a guided tour.

21. Hymn numbers are taken from the Presbyterian hymnal.

- Attend a worship service with your child. This may be a Sunday service or a special evensong or midweek service.
- As your child begins to know letters and numbers, let him/her find the hymns we will be singing on Sunday (listed in the newsletter) in your hymnal at home.
- Read the scriptures for Sunday together (listed in the newsletter).

Prayers and Worship at Home

- Begin to recite for children the Lord's Prayer.
- You may begin to use the Doxology (Tune: Old Hundredth) as a table blessing or at bedtime prayers.

Table Blessings

Johnny Appleseed:

> O, the Lord's been good to me and so I thank the Lord,
> For giving me the things I need, the sun, and the rain and the apple seed,
> The Lord's been good to me. Amen. (said or sung)

"God Is Great": sung to "Jesus Christ Is Risen Today" by Charles Wesley, Hymn #123

> God is great and God is good. A-le-lu-u-ia,
> And we thank God for our food. A-le-lu-u-ia,
> By his hand we all are fed. A-le-lu-u-ia,
> Give us, Lord, our daily bread. A-le-lu-u-ia.

Age Five Through Age Eight

At the beginning of this age group, children are still in the **Experiential** stage of faith development. They are dealing with issues of love and trust regarding their relationship to God. Around the age of eight, children begin to move to another level of faith identified as the **Affiliative** stage. At this point they want to **belong** to their community of faith or their church family. Participation in church activities and being recognized as a part of the community is important.

Bible Passages

Psalms	Psalm 100 Psalm 91:14-16 Psalm 19:14
Old Testament	Deuteronomy 6:4-7 (the Shema) Genesis 1:1–2:3 Leviticus 19:18 1 Samuel 16:7b Micah 6:8
New Testament	Mark 12:28b-31 Matthew 6:9-13 (The Lord's Prayer) Matthew 18:21-22 John 3:16, 17

Hymns

#464 Joyful, Joyful We Adore Thee
#322 Spirit of the Living God
#455 All Creatures of Our God and King
#513 Let Us Break Bread Together

Corporate Worship with Your Family

- Register your kindergartener to sing in the Carol Choir. Explain the importance of giving our time to God and also of helping to lead others in worshiping God.

- Have your child find the hymns in the hymnal and mark them as soon as you get to the sanctuary on Sundays.
- Bring your child to a worship service other than Sunday mornings so they can see other times and ways our church family worships God.
- Practice with your child the responses we say during worship. There are several places in our service where we use the same response week after week: after the scripture readings, passing the peace, during the Prayer of Thanksgiving.
- When you enter the sanctuary, point out to your child familiar people. Introduce your child to people around you once you are seated.
- Show your child how we read hymns by stanzas, not lines. Sing along with your child, underlining the verse we are singing with a card or your bulletin.
- Help your child to understand the words and phrases of, and to memorize, the following:

  Lord's Prayer
  Doxology
  Gloria Patri
  Responses to the Great Prayer of Thanksgiving said in worship:

    The Lord be with you.
    And also with you.
    Lift up your hearts.
    We lift them to the Lord.
    Let us give thanks to the Lord our God.
    It is right to give our thanks and praise.

- Discuss how to pass the peace during worship: Offer your hand and, while shaking hands, say to your neighbor, "**Peace be with you**."

Table Blessings

Thank you for the world so sweet.
Thank you for the food we eat.
Thank you for the birds that sing.
Thank you, God, for everything. Amen.

Lord Jesus, be our morning guest,
Our noontide friend, our nighttime rest.
And with this gift of food impart
Your love and peace to every heart. Amen.

Be present at our table, Lord.
Be here and everywhere adored.
Thy children bless and grant that we
May feast in fellowship with Thee. Amen.

Age Eight Through Age Eleven

Children in this age grouping are generally deeply entrenched in the **Affiliative** stage of faith development. This means they enjoy being part of a church community that loves and accepts them. Actually they just love being part of any group — they have begun to understand the concept of fellowship! Children at this age want to learn ways in which they can belong to the community and to do this they want to participate. Above all they want to feel that they **belong**!

Bible Passages

Psalms	Psalm 1 Psalm 23 Psalm 119:9-16 Psalm 121
Old Testament	Proverbs 3:1-2 Exodus 20:1-17 (Ten Commandments) Isaiah 9:2, 6-11
New Testament	Matthew 5:3-11 Matthew 16:13-17 1 Corinthians 12:4-11

Hymns

#442 The Church's One Foundation
#260 A Mighty Fortress Is Our God
#298 There's a Wideness in God's Mercy
#467 How Great Thou Art
#280 Amazing Grace
#555 Now Thank We All Our God

Corporate Worship with Your Family

- Sign up as a family to:
  - usher/greet
  - bake bread for Communion
  - prepare Communion
  - illustrate a bulletin cover
- Practice with your child to help him or her memorize the Apostles' Creed.
- Talk about what it means to pledge our time, talents, and money to God through the church. Fill out a pledge card with your child. Children can contribute to the church both by committing to help out in some manner and by putting in their own offering. Discuss what tithing means and help your child work out a plan for tithing.

Prayers and Worship at Home

- The Lord's Prayer
- The Apostles' Creed
- The names of all thirteen disciples (see Acts 1:15-26)
- The *Gloria Patri*
- The Doxology
- Begin to memorize the books of the Bible

Table Blessings

O God, bless this food we are about to receive. Give bread to those who hunger, and give hunger for justice to those who have bread.
— A Nicaraguan blessing

For every cup and plateful, God, make us truly grateful. Amen

Lord, through this day, each bite I take,
and through this day each friend I make,
help me remember you. Amen
— Taken from a table blessing

For this food and joy renewed we praise your name, O Lord!
— A monk's table blessing

Age Eleven Through Age Fourteen

Welcome to the teen years with your child! Most youth of this age still want to belong and be accepted into the community and so there is usually a high desire to continue to be active and participate in all aspects of the church. Around fourteen years of age and then into the later teen years, young people begin a time of searching, questioning, and even challenging accepted beliefs and traditions of the church. They are moving away from the faith of their parents and are in search of a faith they themselves can own. There is often doubting and criticism of parents' beliefs. But the operative word here is **commitment**. Though their commitments may seem fickle, their searching is for something to commit to and own. This stage sometimes lasts well into adulthood!

Bible Passages

Psalms	Psalm 119:33-40 Psalm 139:1-18, 23-24

Old Testament	Proverbs 3:5-7
	Jeremiah 1:4-10
	Joshua 24:14-15
	Amos 5:21-24
New Testament	1 Corinthians 12:31b–14:1a
	John 1:1-5, 10-13
	Ephesians 6:10-16
	1 Peter 3:15-16

Hymns

#260 A Mighty Fortress Is Our God
#276 Great Is Thy Faithfulness
#322 Spirit of the Living God
#326 Spirit of God, Descend upon My Heart
#339 Be Thou My Vision
#525 Here I Am, Lord
#282 If Thou but Trust in God to Guide Thee

Corporate Worship with Your Family

- Encourage your child to volunteer to usher/greet.
- Encourage your child to volunteer to be a reader for a worship service.
- If your child is asked to read scripture, practice with him/her beforehand.
- At this time your child may choose to sit with friends or church school class during the worship service. If this arrangement is agreeable with you, be sure to sit where you are able to see your child. This will encourage your child to participate fully in the service and not just to socialize.
- Your child should begin to notice and understand symbols of the church used during the worship service.

Prayers and Worship at Home

- Learn the Nicene Creed
- Be able to read and locate a Bible reference.
- Be able to locate the Old Testament, New Testament, all four Gospels, Psalms, Genesis.
- Know what it means to be Presbyterian.
  – What does the word *presbyterian* mean?
  – What does it mean for our church?
- *Sanctus* #568
- *Gloria in Excelsis* #566

Table Blessings

"Come and dine," the Master calleth, "Come and dine."
To the hungry calleth now, "Come and dine."
He who fed the multitude, turned the water into wine,
"There is plenty at God's table all the time." (sung or said)

I thank you now, dear Lord, for my home and friends and food.
Help me to serve you all this day and show my gratitude.
Amen

To God who gives me food each day
And cares for me in every way:
In all the things I say and do
I'll try to show my love for you.
Amen

Cornerstones is an example of how one congregation is attempting to give parents the support they need to raise children in the faith and to equip them for full participation in corporate worship. It illustrates what can be done when congregations take the theological dimensions of worship seriously.

The congregation that strives to welcome children into corporate worship will likely find itself swimming against the cultural tide. In our consumer culture, churches are feeling the pressure to provide "alternative experiences" for children so that their parents can be free of them during worship. The session of First Presbyterian Church of Tallahassee tells parents that helping their children to worship is a fundamental responsibility, shared by both parents and congregation. The session offers workshops and materials to equip parents for this calling. During Lord's Day worship the session provides childcare for children under the age of kindergarten, but children who have reached kindergarten age are expected to be present in the assembly and to take part as fully as they are able.

This approach, though culturally subversive, is theologically consistent. While no approach is guaranteed to produce pastor-theologians, the congregation of First Presbyterian Church has produced numerous ministers of Word and sacrament through the years. If some have turned out to be pastor-theologians, perhaps some credit is due to a congregation that takes seriously its calling to raise children in the nurture and admonition of the Lord.

Faith and College

Richard R. Crocker

None of us is old enough to remember the days when almost all the colleges in America held, as an explicit purpose, the education of young people (men) to be ministers in the Christian church. Usually the college president was a minister, and many of the professors were also ministers. The curriculum reflected the conviction that all truth was God's truth. Piety was expected of all and was inculcated in regular (sometimes daily) chapel services, where the college president often presided. In those days, so long past it now seems, institutions of higher education reflected and supported a set of cultural assumptions that now exist mainly in small pockets of relative cultural isolation.

In fact, however, those institutions and cultural assumptions persisted until fairly recently. Only in the middle of the nineteenth century did the transition to secular models of education occur, and that, sporadically. The older established private colleges retained required chapel services until the beginning of the twentieth century, and most colleges retained required regular assemblies or convocations with a religious flavor until as late as the 1970s. While the rise of public colleges and universities in the nineteenth century provided a more secular model of education, even these universities were not, at the beginning, avowedly secular. Only in the second half of the nineteenth century did the intellectual division between faith and learning become an accepted part of the educational scene in America, and, even then, in many denominationally affiliated institutions, that great divide was never absolute. Indeed, in some colleges, that divide still does not exist. But in most colleges and universities today, religion has been strictly confined to the curriculum in departments of religious studies that often adhere, even more devotedly than other departments, to a model of "objectivity" that precludes the relevance or importance of any personal perspective. Ministers are rarely on the faculty, though some institutions retain chaplains, or more commonly, coordinators of religious life, or even more commonly, directors of religious and spiritual life who are commissioned to manage the diverse religious groups on campus. Reflecting the marketing realities of the educational business in America, even denominational colleges often minimize their religious affiliation while trumpeting their non-sectarian and diverse constituencies. Occasionally ministers may serve on the board of trustees of institutions, but their formerly central place has given way to other experts whose positions in our culture give them access to the funding on which these institutions depend.

My experience has been primarily in private colleges, and my perspective reflects that experience. I was an undergraduate at Brown University, founded as the Baptist College of Rhode Island. I pursued graduate studies at Vanderbilt University, whose historic association with the Methodist Church was rather bitterly broken in the early twentieth century, and at Oxford University, which, with its Anglican establishment, provided an interesting contrast. Later I worked as college chaplain at Bates College, which was founded as a Free Will Baptist college; as dean at Elizabethtown College, which retains its affiliation with the Church of the Brethren; and, presently, as college chaplain at Dartmouth College, founded by a congregational Great Awakening preacher, with an explicit mission to educate both native Americans (Indians) and the English youth who would minister to them. Each of these institutions, except Oxford, reflects the common pattern of ecclesiastical establishment followed by increasing disestablishment, secularization, and pluralism.[1]

From the point of view of a "representative of faith" on college campuses, the general trajectory of change and accretion that has occurred in their positions in the last three hundred years might be described as follows:

1. For the story of the secularization of American education more generally, see George Marsden, *The Soul of the American University: From Protestant Establishment to Established Unbelief* (New York: Oxford University Press, 1994). For a portrayal of the role of some of the generally small colleges that continue to put a creedal position at their intellectual center, see Naomi Schaefer Riley, *God on the Quad* (Chicago: Ivan R. Dee Press, 2006).

1. fundamental part of the establishment;
2. an integral member of the community;
3. a designated representative of faith in a context of increasing specialization;
4. a designated representative of faith in a context of increasing specialization and skepticism;
5. a designated representative of a particular faith in a context of increasing specialization, skepticism, and pluralism;
6. a designated manager of religious groups in a context of pluralism, skepticism, and specialization;
7. and (contemporarily) a designated representative of religious concern in a context of competing ideologies.

The titles that would represent this trajectory are: founder, president, trustee, faculty member, professor of religion, professor of religious studies, college chaplain, dean of the chapel, campus minister, director of religious life, coordinator of religious and spiritual life, multifaith advisor.

One might think, for example, of Jonathan Edwards, revival preacher of the Great Awakening who became president of Princeton; Eleazar Wheelock, one of Edwards's contemporaries, who founded Dartmouth College; Francis Wayland, Baptist pastor and notable president of Brown; the many faculty who inspired students to become missionaries in the late nineteenth century; William Jewett Tucker, the last minister/president of Dartmouth; Ernest Gordon, postwar Dean of the Chapel at Princeton; activist chaplains like William Sloane Coffin at Yale and Bev Asbury at Vanderbilt, who fundamentally changed and shaped the notion of college chaplain. Following them (all men) have been a variety of men and women, Christian and non-Christian, ordained and lay, who have occasionally (like Peter Gomes at Harvard) distinguished themselves as great preachers, or, more commonly have been subsumed into the vitally important but far less glamorous world of student services.

Early in the twentieth century, YMCA/YWCA "student work" became established on campuses. These "CAs" became Christian Associations or Christian Unions, prevalent on many campuses, and later became secularized as "Campus Associations" (Bates College). At Dartmouth the Christian Union became the William Jewett Tucker Foundation, named after the college's final preacher president and charged with "furthering the moral and spiritual work of Dartmouth College." Dwight Hall at Yale, Faunce House at Brown, and Phillips Brooks House at Harvard were similar. The World Christian Student Federation provided an internationally connected ecumenical (mainly Protestant) student organization that affected many campuses. Later denominations either built their own campus ministry facilities (Baptist Student Unions, Westminster Houses, Wesley Foundations) adjacent to campuses, or they joined in cooperative campus ministry ventures. Today, while denominationally supported campus ministries have declined, there has been a multiplication of external campus ministry groups and institutions, ranging from the venerable Newman Associations for Catholics, Hillels and Chabads for Jewish students, parish-based ministries for many Protestants, and very active evangelical campus ministries such as InterVarsity Christian Fellowship, Navigators, Campus Crusade for Christ, and Fellowship of Christian Athletes.[2] Usually these groups have some recognition from the college and report to the "manager of religious affairs" (or, in the case of Dartmouth, to me as college chaplain). Such reporting is functional and formal rather than substantial. There are agreed-upon procedures that allow groups with very different purposes and creeds to retain a peripheral relationship with the college.

From the point of view of a college student at a typical college (if such exists), the historical trajectory that depicts the changing relationship of a religiously interested student to the general student-body over the last three hundred years might be described as follows:

1. typical student;
2. student with religious concerns among some who do not have such concerns;
3. member of a particular Christian denomination among many others;
4. adherent of a particular tradition among many others;
5. adherent of one particular tradition among adherents of many other traditions as well as adherents of no religious tradition;
6. spiritually interested student;
7. seeker.

2. See Conrad Cherry, Betty A. DeBerg, and Amada Porterfield, *Religion on Campus* (Chapel Hill: University of North Carolina Press, 2001).

How has this general pattern of institutional and cultural change affected the formation of pastor-theologians? One might well argue that, beginning with institutions specifically devoted to training pastors and theologians, colleges became places where one could choose to study religion as one subject among many others, to the place where one could choose to study a variety of religious traditions, to the place where one might well neither study nor practice a faith. In short, the study of religion has become separated from its practice and has moved from the center of the institution to the periphery. What this means is that, while increasing numbers of students are attracted to the study of religion, those who are attracted to the study and practice of a particular religious tradition are now certainly much more the exception than the rule. This does not mean that religious interests have disappeared. It does mean that the student who is or becomes religiously interested now does so, usually, in a context of pluralism, skepticism, and relativism. Religious interests nurtured in such an environment are likely to develop in several different ways. Sometimes students seek an entirely new religious orientation (Buddhism, Islam). Or they may develop into a bold assertion of particularity, which is usually associated with what we call conservatism or, sometimes, fundamentalism. Or they may develop in a way that is necessarily apologetic, because it respects the reality of other perspectives that sometimes conflict with one's own. Or they may develop into relativism. Rarely are they encouraged to develop into a confident faith that, while recognizing its own limitations, still engages the intellectual and ecclesial world with a message of hope and commitment.

College has always been a place where inherited beliefs were examined and criticized, as well as inculcated. What has changed is the balance of those functions. Formation and inculcation now take place in a different context. It is very difficult for a sensitive, intelligent young person to emerge from a contemporary undergraduate education (especially a liberal arts education) without having undergone a process of deconstruction of religious belief. The process by which a reconstruction occurs is haphazard, accidental, or providential.

What are the experiences that shape a pastor-theologian at college today? What are the factors that help to form a thoughtful, faithful person who explores a call to ministry in the church? I will answer this question by reflecting on my own experience, which occurred in the 1960s and 1970s, and then by commenting on the experiences I have observed as teacher, pastor, dean, and chaplain. This personal, anecdotal account is particular, not universal, but it does reveal both the importance and the changing context of college as a time of pastoral-theological formation.

I entered Brown University in the fall of 1965, a white Southern Baptist boy from Alabama. I had grown up in a small town in rural west central Alabama, the black belt, as it is called, in the tense years of the civil rights movement. Selma was the nearest town of any size; that is where I was born. The Selma-Montgomery march began on my 18th birthday. Most of the white people I knew hoped that things would be peaceful, feared change, had frequent and intimate contact with black people, but went to separate schools and to separate churches.[3] And we all went to church. My town had (white) Baptist and Methodist churches, as well as several "colored" Baptist and Methodist churches. Going to church was what everyone did. You saw your schoolteachers and classmates in church. If they were not in your church, you knew they were in another one. You knew this about everyone.

So I entered Brown (1) with a thorough indoctrination into the belief that religion was important; (2) with a sense that religion had to do both with social stability and social change; (3) with an awareness of the universality of religious concern and a belief that Christianity, despite its various patterns of racial and denominational segregation, was for everyone; (4) and with the belief that intellectual life and Christian faith were complementary and mutually reinforcing. I went to Brown because of Roger Williams, who had been my "great man" in high school.[4] I was distressed, after arriving at Brown, to discover that no one among my peers seemed to have any idea at all of who Roger Williams was, nor any knowledge of Brown's Baptist heritage. But I did make a religious connection. Prior to my arrival, I responded to a general invitation from the chaplain, Charlie Baldwin, to attend a "chaplain's retreat" prior to the opening of the school year. I have forgotten the theme but not the occasion. There were about thirty of us who gathered in Newport to listen to speakers and talk. I quickly discovered a pluralism of religious opinion and experience that was new to me.

Brown in many ways turned my life upside down. I arrived as a conser-

3. Although the Supreme Court decision outlawing legal separation in public schools was rendered in 1954 (the year I was in first grade), segregation persisted throughout my high school years. Significant integration in the schools of rural Alabama did not occur until fifteen years later.

4. My high school required that each ninth-grade student choose a "great man" and read a book and write a paper about him each year. I chose Roger Williams. This choice, in itself, probably reflects a religious temperament that is itself a mystery.

vative Southern Baptist boy intent on studying pre-medicine. I thought that the way of life that had formed me in Alabama was self-evidently good — troubled, but good. I encountered a chaplain's office that was enlisting volunteers for the voter rights movement — essentially sending missionaries to the place that I had come from. I attended the college chapel faithfully. Later, with Charlie's help, I started volunteering to teach Sunday school in a struggling Baptist/Congregational congregation in the heavily Cape Verdean Portuguese neighborhood that abutted Brown. I saw an ad in the campus newspaper concerning the formation of a Southern Baptist church meeting in a downtown Providence hotel. I rounded up a few of my Southern friends and took them there. Some of us stayed. It was a place of safety for me — a place of reorientation, where the familiar hymns were sung, and where I could count on traditional Sunday dinner at the pastor's home. This form of nurture sustained me while I was changing.

I experienced my first racially integrated classrooms at Brown. I heard Martin Luther King talk at Brown. I joined a Jewish fraternity where my brothers and I anguished continually about the stupidity of the Vietnam War. My political opinions shifted so decidedly that I found it best simply to be quiet when I went home. I became a conscientious objector, though my draft board in Alabama would not allow my application. My parents divorced. I found that I did not like studying biology and mathematics; I gravitated instead to the classes in the honors program in English and American literature. Literature gave me a way of exploring my own culture safely — and, especially, it allowed me to explore the relationship between religion and culture. Despite knowing a few southern Protestants, my friends were Jewish or Catholic or congregational — most non-practicing. I studied Judaism under Salo Baron, and the sociology of religion under Herbert Gezork. There was no evangelical student group that I knew anything about. Charlie Baldwin once asked me to meet with a representative from InterVarsity (the first time I had ever heard of that organization) who was visiting and who wanted to start a Bible study group. I met with him but had no interest in what he was proposing. Neither did anyone else, as far as I knew.[5]

5. The rise of organizations like InterVarsity and Campus Crusade began in the 1970s and has continued. Now these groups have established chapters at almost every college. While they differ in style and tone, they all combine an intense relational style of Christian fellowship with very simple evangelical doctrine.

Upon graduating in 1969, at the height of the Vietnam War, with my conscientious objection application disallowed, I was drawn to divinity school. This was not simply to avoid the draft. Rather, the Vietnam War and civil rights movement, and the deaths of Martin Luther King and Bobby Kennedy, pushed me inward, to a search for the basis of my values and to the basis of my hope for this world. That search always led me back to Christianity, and to the person of Jesus. Soon, the draft lottery took away my concern, since my number was 347. I wanted and needed to return to the South. I went to Vanderbilt Divinity School. Part of the reason I chose Vanderbilt was because Bev Asbury, the Vanderbilt chaplain, had spoken at the Brown chapel and I, along with a small group of students, had had lunch with him following. I still remember my interchange with him. Having listened to his very politically charged, social activist sermon, I asked him, innocently, whatever became of the notion that ministers should save souls. Bev snapped back (and he did snap): "I don't save souls. God saves souls." Despite being taken aback, I have followed the man ever since. At Vanderbilt I encountered people like Walter Harrelson, Liston Mills, and John Killinger (all Baptists) who also modeled for me the union of mind and heart, Southernness and worldliness, piety and learning, commitment and openness that allowed me to know that I could live in this tension — that, indeed, living within this tension was the only way I could live. It is a model that I also have tried to exemplify ever since.

There was one other formative experience that occurred while I was at Brown. Through the encouragement of a Jewish friend who had been there, I spent a summer as a tour guide on the Isle of Iona, off the coast of Scotland. There I met the head of the Iona community, George McLeod, and entered into the daily worship life of the community. Though ecumenical, it was mainly Presbyterian. This was my introduction to the Presbyterian Church. (There had been a Presbyterian church in my home town, but it had burned down long before my birth, and the members there, seeing this as God's will, dispersed themselves into the Methodist and Baptist churches.)

After one year at Vanderbilt, I won a Rhodes scholarship to study theology at Oxford. My Anglican tutors, admirable though they were, did not shepherd me into their fold. John Macquarrie convinced me to be a Christian existentialist, but not an Anglican. Given who I was — socially, economically, geographically, and theologically, Anglicanism, to use William James's phrase, was not a live option. I faithfully attended the New Road Baptist Church, with occasional excursions to the Quakers, the Presbyterians, and, of course, the weekly sung chapel service at my college. I preached at tiny Baptist churches throughout the countryside. When I returned to Vanderbilt and completed my M.Div., I was still a Baptist and earnestly tried to find a Baptist pulpit, but it was not to be. Vanderbilt counted against me. My opinions and beliefs, like Roger Williams's, were now judged incompatible with the prevailing Southern Baptist doctrines. Married by now, my wife and I moved to another part of Nashville, where we both were teachers. We started attending a neighborhood Presbyterian church, where I found a fit, validation, affirmation. And so I became a Presbyterian minister. Despite the constant arguments and excessively long meetings, I have remained one ever since — serving as pastor of two Presbyterian congregations — and being a chaplain and dean at three colleges.

What useful generalizations about the formation of pastor-theologians might be drawn from this very particular experience, and from the observations of generations of students that I have watched since then? I think, these:

First, college is for all thoughtful people a time of growth and change. Developmentally, late adolescence and early adulthood are crucial times for the tasks of identity formation and intimacy. That is why these years are so precious and so important. The triggers that lead to change may be environmental and cultural, but they are also biological and psychological. It is a very rare person indeed who emerges from college as the same person who entered.

Second, religious interest may be fundamentally a matter of temperament, but it is also a matter of experience. Those people who have been taught by families, schools, and churches that religion is important are apt to continue to believe that religion is important. Lacking those lessons, the discovery that religion is important, while not impossible, is much less likely. We all know of people who have "come to Christ" or made other important religious commitment during their college years, with little or no previous background. In my own personal experience, as well as in the experience of the generations of students whom I know, this is rare. Now that there are well-organized and well-funded evangelical groups (Christian and otherwise) on college campuses, there are, of course, students who move from a secular stance to a religious one, but there are far more students who use these groups as I used the Southern and Baptist church in Providence — as a way of reorienting and stabilizing my growth. Almost every student wants reminders of home — sometimes an idealized home. Students who had significant experiences in high school youth groups often want those to continue. The Bible study that is so often a feature of these groups is quite often really a time for social reinforcement. This is not to say that nothing significant can happen in these contexts. Obviously it can and does. The Word and the Spirit, as we know, are unconstrained. But they are mainly stabilizing influences.

Third, the academic study of religion is, for some people, very destabilizing, while it is, for others, an experience of intellectual growth. I think this depends both upon the teachers, as well as upon the student's particular needs and interests. I have heard, so often over the years, teachers of religious studies who complain that students expected their classes to be a continuation of Sunday school, as well as complaints from students who believe (sometimes accurately) that their teachers have an agenda of unbelief. Thus it is that some religious groups advise their adherents to avoid the religious studies department. But there are those who find that the academic study of religion, whether it is anchored in a religious commitment or not, is intensely interesting to them. Some of these go on to graduate programs in religion without ever intending to unite study and religious commitment. Each year, in every college, I have seen this happen to a small number of people.

Fourth, it is important that those who become pastor-theologians, intentionally or, more often, unintentionally, encounter in college serious challenges to their faith, both intellectual and experiential. An education that does not teach doubt cannot lead to strong faith. People who have never taken doubt seriously, who have never been seriously acquainted with the intellectual questioning that characterizes our culture and our age, can never become thoughtful advocates of faith.[6] Paradoxically, unless one fully and sincerely approaches the abyss of meaninglessness, strong faith cannot take root. Similarly, persons who have never lived in a genuinely pluralistic world can never test their own particularity. This is why a good liberal arts education is an essential preparation for ministry. The groups that have neglected this requirement have sacrificed more than they have gained.

Fifth, for those students who later become pastor-theologians, it is essential that they encounter during their college years role models who combine faith and learning.[7] In some places this may be a teacher, or a campus minister, or a chaplain. It is not essential that the role model be a mentor; it is not essential that there be agreement about beliefs. But it is essential that there be someone who shows, by his or her commitments and practices, that

6. See Rebecca Kuiken's essay in this volume.

7. See Cynthia A. Jarvis's essay in this volume.

it is possible to express faith in terms that acknowledge the importance of intellectual questions. Those role models continue to be found, I hope, on every campus. To be sure, there are probably fewer of them. Increasingly, as women have become theologians and ministers, the importance of female role models has been rightly acknowledged. The fear of imposing beliefs (than which there is apparently nothing worse) inhibits many conversations between faculty and students — unless the beliefs in question happen to be political ones, in which case they fuel conversation. But, just as I needed Charlie Baldwin and Bev Asbury to be people who combined faith and learning, even though at the time I thought they might be defective, and just as I needed Herbert Gezork to show me that one could be a committed Christian (president of Andover Newton seminary) and an objective teacher of sociology, so every budding pastor-theologian needs someone who can model that union. That is why the role of college chaplain, like the role of pastor-theologian, is so important, and it is why I, even without fully knowing it, wanted to be one.

The Education of a Pastor-Theologian: Toward a Learned Ministry

Wallace M. Alston Jr.

Theological education has not lacked for scholarly attention in the recent past. Numerous books and articles, most of which have had a very limited shelf life, have been written on the subject. Foundations, divinity schools, seminaries, and ecumenical consortia of one sort or another have drawn down huge financial grants and invested enormous amounts of time and energy pursuing research projects, institutional analyses, curriculum reviews, and governance evaluations, all aimed at increasing the effectiveness of theological education. Reports of these efforts have been variously constructive, angry, insightful, trivial, and in some cases revolutionary, leading to innovations in the content and delivery of theological education. In most cases, these studies have arisen within the academy, led and staffed by gifted, committed members of institutional administrations and faculties. Only a very few of them have included able pastors currently serving churches as full participants in their processes, and even fewer have originated in the disciplined research and peer discourse of pastors of churches. Furthermore, since only a few of the participants in these studies have ever tried to translate a theological education into pastoral practice, one might argue that any assessment they might make of its usefulness would be incomplete at best and at worst naïve and potentially misleading.

This is not to deny the validity of the work done in and on theological education that originates within the academy. It is to plead for attention to be given by those charged with the responsibility of educating ministers and priests for the church to reflections and recommendations that come from men and women who are attempting to embody a theological education in a ministry to others. The conviction that gives to the various perspectives on ministry represented in this volume its essential unity is that contemporary pastoral practice should be informed by and reflective of the sources, convictions, and practices of the church catholic; that the pastoral calling is a theological vocation; that preaching, teaching, pastoral care, and church administration, far from being merely institutional functions, are theological occasions for the communication of the gospel of Jesus Christ; that theological education should be about preparing and equipping pastor-theologians for a learned ministry in the service of the church.[1]

How might seminaries and divinity schools go about doing that? Theological education is not a monolith and should not be treated as such. Institutions sharing the same theological tradition may offer essentially the same curriculum yet produce very different types of ministers and pastoral perspectives. Some institutions regularly graduate men and women who understand their vocation to be that of a pastor-theologian for the church while others, teaching essentially the same courses, do not. Wherein lies the difference? What are the formative influences in one's theological education that create and nurture the love of theology and an understanding of the pastoral vocation as that of pastor-theologian?

From the vantage point of thirty-three years as a pastor of churches, and on the basis of my experience in the Pastor-Theologian Program sponsored by the Lilly Endowment and the Center of Theological Inquiry, I think it possible to identify four formative influences in theological education that support and encourage students to identify the pastoral office as a theological vocation: (1) the ecumenical appropriation of a particular theological tradition; (2) convictional teaching by faculty with pastoral experience; (3) a curriculum with the Bible and the history of doctrine at its core, integrated by the expectations and demands of pastoral practice; and (4) the advocacy by faculty and administration of pastoral ministry as a compelling theological vocation.

1. When I speak of theological education in this paper, the intended reference is always to undergraduate theological education for which the basic degree (M.Div., B.D., or S.T.B.) in theological studies is awarded. Undergraduate theological education is the context in which most pastor-theologians are formed. Graduate theological education is oriented to research and writing, with an academic vocation in view, and represents a different set of circumstances altogether.

The Ecumenical Appropriation of a Particular Theological Tradition

One of the most influential factors in the formation of the pastor-theologian is the power of a particular theological tradition (e.g., Wesleyan, Lutheran, Mennonite, Reformed, Anabaptist) to provide motivation and conceptualization for self-identification. The pluralism of historical theological traditions should not be an embarrassment if all are portrayed as attempts to recover and restate that which Irenaeus called the "regula veritatis," the apostolic tradition, a canon-like summary of the revelation deposited in scripture. In fact, it is only an ecumenical appropriation of the great historical traditions that adequately represents any one tradition's intent, which is to bear witness to the essential unity of the church.

Theological education is not self-generating. When institutionalized in seminaries and divinity schools it embodies a particular history of faith and life. Interdenominational as well as denominational institutions are rooted in historical communities that were brought into being and shaped, at least in part, by a particular theological consensus. This consensus, which consisted of Bible reading, prayer, regular church attendance, and in some traditions the memorization of catechisms and creeds, was validated and practiced in Christian family life. New generations were given the sources and language of faith in the context of familial love and trust, such that even the rebel was given something to rebel against. When young people left home for school or work, they carried with them, whether consciously or subconsciously, a memory of and a predisposition for Christian faith and life. What this meant for our topic is that students entering upon a theological education brought with them the memory, however vague and unformed, of the essential elements of a particular theological tradition.

This is no longer the case. People entering upon a theological education today, on account of the influence of the times on their parents and grandparents, still bear the marks of the 1960s and 1970s. The revolt against authority and prescription, and particularly the ridicule of habit and routine, called into question the concept of the ordered life as the means by which a historical tradition is practiced and delivered. Not many years ago the ordered life, in contrast to the driven live, the scattered life, or the shiftless life, was not only honored as an expression of authentic piety in the home, but it was generally understood to be a lived confession of the power of the living God to make sense of human living and dying. "Drop thy still dews of quietness, till all our strivings cease," wrote John Greenleaf Whittier. "Take from our souls the strain and stress, and let our *ordered lives* confess the beauty of thy peace."[2] Unfortunately, the ordered life does not have the same appeal in Christian family life today, partly because of the pervasive influence of secularism in and upon the church, but also because the family, which once was the trustee of sacred tradition, lost interest somewhere along the way in making routine connections between their faith tradition and their daily practice. As a consequence, there has not only been a neglect of historical theological traditions in families in the context of which the language and narratives of faith were handed on from generation to generation; there has been an outright rejection of the possibility that tradition is liberating rather than confining.

A similar process of de-traditioning is being experienced in congregations today. Pastors only infrequently understand their task in terms of traditioning the church. Preaching for the most part is first-generational preaching, by which I mean preaching from personal experience with little indication that men and women for centuries have sought insight into the same passage or similar issues and with little anticipation that contemporary people could benefit from making their acquaintance. Teaching, if practiced at all in any systematic or sustained way by the pastor, is mostly oriented to contemporary experience or issues of current concern, e.g., parenting, conflict management, just war, and abortion. There is little indication that the pastor is aware or knowledgeable of the history of interpretation. Pastoral care is essentially governed these days by the rules of psychiatry and the goals of mental health, and church administration has adopted the model of the corporate executive. The traditioning task of the pastor, whereby the centuries of Christian thoughtfulness and belief are delivered into the hands of succeeding generations, has been displaced by indicators of success and replaced by the various guarantors of pastoral longevity. Theological education, which once was a process of redefining and reclaiming, of bringing to life and of engendering new passion for the particular theological tradition in which a person was nurtured and with which the person was at least somewhat familiar, is now challenged to assume the role of the primary bearer of historical theological traditions.

2. These lines from the familiar hymn, "Dear Lord and Father of Mankind," are taken from the larger poem by Whittier titled "The Brewing of Soma."

The unnerving circumstance for those who cherish theological traditions as tutors of theological imagination is that theological education itself is increasingly done at a distance from the theological traditions from which it emerged. Denominational institutions may continue to pay lip service to their founding tradition, but they do not always appear to understand their mission as one of educating men and women to be pastors of churches in that tradition. Denominational institutions no longer expect members of their faculties to be active participants in churches of that tradition. Student bodies even in denominational institutions are increasingly ecumenical, having no relation to the founding theological tradition of the institution, and faculties are increasingly called to teach without either proficiency or practice in the tradition that the institution was established to represent. Seminary and divinity school curricula are theologically scattered rather than oriented to a particular theological tradition, creating a huge crisis of theological competence in the ministry.

John Leith has noted that prior to the Second World War theology in nearly every seminary was taught from a basic text.[3] Whether it was Luther or Calvin, Hodge or Strong or Berkhof, did not really matter. These textbooks, representing particular theological traditions, all contained a basic system or structure that covered the gamut of theology from a perspective that had received the approbation of at least a significant segment of the Christian community. A student with average ability but with diligence in study could not only grasp a coherent view of the faith from the perspective of a particular theological point of view, but also was provided forms of thought and expression against which one was invited to struggle and with which one might become an effective communicator of the gospel. In contrast, more than a few seminary graduates today go forth into ministry having read bits and pieces of several contemporary theologians without having a clear grasp of any coherent pattern of theology that has a track record of benefiting the church. The loss of the family and the congregation as the primary bearers of theological tradition, coupled with the widening gap between theological institutions and the particular historical traditions that gave them rise, largely explains the demise of the concept of the learned minister as the criterion of pastoral competence.

Albert C. Outler, in his treatment of the role and place of tradition in

3. John Leith, *From Generation to Generation* (Louisville: Westminster/John Knox Press, 1990), p. 98.

the ante-Nicene church,[4] notes that the Christian church originated in an act of divine traditioning at Pentecost, when apostolic memories were transformed into the apostolic kerygma and the loyalty of disciples was transmuted into the conviction that Jesus of Nazareth was Israel's long-anticipated Messiah. "Since that day," Outler remarks, "the survival of the Church has depended, always at least in part, on the traditionary process by which its time in the world has been prolonged. Tradition, both as act and process, constitutes both the source and the method by which Christians, since Pentecost, have been enabled to know and to respond to the revelation of God in Christ."[5] There was no time in the second century, Outler goes on to say, "when the odds were better than even that Christianity would simply disintegrate under the twin pressures of doctrinal confusion and social disfavor,"[6] a circumstance, perhaps, analogous to that of the church today. What saved the day was the solid confidence on the part of the leadership in the continuance in history of what God had begun. The leaders of the church "were traditioners — trust officers of the Christian treasure of truth, qualified judges of 'right teaching.' They had a sense of tradition — an intuition of the active presence of the Holy Spirit as resident guarantor in the community, as celebrant of its holy mysteries, as guarantors of its destiny,"[7] which freed them to deal with the challenges and crises of the age. The subordination of particular historical traditions, either to an eclectic theological consensus in the name of ecumenism or to a vocation of assisting people on their spiritual journeys, has both lowered the bar in theological education and contributed to the fading from view of the learned minister.

Convictional Teaching

In his discussion of the Emperor Julian and the schools of the fourth century after Christ, historian Glanville Downey argues that one may learn a great deal about the strength of early Christianity and the reasons for its

4. Albert C. Outler, "The Sense of Tradition in the Ante-Nicene Church," *The Heritage of Christian Thought: Essays in Honor of Robert Lowry Calhoun* (New York: Harper & Row, 1965), pp. 8-30.

5. Outler, "The Sense of Tradition in the Ante-Nicene Church," p. 8.

6. Outler, "The Sense of Tradition in the Ante-Nicene Church," p. 9.

7. Outler, "The Sense of Tradition in the Ante-Nicene Church," pp. 9-10.

success and diffusion by observing the pagan efforts to compete with it or suppress it.[8]

Downey's subject is the Emperor Julian the Apostate (A.D. 361-363) and his conception of the role that education might play in his effort to save paganism and eliminate Christianity. Julian believed that Christianity was not only an erroneous religious doctrine but a subversive political force in the empire in that it alienated the favor of the gods who had granted economic prosperity to the Roman state. The condition of the empire, in Julian's view, was compromised by an inadequate system of education. He was familiar with the care that was taken to train Christian teachers and priests and to provide them with apologetic and instructional material, and he saw the need for paganism, which possessed no organization or hierarchy that could compete with the church, to be provided with adequate means for encountering and combating Christian teaching.

To this end Julian launched a massive attempt to reform education, and particularly the quality of teaching, in the Roman Empire. He took note of the fact that Christian teaching was convictional and considered it absurd that Rome should allow people to teach what they did not believe to be sound. "The emergence of Christianity, followed by the effort to revive paganism, had created an issue which had not existed before the emancipation of Christianity, namely, that of the relationship between the teacher's personal beliefs and his public instruction."[9] In the emperor's mind, convictional teaching had rendered Christians potential if not actual dangers to the stability of the empire. Thus they were not allowed to remain in positions where they might corrupt the young.

One of the most disturbing trends in contemporary theological education is the disappearance of convictional teaching on seminary and divinity school campuses. When asked about their perception of the relationship between their teachers' personal beliefs and their public instruction, students today may be expected either to judge the question inappropriate or to respond that they do not know what you are talking about. What I am talking about is classroom teaching that leaves no doubt in the student's mind concerning where the teacher stands in relation to the subject under consideration, whether it is of life-and-death importance or simply an ob-

8. Glanville Downey, "The Emperor Julian and the Schools," *Classical Journal* 53 (1957-58): 97-103.

9. Downey, "The Emperor Julian and the Schools," p. 100.

ject of dispassionate reflection and evaluation. Convictional teaching is teaching done from the inside of an issue or idea as a sympathetic participant rather than from the outside as a disinterested spectator. It is teaching with such obvious passion for the subject matter that the student is caught up, drawn into it, and brought to the point of personal decision about its meaning and merit. Convictional teaching in theological education is a form of intellectual mentoring whereby the teacher approaches questions of truth in scripture and tradition with a hermeneutics of trust and gratitude that bears witness to the sheer delight of serving God with the life of the mind.

Convictional teaching, which not many years ago was the rule in theological education, now appears to be the exception. This is not to say that seminary and divinity school faculties today are without convictions. Many if not most of them are devout men and women who are committed to the Christian faith and deeply involved in the life and work of the church. What I would venture to say is that a pedagogical style that looks with suspicion at anything less than disinterested objectivity seems to have gained currency in theological education. Several reasons may be advanced to account for this trend. First, seminaries and divinity schools increasingly take their operational bearings from the waypoints of secular education. Second, there is an insatiable desire on the part of teachers of the theological disciplines for respect in and acceptance by the secular academy. Third, an increasing number of seminary and divinity school faculty receive their terminal degree in secular universities that are rightly more oriented to research rather than confession. Finally, faculty appointments are being made by people who are unrelated to the theological tradition of the sponsoring denomination, who are unfamiliar with the constituency that supports the institution, and who have never distinguished themselves as pastors of churches. Seminary and divinity school teachers with experience in the pastorate approach biblical texts, church doctrines, and history in qualitatively different ways than those without this experience. A teacher who has lived, suffered, and died with a constituency that is dependent solely upon him or her for the integration and interpretation of the absurd, the tragic, the ironic twists and turns of life, can be expected to teach the Bible, the doctrines of the church, and the various developments in the church's life and thought through the ages with a passion that one who is not privileged by pastoral experience cannot be expected to exhibit.

Ernest L. Boyer, formerly of the Carnegie Foundation for the Advancement of Teaching, insists on a broadening of our definition of scholarship.[10] He distinguished between a scholarship of discovery that closely resembles research, a scholarship of integration that puts isolated facts in perspective, a scholarship of application such as that practiced by the extension departments of land-grant institutions, and a scholarship of teaching that makes it possible for knowledge to be understood by others. All faculties must establish themselves in one way or another as scholars of discovery, but something more is demanded of seminary and divinity school faculty, namely, a scholarship of teaching, to which I would add, of convictional teaching, which is the only way in which knowledge of the Christian faith is transmitted to the soul as well as the mind of others.

In *Stromateis* I where he develops his basic pedagogical theory that Christian truth is not traditioned as information, Clement of Alexandria gives a brief if rather vague biographical account of his own teachers.[11] The communication of Christian truth, he argues, involves maieutic teaching and learning within the context of a significant human relationship, which means that there is something intensely private and personal in the process of Christian teaching and learning. Augustine had a similar take on theological epistemology.[12] According to Augustine, teaching is not about putting knowledge into words which can then be understood and appropriated. Words are but signs that point beyond themselves to reality. They do not by themselves impute knowledge. Knowledge is gained only as a result of an internal process in the mind of the pupil. All the teacher can do by means of words is to elicit the truth. Truth is interior to the mind, though not at all subjective, and cannot be communicated from without. Truth comes from God, whose eternal Truth, Christ, dwells in minds prepared to receive him. Christ is the inward teacher of all who listen to him. The human teacher can but speak "through faith for faith" (Rom. 1:17) of what is believed and known, confident that the Christ, the inward teacher, will give to all who are open to receive the truth according to the ability of each. Krister Stendahl, New Testament scholar and retired Bishop of Stockholm, in his Edward L.

10. Ernest L. Boyer, *Scholarship Reconsidered: Priorities of the Professorate* (Princeton: The Carnegie Foundation for the Advancement of Teaching, 1990), p. 15. Cited and discussed by John H. Leith, *From Generation to Generation*, pp. 75-76.

11. Clement of Alexandria, *Stromateis* I, 4; cf. also V, 10 and VI, 16.

12. "De Magistro (The Teacher)," *Augustine: Earlier Writings*, The Library of Christian Classics, vol. 6, trans. John H. S. Burleigh (Philadelphia: Westminster Press, 1953), pp. 64-101.

Mark lecture at Harvard-Epworth United Methodist Church, Cambridge, Massachusetts, chose to speak about why he loved the Bible. In so doing he left us a graphic illustration of the scholarship of convictional teaching that Boyer, Clement, and Augustine had advocated before him. "What else can one do — what else can I do," asked Stendahl, "but to tell my story, the story of my love for the Bible: how to read, to study, to ponder, to preach the Bible; how it became my professional, even my professorial career, as that study watered, even lubricated, my soul."[13]

An Integrated Curriculum of Study

A third formative influence in theological education that would support and encourage students to identify the pastoral office as a theological vocation is a curriculum of study with the Bible and the history of doctrine at its core, integrated by the expectations and demands of pastoral practice. In an essay titled "Theological Education as Formation for Ministry," John E. MacInnis provides us with a helpful rereading of Augustine's *De doctrina Christiana* in light of the question: How does theological education shape future ministers?[14] For Augustine, the preparation of competent pastors gives a particular shape to theological education. "Theological literacy meant competence in reading and interpreting sacred texts, but it was intended to accomplish something more. Theological education should draw students into a reflective process which assists them in the quest for a deeper personal faith, for a well-grounded confession of that faith, and for life within a community of faith."[15] This tripartite intentionality of theological education — the shaping of thought, confession, and a life of service — requires a curriculum that manifests sufficient internal coherence and motivational thrust to weld thought and belief to commitment and action. I suggest that any curriculum adequate for this task will be one with studies in the Bible and the history of doctrine at its core, integrated by the expectations and demands of pastoral practice.

In conversation with two seminary professors representing two differ-

13. "Why I Love the Bible," *Harvard Divinity Bulletin* (Winter 2007): 20-28.

14. *Theological Literacy for the Twenty-First Century,* ed. Rodney L. Petersen and Nancy M. Rourke (Grand Rapids: Eerdmans, 2002), pp. 382-91.

15. In Petersen and Rourke, eds., *Theological Literacy for the Twenty-First Century,* p. 382.

ent institutions, one of them alluded to "what we are trying to do at . . . seminary." When I asked the other professor if she could speak of "what we are trying to do" at her institution, she smiled and replied in the negative. Her seminary offered a rich curriculum of courses taught by widely recognized and acclaimed scholars, but her take on that institution was that it was a matter of each member of the faculty, each department, pursuing their individual and not always complementary academic agendas. Another member of that faculty likened this lack of integration in institutional goals and motivation to people working loosely together as "independent contractors." The integrating factor that might interrelate, interconnect, and make vocational sense of the various options and opportunities in a theological curriculum of study is commitment to the preparation of men and women to be learned pastors of Christian congregations.

To say that pastoral practice should be the integrating factor of the theological curriculum is not to say that the number of practical courses needs to be increased. To the contrary, an increase in courses on how to do ministry taught by people who have never done ministry in any sustained or distinguished way is unlikely to contribute very much to the formation of a learned ministry. It is the insight into pastoral practice that comes from the content of the faith itself, communicated in biblical, theological, and historical studies, that is capable of providing a sense of wholeness to a program of study. In other words, and to put the matter bluntly, practical courses do not usually create effective practitioners. The practice of ministry is most effectively taught by convictional teaching in the substantive courses of the curriculum.

To this end, the first and most basic task of theological education is to teach the Bible, not in order to increase the level of competence in dealing with a classic of ancient near eastern literature, but for the formation of believing, intelligent, articulate pastors. The planning and enactment of theological studies will always be incomplete if it fails to take into account the need and opportunity for students to examine the truth-claims of the Christian faith with a view toward their own growth in faith and life.

If the primary task of theological education is to shape thought and facilitate faith, theological education must take seriously the conclusion of pollster George Gallup that the United States is "a nation of biblical illiterates."[16] In a quiz Stephen Prothero administered to undergraduates, students

16. Cited in Stephen Prothero, "Georgia Is Right to Teach the Bible," *The Atlanta Journal-Constitution,* March 19, 2007, p. A9.

told him "that Moses was blinded on the road to Damascus and that Paul led the Israelites out of Egypt. Surveys that are more scientific have found that only one out of three U.S. citizens is able to name the four Gospels, and one out of 10 thinks Joan of Arc was Noah's wife."[17] The first and most basic task of theological education is to hand on the Bible as the narrative of the Christian faith and the language of Christian thought. Teaching about the Bible is always secondary to teaching the Bible. Augustine, whose theology was done under the rubric "We believe in order to understand," knew that belief and understanding were colleagues in Christian pedagogy and that the two were inseparable in theological education. The Bible, its narratives, teachings, poetry, promises, language, and worldview, is the word of God written and its appropriation is basic to the formation of the pastor-theologian.

The second task of theological education is to teach the theology of the church, which is not the same as teaching various theologies. It is important and helpful for the pastor to know what contemporary theologians are saying, but one can only assess the import of these contemporary theologies as one grasps the theology about which the church has reached a degree of consensus through the ages. This is the theology of the ancient creeds: the Apostles' Creed, the Nicene Creed, and the Chalcedonian Definition. It is also the theology of the great creative theologians of the past, such as Augustine, Aquinas, Luther, Calvin, Wesley, and Barth. The task of the pastor is not to advocate his or her own idiosyncratic understanding of the Christian faith. It is to be a faithful interpreter of the ancient theological tradition and of the contemporary attempt either to appropriate or to challenge it, and it is to make that engagement of the present with the past available to people in the language of the present day.

The third task of theological education is to equip men and women to think, to preach, to teach, to exercise pastoral care, and to administer a Christian congregation as representatives of the biblical and theological tradition of the church. The point of grounding theological education in the Bible and the history of Christian thought is not to provide students with facts but to provide them with ecclesial insights and clues in the light of which they may come to understand the world around them. The task of the pastor-theologian is to equip people to think theologically themselves, to understand their own lives and the life of the contemporary world in the light of the scriptural and theological consensus of the church, and only

17. Prothero, "Georgia Is Right to Teach the Bible," p. A9.

then in light of its contemporary critics and reformers. It is to expose the alien faiths by which many people live, including the assumptions and concepts that govern their thinking, and to invite them to consider the Christian faith as a more adequate interpretation of the experiences of life in this world.

These three curricular intentions — to teach the Bible for faith formation as well as for knowledge, to teach the faith of the church in order to facilitate understanding of the manner in which enduring and normative revelation in scripture has been related to specific cultural contexts, and to teach these things for the purpose of preparing people for a learned ministry — constitute the integrating factor that makes the formation of pastor-theologians possible.

The Advocacy of Pastoral Ministry as a Compelling Theological Occasion

Any theological institution that intends to play its part in the formation of pastor-theologians must allow the agenda and context for the study of scripture and doctrine to be set, not by the criteria of the secular academy, but by the faith, needs, and questions of the church. Putting the matter in this way, of course, requires a caveat. The caveat is that the church does not always know what it needs. Its sense of need is often warped by self-justifying self-interest. Its questions are often not the questions elicited by the gospel. Its perspective is often so culturally conditioned that it positions itself in opposition to things that the gospel requires. The point being made here is one of primary orientation. It is not that theological education is to be a tool of the church, but that it is to be a servant of the church, guarding the church against the distortion of Christian faith and life, and leading the church in the way of truth.

The usefulness of highly technical, critical historical and literary studies of the Bible in the formation of pastor-theologians is totally dependent on the narrative reading of the Bible as witness to the acts of God "for us and for our salvation" (Nicene Creed). The needs that people bring to the study of scripture, the questions they ask of scripture, often differ from those of secular scholarship, and they are often the profounder and more important. "School theology, remote from the congregation, is frequently sophisticated, clever, and pedantic. More significant, it often obscures the reality of the human situation and the concrete questions human beings ask. These questions are central to human concerns, and they are very simple but reveal a great deal about a person's theology. One such question is, is it proper to pray for rain, or is it proper to pray for a cure for cancer? Another question that reveals a person's theology is what happens that is worth talking about when a person dies?"[18] Others are, does God intervene in human affairs and how am I to cope with my own failures? These are the questions that people who are up against the stubborn realities of contemporary life regularly ask. It is when theological studies are undertaken with one eye cocked to such questions that the pastor-theologian is formed.

Likewise the test of good theology is its usefulness to the church, namely, its ability to edify, to energize, to heal, and to provide hope for people living amidst the stresses and pressures of contemporary life. It has often been suggested that preachability is the criteria for any theology that matters. A theological book or treatise written by the most erudite theologian in the world is of little use or importance if it is unrelated to the life-and-death issues that all people face and with which they must come to terms. The substantive writings of many contemporary theologians that have been written with life-and-death issues in mind must be contrasted with the impotent theologies that major in innovative subjects and slants, bringing to mind the philosophers Paul addressed in Athens long ago. Such theologies produce ineffective pastors who will likely have little to offer a congregation.

Seminaries and divinity schools that graduate theologically able men and women whose vocation it is to be pastor-theologians are those that advocate without embarrassment or apology the pastoral ministry as a theological occasion. The extent to which this is true is difficult to fathom unless one has personally experienced the practical affairs of pastoral life as occasions for the gospel. Preaching and teaching are obviously occasions when the biblical and theological tradition of the church are brought into play, but so also are pastoral care and church administration. When an individual seeks pastoral counsel, the person is not simply looking for professional counsel from a psychiatrist or social worker. The person wants a pastor who is competent to reflect upon the situation at hand from the standpoint of the gospel. This is not to say that pastor is to evangelize the person who seeks counsel or care, but it is to say that the pastor approaches the situation as a

18. John H. Leith, *Crisis in the Church* (Louisville: Westminster/John Knox Press, 1997), pp. 31-32.

representative of the Christian faith, not as a professional clinician or social change agent. Pastoral care is an opportunity to communicate, verbally or non-verbally, directly or indirectly, the faith of the church.

Likewise, church administration is a theological occasion. Staff meetings are theological discussion groups and ecclesial planning events. Christian stewardship and the making of a church budget have to do with the meaning of discipleship in relation to the needs of both the church and those in need in the world beyond the church. The property committee has before it the Christian doctrine of creation, namely, what is to be done with that part of God's creation for which it is responsible, and how the tender care of church property might bear witness to the glory of God in the community at large.

The teaching of pastoral practice is best done by men and women who have years of experience in assisting congregations to become theological communities.[19] In the sacraments, the liturgies, and the everyday devotional activities, as well as in the mundane affairs of the church mentioned above, the minister is called upon to function as a theologian for the church by bringing the scriptural and theological tradition to bear on ecclesial practices. These practices, even an enlightened interpretation of them by a pastor-theologian, do not guarantee Christian existence. Nevertheless, it is more likely that one who is nurtured in them and by them will be able to meet the challenges of life constructively and faithfully than those who have not been nurtured by these basic disciplines.

Nathan Pusey, the former President of Harvard University, in his speech at the dedication of the Speer Library of Princeton Theological Seminary, said that

> the enduring first need of the church is for a learned ministry, for a continuing succession of those scholar-teachers who shall not need to be ashamed and shall not fail to help the churches to do their work in the world because they will have been qualified rightly to divide the word of truth. . . . Many circumstances of our lives suggest that today the informed, compassionate, understanding scholar-minister is the professional of whom all other professionals stand most in need, whether they know it yet or not, for it is (the minister's) function to speak to them of that kind of redemption or redirection which alone can give acceptable

19. See the essay on theological mentors by Cynthia Jarvis in this volume.

meaning to their efforts and which it is in the gospel's power, helped by a truly learned ministry, widely to mediate.[20]

We do not often use that sort of language when speaking of theological education these days, nor do we often hear comments like that from laypersons, calling for a recovery of theological competence in the Christian ministry. It is as though the whole point of it all has been missed by those involved in theological education. It is as if someone at the controls of things is simply not listening. "What in hell do seminaries think they are doing in putting out people like that?" asked one congregant in the context of a discussion of the difficulty people have today in finding good preaching.

Perhaps in the minds of some the idea that the church might once again benefit from the substantive influence of a learned ministry is unrealistic at best, and at worst naïve. After all, so the argument goes, times have changed. The respect once accorded to theology as "the queen of the sciences" and to the office of pastor in Western culture, to say nothing of the ways that both were privileged by the culture, no longer exists. The ministry no longer attracts the top talent. The ablest college and university graduates no longer consider theological education as an attractive and challenging option. Furthermore, the church has played its own part in the degradation of the pastoral vocation by lowering the standards for ordination to the extent that a pleasing personality and effective interpersonal skills are more highly valued than biblical and theological competence. Search committees, as a matter of fact, tend to shy away from competence, feeling far more comfortable with mediocrity and style. The idea of the learned minister, who is equally competent to represent the biblical and theological tradition of the church as a neurosurgeon is to excise a tumor from the brain or a chief executive to preside over a transnational corporation, is not what most search committees have in mind when looking for a minister.

New initiatives in alternative theological education are needed. These new initiatives should not be identical in content or form to theological education done in established institutions, nor should they be understood as threats to the good work being done in many of these institutions. They should complement, supplement, and extend what is being done in ways that stimulate and encourage the development of a distinctive pastoral theo-

20. Reprint of "The Dedication of the Robert E. Speer Library," October 8, 1977, Princeton Theological Seminary, Princeton, New Jersey.

logical voice on the part of those already in ministry. The model I have in mind is the Finkenwalde experience under the leadership of Dietrich Bonhoeffer, redesigned and made available to existing pastors of churches who are attempting to offer a learned ministry to the church in spite of cultural and ecclesiastical pressures to define the vocation otherwise.

The Pastor-Theologian Program, funded by the Lilly Endowment and sponsored by the Center of Theological Inquiry for nine years, was never intended to be a continuing education program. Continuing education programs are intentionally episodic and cannot adequately contend with the continuing crisis of the contemporary church. The Pastor Theologian Program was designed, with Finkenwalde in full view, to be an extensive pedagogical experiment, offering pastors opportunities for identifying, clarifying, and incorporating their reading, discussing, and writing in a process of quickening faith and reforming practice. That is to say, it sought to explore a strategy for learning in the context of difference and diversity that is designed not simply to inform but also to renew. The church may well choose to remain complacent and satisfied with the current caliber of its ministry, rewarding style over substance and tolerating mediocrity in pastoral practice. But if the church should determine that it must be otherwise, experiments in alternate forms of theological education such as this must be pursued and given sufficient survival time to have a lasting influence on the church.

There are many valid and useful forms of Christian ministry, and the church needs them all. The importance of ministries of compassion and comfort, of social service and prophetic protest, cannot be minimized. That said, the recovery of a learned ministry, pastor-theologians who are "qualified rightly to divide the word of truth," must be high on the church's missional agenda if it is to contend with the various claims and challenges of an increasingly secular, pluralistic world. Theological education, because it is so central to the formation of the pastoral imagination, is currently on trial. Whether it is sufficiently aware of the role it has played in the loss of the learned pastor as the controlling image of the ministry is unclear. What is clear, at least to me, is that apart from the recovery of the theological competence and skill represented by that image, the church will not likely be able to recognize and receive the new life for which it prays.

The Role of Theological Masters in the Formation of the Pastor-Theologian

Cynthia A. Jarvis

> *To become and be a theologian is not a natural process but an incomparably concrete fact of grace [marking a person] with a* character indelebilis, *an indelible quality. Whoever has eyes to see will recognize even at a distance the [person] who has been afflicted and irreparably wounded by theology and the Word of God. . . . But the* process and the way *in which it was possible for him [or her] to become such a [person] will always be hidden, even from the theologian himself [or herself].*
>
> Karl Barth[1]

There is no doubt in my mind that a pastor-theologian is formed, in part, by a relationship with one other or many others who have been afflicted and irreparably wounded by theology and the Word of God. Whether that one is the minister of a congregation, a professor in college, seminary, or divinity school or a colleague in the early years of ministry, this relationship will be marked by the other's willingness to lay open her own wrestling with God's reality, neither suppressing the negative experiences and the dark nights of the soul nor hiding his positive delight in God. And though the process and the way of this relationship's shaping of a pastor-theologian remains hidden

1. *Evangelical Theology: An Introduction* (Grand Rapids: Eerdmans, 1979), pp. 72-73.

and cannot be prescribed, the formative relationships surrounding the lives of pastor-theologians in the history of the church may provide a clue about what is most missed today in the two institutions charged with raising up and equipping pastor-theologians for such a time as this, namely the church and the academy.

Wisdom without Wrestling

In his seventieth year, Douglas John Hall set out to look back on a life given to teaching theology convictionally in a seminary and in a secular institution. Writing on "Theology as Vocation," Hall reflects on his own wrestling with *gratia irresistibilis,* a wrestling that led him not simply to be a theologian but to understand himself as called to be a servant and teacher of the church. Hall notes that he pursued this calling even though the Protestant churches in the latter half of the twentieth century were increasingly indifferent to the vocation of theology. "With few exceptions," he observes, "[the churches] have shown every inclination to avoid theologians wherever possible, including clergy who see their chief role as that of theologians of the congregation. Indeed, one suspects that congregations have been hardest of all on parish ministers who really tried to be 'teaching elders.'"[2]

Moreover, Hall indicts those who have chosen to live out their theological vocation in academic institutions. Too many of the best-educated theological, biblical, historical, and other scholars "have seen their vocation not primarily as a call but a career — and often in individualistic terms.

> Their community of discourse and concern is not a particular denomination or even the ecumenical church broadly conceived, but the academy, with its own well-known system of rewards and punishments, its own language, its own (usually ambiguous) communality. In fact, many who are working in theological or paratheological situations today have little or no connection with institutional religion. They do not write for the churches; they do not write about the churches; they do not seek personal satisfaction or a sense of belonging in that direction at all.[3]

2. Douglas John Hall, *Bound and Free: A Theologian's Journey* (Minneapolis: Fortress Press, 2005), pp. 7-8.

3. Hall, *Bound and Free,* p. 10

That said, the voluminous analysis of the present theological malaise afflicting the church and its preachers has been proffered in the last quarter century almost exclusively by academics. Most have held that the *process and the way to becoming a theologian can be known* (to misquote Karl Barth) and is to be located in sweeping or not so sweeping curricular reform. The impetus for this multifaceted debate seems to have been *Theologia: The Fragmentation and Unity of Theological Education,* Edward Farley's scathing indictment of current practices both in seminaries and schools of divinity. Farley proposes that "theological education needs to recover *theologia* [what I take to be a unity of theological understanding], a recovery which will call forth a new course of studies and a new way of structuring catalogue fields." More questions than answers ensue: "Does this imply that *theologia,* a *habitus* of faith itself, can be taught? Does it mean that *theologia* or theological understanding can itself be the subject matter of a course of studies, thus placing scholarly matters in the background? Does the recovery of *theologia* occur at the expense of the distinctive needs of clergy education?"[4]

In response, Farley argues that "*theologia* is restored to the overall program of studies as that which evokes *paideia* [the 'culturing' of a person in theological understanding] as an element in the educational process, as that which permeates and guides what church leadership is called to do and be, as the criterion (in its connection with church leadership) for determining pertinent areas of inquiry and knowledge (sciences) and with them, areas of teaching."[5] He rejects the clerical model of theological education that has been the lot of North American seminaries and, in its stead, briefly enumerates what he calls "criteria and desiderata" for a course of study whose aim is the cultivation of *theologia.* The next step is presumed to be a detailed rethinking of a curriculum that would promote a culture of theological understanding directed by a theological faculty no longer divided into the discrete departments of Bible, church history, dogmatics, and practical theology.

In response to those same questions, I would argue that *paideia,* the cultivation of *theologia,* the *habitus* of faith are gifts given in the context of a relationship where the faith of both teacher and student, mentor and mentored seeks understanding. Because the center of this faith is the revelation of the God whose self-giving of the only-begotten Son and whose re-

4. Edward Farley, *Theologia: The Fragmentation and Unity of Theological Education* (Philadelphia: Fortress Press, 1983), p. 178.

5. Farley, *Theologia,* p. 180.

ceptive love in the Son reveals the nature of the relationship for which we were made, theological existence is communicated to the other in a relationship of self-giving. This relationship, of course, is not without sacrifice. Hall's vocational identity led him, in his early years of teaching, to open his door at the cost of his own scholarly pursuits and publications. Yet Hall offers an image of a life opened for the sake of the other who, in seeking to live the life given her by God to live, may recognize that life as it is being lived out on the other side of an open door. Living alongside the other's flawed but faithful incarnation of theological existence seems to be the forgotten factor in every recent analysis of theological education.

Wrestling That Leads to Wisdom

What might this relationship look like? Huston Smith offers some helpful distinctions and heads us down a path that turns from the academy's discussion of curricular reform to a consideration of the character of those whose mentoring or mastership is significant in the formation of a pastor-theologian. In an essay titled "The Master-Disciple Relationship," Smith begins by noting that a student seeks out a *teacher* on the basis of "the body of knowledge or a skill that the teacher has mastered and to which the student aspires."[6] The center of the relationship is the object of study; the persons who have entered into that study are random and replaceable.

By contrast, the *master-disciple relationship* is a situation in which "the personhood of both parties is central. . . . The master does not enjoy the disciple's esteem because he conveys something that is useful in any utilitarian respect. Nor is it a distinguishable attribute of his total self that he seeks to transfer to the disciple — to repeat, a specifiable skill or body of knowledge. What is significant for the disciple is the master's total self, whose character and activity are unique and irreplaceable."[7] In this regard, I think of the indelible character that marks one whose life, in Barth's words, has been wounded by theology and the Word of God. The formation of a pastor-theologian has something to do with living, for a time, in relationship to a person or a community of persons whose amazement before the Word of

6. Huston Smith, "The Master-Disciple Relationship," in *The Best American Spiritual Writing 2006,* ed. Philip Zaleski (Boston: Houghton Mifflin, 2005), p. 170.

7. Smith, "The Master-Disciple Relationship," p. 171.

God invites, nurtures, and calls forth an amazement that becomes a way of seeing, thinking, reflecting, and being in the world.

In the second place, "Students make up their minds and intend to study, whereas disciples are called to discipleship"[8] and become essentially who they were destined to be only in relation to the master. From the other direction, the master is only who he or she is by virtue of the relationship with the disciple. There is a mutually dependent vocation that need not be so between teacher and student. A teacher may pursue a career of writing and research in total independence from the person the student is becoming. In Smith's words, "the master-disciple relationship centers in mutuality in principle. . . . The master only becomes a master in his relationship to his disciples, and only through perceptive and comprehending disciples does he become fully aware of his mastership."[9] Here I think of those whose sense of vocation results in a kind of convictional teaching (what Farley identified in the early Christian centuries as a salvifically oriented knowledge of God and what Wallace Alston discusses in his chapter on Theological Education) that engages the student/disciple in a mutual pilgrimage of faith seeking understanding.

In the third place, Smith notes that "the teacher gives of his knowledge and ability, whereas the master gives — not *of* himself, as we are likely to say, as if his gifts could be isolated from the wholeness of his being, but *himself,* period."[10] I would also note, in this regard, the community that first turned my own life in the direction of theological amazement. From the classroom to the refectory to the bar across the street to late evenings at students' apartments, the faculty, including Edward Farley, engaged us in theological conversation that became the air we breathed. By being with these "masters" who were "intending the world theologically," the person I became was marked by the same *character indelebilis.*

From Smith's more general analysis of the master/disciple relationship, we turn specifically to that relationship in the context of the Christian community. In a series of lectures given at the conclusion of Karl Barth's academic career, Barth asks how theology encounters, confronts, enters into, and assumes concrete form in a person. To repeat his words from the beginning of this essay: "To become and be a theologian is not a natural process

8. Smith, "The Master-Disciple Relationship," p. 171.
9. Smith, "The Master-Disciple Relationship," p. 173.
10. Smith, "The Master-Disciple Relationship," pp. 173-74.

but an incomparably concrete fact of grace."[11] When that fact of grace claims a person's life, that person is marked with "a *character indelebilis*, an indelible quality. Whoever has eyes to see will recognize even at a distance the [person] who has been afflicted and irreparably wounded by theology and the Word of God. . . . But the *process and the way* in which it was possible for him [or her] to become such a [person] will always be hidden, even from the theologian himself [or herself]."[12]

No doubt taking his cue from Barth and also looking back on a life given to teaching theology, Jürgen Moltmann asks a similar question: "How does someone become a true theologian?" His answer is twofold. God, he says, is "the passion of theologians, their *torment* and their *delight*."[13] Concerning the torment, Moltmann cites Luther's lecture to his students in a class on psalms in which Luther offers the students his own experience: "By living, no — more — by dying and being damned to hell doth a man become a theologian, not by knowing, reading or speculation" (WA 5, 163). This is not to downplay the study, reading, reflection and understanding of scripture necessary to becoming a theologian, says Moltmann; but it is to say that the theologian's personal wrestling with God must be central if theology is to become "not just a scholarly study which teaches, but also a *wisdom* which makes wise out of the experience of God."[14] Put another way, Moltmann contends that true theologians must lay themselves open personally to the things they maintain, and "must neither suppress the negative experiences of their own selves before God nor hide their positive delight in God."[15] The theology of those who experience delight, Moltmann concludes, "becomes a kind of intellectual love for God."[16]

If we now turn to scripture and the history of the church in search of a pastoral identity that was theologically formed by way of a relationship between master and disciple, Paul and Timothy come first to mind. In Acts 16, Timothy is introduced by Luke as "a disciple, the son of a Jewish woman who was a believer; but his father was a Greek." Clearly Timothy stood out as one claimed in a particular way by God for service. Paul recognized this and

11. Barth, *Evangelical Theology,* p. 73.

12. Barth, *Evangelical Theology,* pp. 72-73.

13. Jürgen Moltmann, *Experiences in Theology* (Minneapolis: Fortress Press, 2000), p. 23.

14. Moltmann, *Experiences in Theology,* p. 24.

15. Moltmann, *Experiences in Theology,* p. 24.

16. Moltmann, *Experiences in Theology,* p. 25.

so "wanted Timothy to *accompany* him." The word suggests not only the act of traveling together but of living the life given them by God to live *together.* A relationship of un-equals is begun. If one reads the next few chapters of Acts through the person of Timothy, there unfolds a theological education few seminaries could equal: witnessing the conversion of Lydia in Macedonia because of the substance of what Paul said; seeing Paul and Silas imprisoned after performing an economically threatening exorcism and watching as he baptized the family of his jailer; listening as Paul argued from the scriptures in the synagogue in Thessalonica; living with Paul for a year and a half in Corinth as he built up the church through preaching.

Reading of Timothy in Paul's letters, we find that this student grows into a trusted colleague: a co-worker (Rom. 16:21), a beloved and faithful child in the Lord (1 Cor. 4:17), a fellow preacher (2 Cor. 1:19), and a co-correspondent (Phil. 1:1; Col. 1:1; 1 and 2 Thessalonians; Philem. 1:1). And even though the letters to Timothy are not from Paul's hand, the author presumes a known relationship between Paul and "my loyal child in the faith." A model has been established. Paul is portrayed as both trusting this child in the faith to handle a very difficult situation in Ephesus while remaining his teacher to the end. Therefore he reminds Timothy of the substance of the faith to be defended and the purpose of Timothy's witness: "the aim of such instruction is love that comes from a pure heart, a good conscience, and sincere faith" (1 Tim. 1:5). Timothy is addressed again as "my child, in accordance with the prophecies made earlier about you, so that by following them you might fight the good fight, having faith and a good conscience." Clearly 1 Timothy goes on to address subjects of interest to the church at the beginning of the second century, but the premise of the letter underlines the ongoing relationship of master to disciple.

The text of 2 Timothy is different altogether and arrestingly personal. Again, the writer is not Paul but presumes to be Paul, perhaps addressing Timothy for the last time from prison. Here Paul's intimate relationship to Timothy's family of origin is evident and poignant: "I am reminded of your sincere faith, a faith that lived first in your grandmother Lois and your mother Eunice and now, I am sure, lives in you" (1:5). This remembrance is followed by fatherly advice: "I remind you to rekindle the gift of God that is within you through the laying on of hands . . ." (1:6). Timothy is admonished not to be ashamed of the gospel or of Paul's imprisonment, but rather to take Paul's suffering as an example. Furthermore he is told to "hold to the standard of sound teaching that you have heard from me in faith and love that are in Christ Jesus; guard the good treasure entrusted to you . . ." (1:13-14a); "be strong in the grace that is in Christ Jesus . . . share in suffering . . . and think over what I say, for the Lord will give you understanding in all things" (2:1, 3, 7). In each of these instructions, the mark of Paul's life upon Timothy is central. Then as he summarizes the faith in the form of an ancient hymn, it is as though this master means to make certain, one last time, that the substance of faith is clear to the one who will bear that faith to the next generation after his death.

All of these words reach their climax in Paul's final charge: "Now you have observed my teaching, my conduct, my aim in life, my faith, my patience, my love, my steadfastness, my persecutions and my sufferings" (4:10-11). Paul's words underscore the observations with which we began, for here is one afflicted and irreparably wounded by theology and the Word of God, one personally laid open to the things he maintained, neither suppressing the negative nor hiding the delight, one who gave not *of* himself but *himself* to a relationship in which the *personhood* of both parties was central to a relationship in which discipleship to the one Lord was all in all.

Augustine and Ambrose come next to mind. According to Peter Brown, when Augustine arrived in Milan, Ambrose greeted him "with more affability than Augustine had expected from this distant, paternal figure: 'and I first began to love him,'" Augustine wrote in his confessions, "'as a man who showed me kindness.'"[17] Yet in trying to engage Ambrose after a disturbing sermon, Augustine found him hard to reach and remote, "suddenly drawn to himself at the end of the day, and reading a book in complete silence: 'When he read, his eyes traveled over the page and his heart sought out the sense, but voice and tongue were silent . . . and after we had sat long in silence, unwilling to interrupt a word on which he was so intent, we would depart again.'"[18] "What [the master] is to the disciple," writes Smith, "he is through the presence of his total selfhood in his every word and deed, right down to what is seemingly trivial."[19]

Ambrose preached some of the most learned sermons in the Latin world, writes Brown, though we do not know which of those sermons Augustine heard. What we do know is that Ambrose "showed himself a com-

17. Peter Brown, *Augustine of Hippo* (Berkeley and Los Angeles: University of California Press, 1969), p. 82.

18. Brown, *Augustine of Hippo,* p. 82.

19. Smith, "The Master-Disciple Relationship," p. 174.

plete master of the [theological] situation; he could parade all the great 'names' and their opinions, only to dismiss them with contempt; how could these frail quibblings stand against the word of Moses, who had spoken 'mouth to mouth' with God?"[20] In the end Brown finds it to be "exceptionally difficult to assess the precise influence of Ambrose in provoking [Augustine's theological] evolution. . . . We are dealing, here, with a relationship between two people whose eddies may escape the historian. The influence of Ambrose on Augustine is far out of proportion to any direct contact which the two men may have had."[21] [*"But the process and the way in which it is possible for a person to become such a theologian will always be hidden."*] Yet Augustine once told a correspondent that when asking Ambrose for advice on behalf of his mother, Ambrose replied that "he could only teach me to do what he himself did, for if he knew of any better rule, he would have observed it." Augustine admitted that, looking back on this exchange, he "always treated it as if it were an oracle from heaven."[22] What I take from this is the indelible character of a man wounded by theology and the Word of God upon the character of another man who, in turn, would be master to a multitude of pastor-theologians down the ages.

The monastic movement and, in particular, the Dominicans (the Order of Preachers) in fifteenth-century Florence cannot be overlooked as a more developed model for the mentoring of novices. According to *The Constitutions of the Order of Friars of Preachers,* the Order was founded "for the sake of preaching and the salvation of souls."[23] Therefore the ordering of the common life and the architecture of the Cloisters at San Marco were directed toward the education of novices and the preparation of friars for the pulpit.

Three halls on the upper level of the Cloisters were lined with cells that housed the novices, the clerics, and the lay brothers. Although the dormitory is best known for the Fra Angelico frescoes that adorn the walls of each cell, one soon understands that art was central to the formation of these preachers. The theological intent of the frescoes in the clerics' cells was to explicate the church's doctrines. Narrative frescoes adorned the walls of the lay brothers' cells and told the story of salvation. The cells of the novices were

20. Brown, *Augustine of Hippo,* p. 84.

21. Brown, *Augustine of Hippo,* p. 86.

22. Brown, *Augustine of Hippo,* p. 87.

23. William Hood, *Fra Angelico at San Marco* (New Haven: Yale University Press, 1993), p. 290.

adorned with St. Dominic in one of the nine attitudes of Dominican prayer at the foot of the cross.

According to art historian William Hood, the architecture of the dormitory as well as Fra Angelico's art became significant in the formation and practice of Dominicans. In fact, the Cloisters at San Marco and the Dominicans' commitment to study and prayer changed monastic architecture and the organization of religious communities throughout Europe.[24] Living in solitude yet side by side in cells, the friars and novices were to "write, read, pray, sleep, and even have a lamp and stay up at night if they wanted to, to study."[25] Reading in particular was a form of prayer for the Dominicans, and so "what might be called prayerful study was in many cases the day's chief occupation."[26] In fact, one of the cells on the novices' corridor has an illustration that depicts St. Dominic reading theology as a mode of prayer.

As specified in the Constitution of the Order, a master was to be appointed to take charge of the formation of the novices. The master's double cell, located at the end of the clerics' hall and facing the cells of the novices, was adorned with the *Presentation in the Temple,* Simeon holding the Christ child with the prophetess Anna, Mary, Joseph, and St. Dominic looking on. In like manner, the novices were babes being presented for initiation. The master was to teach them the Order's way of life, a life marked by the discipline of both body and mind. Yet the life of the mind was deemed to be so crucial to the formation of the preacher that novices were to be relieved of chanting the Hours in favor of reading. The Order decreed that "no one is to become a preacher general until he has studied theology for three years and then only if he is balanced and sensible enough to discuss the Order's affairs at Chapter."[27]

The novices were readied for theological discussion by coming together in the presence of the student master "after the disputation or after vespers or at any other time when he is free, to put forward their doubts and questions or to give talks."[28] Moreover, the novices were not to offer "any literal interpretation of the psalms and prophets other than that approved and confirmed by the saints."[29] In other words, they were to be

24. Hood, *Fra Angelico at San Marco,* p. 290.
25. Hood, *Fra Angelico at San Marco,* p. 300.
26. Hood, *Fra Angelico at San Marco,* p. 205.
27. Hood, *Fra Angelico at San Marco,* p. 299.
28. Hood, *Fra Angelico at San Marco,* p. 300.
29. Hood, *Fra Angelico at San Marco,* p. 300.

formed by the theological tradition of which they were a part, and their subsequent preaching was to be marked by the intelligent transmission of the faith they had received.

In the monastic movement, what we see is the institutionalization of the master/novice relationship. The Dominican novices are of special interest to this volume because these were young men being prepared for the pulpit. Such preparation required rigorous study under the watchful eye of a master who resided at the end of the hallway. This formation encompassed the whole of both the master's life and the novice's future. As we shall see later, such a model was in the mind of Dietrich Bonhoeffer as he ordered the life of seminarians at Finkenwalde.

Another insight into the nature of the master/disciple relationship on the nurturing of theological understanding is to be found in Luther's *Table Talk.* In Luther's household "about five o'clock in the afternoon supper was served, and this meal was often shared by exiled clergymen, escaped nuns, government officials, visitors from abroad, and colleagues of Luther in the university who frequently stopped in, men like Philip Melanchthon, John Bugenhagen, and Justus Jonas. The relaxed atmosphere of the hospitable home," notes Theodore Tappert, "was conducive to spirited conversation," and John Mathesius, who was often present in 1540, has left us this description of what the scene was like:

> Although our doctor often took weighty and profound thoughts to table with him and sometimes maintained the silence of the monastery during the entire meal, so that not a word was spoken, yet at appropriate times he spoke in a very jovial way. . . . When he wished to get us to talk he would throw out a question, "What's new?" The first time, we let this remark pass, but if he repeated it — "You prelates, what's new in the land?" — the oldest ones at the table would start talking. . . . If the conversation was animated, it was nevertheless conducted with decent propriety and courtesy, and others would contribute their share until the doctor started to talk. Often good questions were put to him from the Bible, and he provided expert and concise answers. When at times somebody took exception to what had been said, the doctor was able to bear this patiently and refute him with a skilful answer.[30]

30. Theodore G. Tappert, *Luther's Works,* Volume 54: *Table Talk* (Philadelphia: Fortress Press, 1967), pp. ix-x.

Those at table took notes that became *Table Talk,* a running dialogue with implied conversation partners. Though we know only what we can infer from the notes of his students, this table talk uncovers the sort of theological relationship in which a master's astonishment enters language and acts to shape those who have been called to his table.

Finally and most notably, I think of Dietrich Bonhoeffer and the Confessing Church's seminary at Finkenwalde. Says Eberhard Bethge in his introduction to this period in Bonhoeffer's life, "It was a delight to him to confirm young theologians in their calling in the hard-pressed Church and to share with them, not only his gifts, *but everything he possessed.* Those students who were meeting him for the first time were surprised to find that the director of their seminary was *always ready to make himself available.*"[31]

No doubt the seminary at Finkenwalde was unique to its time and circumstance. The Confessing Church's witness to the God who "wonderfully preserves the church as it were in a hiding place"[32] formed ministers in a way no ordinary time can. Nevertheless, the Preachers' Seminary and the House of the Brethren provide insight — by way of an intense experience of the master-student relationship — that might lead us, during less pressing times, to understand how that relationship is significant for the formation of a pastor-theologian.

In the first place, there was a common life whose details unfolded not by chance. Bonhoeffer ordered and framed each day at Finkenwalde by morning and evening worship. The ordinands gathered not in a sanctuary but around the dinner table to read a psalm, sing a hymn, listen to a lesson *(lectio continua),* and pray. Here, for instance, the ordinands began to understand that scripture was not just a "tool of their trade." Bethge reports that Bonhoeffer insisted on this order, an order that met with resistance at first, because he believed such was a suitable form of worship for theologians. On Saturdays, a sermon would be delivered by Bonhoeffer "which was usually very direct."[33] In other words, Bonhoeffer was the preacher to his students in such a way that his preaching both form and inform their own.

Related to this was Bonhoeffer's insistence that prayer had to be taught

31. Eberhard Bethge, *Dietrich Bonhoeffer* (New York: Harper & Row, 1985), p. 341.

32. John Calvin, *Institutes of the Christian Religion* (Philadelphia: Presbyterian Board of Christian Education, 1930), 4.1.2.

33. Bethge, *Dietrich Bonhoeffer,* p. 349.

and learned. He took responsibility for the morning and evening prayers, giving "much time and trouble to the preparation of these prayers and their inner order. His language was wholly appropriate to the matter in hand and seemed completely free from all manifestations of self. Into these prayers he would put his will, his understanding and his heart."[34]

Bethge goes on to mention the lessons broken off in favor of a walk in the woods or on the coast as well as Bonhoeffer's love of and inclusion of music in the common life. An evening every week was given to a discussion whose subject was often political. Weekends often were times to host other clergy or clergy conferences or students from other seminaries. In one instance, students from Greifswald asked the seminary to offer study seminars that would help them reflect theologically on church politics. Suggestive of the Pastor-Theologian Program that has spawned this volume, neighboring pastors quit administrative gatherings in favor of theological discussions that would continue the theological reflection they had begun under Bonhoeffer's guidance.

"Clearly this was all part of the practice of communal and fraternal living as also of the personal education of future preachers. The process, however, relied more on indirect intimations than on actual instruction."[35] That is to say, Bonhoeffer quietly lived out among both ordinands and his colleagues the discipleship and mutual service that were to become the substance of his lectures. Much was to be learned simply by observing this master: his ability to produce a well-constructed lecture or sermon in a matter of hours; his clarity of purpose; his ability to interrupt work for play without falling behind. His impatience with the lack of these qualities in the ordinands had the effect of making them "discover resources within themselves which they had never previously suspected."[36]

Concerning the more formal course of study, Finkenwalde was, on one hand, unique because of the master who set its curriculum; on the other hand, that which was unique is precisely that which is missing in our current understanding of pastoral formation. The courses themselves mirrored the courses in most seminaries of that time: homiletics and catechetical studies, pastoral care and liturgical studies, lectures on church, ministry, and community. Because of Bonhoeffer's insistence that "only he who cries out for

34. Bethge, *Dietrich Bonhoeffer,* pp. 382-83.
35. Bethge, *Dietrich Bonhoeffer,* p. 350.
36. Bethge, *Dietrich Bonhoeffer,* p. 351.

the Jews can sing Gregorian chant,"[37] even lectures that could have focused narrowly on the church's inner life were shot through with what was at stake in the worship of God alone. Yet the theological struggle and the practice of prayer of this pastor also marked each subject.

The teaching of homiletics was a case in point. Though he might allow an assistant to lead discussions about preaching, he delivered the course lectures. Committed to listening for God's address through the words of the sermon, even the most hesitant sermons and those most wanting practice were received with gratitude. Sermons were to be "listened to in all humility . . . not analyzed. The only sermons he allowed to be discussed were those that were read aloud, never those that had been delivered before a congregation. . . . Needless to say, he gave due attention to problems of method and form, but nothing exerted so chastening an effect as Bonhoeffer's method of listening to sermons. He himself demonstrated daily what he required in the way of expression, taste, imaginativeness. Thus homiletics began with the most difficult lesson of all — one's own listening to sermons."[38]

Yet beyond the normal course offerings was the pressing theological work that was Bonhoeffer's own wrestling with faith and obedience. "There was only one theme which distinguished Bonhoeffer's seminary from the rest for the first two and a half years, and that was the series of lectures on discipleship. After only a few hours, newcomers would realize that this was the nerve-centre of the whole, that they were witnessing a theological event which would stimulate every area of their personal life."[39] It was in Bonhoeffer's lectures, which were to be published as *The Cost of Discipleship,* that these ordinands grasped the theological breadth and depth of their call to ministry. In Bethge's words, "Suddenly the realization burst upon them that they were not there simply to learn new techniques of preaching and instruction, but were to be initiated into something that represented altogether revolutionary prerequisites for those activities."[40]

When the doors of Finkenwalde were bolted by the Nazis in September of 1937, the dispersed community was well represented in the 800 members of the Confessing Church imprisoned. As it was to be with Bonhoeffer, so it

37. Bethge, *Dietrich Bonhoeffer,* p. 512.
38. Bethge, *Dietrich Bonhoeffer,* p. 361.
39. Bethge, *Dietrich Bonhoeffer,* p. 360.
40. Bethge, *Dietrich Bonhoeffer,* p. 369.

was with the pastors who had been formed theologically by him: each had been equipped for discipleship in the church and in the world.

The Wrestling Ahead of Us

At the heart of pastoral and theological formation is a person whose vocation is theology. That vocation may be practiced in the church, the academy, or the world (a tent-making theologian). No matter the setting, the one whose vocation is theology in the service of the church is the one whose character is marked by amazement before the Word of God (Barth). Such amazement has a way of taking the initiative with any who find themselves drawn to a theological way of seeing, reflecting, and being in the world. Such was the case with Timothy in relation to Paul, with Augustine in relation to Ambrose, with novices in relation to senior friars, as well as with ordinands in relation to Luther and Bonhoeffer.

What unfolds is a mutual pilgrimage or discipleship. As the theological mentor dares a kind of intellectual and personal wrestling with the substance of the faith, the person being formed is given an understanding that can only be described as incarnational — a flawed incarnation, no doubt — nevertheless a life claimed by God in one whose vocation is theology. So Timothy accompanied Paul in every sense of that word and Augustine watched Ambrose read or simply "do what he himself did." In the process Timothy and Augustine became who they were destined to be! In the hushed hallways of the cloister, Dominicans formed their own successors as they prayed by reading theology. Around the table in Luther's home, learned and laity, clergy and ordinands were prompted to think theologically by Luther's questions and his silence. Quitting the classroom for a walk along the beach, Finkenwalde's ordinands caught Bonhoeffer's ruminations and wrestling with the cost of discipleship in a way no mere academic lecture could convey.

Common to these relationships and the relationships that have shaped generations of pastor-theologians are a number of qualities. The first is a vulnerability and an availability that respects neither office nor office hours! As Hall exclaims at the end of his autobiographical reflections, "It is a matter of *vocation*."[41] That is to say, theology and the shaping of pastor-theologians comprise a way of life that all are not called by God to live. Short of the inten-

41. Hall, *Bound and Free*, p. 131.

sity of Finkenwalde's *life together,* there is a way of seeing and intending the world theologically at work in theological mentors that never quits. "For ten years in the small seminary in Saskatoon," Hall writes, "I spent more time listening to students than I did writing books. I wrote no books at all, in fact, until I was in my mid-forties, and *part of the reason for that was that my door was open to my students, perhaps to a fault.*"[42] Whether in a study or on a sailboat, around a kitchen table or lingering at the refectory, at the bar across the street from the seminary or in a car on the way to a church meeting, the *character indelebilis* of theology is available to any who would be shaped by it.

In the second place, theological mentors tend to be persons who are deeply engaged in the great questions of any time and place. Again Hall notes that the vocation of theology entails exposure "to the heights and depths, the hopes and despairs, the beauties and terrors of life as it is lived *hic et nunc.* It is no safe profession! . . . One has to enter the unknown land, the terra incognita, of the present and impending future and to confront, as though one had no ready-made religious responses, the searing dilemmas of today and tomorrow."[43] In every mentor cited — Paul, Ambrose, Augustine, Dominic, Luther, and Bonhoeffer — each was a theologian deeply engaged in the religious and political currents, even to the point of death. The risk that must be involved in daring to think about and speak of God is part of the necessity that presses itself upon those who do theology in the service of the crucified and of his church.

Finally, though not exhaustively, the relationship of theological mentor to the pastor-theologian being formed — if that relationship is dared in the reality of the church and the world — exists always in a dialectic of doubt and delight that inhabits the question: Could this *really* be true? More than three decades after my own ordination, I can recall — almost word for word — the letter written to me by one of my mentors at Vanderbilt Divinity School. A Jesuit priest and professor of New Testament, John Donahue was singular in his understanding of my decision to accept a call rather than pursue a doctorate in theology. During my years at the Divinity School, he had accepted every invitation to dinner after class or to a student party and was often still reflecting on the language event of a parable with beer in hand at 2 a.m. in the morning.

At the end of my seminary days, Professor Donahue's car transported

42. Hall, *Bound and Free,* p. 49.
43. Hall, *Bound and Free,* p. 49.

my fellow students a day's drive to my ordination where he participated in the laying on of hands. Weeks after that day, I received a letter from him that said, in effect, "I could not separate my tears from my joy as my hand joined the others on your head. I thought of the babies you would baptize, the lives you would join together in marriage, the sorrowful you would comfort, the self-satisfied you would trouble and the hands you would hold for the last time in death. I wanted to spare you the abiding loneliness and yet rejoice with you before the calling that alone is worthy of your life."

With those few details noted, we must return full circle to Barth's initial warning that the process and the way of becoming a theologian and so a pastor-theologian will always be hidden, even from the theologian himself or herself. The same must be said of theological mentors. One cannot set out to be vulnerable and so radically available to the generations that are yet to be formed theologically. One does not decide to risk one's self in the great issues of the day but is chosen for such service. One can never conjure the astonishment that is known by those who will never become accustomed to the claims of the gospel.

What *is* possible is that the institution responsible for the identification of those whom God may be calling into ministry, namely the congregation, and the institution charged with the education of future ministers, namely the seminary, might seek out and call those theological mentors whose vulnerability and availability, whose social conscience and courage, whose own wrestling with doubt and astonished belief will lead congregants and ordinands to the realization that they have been called out not simply to learn new techniques of preaching and instruction, but to be initiated into something that represents altogether revolutionary prerequisites for the practice of ministry and the life of discipleship.

Follow Him through the Land of Unlikeness: "Passing Over" as a Way of Truth in the Practice of Ministry

Albert H. Keller

> *"Have you [disciples] understood all this?" They answered, "Yes." And Jesus said to them, "Therefore every scribe who has been trained for the kingdom of heaven is like the master of a household who brings out of his treasure what is new and what is old."*
>
> Matthew 13:51-52

Theological Crisis in the Church

Jesus says to disciples: every teacher trained for kingdom-work in the school of Christ is like a homemaker who brings out of the pantry what is new and what is old. How do we understand "what is new and what is old"? When Karl Barth says the pastor should hold the Bible in one hand and the newspaper in the other, we know what he means: the pastor-theologian should have the skill to draw deeply and truthfully from the well of scripture and tradition, and also command the skill to discern what is happening today in a world in which God is active. Neither skill comes easily but requires disciplined approaches. In other words, holding the Bible is a figure of speech meaning that one can read it, interpret it, and use it effectively; holding the newspaper means possessing the interpretive ability to discern what John F. Kennedy called "the profound tendencies of history" and to harness that insight, in dialogue with scripture, to do the work of ministry. Could Jesus have meant something like that with his parable? Kingdom work requires both the "new" of understanding our world and the "old" of attending to scripture.

In this paper I propose to show how a pastor who is grounded in a scripture-based tradition or canon can become fluent or "at home" in a contemporary domain, discipline, or practice, and thus become a theologian after Jesus' intention — able to bring out not only the old but the new. The method is not easy and it is risky. Why make the effort? A great deal depends on whether one sees Christian theology standing at a critical crossroads today. If *not,* then theological discovery (such as a seminary education) is unto *knowledge,* and the process of formation amounts to downloading what one's church tradition believes and teaches so one can pass it on. If *so* — if theology has been brought to a crossroads by globalization, modern science, radical potentialities in pharmacology and genetics, nanotechnology, artificial intelligence, and indeed the whole postmodern world — then knowledge is unto *discovery.* All we have inherited from the tradition must be seen as a foundation upon which we stand to reach for the yet undiscovered, unthought, and unarticulated.

Theology, in my view, stands at that crossroads today. The theological crisis (read *opportunity*) may be no less than its first-century passage from Judaism into the Hellenistic and Roman world, when the Apostle Paul struggled to give the Way a voice that would be intelligible and compelling to Gentiles. There were undoubtedly many who could not follow the startling leaps his mind took in using the alien categories of Hellenistic philosophy and culture to interpret the gospel — even to *recast* the gospel. Perhaps Paul was encouraged by the thorough recasting of the former Hebrew religion performed by exiled Jews after the destruction of Jerusalem, when the prophet heard God say, "Behold, I am doing a new thing!" (Isaiah 42:9). Our times are just that new, our God is just that creative, and our challenge is just that great.

In his 1975 autobiography *All the Strange Hours,* social scientist Loren Eiseley creates a striking image about how resistant scientists can be to thinking out of the box. "Sir Francis Bacon once spoke of those drawn into some powerful circle of thought as 'dancing in little rings like persons bewitched.' Our scientific models do simulate a kind of fairy ring or magic circle which, once it has encompassed us, is hard to view objectively."[1] Theolog-

1. Loren Eiseley, *All the Strange Hours* (New York: Charles Scribner's Sons, 1975), p. 192.

ical models and canons can be magic circles! Today the enemy of theological innovation in the face of rapid and global change — *paradigm* change, to borrow again from science — is magic circle thinking. How can the pastor-theologian escape the charm of the conventional and the "authority" of the orthodox to help bring the living tradition into a radically new world? How can we use what we have received to the end of discovery?

Theology as "Passing Over"

John S. Dunne, theologian at Notre Dame University, wrote a series of books that could be called spiritual theology, tracing as they do his own intellectual and spiritual quest for God. They also suggest a way that the practice of ministry can bring new truth into theological tradition.

In his second and third books, *A Search for God in Time and Memory*[2] and *The Way of All the Earth*,[3] Dunne develops the idea of "passing over" and "coming back." This means that one can intentionally pass over into the standpoint of other lives and times and then come back to the standpoint of one's own life and times, but with a difference from having immersed oneself in the other's point of view. This process is one of radical dialogue; it is risky but consistent with growth in the knowledge and love of God. An example of the process is the path taken by Gandhi who, when he lived in South Africa as a young man, immersed himself in the life and teaching of Jesus. He learned from Jesus the principles of love and non-violence. When he returned to India, he continued his life as a Hindu but with a difference: he introduced new insight into his tradition and was himself infused with new energy and direction for leading millions of his faith into the practice of non-violent resistance.

What does the process of passing over and coming back entail? Ashok Gangadean, an Indian Christian teaching at Haverford College, spells out the method (or spiritual adventure) from his own research. The first encounter with the other, he says, often comes as a shock because the alien worldview or way of life disrupts one's settled patterns of perceiving the

2. John S. Dunne, *A Search for God in Time and Memory* (Notre Dame: University of Notre Dame Press, 1969).

3. John S. Dunne, *The Way of All the Earth* (Notre Dame: University of Notre Dame Press, 1978).

world. The encounter is challenging. It makes one pause, it creates uncertainty; it causes one to weigh the risk of moving forward in the encounter.[4]

If, though, one feels positively challenged to inquire, investigate, and engage this new thing, then one realizes one's need to stand back from former habits and patterns of minding the world. This other that I have encountered organizes and processes the world differently from my way. I realize that to understand this new world, I need a different language. Indeed, says Gangadean, "I must translate myself into a different form of life that sees the world differently. This involves a bracketing of my prejudices."[5] This step might be called radical empathy: crossing over, letting go, and entering the world of the other.

As the empathy increases, one feels keen to free oneself to enter, experiment, learn, and grasp this new way of being. There is excitement in discovering, even more in inhabiting a new worldview. One can experience a profound sense of the other and appreciate an alternative reality to what one has known. This is akin to the passion of an actor taking on a great role and making that character live on the stage.

Ultimately, however, one realizes that this other is not one's home. One moves back into one's own world voluntarily, but with the revolutionary awareness that there are other ways to understand or construct reality. This opens one to rethinking how one sees self, others in the world, and the ultimate reality upon which the world rests. Encounter with radical difference (the other's religious identity, ethnic and socioeconomic self-definition, cultural assumptions) challenges one's former identity and possibly enlarges it. There is no return to a former unilateral (and naïve) way of minding. I cannot forget the reality of the other.

Theology as Transformation

The awareness of plurality not only provides new avenues of insight and metaphors to shape knowledge; it is also transformative of the self. I think the reason for this is that certitudes are relativized and the self is grounded in a new and expanded ecological community. This irrevocably changes

4. Ashok Gangadean, unpublished lecture, "A Universal Grammar for Spiritual Transformation," August 1, 2005.

5. Gangadean, "A Universal Grammar for Spiritual Transformation."

one's sense of self: a new reality has broken in and called one to live in terms of it. While coming back to one's "home," as Gandhi did to his Indian culture and worldview, one can never be the same.

What is the content of this transformative awakening? Some of its features can be described this way (and in this analysis I acknowledge again my debt to Gangadean).[6]

(1) Discovery of a deeper inner dialogue within the self among the rich multiplicity and diversity of perspectives in one's inner life. Identity is enriched with the ensuing complexity, not diminished, and one can actually feel more grounded in the expanded world of relationality. It has been said that the mind needs many vocabularies — not to chatter away to oneself but to establish a sustained inner dialogue that can true up the self.

In this regard, I recall a conversation I had with a young artist who is also a practicing physician and an inactive member of our congregation. She wanted me to know why she had stopped coming to worship and withdrawn from church life. She said that over the years, church had become like a box for her, especially the underlying assumption in both Bible and Christian tradition that the masculine is humanity's default position. Her feminine self had no room to breathe. Since I've begun painting, she said, I've been free and able to go places in myself that were undiscovered, and that have begun to speak in voices I desperately want to hear. Art has taken me to another country within myself.

(2) Discovery of a different and more ambiguous relation to one's community (faith tradition, culture, ethnicity). When one grows in understanding oneself, this often causes disconcerting changes with one's community of origin. Paradoxically, as one is experiencing even deeper connectedness with the self and with the other, there are often tensions with those whose mentality is more collective than communal, whose faith development is more affiliative than creative and relational, or whose cognitive approach is literal rather than metaphorical.

If my artist friend comes back into the church community, she will come as a different person, or more precisely as a changed person. She will return because she chooses to draw from the living tradition of Christian faith, not to "belong" to it. And she will bring fresh, perhaps jarring gifts so that the community itself will change and the living tradition will proceed differently.

6. Gangadean, "A Universal Grammar for Spiritual Transformation."

(3) Discovery of God in a lighter way. A consciousness of God that is more relational and personal may become less dogmatic and exclusive. We realize that our *concepts* of God are analogical — true of the Bible, true of Nicaea and Chalcedon, true of the Reformers and true today. They are derived from images and relational patterns with which we are familiar. Therefore the seeker who would generate theology and not just repeat it is blessed by *passing over* to a wider range of metaphorical material, using fresh sets of metaphors with understanding and nuance. What feeds a living theology is one's ability to use the things of the world richly and discriminately in order to glimpse and speak of God in imaginative ways that people of our generation find illuminating.

The movement of passing over is a move of the soul as well as the mind. In it the soul is opened to the reality of God in ways that are packaged differently from familiar ways. Concepts are softened as new ways become meaningful, and faith becomes less like ideology and more like trust. One doesn't take oneself so seriously in believing. One may even come to the point of realizing that truth is served best not by defending it but by loving and seeking it.

In sum, theology as "passing over," in John Dunne's suggestive phrase, describes a method that takes dialogue to its deepest level. In a sense, it brings out the new and the old and holds them in creative tension. It is a theology of transformation because it invites new reality to break into consciousness, and that changes identity, faith, and practice.

Pastoral Formation for a Practice of Dialogue

How does it happen, this theology of dialogue? And can we intentionally foster its happening to contribute to the formation (or transformation) of a pastor-theologian? Almost every pastoral conversation models the dialogue at the heart of theology. I bring something from my experience; she brings something from hers. Differences excite the spiritual imagination. But the empathy of most pastoral conversations is not the same as the sustained empathy, the sustained conversation, that happens in the experience of *passing over.* Passing over not only excites but informs the spiritual imagination because the process is developed more fully and longitudinally.

I will mention three ways in which "passing over" can be significant in the formation of a theologian. It seems appropriate to speak autobiographically in doing so, not because my experience is in any way a paradigm, but the personal experience of one person connects naturally to the personal narrative of others and suggests new possibilities.

(1) Other Cultures

At three critical moments in my life an immersion in another culture has opened within me new levels of awareness.

The summer after graduating from college and before entering seminary, I lived with a group of graduate students in New York City in an urban studies program sponsored by the United Presbyterian Church. Never before had I been out of the South. My job was to work with children in the neighborhood of the Hispanic Presbyterian Church in Harlem. The disruptive challenges of the neighborhood, culture, and language were compounded by the intense urban exposure. My "passing over" was facilitated by warm friendships. Puerto Rican families invited me in and introduced me to customs foreign to an Alabama boyhood. That three-month stretch allowed me to "come back" to graduate theological education in a Southern seminary with a degree of criticism and openness of mind I would not otherwise have had.

After two years of seminary, the faculty nominated me as the exchange student to the Faculty of Theology of the Reformed Church of France in Montpellier. I was resistant, and the president had to ask me three times in as many weeks. I felt such a year would be "time out" and contribute little to my call to pastoral ministry. Finally persuaded to go, I had scarcely landed in France when my father died. The year ahead was marked by grieving, both for my father and for John F. Kennedy, who was assassinated several months later. I mention this aspect of the year's experience because grieving more radically opened me to the present and the future. It was as though past chapters of my life were closing irrevocably behind me. Scarcely able to communicate in French, I felt more isolated, anxious, and depleted than I ever thought was possible.

As the year progressed I began to pray and even dream in French. The consolations of several spiritual retreats at Taizé and the Benedictine monastery En Calcat, as well as the unfamiliar resources available to me for rebuilding my sense of wholeness, moved me out of my native religious culture into a different world. The symbols may have been the same, but their presentation in a different cultural setting was new. Given my raw neediness and the intensity of coming to life again, like springtime after lifeless winter, I plunged more deeply into French (and Catholic) spirituality than I might otherwise have been able. I returned to Richmond a different person belonging to a larger Church, a larger world.

Two years later I was in the Congo on assignment to teach Greek and New Testament studies, ethics and moral philosophy, in the new Protestant university at Kisangani. The experience of passing over was not complete there but significant. Expatriates in Africa normally lived in compounds that resembled islands of Western culture in a mysterious if not threatening sea. Life on the university campus was no exception. Fortunately I was able to live in the Congo for almost three years, to travel extensively outside the compounds, and to gain the confidence of students who were willing to tell their stories and describe their heritage over time. I came to love them and to love the land and rivers, the food, the customs, the drumming and dancing, the sounds and smells. Essential to passing over is the love that begins in empathy but becomes more than that. I think it becomes an incarnation of God's fierce love that changes life. My soul was graced by the Congo.

When a new order of intelligibility breaks into one's settled way of looking at things — when transformation begins, that is — familiar things become unfamiliar and may be approached in new ways. Confident enough in my biblical foundation to risk teaching Greek and New Testament studies, I found myself virtually starting over. Exegesis of Mark was an adventure of constant surprises in dialogue with students whose worldview bore striking similarities to that of the author. I could give them the original language but they translated it into new idioms, new meanings that gradually became mine.

Experiences such as these three connect with similar and perhaps more profound experiences of other people — passing over into a different culture and coming back into one's own, bearing marks of transformation. Barbara Kingsolver's canny novel *The Poisonwood Bible*[7] shows that not everyone makes the journey back, and some find the very act of passing over destructive to the self. Joseph Conrad's earlier novel of the Congo, *Heart of Darkness*[8] (his "inner station" was Kisangani), makes the risk even more dramatic. But the risks are put in perspective by many more testimonies to

7. Barbara Kingsolver, *The Poisonwood Bible* (New York: HarperCollins, 2003).

8. Joseph Conrad, *Heart of Darkness* (New York: Harper & Brothers, 1910).

the expansion of consciousness and the growth of spirit and intellect that result from a sustained conversation with another culture, especially as that conversation becomes an inner dialogue.

In an increasingly multicultural society such as ours, it is no longer necessary to travel abroad to experience the benefits of passing over into a different culture. The world is coming to us through immigration, cultural exchanges, even increased sensitivity to minority communities next door. In addition to the intellectual and spiritual stretch that comes of passing over and coming back, these possibilities right at our doorstep bring new potential for prophetic vision and social action by pastors and churches.

(2) Other Faith Traditions or Religions

Everyone has experiences or knows stories of others who have had a profound engagement with a faith other than the one in which they were raised, and who then imported values of that tradition back into their own. No one represents this process of passing over better than Fr. Bede Griffiths. In his books *The Golden String*[9] and *The Marriage of East and West,*[10] Griffiths describes his conversion to Catholicism and Benedictine monasticism. He then intentionally moved to India and immersed himself in the spiritual culture of Hinduism, planting on the banks of a holy river what he called a Christian ashram. There he lived, working out his salvation with fear and trembling, bringing the spiritual path of the West into "marriage" with that of the East.

My experience is incomparably less rigorous but critical nonetheless in my faith journey and theological development. It began as Griffiths's did with exposure to Catholicism. The culture of the Protestant church of my early years was rigidly separatist and fearfully suspicious of "popery." My first substantive conversation with a Roman Catholic occurred when I was 23. Conversely, those two seminarians with whom I spent long hours talking had never had any sustained conversation with a Protestant. We met at the Taizé Community. The heightened significance of the encounter, owing to the novel, forbidden nature of it, influenced me to use a detailed commentary of the Benedictine canonical hours during the season of Advent, 1963. I

9. Bede Griffiths, *The Golden String: An Autobiography* (London: Harvill Press, 1954).

10. Bede Griffiths, *The Marriage of East and West* (Springfield, IL: Templegate Publishers, 1982).

then spent the fourth week of Advent and first days of Christmas in a Benedictine monastery with spiritual direction from a monk. From this experience and repeated visits to Taizé, I felt the tug of a monastic vocation.

Ten years later, in a desultory campus ministry in Charleston, South Carolina, feeling spiritually depleted and theologically dead-ended, I attended a one-week seminar on Thomas Merton led by Parker Palmer, a Quaker. When I began to read the work of Merton (who had died seven years earlier) and other contemplative Catholics, I discovered both a practice of prayer and style of theological reflection that nourished my soul: "a prayer of silence, simplicity, contemplative and meditative unity, a deep personal integration in an attentive, watchful listening of 'the heart.'"[11] My earlier experience of "passing over" and coming back had prepared me, I believe, to receive the particular gift of the Spirit that I would need later, one that I may not otherwise have been able to accept and make my own.

(3) Other Domains or Disciplines of Thought

"Passing over" into practices or academic disciplines other than theology, then coming back into pastoral ministry, may seem almost unnecessary to talk about at a time when most candidates for ministry are launching a second or third career. Seminary or divinity school students are not only older but more worldly-wise than a generation ago when seminary was usually continuous with college. They are teachers, lawyers, healthcare workers, engineers, artists, and business people before they "feel the call" and report to seminary. But must it be "*before* they feel the call"? Could not the call to ministry encompass the discipline or practice in which they have already become engaged?

My passage to seminary was seamless from college. I had no thought in mind other than pastoral ministry. Yet when I graduated with a degree in theology, I began teaching. With only brief interruptions, my teaching for forty years has been parallel to, and interwoven with, congregational ministry. I cannot claim to have planned it that way. Nevertheless, the unexpected bi-vocational nature of my ministry has unfolded a model that was bracing in the practice of it and has made sense in hindsight. Teaching has meant an

11. Thomas Merton, *Contemplative Prayer* (New York: Image Books/Doubleday, 1996), p. 33.

alternate practice, a foothold or base in the secular world, a second community of colleagues, an explicit system of accountability, and a complementary and demanding discipline of study. Each one of these things can readily be imported into the church and into ministry with advantage.

Today the majority of Protestant congregations comprise fewer than one hundred active members. Realistic responses to this demographic fact include yoked parishes, federated churches, and tent-making ministries. Tent-making, alluding to Paul's way of supporting himself on his missionary journeys, suggests that one's parallel, secular occupation is a way to make a living without having to burden the church with full salary responsibilities. That may be a good starting place for bi-vocational ministry if the minister and the church can be helped to see that ministry can happen in both workplaces and can happen better because of both places.

Practical problems cannot be avoided. The minister with regular job responsibilities outside the church is not "on call" all the time and is not available at every hour for church meetings, funerals, visiting, or counseling appointments. That is not altogether a bad thing. Many church jobs foisted on the pastor can and perhaps should be performed by prepared laity. The minister who goes to work outside the church on weekdays may also find that regular study hours suffer. The question may be raised whether or not the study and/or practice of another discipline compensates for a reduction in theological reading or exegesis. When the dialogic style of theology and ministry is valued, practical matters can be resolved with a willing congregation.

Bi-vocational ministry, as an expression of "passing over" and coming back, regards the pastor's ministry in the world as theological vocation, not just grocery money. Mastery of a second practice or discipline enlarges the theological mind by extending it into another domain of knowledge or skill. A stimulus to analogical reflection, a source of creative metaphors (not just sermon illustrations but new ways and images of understanding God), even pathways to better method may be gained. Just as there is a risk of getting lost in passing over into foreign cultures such as "going native," and risks of getting lost when passing over into other religious traditions, there are risks inherent in moving as a theologian into literature or science, school teaching or business, labor or counseling. When one does so, however, with purpose and a clear sense of the integrity of dialogue, the risk may become a green edge pushing the living tradition forward.

Examples of Christian theologians who are also accomplished scientists prove that the benefit is not just to the living tradition of theology. Arthur Peacocke, John Polkinghorne, and Robert Russell, to name a few, have also advanced theoretical scientific thinking substantively because of their theological insight. Dialogue is reciprocal. Pastor-theologians may not move in those academic circles, but that is not the point. The point is that when masters of a discipline such as evolutionary biology (Peacocke) have had the courage to study theology and bring their discipline into dialogue with it, when pastors have had the courage (and opportunity) to pass over into another field and "bring every thought into captivity to Christ," they are like homemakers who follow Jesus by bringing out of their pantry something old and something new.

At the end of W. H. Auden's poem, *For the Time Being: A Christmas Oratorio,*[12] the poet invites the reader to undertake the journey of faith personally in his or her own day. One may read this challenging chorus also as an invitation to experience the peculiar blessings of *passing over.*

> He is the Way.
> Follow Him through the Land of Unlikeness:
> You will see rare beasts, and have unique adventures.

12. W. H. Auden, *For the Time Being* (London: Faber & Faber, 1945), p. 124.

The Living Edge of Faith: Doubt and Skepticism in the Formation of Pastor-Theologians

Rebecca Kuiken

> *It is not as a child that I believe and confess Jesus Christ. My hosanna is born of a furnace of doubt.*
>
> Fyodor Dostoyevsky[1]

> *The Christian intellectual provides our best hope because he has access to both the reasons of the heart and the reasons of the head, and if he is worthy of his vocation he knows how to combine them. He can hold in one context both intellectual integrity and depth of spiritual experience, with no sense of incompatibility. In short, he can both pray and think! He will be keenly aware of the appeals of both agnosticism and dogmatism, but he will resist both, because both represent escape from the struggle for an intelligent faith. What we need is thoughtful people who belong to the fellowship of perplexity, yet have discovered points of clarity in the midst of the confusion.*
>
> Elton Trueblood[2]

Doubt is an ever-present companion to the thoughtful Christian. How this companion is imaged has much to do with one's season in life, the depth of

1. *Literaturnoe nasledstro,* no. 83 (Moscow: Nauka, 1971), p. 696.
2. *A Place to Stand* (New York: Harper & Row, 1969), pp. 31-32.

the skeptical arrow currently lodged in the heart of one's faith, and the theological climate of the age. Doubt can be the enemy with whom one must battle for victory. Doubt can be the dangerous voice (of Satan or of God?) to be suppressed, repressed, or addressed at one's peril. Doubt can be the careful pruning tool that cuts away the dead theological debris so that new and vibrant life begins. Doubt can be the anvil upon which faith or atheism is finally forged. Doubt can be the clever student whose mind and mouth, ever open, cannot close upon solid spiritual truth. Doubt can also be the elderly mentor, carrying the burden of questions for which only God holds the final response, and in doing so displays a tolerance for ambiguity and a deep commitment to Christ.

> Doubt comes in these and many other forms for a Christian, whether an ordained minister of Word and Sacrament or a person in the pew. When Christian faith — and its proclamation — is part and parcel of our daily leadership, livelihood and care of souls, good spiritual hygiene requires pastors to appreciate how we are formed, deformed and reformed theologically by our skepticism and doubt. For contrary to the encouragement of a kind teacher, there *are* stupid questions in Christian faith and theology. There are also stale questions, boring questions, and most frequently, harmful questions that emerge out of cynicism and spitefulness. For our own sakes as well as Christ's, we need to discover the boundaries where our doubts and those of our flock have either run amok or are root-bound in a deadly culture. Tracing the history and nature of our doubts, we may discover where our theological acuity has petrified or turned morbid. We equally may discover how doubt and skepticism have helped us to cast down idols or root out demons — offering fruitful engagement for spiritual growth.[3]

As I reflect on the role doubt and skepticism have played in my formation as a pastor-theologian and in the formation of the congregations I have served, I return to the writings of two theologians. Ted Peters, author of *God — the World's Future,* speaks of different stages of consciousness both historically and individually in the construction of faith. His work provides me with a broader contextual understanding of doubt in my life of faith as well

3. Ted Peters, *God — the World's Future: Systematic Theology for a Postmodern Era* (Minneapolis: Fortress Press, 1992).

as that of the people in my congregations. Yet another underpinning is Paul Tillich's *Dynamics of Faith,*[4] a work that has provided deep reassurance to me. Most significantly for this paper, Tillich's insights, more than those of any other theologian, have provided a compassionate theological compass for many thoughtful members of churches I have served, by demonstrating that doubt and skepticism are necessary allies to the life of faith. Tillich has helped us all to see that the liveliness of faith is measured by the ability to dance with doubt. Where there is no dancing partner, no movement, there is no life.

Life on the Edge of Faith for the Pastor

Without faith, there is no content or jumping-off place for doubt! In his work *God — the World's Future: Systematic Theology for a Postmodern Era,*[5] Ted Peters describes this launching stage of faith as *naïve world-construction.* It is important to note that "naïve" is not pejorative but descriptive. Peters insists that each stage of faith development retains its own integrity and power.

For me, the world of faith was constructed from childhood. I attended a Presbyterian church weekly with my parents. We went to worship as a family, and then off to our respective Sunday school classes. My Christian world was built brick by brick out of family prayer and a rich musical heritage that began at mealtime and ended at bedtime. I cannot remember a time when I did not know the Lord's Prayer, the 23rd Psalm, and more hymns than popular songs or television commercials. Given that we did not have extended family locally, our church friends functioned as aunts and uncles.

Christianity was part and parcel of my family tree. I was shown the genealogy and told the stories of Huguenots who left France to go to Holland. I met our family's Christian heroes and heroines — Dutch Reformed missionaries who from the 1920s forward had been pioneers in India, Iraq, and China as agricultural and medical missionaries.

Ted Peters reminds cradle Christians like me, and new Christians in our congregations (who may be memorizing the Lord's Prayer at 30 rather than age 3) to honor the beginning stage of faith. He says: "The fundamental existential issue at the level of the first naïveté becomes the degree of per-

4. Paul Tillich, *Dynamics of Faith* (New York: Harper & Row, 1957).

5. Peters, *God — the World's Future.*

sonal commitment."[6] Etched in the deepest layers of my soul are memories of pastors, people, and family who built my trust and faith in a God who is *for* me, who loves me, and keeps promises to and with me. Thus, my identity as a "child of the covenant" was made visible, tactile, and auditory in Christian community.

Every pastor is spiritually formed, and indebted to the people and communities that first told the Christian story. For cradle Christians it is the world of Sunday school teachers and Vacation Bible School. It smells like glue and felt. I currently see this world highly developed and honored through wonder and reverence in the work of Jerome Berryman and those teachers adept in his curriculum of *Godly Play.*[7]

Doubts and questions may come during this stage: "How much faith do I have?" "Am I sincere in my belief?" To describe our beginnings in faith as naïve — at whatever age they occur — does not imply this is an anti-intellectual nor spiritually shallow way of faith and life. It is a way of communicating and participating in Christian worship, prayer, and confession that is meaningful for children and naïve adults (perhaps a better way of putting this would be "adults with a beginner's mind"). Peters describes the role of theology in this stage:

> For theology to serve the task of world-construction, then, means that it will seek to present, re-present, and think through the primary symbols of the Christian faith in terms of naïve realism. By retelling the Bible's stories and by reciting the creeds it will provide a vocabulary through which we can bring to articulation our innermost thoughts and personal feelings in conjunction with a mental picture of how God's world works.[8]

There are some real dangers, however, in romanticizing the *naïve world construction* stage. Not everyone had happy childhoods or positive initiations into the Christian story. Naïve faith may be formed by kind pastors who resemble Mr. Rogers, but also by thundering orators with frightening visions of God. Popular culture expresses a homey first naiveté in Prairie

6. Peters, *God — the World's Future,* p. 22.

7. Jerome Berryman, *Godly Play: An Imaginative Approach to Religious Education* (San Francisco: HarperCollins, 1991).

8. Peters, *God — the World's Future,* p. 22.

Home Companion's Pastor Inkvest of Lake Wobegon or in the Mitford books by Jan Karon. For good or ill, this is the place where many who are called to pastoral ministry begin in faith. Yet for those whose expertise and responsibility involve critical thinking and biblical literacy, it would be unconscionable, if not impossible, to rest in this stage.

Every pastor can tell the tale of his or her entry into the next stage of faith, what Peters calls *critical deconstruction.* It marks the time when the symbols of Christian life, once uncritically accepted as God's truth, come to be tested and questioned. In Western culture, it frequently is part of the individuation process into young adulthood for religiously raised youth. It takes place when a person encounters the purging fires of modernism.

For me, critical deconstruction first occurred as an 18-year-old exchange student in France where I lived with a Socialist-Catholic professor and his family. I was befriended by "Le Cercle Rouge," a group of charming and naïve teen-age Marxists. Away from family, native tongue, and customs, I first recognized that I had a decision and a choice to make about faith. I was challenged from the top of my head to the very foundation of my soul. I was asked to sort through deeply held assumptions about God, Jesus, and America. I was thrown into doubt and made to raise questions about all that had formed my religious and cultural identity. I remain to this day grateful for these French voices.

I once saw this as my very particular story. (The hubris of adolescence!) It was and it was not. What Peters calls to mind is that the characteristics of freedom, autonomy, and skepticism are traits that distinguish modern sensibilities. My story had become the larger story of faith's deconstruction in the Western world. Doubt had been elevated to the governing principle of modern critical thinking. Karl Marx, Friedrich Nietzsche, and Sigmund Freud all added subjectivity itself to Descartes's old list of things to be doubted. Today if I bring up the subject of "the will of God," Marxists might respond that it is all an illusion cloaking my class identity. Cultured despisers of religion might argue that God-talk is only fantasy since God is dead, and psychologists might speak of projection and transference from father to Father.

A pastor's first personal encounter with critical modernism is peculiarly life changing. Like the loss of innocence, one can never return. For some it arrives in a sudden shock, a singular event like a tragedy or a simple conversation. Others may experience this as a slow sea change, an awareness that the faith of one's childhood has worn thin. Seminary life is chock full of such encounters. The shock of critical modernism happens over and over again as pluralism here, scientific breakthroughs there, and the unexpected force of personal suffering or tragedy make their various challenges to faith as it has been received.

I am heartened to know that Ernst Troeltsch wrestled throughout his life with the impact and significance of the historical-critical method for Christian faith. He knew that the method was incompatible with naïve pre-critical faith. "Once the historical method is applied to Biblical science and church history," he said, "it is a leaven that alters everything, and finally, bursts apart the entire structure of theological methods employed until the present."[9] He understood his personal role in critical deconstruction.

In response to this modernist challenge, pastors and congregations can find it tempting simply to retreat into a pre-critical naïve faith and to place a hermeneutical bubble over things religious. Bibliolatry and reactionary literalism are sometimes the result. Peters warns, however, that we should not misunderstand or misrepresent what is really going on in the neo-orthodox-liberal-fundamentalist debate:

> One aspect of the debate that makes it unnecessarily bitter is the frequent failure on the part of liberal and neoorthodox proponents to distinguish between the first naïveté and fundamentalism. These two are not exactly the same. Naïve literalism is precritical. Fundamentalism is anticritical. There can still be considerable intellectual integrity at the level of compact naiveté. The problem of bibliolatry arises only as a defiant response to the attack launched by critical consciousness. Bibliolatry does not belong to the first naiveté proper.[10]

What is harmed and healed in faith's dissection and examination? "The task of theology at the level of critical consciousness . . . is to be world-destroying."[11] In seminary, feminist theology marked serious challenges and a few deathblows to my inherited faith. I lost the easy connection to the treasure-trove of hymns and stories because all I could see was "He." Far too readily, fear, anger, and righteous skepticism became my knee-jerk response to the church's tradition rather than critical theological reflection. In retro-

9. Quoted by Van A. Harvey in *The Historian and the Believer* (New York: Macmillan, 1966), p. 5.

10. Peters, *God — the World's Future*, p. 27.

11. Peters, *God — the World's Future*, p. 29.

spect, I have both been harmed and done harm out of this quest. In retrospect, I have been healed and enlivened, and given a larger portion of the Christian tradition with which to pray, preach, and worship.

Doubt fueled my feminist excavations into the "shekinah." I researched the linguistic connections between "Logos" and "Sophia" as well as the writing of female mystics from Julian of Norwich to Hildegard of Bingen. My "first Christian" world was destroyed, but it was a very small world indeed. As the years go by, I have drawn upon the riches of feminist scholarship and the prayers and words of these ancient women mystics to enliven and heal broken and searching people. I have also gratefully drawn upon the richness of both Bible and tradition in order to heal damaged souls and to renew congregational worship. Sometimes doubt functions as a faithful exercise of the first commandment's call, "You shall have no other gods before me" (Exod. 20:1). We must step out of the comfortable and familiar language and images, in order to return again with fresh eyes.

Critical deconstruction is a tender and risky stage. Beyond seminary, particularly during my father's diagnosis and dying of Lou Gehrig's disease, I have relied upon mentors and friends to navigate the critical theological turbulence lest I dwell too long in angry cynicism, irresponsible adolescent questioning, or personal victimization. These have been my theological and emotional temptations when my world and faith are under assault.

This critical stage is experienced in the collective as well. While pastor of an intellectually rigorous liberal church, I discovered many leaders whose faith languished in this deconstructive stage. Doubt and skepticism were held in such high esteem that they were no longer willing to recite the Apostles' Creed, or they argued against placing a cross in the sanctuary during a newly developed Taizé service. Doubt had petrified people's ability to bring lively questions to the biblical text for Bible study. Many skeptics had essentially left the Christian tradition while remaining in place in the church.

What does faith look like once a person passes through the naïve pre-critical arena of faith and on through the valley of the shadow of doubt and skepticism?[12] Are we left with modernist skeptical communities that maintain fellowship and an empty shell of practices that are no longer meaningful?

Individually and collectively, Christians are helpfully moved into the

12. See essay by Albert H. Keller on "passing over" in this volume.

stage that Peters calls *post-critical consciousness.* Here we discover a new entry point into the Christian world. The modern quest, Peters says, has left many believers and non-believers with a hangover, composed of equal parts meaninglessness and subjectivity. Now, we are asked to doubt our doubts! Perhaps it is not true that isolated subjective and relative truth — yours being no better than mine — holds the key to the truth of human existence. Perhaps there is common ground, common language, and a way through to a more mature faith. Perhaps you and I can hold our critical thinking and doubts, and receive, by grace, the freedom to choose faith again.

In this regard, Paul Ricoeur reminded me of Pascal's wager: "Beyond the desert of criticism we wish to be called again."[13] Somehow, I knew myself to be asked simply to bet again that there is more truth on the side of faith than doubt. My doubts remain, but I am returned to a world that bears resemblance to that of naïve pre-critical faith. As pastor, I am set apart to hold up the symbols and tell the stories. I even find peace in politically incorrect hymns as well as solace in prayers new and old. There is a greater spaciousness in my pastoral tent both for those whose stories are like mine, and those whose stories differ widely from my own.

We are called to participate in the faith in order to understand the faith, for it is only by entering into the strange ancient biblical world that we come to discover its voice. My pastoral call is embedded in this deep longing to find God's presence in this ancient world of font, creed, psalms, and gospel. In this way, Christian symbols function as reality detectors, akin to Berger's signals of transcendence that help us to discern and confront life's meaning:

> Once we have entered the belief-understanding circle, the process of interpreting Christian symbols begins to illumine our own life and makes it understandable in relation to the divine reality. . . . If we treat Christian symbols only from a distance, only across the gap of twenty centuries, only as meaningful to another culture of another time with another worldview, then we will be unable to hear what they might be saying to us. By betting that the gospel can be meaningful, we will open ourselves to the possibility of constructing a new self-understanding and a new world-understanding. Post-critical thinking is both personally partici-

13. Paul Ricoeur, *The Symbolism of Evil,* trans. Emerson Buchanan (Boston: Beacon Press, 1969), p. 349.

patory and world-constructive, or better, world-reconstructive. It is integrative and holistic consciousness at work.[14]

Post-critical consciousness is a twenty-first-century way of speaking of homecoming. For me as pastor, my calling is a constant returning to the Christian community that nurtures a new generation of "cradle Christians" and encourages disciples of all ages in their spiritual maturation to live out their identity as children of the covenant. In the words of T. S. Eliot: "We shall not cease from exploration/And the end of all our exploring/Will be to arrive where we started/And know the place for the first time."[15]

Life on the Edge of Faith for a Congregant

Where Peters's work paints broad brushstrokes to help us see doubt as a developmental process in contemporary faith, Tillich's gift to me as a pastor is the provision of detailed theological tools. These tools have helped me to work with congregants in many congregations, all of whom struggle with doubt as if it were a mortal enemy.

Far too often, our best and brightest congregants view faith and doubt as polar opposites. Faith is something one "has" and "loses," as if it were a consumer good, rather than a dynamic trusting in the living Christ. Doubt and skepticism become linked with shame and remain in the closet. Questions remain in the dark shadows of silence where they fester and fray the healthy life of faith. Many Christians need permission to doubt. They come to the pastor's study seeking absolution for the guilt they experience, or seeking approval for their quest.

Paul Tillich's *Dynamics of Faith* offered me a way to articulate theologically the necessity of doubt within faith for these conscientious church members. Three of his insights have given me that theological foundation: (1) his definition of faith as "ultimate concern"; (2) his insistence on the necessity of idolatry-smashing in the Protestant principle; and (3) his lifting up of existential doubt as a necessary interplay in the life of faith.

In his exposition of the First Commandment, Martin Luther asked, What does it mean to have a God? "To have a God," Luther explains, "prop-

14. Peters, *God — the World's Future*, p. 28.

15. T. S. Eliot, *Four Quartets* (London: Faber & Faber, 2000).

erly means to have something in which the heart trusts completely."[16] Tillich, following Luther, defined faith as ultimate concern. In so doing he redefined the locus of faith in one's lived experience. Faith is more than creed, tradition, or church. It is a profoundly human activity, embracing cognitive, aesthetic, social, and political experience. Nationalism, individual success, and secular humanism can all be objects of ultimate concern. "Our ultimate concern can destroy us as it can heal us. But we never can be without it."[17] Our ultimate concern is that which gets us up in the morning, keeps us going through the day, and assures us that life is not fundamentally shallow. We navigate life's meaning by its compass. It may be duty, work, ideology, or a person. It is that in which we place our ultimate trust and confidence, and for which we are willing to risk our lives. Faith, then, is an act that involves risk and courage in that it privileges a particular concrete concern as that which gives meaning and direction to life.

> If it claims ultimacy it demands the total surrender of him who accepts this claim, and it promises total fulfillment even if all other claims have to be subjected to it or rejected in its name.[18]

Faith is a longing and a yearning for God. As Tillich noted in one of his most compelling sermons, sometimes one experiences this yearning without knowing the name of that for which one yearns. Sometimes one ventures a name: the Infinite, the Absolute, Christ, God, Spirit, or Higher Power. (Alcoholics Anonymous helpfully gives recovering people greater leeway in this naming than most churches!) Our internal, subjective, and deeply personal longing, however, at least in Tillich's mind, cannot be separated from the "objective" Holy One for whom we yearn. Somewhere, I know not where, Augustine is reported to have said, "A man doubts, therefore God is."

E— was recently was diagnosed with breast cancer. She sits in my study and unburdens: "I pray and feel nothing. I've been told that God will only give us as much as we can bear. But I'm not sure. I'm so scared, and I don't feel God's presence. Not a damn thing but my anxiety level rising sky high. I guess I'm just a weak person, but I don't know how or what to pray."

16. Martin Luther's Large Catechism, The Book of Concord, trans. and ed. Theodore G. Tappert (Philadelphia: Fortress Press, 1959), p. 366, par. 10.

17. Peters, *God — the World's Future*, p. 16.

18. Tillich, *Dynamics of Faith*, p. 1.

We remember together the prayers of the psalmists who felt abandoned and angry with God. We talk about the longing for healing and economic security. Finally, I remind her that all this conversation — listening, talking, longing, and hoping, is God as Spirit praying within us. Sitting in the silence of the study, she cries. Together we light a candle and offer a formal prayer to the living Christ, who has been with us in this sacred hour.

By understanding faith as a deep yearning in which the one who longs and the One who is longed for cannot be separated, Tillich helps me pastorally to reframe the issues at stake in times of doubt. Who is the God for whom you yearn and what are the doubts that help or hinder your longing? What difference does it make to you to know that the longing in and of itself can be a sign of faith? In myself, and others, I have increasingly come to appreciate doubt as a partner in uncovering one's authentic growth in Christian life, most particularly in critical times.

When I enter the pulpit, or when I offer pastoral care to the confused, I have also found help in Tillich's Protestant principle, which recognizes doubt and skepticism as robust theological forces in unmasking false gods. We are always in danger of placing penultimate concerns in place of God. Martin Luther, who was Tillich's theological mentor in these matters, said, "To have a God does not mean to lay hands upon him, or put him into a purse, or shut him up in a chest. . . . To cling to him with all our heart is nothing else than to entrust ourselves to him completely. He wishes to turn us away from everything else, and to draw us to himself, because he is the one, eternal good."[19]

Faith is an ambiguous reality for us, involving a push-pull dynamic where we approach the Holy only to frequently draw back into our fear and finitude. There is both creativity and destruction in this encounter with the Holy. The Protestant principle's vigilance regarding the dangers of idolatry and its insistence upon constant renewal, clarity, and redirection to our yearnings for the Holy are strong reminders of the necessity of doubt to faithfulness.

H. Richard Niebuhr in *Radical Monotheism and Western Culture* also acknowledges doubt to be a dynamic process in revealing idolatry. "So long as we try to maintain faith in the gods, we fear to examine them too closely lest their relativity in goodness and in power become evident, as when Bible worshipers fear Biblical criticism, or democracy worshipers fear objective

19. Luther's Large Catechism, The Book of Concord, p. 366, par. 13-15.

examination of democracy."[20] During the "dot com gold rush" in Silicon Valley, pastors and congregations witnessed tremendous faith invested in the gods of technology and venture capital. With the 2002 economic bust came the toppling of a few idols, but California's sunshine and ever-present "possibility culture" is a robust and fast-paced engine for idolatry. Personal failures, illness, and death most frequently unmask these Silicon Valley gods, with their accompanying illusions of control and power. When the corporate executive loses his or her job, or the teenage child acts out, or homelessness displays the economy's harsh underbelly, a pastoral opportunity presents itself to reexamine the old gods and search once again for the living Christ. In this sense, doubt proves a helpful tool in my pastoral arsenal, used gently to prune the deadwood and to find the living bud. As Christians, together we can find our way clear of the consumerism or nationalism or just plain stubbornness that blocks our theological clarity. "But when man's faith is attached to the One, all relative beings may be received at his hands for nurture and for understanding. Understanding is not automatically given with faith; faith makes possible and demands the labor of the intellect that it may understand."[21]

Discernment of the quality and kind of doubt that may prove life-giving has also been a significant aspect of my ministry in the church. In his definition of doubt, Tillich offers me a theological gift and pastoral tool. There are forms of doubt, he says, that are not helpful to spiritual growth and maturity, but rather lead a person to be spiritually adrift. Skeptical doubt, he says, can be a dangerous attitude that leads to indifference or despair. He describes the skeptical doubter as a person who is liberated and awakened yet lacks a centered personality.

I am reminded of B—, a middle-aged skeptic who was intellectually brilliant and filled with theological "ifs and buts." He wandered from congregation to congregation, filled with questions, reading tome after tome of philosophy, and yet seemingly unable to find solid ground. My pastoral heart went out to him, so worn down by his cynicism and nomadic spiritual life, yet so keenly passionate to seek and find the truth. Even his inability to cast an anchor in a church, a tradition, or a creed served as living proof of an inherent faithfulness. Amidst his skepticism, his passionate questing showed that truth was taken seriously.

20. Quoted by Van A. Harvey in *The Historian and the Believer,* p. 5.

21. Harvey, *The Historian and the Believer,* p. 5.

I suspect many pastors find such skeptics woven into or alongside the life of their congregation. We love them for their passion, and seek to provide them with some concrete content so that their lives are secured in the faith that has held people fast down through the ages.

Another form that doubt may take is what Tillich calls "existential doubt." Unlike skeptical doubt, existential doubt is part of the dynamic ebb and flow of faith, in all its risk and courage. My model for giving people the assurance that the presence of existential doubt was not a sign of faithlessness took place at the University of Oregon. I had gone to my college pastor for guidance saying, "I am not faithful or disciplined enough. Right now I cannot say 'Jesus Christ is my Lord and Savior.'" He replied, "This is not about discipline, and I think you are faithful enough to be asking questions." While it may not always be expressed, existential doubt is part of the underlying bone structure of faith: "There is no faith without an intrinsic 'in spite of' and the courageous affirmation of oneself in the state of ultimate concern."[22]

This theological legacy is one I treasure, and pass on. People come into my study who simply need permission to doubt, and to be reassured that this is not bad or crazy or faithless, but an act of courageous risk-taking. Faithfulness to the One who healed the child of a man that exclaimed "I believe; help thou my unbelief" embraces doubt and questions. Within this embrace, one can rest assured of a committed relationship to Christ, even amidst intellectual and emotional wanderings and travels.

Tillich insists that the search for God is fraught with ambiguity. This is not a surprise. In truth, ambiguity enters into any and all human activity. In art and architecture, there is the interplay of light and shadow. In music it is dissonance and unresolved sound that all play off against harmony and resolution. Peace is not necessarily the final product of faithfulness. To be sure, there is a "peace that passes all understanding" yet it is not achieved by the complete removal of doubt. Rather, this peace is given us by God in the courageous risk of believing, knowing that one can never have all the facts, all the data, all the answers.

This is why the early stories of saints and ascetics frequently tell of doubt's persistent presence in the form of temptation. As the monk or sister deepens in relationship with God, the voice of doubt steadily increases. Existential doubt somehow keeps pace with the functioning, living presence of faith. It may even provide the leaven of humility. Why is it that the religious

22. Tillich, *Dynamics of Faith*, p. 21.

people who readily claim to have repelled all doubt and boast of their unshakeable convictions also seem to have the least ability to tolerate those of differing views? I am reminded of my eighth-grade Sunday school teacher who carried the loudest Christian megaphone in our small town, and who regularly scared us by praying that our class would "all come to Christ so that if a truck ran over us we'd go to heaven." One would have wished upon her a larger dose of existential doubt — and understanding of adolescent psychology! We find in fanaticism and pharisaism the absence of doubt. This says less about the presence of genuine faith than about the power of repression to uphold scaffolding for a spiritually rigid and fragile person. Courage consists of saying "yes" to doubt as a way of acknowledging human limits and finitude. We are the clay and not the Potter. We can risk belief even in the absence of unquestionable conviction.

For the Christian pastor, the life of faith may wobble and veer across the theological and existential landscape, but we are nevertheless linked to a community and a content, e.g., the gospel message. Doubt may be an ever-present reality. Nonetheless, we are also given anchors amidst the turbulence.

Finding Theological Anchors

Anchor #1: Creed and Community, or, "It's not about me. It's about us."

One of the blessings and burdens of pastoral ministry is that our dancing faith, with its full interplay of faith and doubt, takes place so publicly. In our preaching, teaching, and prayer, we give new life to a centuries-old linguistic and historic faith community. (I once reminded a slightly ornery and eccentric couple in pre-marital counseling that it wasn't "their" wedding nor "my" service, but a form of worship, and that we were all beholden to a 2000-year-old Christian community that had given us the beautiful sanctuary.) As pastor-theologians, our vocation constantly seeks to uphold a living conversation between ancient creed and contemporary community. May I change prayers? Worship? My pastoral mind? Of course! Must I also be mindful of the Protestant principle's unmasking of idolatry, and the dangers of becoming rigid and inflexible? Yes! As pastors, we are anchored to more than our personal creativity, or the current programmatic device for providing easy comfort to incoming worshipers. To exercise our vocation responsibly, we tether ourselves to the "us" that comes from a deeper Christian past and geography than our individual congregations, or our personal quest. It is this large "us" that offers protection from the distortions of the deep currents of individualism (our own and others') that seek to fray community, creed, and any mutual quest for a common language in Christ.

Kathleen Norris tells the story of a heated exchange between a seminary student and an Orthodox theologian at Yale Divinity School. "What can one do," the student asked, "when one finds it impossible to affirm certain tenets of the Creed?" The priest responded, "Well, you just say it. It's not that hard to master. With a little effort, most can learn it by heart." Norris continues:

> To learn something by heart is a concept more in tune with the ancient world than our own, and the student, apparently feeling that he had been misunderstood, asked with some exasperation, "What am I to do . . . when I have difficulty affirming parts of the Creed — like the Virgin Birth?" And he got the same response. "You just say it. Particularly when you have difficulty believing it. You just keep saying it. It will come to you eventually." The student raised his voice: "How can I with integrity affirm a creed in which I do not believe?" And the priest replied, "It's not your creed, it's our creed," meaning the Creed of the entire Christian church. I can picture the theologian shrugging, as only the Orthodox can shrug, carrying so lightly the thousand-plus years of their liturgical tradition: "Eventually it may come to you," he told the student. "For some, it takes longer than for others. . . ."[23]

I confess that my visceral reaction to this story has varied over the years. It may have to do with my development along Peters's three stages of faith. I note places of trust and resistance. In some sense, my reciting and understanding of this story, and the Apostles' Creed, serves as a Rorschach test for the way I am able, at various times, to take my place within the broader church.

Without creed and common language, there is no theological compass for faith and ultimately, no church. I am reminded of the adult youth advisor who brought pictures of crystals that had changed shape in response to positive thoughts as the spiritual content for the youth group. In the adult committee discussion, my advocacy for Bible study rather than cultural spiritual-

23. Kathleen Norris, *Amazing Grace* (New York: Riverhead Books, 1998), p. 64.

ity with our youth prompted an advisor to ask, "Why do we have to talk about Jesus?" Over the years, I notice a spiritual pleasure when I rest within the ancient language of Christian tradition, even lines and verses that once annoyed me. Were I to describe my soul today, the old song "Deep and wide, deep and wide, there's a fountain flowing deep and wide" comes most readily to mind.

Anchor #2: "God is God . . . and I am not." The Protestant Principle

In the contemporary climate, pastors come dangerously close to providing the sole anchor for congregational life. Our vocation places us squarely at the intersection of the ebb and flow of congregants' souls seeking nurture and voice in disparate ways. We care for skeptical congregants who may wear away at the center of the church's confession and to the firmly faithful whose convictions may provide a stranglehold grasp impeding the church's future.

In my pastorates, I found grace by holding fast to the Protestant principle. God is God, and all other loyalties are penultimate. If we place ourselves in the center — where only God's living flame resides — we do so at our peril, for we shall be consumed. "God is God . . . and I am not." This simple truth bears prayerful repetition. As congregants seek the God of his/her understanding, familial memories, biblical stories, songs and communities rise up, often with great emotional turbulence. The Protestant principle calls me to a necessary theological humility.

Doubts, my own and those of my congregants, may present themselves as a gift and a grace, offering a way of holding back the forces of fanaticism, and providing a measured restraint in order to prevent idolatry. Tillich expresses it like this: "He should not even have faith in the Bible. For faith is more than trust in even the most sacred authority. It is participation in the subject of one's ultimate concern with one's whole being."[24] In other words, faith is not our intellectual "yes" to an external authority. Faith is neither an act of the will nor a sentimental subjective experience of "loving feeling." Given that faith constitutes such powerful and full engagement of any human person, I, as pastor, am well advised to befriend my doubts and to honor their ability to keep my human limitations ever before me.

24. Tillich, *Dynamics of Faith,* p. 32.

Anchor #3: The Value of Symbol: "What points us to God?"

Centuries ago, Christians lived in a linguistic universe that did not neatly separate fact and symbol, history and myth. Today, faith must account for itself in a culture where truth means "fact" and symbol means "fairy tale." My third anchor, in conversations of faith and doubt, is a deep appreciation of symbols and their evocative power-filled reality.

> The modern mind poses a challenge to Christian theology because it makes assumptions that are essentially hostile to the symbols of the Christian faith. The most devastating assumption is that Christian symbols are old-fashioned and out-of-date. In fact, it is only because of modern thinking that one could even suggest the possibility that the Bible's meaning is strange, anachronistic, or no longer valid. Augustine in the fifth century did not think the Bible was out-of-date. Nor did Thomas Aquinas in the thirteenth century or Martin Luther and John Calvin in the sixteenth century think of the Bible as old-fashioned. Only those who come after the rise of natural science and the Enlightenment pit what scripture says against what we learn from other sources.[25]

I remember a congregation where worship leaders were initially uncomfortable about holding prayers at the cross during a Taizé service. In subsequent years, the prayer at the cross became the heart and soul of the service, with people standing, kneeling, bending forehead to wood. The cross, now as in earlier times, witnessed to the living Christ. Symbols point beyond themselves. They participate in the reality to which they point. Symbols open up new depths and heights of reality that are closed for us. They unlock keys to our souls, ways of appreciating reality and dimensions of its beauty and tragedy that we could not get access to in other ways. Finally, they cannot be invented or produced.[26]

In recent years, writers such as Richard Dawkins (*The God Delusion:* [Houghton Mifflin, 2006]) and Christopher Hitchens (*God Is Not Great: How Religion Has Poisoned Everything* [HachetteBookGroup, 2007]) have launched a full-blown assault on the life of faith. Dawkins places all the world's ills at the doorstep of the church, mosque, and synagogue. This "God

25. Peters, *God — the World's Future,* p. 7.
26. Tillich, *Dynamics of Faith,* pp. 42-43.

delusion" has afflicted humankind. Ironically, Dawkins is a faithful and zealous believer in "scientism," a worldview that sees Science, or rather a version of Darwinism, as the world's salvation. It is a problematic fundamentalism for many believers and scientists.

To counter these and other challenges, Tillich reminds us that the truth of faith is not like scientific truth, historical truth, or even philosophical truth:

> Faith includes certitude about its own foundation — for example, an event in history which has transformed history — for the faithful. But faith does not include historical knowledge about the way in which this event took place. Therefore, faith cannot be shaken by historical research even if its results are critical of the traditions in which the event is reported. This independence of historical truth is one of the most important consequences of the understanding of faith as the state of ultimate concern. It liberates the faithful from a burden they cannot carry after the demands of scholarly honesty have shaped their conscience.[27]

What about the historical reality of Jesus of Nazareth? What about the Resurrection? For Tillich, my guess is that he saw Jesus of Nazareth as a historical event, and shared the theological spectrum found in Rudolf Bultmann who argued that the resurrection narrative held power in transforming a person's life. So when Christians preached how faith in Jesus could change lives, Jesus "was raised" in the preaching event, and not in a miraculous historical moment that preceded it.[28] At the other end of the theological spectrum are Christians who believe that, had a camera been present, evidence of Jesus' resurrected body would have been obtained. For my own part, I lean most comfortably into Calvin's theological humility:

> Calvin once wrote that he would try to give "some suggestion of the manner of resurrection. I use this language because Paul, calling it 'a mystery,' urges us to sobriety and restrains us from philosophizing too freely and subtly." Sobriety and restraint indeed seem like a good idea when talking about this topic. A resurrection from the dead, a transfor-

27. Tillich, *Dynamics of Faith,* p. 89.

28. William C. Placher, *Jesus the Savior: The Meaning of Jesus Christ for Christian Faith* (Louisville: Westminster/John Knox Press, 2001), p. 166.

mation of the meaning of things, an inbreaking of the ultimate triumph of God into the midst of history — we might expect that such an event would be a little hard to describe. . . . Moreover, the biblical texts themselves invite caution.[29]

Final Thoughts

Certainly as pastor-theologians we must have some criteria for whether our doubts are allowing us simply to blow in the wind or whether they are leading us toward a less idolatrous, more Christ-like faith. One criterion is whether faith is adequate to express an ultimate concern "in such a way that it creates reply, action, communication. Symbols which are able to do this are alive."[30] Given the danger of this first criterion (where even a destructive cult could be called adequate), Tillich quickly states a second criterion: faith must contain some element of idolatry-detection. To twenty-first-century pluralistic, ecumenical, and interfaith ears, it is both disconcerting and refreshing to receive this nugget of Christian apologetics:

> The criterion contains a Yes — it does not reject any truth of faith in whatever form it may appear in the history of faith — and it contains a No — it does not accept any truth of faith as ultimate except the one that no man possess it. The fact that this criterion is identical with the Protestant principle and has become reality in the Cross of the Christ constitutes the superiority of Protestant Christianity.[31]

Postmodern currents may be pressing us in new directions, but most pastors carry in their theological bones the hermeneutical questions that first emerged in the nineteenth century. If the early church struggled with the ontological understanding of Jesus in terms of *how* he was human and *how* divine, intellectual squabbles between liberalism and neo-orthodoxy over Christology have left a chilling climate within denominations. Here postmodernism is barely on the horizon! The theological polarization of the last century continues to offer a chilling climate for faith and doubt.

29. Placher, *Jesus the Savior,* p. 167.
30. Tillich, *Dynamics of Faith,* p. 96.
31. Tillich, *Dynamics of Faith,* p. 98.

For pastors inside the church, and those coming into its leadership, one hopes for a greater thaw. Constructive doubt has multiple conversation partners, both inside and outside the church. Signs of theological morbidity for pastors include indifference, resignation, or rigid defensiveness. Theological liveliness in the pastor requires a horizontal and vertical axis, a cruciform life that involves both prayer and community. Out of the dialogue in each emerge the living relationship that includes doubt, skepticism, and questions.

Reading as *Habitus:* On the Formative Practice of Reading Theology Today

Kristine Suna-Koro

> *Quality is the greatest enemy of any kind of mass-leveling. . . . Culturally it means a return from the newspaper and the radio to the book, from feverish activity to unhurried leisure, from dispersion to concentration, from sensationalism to reflection, from virtuosity to art, from snobbery to modesty, from extravagance to moderation.*
>
> Dietrich Bonhoeffer[1]

Even though things like newspapers and radio exude the refined air of nostalgia and sophistication of a bygone era in this age of instant messaging, blogging, YouTube, and the omniscient Wikipedia, Bonhoeffer's concern with "quality" is by no means nostalgic. Christians love to proclaim near and far their being "in the world" but not "of the world." By extension, in pondering the state of the pastorate and its educational and professional training practices in the first decade of twenty-first-century North America, it is dangerously easy to resort to the utopian comfort of the above axiom too quickly. Bonhoeffer's old worry mandates a closer look at the status of "in" versus "of": Is it how things are or is it how we wish/hope they would be in the theological formation of pastors?

1. "After Ten Years: A Reckoning Made at New Year 1943," *Letters and Papers from Prison,* ed. Eberhard Bethge (New York: Touchstone/Simon & Schuster, 1997), p. 13.

The aim of my contribution to this volume is to interrogate some of the contemporary challenges through the lens of the formative practice of reading as a major component of the theological training and formation of pastors. It is obvious to all who have worked their way through the system of higher education in the West, including theological education, that reading consumes countless hours of our waking time. Moreover, Christianity as a "religion of the book" already presupposes reading as a core practice that potentially includes the whole polyphonous tradition of Christian theological thought spanning two millennia, with its rich array of cultural and historical configurations.

Even though we all read, whether voraciously for the love of it or only because we must, reading is by no means a practice that can be assumed to be automatically mastered and available for those pursuing theological inquiry as part of their training and pastoral ministry. Among fellow pastors, seminarians, and undergraduates alike, I have seen eyes being rolled time and again over the fact that reading undiluted and unabridged theological texts, especially written in languages other than one's native and in other contexts than one's own, is perceived as a frustrating, time-consuming, and boring endeavor, a duty rather than an opportunity for joy and transformation, conversation, and contemplation.

My observations in parish and academic settings over the past decade, both in Europe and North America, have led me to question the *"how"* of reading precisely as a formative discipline *today* — particularly among those who, like myself, actively inhabit the late modern culture with its parallel cyber-universes, informationism, and the constant lure of life on the surface. My primary concern is with the pastoral formation of those who are currently entering into or preparing for their ministries. To start with, this particular culture that most of us indwell and engage on a daily basis, as doubtlessly all cultures are, is deeply and pervasively formative as it ingrains in us certain habits that very often go unnoticed and unreflected upon. It forms the *"how"* of our living, relating, consuming, loving, inquiring, discerning . . . and — also reading. Once more, for the sake and love of all things ecclesiastical, the "in the world" ought not to be underestimated, unless there is a wish to promote self-righteous and nostalgic illusions. In what follows I will first look at a few distinctive features of the present cultural landscape — of which we all to a greater or lesser degree are a part — and subsequently suggest that the inescapable activity of reading could be viewed as a generous opportunity for engaging in a *trans*-formative practice. Reading can transform the ways of *"how"* we as pastoral theologians relate to other people, other times and cultures, other ideas; but beyond all this and through all this and amidst all this, reading can transform how we relate to the Triune God from within God's world.

Status Quo

Not many would claim that the enclaves of theological training are immune from the trends (ills?) of the present growing divide between the pastorate and institutions of theological education, a divide that issues in mutual impoverishment and disappointment and, in some cases, even unnecessary antagonism. It is precisely the theological component that suffers the most alongside this divide. Occasionally the disappointment on the ecclesiastical side translates into a wish to "go it alone," as if the educational institutions were a necessary purgatory beyond repair to be endured while being on a pilgrim's progress towards a pulpit. But perhaps in the church that is *in* the world, but not *of* it, the damage control could be gracefully performed in a collaborative effort of both academy and church. In a sense, the very impetus of the Pastor-Theologian Program has been to provide a space for such a creative and timely damage control.

But let us not forget Bonhoeffer's worry and let us not wishfully or nostalgically overestimate the "not of" over the "in" as far as both church and academy are concerned. The churches are not immune to the penetration of the culture characterized by consumerism with its skillfully commodified desires, mass entertainment, and techno-triumphalism. Vincent Miller has called this the postmodern religious peasantry — the ubiquity of passive believers who take what they find privately useful or desirable from faith traditions while paying little attention to the consistency and depth of pretty much everything else.[2] In other words, believers themselves, and especially the younger generations, are often schooled and formed by the consumer culture with all its shallow glamour and tricks of inciting the desires to possess, to achieve, to manage, to profit, to win, and above all to have the sort of fun that never results in boredom.

To ignore being "in" the world that is crisscrossed by these formative idols and practices seems to underestimate the powers and principalities of

2. Vincent J. Miller, *Consuming Religion: Christian Faith and Practice in a Consumer Culture* (New York and London: Continuum, 2005), p. 10.

everyday routine living as we know it here and now. Analyzing the pervasive impact of consumer culture precisely on religious practices, Miller points out that this culture is not primarily about some specific consumerist values or ideologies — that would be an easy target for inspired preaching! Rather, this culture and *its formative practices are about our ways of relating to beliefs, our habits of interpretation, and our use of everything.* Here it is worth quoting Miller at some length:

> The problem is not simply a clash of beliefs, values, or cultures that pits consumerism against Christianity. Although very real conflicts in values exist, the problem is deeper and more subtle. Rather than a conflict between cultures, we face a cultural infrastructure that is capable of absorbing all other cultures as "content" to be commodified, distributed, and consumed. This changes our relationship to religious beliefs and practices profoundly. . . . *Consumer culture forms people in consumerist habits of use and interpretation, which believers in turn bring to their religious beliefs and practice.* Thus while theology can offer daring and radical counternarratives by drawing on the rich wisdom of religious traditions, these responses are subject to the same fate as other cultural objects within consumer culture. For that reason, Christian counternarratives, metanarratives, or even master narratives are in danger of becoming ineffectual and, more than that, of functioning as comforting delusions that are nothing more than a way for religious believers to convince themselves that, appearances notwithstanding, their religious faith is impervious to the erosions of commodification. Indeed such reassuring narratives are very marketable commodities in the cultural turmoil of advanced capitalism. Theology has to learn the lesson that the market has taught other subversives who have attempted to reach a mass audience: this system greets subversion and denunciation with mercantile enthusiasm.[3]

Another aspect deserves to be mentioned here, precisely as it relates to education. What about the models of pastors as theologians available in the popular culture that reach into the homes and classrooms through television and Internet? In the contemporary North Atlantic culture we live on the digital side of the cultural watershed. While our learning unstoppably drifts

3. Miller, *Consuming Religion*, pp. 179-80. Italics added.

away from the page to the screen, it is also intensely and at the same time precariously formed by the electronic mass-produced entertainment. As never before, observes Sven Birkerts, we live in the "entertainment environment, among myriad spin-offs and products and commercial references, all of which reinforce the power, or should I say tyranny of the movie."[4] Overall, the above tyranny has been rather forgetful about the lives, times, sins, and victories of pastors and theologians, preferring those of lawyers, crime scene investigators, desperate housewives, and ER medics. All commercial and other reasons notwithstanding, those few attempts to portray a contemporary clergyperson usually succeed in reaffirming the stereotypes already reified. Consider this by no means exhaustive list: a Catholic priest struggling with the issues of love, friendship, and boundaries ("Keeping the Faith") or sexual identity ("The Priest"), a Lutheran minister falling in love with an overwhelmed and glamorous step-mom at her most vulnerable moment ("Raising Helen"), and an Episcopalian priest trying to keep his head above water at home, in the ministry, and in church politics with the aid of chats with Jesus now and then in his very own church office ("The Book of Daniel"). Then there was a female bishop (it was about time to have one in a primetime TV show!) to deal with when he was not busy straightening up the teenage son or talking to Jesus in his office. There was also the miserable British vicar, terrorized by his keeping-up-upper-class-appearances parishioner and by the stinginess of his parish ladies' group ("Keeping Up Appearances"). On top of it all, there was the indefatigable first female "Vicar of Dibley" in the BBC series as well as the politically unsavvy priest in the boonies of "Ballykissangel," whose confessional with a fax machine and air conditioning lacked only the wireless Internet and an online option for the "forgive me, Father, for I have sinned."

All things considered, the effort obviously is to show the accessible "modern" clergy as "one of us," as "normal guys" with a couple of mandatory office shots against an impressive, well-stocked mahogany bookcase with perfectly aligned, leather-bound volumes that are virtually never seen in action. What is glaringly missing from the portrayals of those ministries full of ceaseless socializing, administrative juggling, therapeutic *modus operandi* in the pulpit and outside of it, constantly lurking sexual sidesteps, corny schmoozing with the VIP church members for fundraising purposes, and

4. Sven Birkerts, *The Gutenberg Elegies: The Fate of Reading in an Electronic Age* (New York: Fawcett Columbine, 1994), pp. 29-30.

genuinely incomprehensible perseverance amidst all this, is a fair and unpretentious exposé of prayer life and theological inquiry, reading, preparing for sermons and Bible studies, etc. Of course, these are not at all glamorous and thus, hardly profitable or fascinating.

Ellen Charry is on target when she reminds us that "theology today lives on the margins of the secular culture, the margins of the academy, and the margins of the church."[5] In its own way the mainstream movie industry corroborates her point by its choice of clergy figures that apparently reflect what the viewers applaud. There *is* a certain theology in those models of pastors that millions of viewers absorb from their screens. Instead of secretive, detached, out-of-touch, and out-of-date clerics engaging in obscure spiritual disciplines as well as abstract and impractical intra-ecclesial escapades, relevant church ministry in the contemporary, high-tech, and democratic society must be "purpose driven," i.e., responsive to the spiritual needs of the (consumerist) society twenty-four hours a day! Perhaps it should bother theologians a bit more deeply that the industry's preferences might be mirroring the pervasive consumerist relativism and superficiality about all sorts of theologies and spiritualities — which, unfortunately, coincide rather nicely with the present mainline commodification of everything, including things divine.

From the "How" of Culture to the "How" of Reading

How is one predisposed or at least tempted to study and read today when the graphic novel (imagine, Franz Kafka's *The Metamorphosis* or *The 9/11 Report* in comic format!) becomes the omnipresent fixture in public libraries across the country? My ruminations on the subject are stimulated by a fellow Latvian-American, the literary critic Sven Birkerts, and his reflections on the impact of cyber-culture. Outside the church and occasionally also inside it, we are thoroughly surrounded by the speeded-up and thinned-out culture of techno-triumphalism.[6] Not only are the ways of processing information changing rapidly; the ways of learning and acquiring knowledge also partici-

5. Ellen T. Charry, *By the Renewing of Your Minds: The Pastoral Function of Christian Doctrine* (New York and Oxford: Oxford University Press, 1997), p. 245.

6. Jean Bethke Elshtain, Foreword to Quentin J. Schultze, *Habits of the High-Tech Heart: Living Virtuously in the Information Age* (Grand Rapids: Baker Academic, 2002), pp. 9-10.

pate in the same systemic change. The electronic age has inaugurated an unprecedented access to information, at least in the Western world, and therefore to knowledge in the modern sense. Yet as Birkerts warns, the flipside of the global electronic age is the "lateral age" with its features of a fragmented sense of time, a loss of the duration experience, a reduced attention span, and a general impatience with sustained inquiry, among others.[7] While "we train ourselves to computer literacy, find ways to speed up our performance, accept higher levels of stress as a kind of necessary tax burden,"[8] we come dangerously close to "believing that the speed and wizardry of our gadgets have freed us from the sometimes arduous work of turning pages in silence."[9] In Birkerts's view, the cyber-culture entails the sacrifice of depth: the practice of reading is fundamentally altered, falling into the "lateral range."[10] The contemporary reader "tends to move across surfaces, skimming, hastening from one site to the next without allowing the words to resonate,"[11] thus inhabiting "lateral vistas of information that stretch endlessly in every direction,"[12] where data substitute for knowledge and information for wisdom. The lateral orientation of what is perceived as knowledge fits well with the attention span formed by MTV and the "untaught body"[13] of those preferring readers' digests, "idiot guides," and "for dummies" kind of texts.

Already more than twenty years ago theologian Edward Farley keenly warned that it is the institutional and administrative view of ministry that dominates the culture of theological education of pastors in this country.[14] Philosopher John D. Caputo detects more of same, in a rather stark contrast to the ancient paradigm of pastor as theologian working within a living conversation with the community of faith:

> Nowadays that paradigm has degenerated on both fronts. On the one hand, the bishops have become bureaucrats, financial officers, CEOs,

7. Birkerts, *The Gutenberg Elegies,* p. 27.
8. Birkerts, *The Gutenberg Elegies,* p. 16.
9. Birkerts, *The Gutenberg Elegies,* p. 32.
10. Birkerts, *The Gutenberg Elegies,* p. 72.
11. Birkerts, *The Gutenberg Elegies,* p. 72.
12. Birkerts, *The Gutenberg Elegies,* p. 75.
13. Talal Asad, "Remarks on the Anthropology of the Body," in *Religion and the Body,* ed. Sarah Coakley (Cambridge: Cambridge University Press, 1997), p. 42.
14. Edward Farley, *Theologia: The Fragmentation and Unity of Theological Knowledge* (Philadelphia: Fortress Press, 1983).

> fund-raisers, administrators, damage-control specialists, almost anything but theologians. The theologians, on the other hand, are busy getting tenure and promotion in academic institutions, writing papers that practically nobody can read except other academics, and they have next to no contact with the actual practice of faith in the churches. So there is an important divide between religion and academic theology that is not healthy for either party and that we should not overlook.[15]

Both Farley and Caputo point out that the knowledge required for a successful pastoral performance has acquired a "strategic, technical character."[16] Farley's observation of what has happened to theology as a discipline traditionally related to wisdom and sapiential knowledge up until modernity is aptly and still relevantly stated in the title of a chapter in *Theologia:* "Theology/Knowledge: From Sapiential Habitus to Practical Know-how." Theology and wisdom have become *Kunstlehre* or a technology.[17]

These pragmatically chosen dispositions issue in a calculated consumerist self-interested and efficient *"habitus"* of sorts. Control, calculated risk, and profit outweigh and write off the classical or open rationality which can by no means be reduced to techniques, procedures, and technologies serving the ends of one's own choice. Under the sway of consumerist rationality, the main(old)line and even more noticeably the shrinking ethnic denominations, begin to succumb to the models of organizations prescribed by feasibility studies and development plans designed to make them competitively attractive with other leisure activities. The main preoccupation here is managed "church growth" or, in case of the ethnic churches, continued survival in the present state of affairs (as my own experience serving an ethnic faith community has shown).

An equally significant concern about the increasing role of techno-rationality in pastoral and theological formation blurs the boundaries with the management models akin to economic institutions. In this context, the ubiquitous techno-rationality in whose waters children grow up, teenagers mature, and thirty-somethings like me swim extensively these days in this part of the world, is also present in faith communities. The communities of

15. John D. Caputo, *Philosophy and Theology* (Nashville: Abingdon Press, 2006), pp. 53-54.

16. Farley, *Theologia,* p. 43; see also p. 39.

17. Farley, *Theologia,* p. 43.

faith are malleable due to their *de facto* participation in both the goods and ills of our culture. All these habits are formed in close proximity with consumerism. Cyber-culture, as described by Quentin Schultze, is an environment structured by technique-laden values and practices that foster information-intensive, technique-oriented habits.[18] Although I do not share the view of the Internet as the largest functioning anarchy in the history of the world with all imaginable vices attributed to it, a view that Schultze seems to endorse, he is prudent to warn against the "lightness of our digital being" and its "cosmic and moral shallowness."[19] With it comes a quasi-religious philosophy of what Schultze defines as "informationism" — "a 'faith' in the collection and dissemination of information as a route to social progress and personal happiness."[20] Such a disposition emphasizes the "is" over the "ought to," observation over intimacy, and measurement over meaning.[21] The result is "promiscuous knowing"[22] which promotes instrumental habits while eclipsing virtuous practices at the expense of that "quality" about which Dietrich Bonhoeffer was so concerned more than half a century ago.

Quo vadis?

Where does that leave us in relation to reading as a (trans)formative practice? What kind of *habitus* can the practice of reading form? The view of Pierre Bourdieu might be helpful here. *Habitus,* Bourdieu suggests, functions as "durable, transposable disposition, . . . as principles of the generation and structuring of practices and representations."[23] *Habitus* is also the term chosen by the medieval theologians to denote theological knowledge. Edward Farley reminds us that *habitus* is the "enduring orientation," "dexterity of the soul."[24] In this context theology itself is a *habitus;* it is a cognitive disposition and orientation of the soul that has the character of sapiential knowl-

18. Schultze, *Habits of the High-Tech Heart,* p. 18.

19. Schultze, *Habits of the High-Tech Heart,* p. 24.

20. Schultze, *Habits of the High-Tech Heart,* p. 21.

21. Schultze, *Habits of the High-Tech Heart,* p. 21.

22. Schultze, *Habits of the High-Tech Heart,* p. 22.

23. Pierre Bourdieu, *Outline of a Theory of Practice,* trans. Richard Nice (New York: Cambridge University Press, 1977), p. 72.

24. Farley, *Theologia,* p. 35.

edge of God.[25] As Farley hastens to add, the modern world has had difficulty grasping this sort of knowledge, i.e., *habitus* as wisdom and salvation-oriented, or existential-personal, knowledge of God.[26] This kind of knowledge is not a utilitarian construal of truth but is rather "engendered by grace and divine self-disclosure."[27] Theology thus conceived is not a purely intellectual skill or descriptive science, which usually separates doctrine from practice, but rather a transposable disposition that is made durable and transformative by enactment, by practice. Farley has rightly pointed out that modern theological education has lost precisely its *theologia:*

> The view that education (the course of studies) means the exposure to sciences or realms of scholarship tends to promote a technological view of education. Education as mere scholarly learning is not a process affecting and shaping the human being under an ideal, but a grasping of the methods and contents of a plurality of regions of scholarship.[28]

Even if the lateral orientation proves itself fruitful in business administration where speed and accessibility of the "bottom line" appear so attractive, we should ask another question. What is the impact of the visual and attention-deficit-ridden mind so ardently cultivated by popular culture which itself is part and parcel of the electronic age? In theological formation this orientation is rather detrimental. While I do not see a profound difference between reading *Summa Theologiae* on my laptop and perhaps rereading some of my favorite sermons of Meister Eckhart downloaded on my PDA, or reading the same texts in a printed book, what is at stake here is the ability to "resist the skimming tendency and delve,"[29] as Birkerts proposes. This is the "*how*" that is pivotal to remember. Again, for the mind trained by MTV and readers' digests, true reading cannot be other than painstakingly hard. It must be practiced, for reading does not always sweep us up in the same way as the Imax format thrill does. For many people it requires an acquired taste. Yet the practice of sustained and reflective reading so essential in theological formation is transformative for mind and body. It is one of the ways theological formation happens in a sustained and disciplined manner. In reading we are consciously

25. Farley, *Theologia*, p. 35.
26. Farley, *Theologia*, p. 36.
27. Farley, *Theologia*, p. 153.
28. Farley, *Theologia*, p. 153.
29. Birkerts, *The Gutenberg Elegies*, p. 76.

unlearning the habit of being constantly distracted and craving "infotainment" by the arduous work of turning the pages (or clicking the mouse) in silence! Considering the breadth, depth, and variety of texts that come across the desk or desktop of a contemporary pastor-theologian, reading is a communicative practice with an extremely wide range of otherness. The styles of theologizing, the genre and the vocabularies are truly exhaustive in their richness. Yet it is precisely this richness that relentlessly frustrates all inattentive and presumptuous attempts to speed-read Gregory of Nyssa or search for the quick bottom line in Marguerite Porete. To delve is the willingness to give the benefit of the doubt to the voice that does not immediately resonate with my own. It is to linger a bit longer, taking the tradition's word about the importance of reading texts that could not possibly seem further from everyday life as we now experience it. To delve is to cultivate a respectful openness to being questioned, especially when and where my habits of hearing strange and seemingly irrelevant voices and ideas clearly reveal an attenuated attention span. But is not the art of genuine listening one of the cardinal dispositions, or at least a painstakingly acquired bodily and mental skill, necessary for pastoral ministry? In short, resisting the temptation to skim the surface is an exercise in humility facing the two millennia of Christian theological thought, even if it sometimes must come at the cost of being made aware of my own ignorance or at least my limited historical and cultural location.

Reading strange and difficult texts can be an effective remedy against a particularly modern sin of arrogant epochalism. Edward Farley, among others, has again wisely warned against this widespread self-congratulatory vice. He describes this as the effort to interpret the relation with the past in such a way as to discredit it while extolling the righteousness of one's own time, method, and taste. Such attitudes and dispositions "sell themselves as the movement that once and for all discovered and corrected the fallacy of all previous modes of thought"; the outcome, no surprise, is "*hubris.*"[30] This sort of *hubris* does not need to be embodied in elaborate philosophical methodologies that by inertia dismiss everything else but itself; a mind formed by systemic superficiality will do just as fine, since the arrival of boredom and the encounter with complexity has come dangerously close to being synonymous with irrelevance and burden.

Meanwhile, the (trans)formative practice of reading is akin to what

30. Edward Farley, *Good and Evil: Interpreting a Human Condition* (Minneapolis: Fortress Press, 1990), pp. 18-19.

Birkerts denotes broadly as the "repositioning of the self."[31] It has become, if you will, an ascetical practice. Even more, the *habitus* developed and practiced by delving as opposed to skimming is a liturgical attitude. In a profoundly practical way it extends well into the Pastor-Theologian's exegetical and homiletic work as a doxological openness for worship and a personal openness to being addressed. The work of praise — liturgy — and intellectual work need not be juxtaposed against one another as has been the perennial modern temptation. Rather, one enriches the other and feeds off the other without becoming identical. In the act of reading,

> beyond the obvious instrumentality of the act, the immersion of the self in a text has certain fundamental metaphysical implications. To read, when one does so of one's free will, is to make a volitional statement, to cast a vote; it is to posit an elsewhere and to set off toward it. And like any traveling, reading is at once a movement and a comment of sorts about the place one has left. To open a book voluntarily is at some level to remark the insufficiency either of one's life or of one's orientation toward it. The distinction must be recognized, for when we read we not only transplant ourselves to the place of the text, but we modify our natural angle of regard upon all things; we reposition the self in order to *see* differently.[32]

This sort of formative reading — as an ongoing practice of repositioning the self — ought to be encouraged to counterbalance the imprint of the culture of systemic superficiality. As such it is a deliberate counter-practice, not simply a leisurely entertainment or a thoroughly pragmatic necessity before the final exams. What is at stake is an ethical question: How do we relate in theological conversation, in spoken or written words, without assuming that we already know what will be said/read or even worse, without presuming that what will be said/read is irrelevant just because it is not easily understood? If we go along with Hans Urs von Balthasar's view that the vocation of theology is to be, in its form and pattern, "a prolongation of the message of revelation . . . through a delicate sense of all its nuances"[33] then the question becomes far more loaded. Given the permanent disclaimers of apo-

31. Birkerts, *The Gutenberg Elegies,* p. 80.

32. Birkerts, *The Gutenberg Elegies,* p. 80.

33. Hans Urs von Balthasar, *Explorations in Theology: I The Word Made Flesh* (San Francisco: Ignatius Press, 1989), pp. 196-97.

phatic reserve that all theologies by definition are a case of *finitum non capax infiniti,* who is then being listened to presumptively and inattentively in those difficult, strange, and boring voices/texts from a different era or a different culture? Could it be that the question of reading here becomes again the question of listening; this time, however, not only of how do we listen to others but, preeminently, how do we listen to God?

(Trans)formative reading is relevant precisely in the situation, described presently in some theological quarters as the "crisis of reason in faith and the overall decline of a thoroughly conceptual rigor and a genuine intellectual yearning for truth among pastors and priests."[34] The marginalization and utter eclipse of the programmatic role of philosophical training in contemporary Roman Catholic and Protestant theological education respectively are seen as a contributing factor for the crisis.[35] These sentiments are not voiced within the Western Christian traditions alone. Drawing from his research of the theological education in the early Christian East, Bishop Hilarion (Alfeyev) of Podolsk has concluded that "it is patently obvious that we should give further thought to ensuring a substantial improvement in the standards of teaching philosophy to our students."[36] Yet, the mitigation of the crisis would involve a mêlée with the complexity curve involving impediments like difficulties with complicated sentences, compound grammatical constructions, and intricacies of syntax. All of those are unapologetically present in our theological tradition from Athanasius to Karl Barth and on to contemporary feminist theologies, and beyond. In the North American context one must also add the pervasive *dis*-ease around languages other than one's native, which often leads to far-too-premature assumptions of cultural, political, and historical similarities among theological traditions, genres of writing, and patterns of acting.

Reinhard Hütter has recently directed attention to Thomas Aquinas's interpretation of the virtue of studiousness. "The obscene inundation of every aspect of human life by pictures and sounds have turned the vice of

34. Paul J. Griffiths, Introduction, in *Reason and the Reasons of Faith,* ed. Paul J. Griffiths and Reinhard Hütter, Theology for the Twenty-First Century Series, CTI (New York and London: T. & T. Clark, 2005), p. 21.

35. Griffiths, *Reason and the Reasons of Faith,* p. 21.

36. Bishop Hilarion (Alfeyev) of Podolsk, "Theological Education in the Christian East: First to Sixth Centuries," in *Abba: The Tradition of Orthodoxy in the West,* Festschrift for Bishop Kallistos (Ware) of Diokleia, ed. John Behr, Andrew Louth, and Dimitri Conomos (Crestwood, NY: St. Vladimir's Seminary Press, 2003), p. 64.

curiosity into a prescribed way of life,"[37] Hütter observes, emphasizing the critical potential inherent in Aquinas's discussion of curiosity and studiousness. First of all, knowledge as the "matter" of studiousness is not a purely intellectual, but also an ethical matter, as the whole framework of virtues suggests. Studiousness "restrains, channels, directs, and applies the cognitive power in a concentrated, sustained, and keenly interested way to the arduous task of gaining knowledge that is appropriate as well as profound."[38] Studiousness as a sustained and habitual attitude once more brings the attention back to the adjective "arduous." The practice of reading within the broader horizon of studiousness is a wide-ranging and arduous counter-cultural move toward a certain *habitus* — a durable disposition within which neither the divine revelation, nor wisdom as the gift of the Holy Spirit, nor rigorous intellectual study are mutually exclusive and superfluous. In the present cultural situation in particular, reading is not only arduous but, to use another term by Hütter and further expanded by Fergus Kerr, it is also "pathic." Theology as *habitus,* as a durable disposition, is a mode of spiritual, intellectual, and emotional suffering. Above all this is so because it includes a constant exposition and renunciation of idolatries — "the renunciation of the creaturely attributes which we naturally project upon 'God'";[39] but it is secondarily so because it conflicts mightily with those habits formed by the steady diet of systemic superficiality of mass-produced entertainment and endlessly proliferating slick clichés of instrumental rationality.

Why is all of this important? We do this in order not to underestimate the strictures of being "in the world." We do this with a sober awareness of the contemporary ways of life while aspiring and praying to be able to live "not of the world." Of course, "not of the world" does not simply mean living in an (imagined) pristine past! Where else if not in and by these faith communities, which exist in our world come of electronic consumerist age, will the formation of pastors be implemented? It is naïve to dismiss the present cultural realities as formative factors in any type of education and formation, including theological. It is nostalgic to dismiss the competitive impact of popular culture on the communities of faith regarding what kinds of

37. Reinhard Hütter, "The Directedness of Reasoning and the Metaphysics of Creation," in Griffiths and Hütter, eds., *Reason and the Reasons of Faith,* p. 178.

38. Hütter, "The Directedness of Reasoning and the Metaphysics of Creation," p. 180.

39. Fergus Kerr, "Tradition and Reason: Two Uses of Reason, Critical and Contemplative," *International Journal of Systematic Theology* 6, no. 1 (January 2004): 49.

activities their pastors might be expected to engage in and what goals are to be their primary objectives in ministry.

Thus it is timely to consider the cultural issues in theological discourse precisely in the context of a discussion of the theological formation of pastors, and to search for alternative and balancing practices such as reclaiming the practice of reading as the repositioning of self. Given the overpacked seminary curricula, it is hard to avoid the sad realization that the very educational system in most of its present institutional incarnations proliferates precisely those habits of speed and measurable efficiency that cultivate systematic overwork and forced superficiality. The possibility of finding and spending time to delve rather than being rushed too often to skim the surface increasingly appears to be an unaffordable luxury. That itself is yet another sign of our times.

As Vincent Miller so cleverly warned, all kinds of counter-practices can be accommodated and assimilated to produce consumerist desire and profit. Accordingly, the modest hope here is not to advocate nostalgically some escapist regurgitations of the premodern past or campaign for overburdening the already overextended pastoral theologians, but rather to apprehend the call pertaining to the faithful advance of the great Christian tradition as the process of incessant recontextualization that has to be undertaken anew every time a change occurs.

In Place of a Conclusion

The underlying concern of these reflections is the observation that theological education perceived as basically technological or instrumental purpose-driven knowledge (the necessity of the tricks-of-the-trade in parish administration notwithstanding) can only replicate "the saturation of market forces and market moralities"[40] in its adepts. Any explorations as to what could and should be recovered, reemphasized, and reintroduced as creative counter-practices in the name of what Bonhoeffer called "quality" cannot be just a simple appeal to the golden ages that probably exist only in nostalgic imagination. Even though it will require effort and hope to search for contextually prudent and creative advances to engage the widespread frustra-

40. Cornel West, *Democracy Matters: Winning the Fight Against Imperialism* (New York: Penguin Books, 2004), p. 26.

tion regarding the state of theological education, one thing appears not to be a part of such efforts. It ought not to be yet another strategy of calculated ecclesiastical efficiency or a stab at self-preservation or a cosmetic return to the premodern modes of theological formation. Also, the intentions to recover, reemphasize, reclaim ought not to entail or advocate an eccentric and futile gesture of wholesale dismissal of technological development and denial of the presence and influence of the cyber-reality. On the contrary, these reflections aim only at encouraging an inquiry into the ways we might critically and intelligently appropriate the opportunities and challenges this cyber-age opens without forgetting for a second the devious workings of late modern *habitus* of advanced Western capitalism. To put it somewhat lightheartedly in the terms of the Augustinian distinction between *uti* and *frui,* the point here is to suggest some possible trajectories to be able to *use* the present opportunities wisely while *enjoying* them maturely.

Of Struggle, Surrender, and the Spirit

Anita R. Warner

This volume is offered in support of a theologically substantive ministry in the church in and through the pastorate. It is an attempt to explore what it is that forms a pastor who views ministry as an occasion for theology. How is the daily work of a pastor, so formed, lived out from a theological grounding that takes shape in the particular practices of ministry? I wish to address one aspect of the first question in this essay. I will probe whether *the experience of personal struggle with and in the church as it is* may have a significant effect upon such formation. By struggle I mean awareness of sin and brokenness within one's experience of life in the church, lived in tension with and in awareness of God's call to righteousness received through God's word. I suggest that this struggle may set in motion a movement from struggle, through surrender to God, to the receiving of the gift of the Holy Spirit. I also believe that the repetition of this cycle of struggle, surrender, and the inbreaking deliverance of the Spirit forms and re-forms a pastor-theologian throughout his or her ministry.

This movement of struggle, surrender, and Spirit may be discerned through an imaginative reading of a poem by Gerard Manley Hopkins:

The Windhover
To Christ Our Lord

I caught this morning morning's minion, king-
 dom of daylight's dauphin, dapple-dawn-drawn Falcon, in his riding

Of the rolling level underneath him steady air, and striding
High there, how he rung upon the rein of a wimpling wing
In his ecstasy! then off, off forth on swing,
As a skate's heel sweeps smooth on a bow-bend: the hurl and gliding
Rebuffed the big wind. My heart in hiding
Stirred for a bird, — the achieve of, the mastery of the thing!

Brute beauty and valour and act, oh, air, pride, plume, here
Buckle! AND the fire that breaks from thee then, a billion
Times told lovelier, more dangerous, O my chevalier!

No wonder of it: sheer plod makes plough down sillion
Shine, and blue-bleak embers, ah my dear,
Fall, gall themselves, and gash gold-vermilion.

In his unique playfulness and profundity with the English language, Hopkins shares the delight he experiences in witnessing a creature being what it is and doing what it was created to do. The falcon of majestic flight is caught in the poet's imagination doing what it does naturally several times each day: flying easily, then again with greater spectacle, then again with masterful daring. The bird meets with the elements of its environment and creates flight — again, sometimes with ease riding the wind as it is, and sometimes with drama, and sometimes with valor, opposing the currents to its own endangerment. The bird and the wind together create a moving life that is a parable for a life in the Spirit. The bird's wondrous physical abilities are perhaps in contrast to the poet's oft-felt pedestrian, gravity-bound existence. Witnessing the bird's natural act of flight draws the poet into adoration of Christ ("the fire that breaks from thee then, a billion Times told lovelier, more dangerous, O my chevalier!") and the Spirit-fire that Christ pours out on him.

However, this work of the Spirit often may not be apparent or visible. The "blue-bleak embers" are dusty and gray and the fire they contain is not perceived until they "fall, gall themselves, and gash gold-vermilion." This is analogous to Luther's conception of the hidden and the revealing God. "God conceals Godself under the opposite of what both religion and reason imagine God to be, namely the Almighty, the majestic transcendent, the absolutely other. . . . But God's otherness, for Luther, is not to be found in God's absolute distance from us but in God's willed and costly *proximity* to us. . . . God is other than we because God *loves* . . . without ulterior motive, spontaneously."[1] In the birth, life and teaching, and death by crucifixion of Jesus of Nazareth God was incarnate and Christ is revealed to those who by the work of the Holy Spirit receive this revelation in faith and who, by the Spirit, respond to the call to faith.

Moreover, the Spirit's work in one's life may be accomplished in large measure through repetition. There is no wonder or surprise in a plough blade (sillion) that becomes shiny through use in dragging through the furrows of the soil (sheer plod). Just so, the falcon is not sensible of its spectacular flight as it is a creature much practiced in flight in a variety of conditions, all day, every day. I propose that the Spirit's work of transformation in a person is wrought through cycles of struggle, surrender, and the inbreaking delivering, liberating work of the Spirit.

A pastor who works theologically is, I believe, one who has experienced the grace of God as a death of the old self, a free and often surprising gift of God, and has received a new life in Christ through the gift of the Holy Spirit. This gift has come through Christ's crucifixion and not through his glory; with Paul, our experience is that "the message about the cross is foolishness to those who are perishing, but to us who are being saved it is the power of God" (1 Cor. 1:17). This saving activity itself may appear to oneself and to others most often as a blue-bleak ember; a humble, hidden gift of the life and energy of the Spirit poured into us as into the world in that saving event (cf. John 19:30).

So a pastor-theologian bears all these similarities to many human beings who have been made new in Christ: One receives the grace of God and becomes convicted of its saving life for the sake of the world. One receives this grace through the word of God, not just once, but time and again one finds in the word a wellspring of life and delight as well as struggle, for the word both accuses us and announces grace. One learns to cling to this Word and turn to it again and again. This word comes in and through the community of faith, that is, the church of Jesus Christ, especially in its preaching/proclamation. This word comes alive in history through the theological work Luther asked of all who proclaim God's word, "allowing the Scriptures of the past to become the tidings of the present."[2] One is given this grace in the death of the glorified self,

1. Douglas John Hall, *The Cross in Our Context: Jesus and the Suffering World* (Minneapolis: Fortress Press, 2003), pp. 20-21.

2. Heiko Oberman, *Luther: Man Between God and the Devil* (New York: Image/Doubleday, 1982), p. 173.

or in its surrender to the mercy of God. The righteousness of Christ given to us then gives one (though not perfectly) a more humble, sober, and realistic estimation of oneself both in one's poverty and in one's belovedness by God.

For some, this results in these further developments. Having experienced one's own poverty, one begins keeping company with those who are poor — in the various kinds of poverty human beings experience. One experiences with them the oppression they receive not only in the world but also, at times, at the hands of the church. This drives one back to the source: one turns again to the word of God with vigor to listen for God in this new experience of poverty and oppression and in one's struggle with the sinfulness of oneself, one's church, and the world. One is disabused of any claim to righteousness of self and freed for proclamation of the love and righteousness of God. One keeps dialogue with God's word as one lives as a part of the church.

Luther wrote in the section on the third article of the Creed in the Large Catechism, "Creation is past and redemption is accomplished, but the Holy Spirit carries on his work unceasingly until the last day. For this purpose he has appointed a community on earth, through which he speaks and does all his work. For he has not yet gathered together all his Christian people, nor has he completed the granting of forgiveness."[3]

Just as the Spirit enables us to receive and hear the saving word of God, so the Spirit brings us again and again back to the word of God in our struggle with our own brokenness. That word is both law and gospel for us individually and communally. The word itself may initiate the struggle when as law it shows us our sin and rebellion against God. If we allow ourselves to hear the prophet's words they still expose us as hopeless before the righteousness of God, with no righteousness of our own. The sense of integrity of faith leads one to the conviction that the life of the church must not contradict the faith of the church.[4] So, out of fear and

3. *The Book of Concord: The Confessions of the Evangelical Lutheran Church,* ed. Theodore G. Tappert (Philadelphia: Fortress Press, 1959), p. 419.

4. Barmen Declaration, 3. "The Christian Church is the congregation of the brethren in which Jesus Christ acts presently as the Lord in Word and sacrament through the Holy Spirit. As the Church of pardoned sinners, it has to testify in the midst of a sinful world, with its faith as with its obedience, with its message as with its order, that it is solely his property, and that it lives and wants to live solely from his comfort and from his direction in the expectation of his appearance. We reject the false doctrine, as though the Church were permitted to abandon the form of its message and order to its own pleasure or to changes in prevailing ideological and political convictions" (1934).

love for God, one might pray, preach, teach, act, and speak on behalf of the need for repentance and amendment of the life of the church. Undoubtedly this activity will meet with resistance of many kinds. Undoubtedly in the process one's own rebellion against God is mixed into one's work. At some point, one comes to the end of one's own power and surrenders the outcome to God. It is at this point that the Spirit of Christ meets us in our defeat and death and creates from the struggle not our intended outcome but something better: the church as a new creation, and for the pastor, a renewed ministry. A saving word can be spoken. A saving act can be engaged, in humility and hope.

Let us look more closely at the dynamics of the Holy Spirit in struggle, surrender, and receiving new life.

Struggle

Struggle is the result of one's lived experience in the church and the world along with one's encounter with the word of God whenever that life is experienced as broken or whenever the word of God exposes the brokenness of that life. The scriptures speak into our lives with truth only through the Spirit's work. Martin Luther writes:

> We preach and open the Scriptures to you through the Holy Spirit, so that you yourselves may read and see what is in them. . . . Christ, in John 10, declares that he is the door by which one must enter, and whoever enters by him, to him the gatekeeper (the Holy Spirit) opens in order that he might find pasture and blessedness.[5]

Reading the Bible in faith for the sake of oneself and others is a complex and tricky business: complex because of the interplay between academic scholarship and lived faith, tricky because the enemy, the world opposed to God and our own self turned in upon itself, are all deceitful. The risks involved in paying careful heed to the scriptures, and in finding the thin line between using and abusing, were described unmistakably by Luther in a sermon he preached in 1515 on the anniversary of his baptism:[6]

5. *Luther's Works,* ed. E. Theodore Bachmann (Philadelphia: Muhlenberg Press, 1960), 35:123.

6. Oberman, *Luther: Man Between God and the Devil,* p. 173.

> Whoever wants to read the Bible must make sure he is not wrong, for the Scriptures can easily be stretched and guided, but no one should guide them according to his emotions; he should lead them to the well, that is to the cross of Christ, then he will certainly be right and cannot fail.[7]

Again, Luther here is pointing to a theology of the cross as the interpretive principle most resistant to the deceptions that come from within and without. The Spirit brings into our consciousness the word of God that critiques the church's life in the world.

A theology of the cross not only provides an interpretive principle when reading scripture; a theology of the cross also provides the church with its calling and stance vis-à-vis the suffering of the world. By "the church" I am here referring to the church in all its meanings, including the local congregation, the local body of believers, the larger political, social, and ecclesial body, and the one, holy, catholic, and apostolic church. One must note the *Sitz im Leben* of one's congregation and the larger church geographically, culturally, politically, and socially as well as in the historical moment. Walter Brueggemann has written, "The dominant script of both selves and communities in our society, for both liberals and conservatives, is the script of therapeutic, technological, consumerist militarism that permeates every dimension of our common life."[8]

A church heavily captive to a therapeutic, technological, consumerist militarism of our society is the context in which we in North America find ourselves living and serving as pastors. This will cause a pastor to struggle with brokenness in more than one dimension. If one sees these cultural forces (with some exceptions) as inimical to the gospel, then one will struggle against the broad direction of a church that is entrapped in these idolatries or props up these idolatries to the detriment and suffering of human beings and the broader creation. In the local expression of the church, one presses against this tide in individuals within the church, governing boards, and in those from outside the organized church who come seeking to understand the church's *raison d'être.*

As Christ was and is the presence of God in solidarity with human suffering, so the body of Christ is called to be present with those suffering in the

7. D. Martin Luthers Werke: Kritische Gesamtausgabe, Abteilung Werke, 1.52, 15-18.

8. Walter Brueggemann, "Counterscript," *The Christian Century*, November 29, 2005, pp. 22-28.

world. In fact, for the church, suffering with Christ in the world is a distinguishing mark, as Douglas John Hall writes:

> For centuries theology has maintained that the true marks of the church are the four that are mentioned in the Nicene Creed: "one, holy, catholic, and apostolic church" (unity, holiness, catholicity, and apostolicity). Each of these *notae ecclesia* can find some biblical basis, but none of them can claim a fraction of the attention paid to the theme of the church's suffering in these sacred writings. They are all latecomers on the scene of Christian ecclesiology. The earliest and most prominent manner of discerning the true church and distinguishing it from false claims to Christian identity was to observe the nature and suffering experienced by the community of faith. Why? Because, of course, as Paul makes clear [e.g., in Rom. 5:1-5 and 2 Cor. 4:5-11] . . . if you claim to be a disciple of the crucified one you must expect to participate in his sufferings; if you preach a *theology* of the cross, you will have to become a *community* of the cross.[9]

God's humanity was incarnate in Jesus Christ and his murder revealed God's humanity enclosed in divinity. In the church the humanity of God still delights to take on human form. As Barth taught, the Living God in Jesus Christ says "Yes" to humanity and thus the church is called to say "No" to things that deny people's humanity. Thus the struggle sometimes lies between the church and the world when the church says "No" and thus resists worldly powers. Yet the struggle sometimes lies between the church and God's demands when the church refuses to say "No" to things that deny people's humanity. Dirk Smit, a pastor and teaching theologian of the Reformed Church in South Africa in the days of apartheid as well as in this post-apartheid era, said, "The humanity of God is in the weakness of the church, which is its humanity. . . . There is only this broken church. It is the witness of this church that is the mystery of the living God, deeply human, imperfect, fragile, problematic, lacking in faith, hope, and love, silent when it should speak, confused, etc."[10]

However that may be, one ought not, because of one's knowing the

9. Douglas John Hall, *The Cross in Our Context,* p. 140.

10. Dirk J. Smit, "On the Humanity of the Church," address at the Pastor-Theologian Annual Conference, June 2006, Sedona, Arizona.

finitude and sinfulness of self and others, succumb to the temptation to deny the reality of the struggle, or refuse to engage in it. Just as the Spirit brings understanding to us in hearing God's word and enables us to receive the gift of faith, so also we are called to trust the Spirit to accompany us in this kind of struggle. In *God the Spirit,* Michael Welker wrote, "We can and must perceive God's action and the presence of God's reign under the conditions of human finitude, and only under such conditions. It is an error to seek an unearthly, abstract, and in this sense 'pure' knowledge of God."[11] The struggle will involve prayer and scripture reading, conversation and action. The struggle and the Spirit's presence will reframe for us the gifts we are given for this moment as well as our limitations. The struggle and the Spirit's presence may also be occasions of broadening the life of the faith community to include others. While recognizing the church's humanity, Dirk Smit said to a gathering of pastor-theologians in the summer of 2006, "So I am pleading that the struggle of people and pastors with the church as it is — broadly as well as locally (in its humanity) be an occasion for dialogue and life together that does not cover over important issues and questions because they are beyond us but that allows and invites in all."[12] Both the experience and promise of salvation by grace allow us to engage the humanity of the church, including those newly gathered to the church, precisely where it is difficult, and to take up courage for the engagement.

We began by saying that struggle is the result of one's lived experience in the church and the world, along with one's encounter with the word of God whenever that life is experienced as broken. I offer at the end of this discussion of struggle an experience from my own ministry.

On the morning September 11, 2001, I was to lead a lectionary text study for a group of local Lutheran pastors in my area of northern California. Upon waking that morning, I heard the news of one airplane crash into one tower of the World Trade Center and saw, on live television, the second airplane crash into the second tower. This cataclysmic event opened a new era of struggle.

Even as I struggled personally with the events of the day, their meaning and future implications, I also had to redefine the task before me. What I had thought would be a rather routine scripture study that morning was

11. Michael Welker, *God the Spirit,* trans. John Hoffmeyer (Minneapolis: Fortress Press, 1992), p. 218.

12. Smit, "On the Humanity of the Church."

now an occasion for asking one another with heightened urgency, what is the word of the Lord that we will speak this week? Within myself, I struggled with the evil surrounding the event, the brokenness at many levels of humanity and the systems we humans create that contributed toward this tragedy. I also struggled with my personal fear of a simplistic military response or reprisal on the part of our government that I believed would exacerbate rather than alleviate some of the systemic roots of terrorism. I wrestled with what words I would speak in my congregation, a diverse community where some of the most vocal members are militaristic in their philosophy. And I struggled with my own self, knowing how vulnerable I was in this moment either to be too quiet or too strident and self-righteous.

In the struggle, I was driven to reach into the Christian tradition. The events of the day were violently opening a new era in the world; however, I believed that the tradition had something to say to us in this new moment of struggle. In the hour I had to revise my approach in leading a study with local pastors to suit the moment before us, I prepared a handout with resources from the tradition that spoke to me and could speak to our various congregations and ministries. The handout included collects, Psalm 46, a section from the Augsburg Confession on Civil Government, and a section from Luther's Large Catechism on the fourth petition of the Lord's Prayer, "Give us this day our daily bread."

Looking ahead, and considering the likelihood of a military response, and how many people in our congregations and communities could be moved to enlist, I again delved into the tradition to analyze whether or not various kinds of military engagement in this moment would constitute a just war. The weeks ahead included comforting and praying with people seeking God in their fear and horror at what their world had become. In the weeks ahead I also looked to understand anew a just war philosophy, especially from Augustine and Aquinas, as well as Christian pacifism, as well as other prevalent philosophies of militarism and realism, in relation to the struggle of the day.

Surrender

In any case of struggle, the struggle must drive one to the cross and righteousness of Christ, surrendering any righteousness of one's own. One is engaged in the struggle because of the word of God. The word functioning as law shows us our sin. The word functioning as gospel announces the free gift of God's grace. Over time and repeated experience, and especially through the faithful witness of others, we even learn to trust that struggle may be the birth pangs of Christ being born into our life again. Because God is a God who suffers, we can live *coram Deo* even in our despair and finitude and at the end of the struggle.

Engaging the struggles of living in the post-9/11 world drove me to a more vital practice of daily confession. The demands of speaking truthfully in the confusion of that time were truly beyond my capability and will, and still a word had to be spoken. Each day I confessed to God sorrow for things done and things left undone, and turned again to God for forgiveness, salvation, and new life.

In the weeks, months, and years that have ensued, our congregation has prayed each Sunday for peace. We have had conversations that have laid bare deep divisions in our various views of the world and God's action in the world. The responses of people in the congregation have been varied. Some members of our congregation enlisted and had active-duty military service in Iraq. We have prayed for them and have attempted to provide spiritual support during and after their tours of duty. Others have actively protested the wars in which our country has been engaged. Others have sought to build bridges of understanding. Others have fearfully crept away from this community that is seriously engaging these questions. Others have taken up scripture study and study of the theological writings of the tradition, such as Augustine and Niebuhr. And yet, even as we faithfully struggle in these ways with the devil, the world, and ourselves, we are also learning more deeply to surrender to living in the grace of God.

In the struggle I often surrender, come to the end of my powers. And in that surrender I am refreshed by God, strengthened for a new day of service, and called to serve in new ways with compassion and hope. None of this is my doing, but all is a gracious gift of God, who attends to our needs even without our asking.

I had spent September 10, 2001, in prayer at a local retreat center. Spending a day in prayer for the sake of my ministry was something I had long wanted to do but had not actually scheduled before. My prayer and reading that day did not have a specific focus or direction, but it was for me a day of resting in the promises of God and praying through the implications of those promises for myself and others. I had ended the day praying at the "peace pole" of the retreat center for peace among the nations of the world.

This day before 9/11 proved to be a gracious gift of God to me. I was deeply strengthened for serving in the time ahead, not through my doing but through this gift of God. The deep fractures of the world were exposed on 9/11, and in response fracturing and polarization threatened at every level of community we experienced. It was never clearer to me that only God could save us.

Spirit

God's Spirit is experienced as a power that exercises deliverance often in processes that are difficult to grasp, much less describe. Perhaps not unrelated to our struggle in times such as these, a more robust pneumatology is developing, and by the gift and leading of the Spirit we may find adequate ways to give witness to this phenomenon. The theologian Michael Welker writes:

> In the midst of disintegration, the Spirit restores community in an unexpected, improbable way. The Spirit connects human beings, interweaving them in an unforeseen manner in diverse structural patterns of life. The Spirit is "poured out" on human beings in diverse structural patterns of life. The Spirit comes bringing life "from all sides." Thus the Spirit heals and revives human hearts and human societies, causing them to grow together anew. The Spirit restores and strengthens communities of creaturely solidarity. The Spirit produces communities of faith and hope among the living and the dead. These communities are realities, even if they sometimes surpass contemporary and finite conceptual capacities.[13]

In our congregation we have been describing the power of God's Spirit that exercises deliverance as the "healing, liberating, life-giving, and revelatory" work of the Spirit.[14] Most people in our congregation who were raised in the church regard the Holy Spirit as the most hidden mystery within the Trinity. In contrast to this opinion is "the biblical conviction that the Holy Spirit represents the presence and reality of the salvation event in a way that can be experienced with the senses."[15] Indeed, the songs of deliverance of

13. Welker, *God the Spirit*, pp. 28-29.

14. This is especially due to the writing of my colleague, Marie Juncker.

15. F. J. Schierse, "Die neutestementliche Trinitätsoffenbarung," in *Mysterium Salutis* 2, 112, quoted in Welker, *God the Spirit*, p. 184.

God's people, as the scriptures testify, describe in concrete fashion the saving work of the Spirit. Think, for instance, of the song of Moses and song of Miriam; of the many deliverance psalms, of Mary's Magnificat. A pastor-theologian does well to listen and speak within the community of faith in order to give witness to the concrete work of the Spirit that accompanies the Spirit's outpouring. "To the presence of God through the Spirit and to the pouring out of the Spirit corresponds a complex process of mutual illumination, strengthening, edification, liberation, and the enlivenment of individual persons," Welker writes.[16] In disseminating basic teaching on the Christian faith to households of his day, Luther describes the Spirit's work in this way:

> I believe that by my own understanding or strength I cannot believe in Jesus Christ my Lord or come to him, but instead the Holy Spirit has called me by the gospel, enlightened me with his gifts, made me holy, and kept me in the true faith, just as he calls, gathers, enlightens, and makes holy the whole Christian church on earth and keeps it with Jesus Christ in the one common, true faith. Daily in this Christian church the Holy Spirit abundantly forgives all sins — mine and those of all believers. On the last day the Holy Spirit will raise me and all the dead and will give to me and all believers in Christ eternal life. This is most certainly true.[17]

We who experience the delivering power of God in the Spirit are often surprised that the selfless work of the Spirit is broader than we may have conceived. The liberation God brings to human beings is unbounded but by the sinful bounds imposed by unholy spirits among the people of God. Yet the Spirit continues to work in and among us, showing us our sin (individually and corporately), enabling us to receive the free gift of God's grace and calling, gathering and sanctifying the church — a church that is God's creation (the Spirit calls, gathers, enlightens, and makes holy the whole Christian church on earth). The way in which the Spirit calls, gathers, enlightens, and makes holy, and who the Spirit calls, gathers, enlightens, and makes holy normally goes beyond church as usual and thus makes of the church a new creation.

16. Welker, *God the Spirit,* p. 156.

17. *A Contemporary Translation of Luther's Small Catechism,* trans. Timothy Wengert (Minneapolis: Augsburg Fortress, 1996), p. 23.

The deep and wide action of the Spirit is described by Michael Welker in this way:

> The Spirit of Christ is a power that:
> - brings help in various forms of individually and communally experienced powerlessness, captivity, and entrapment;
> - in total selflessness and without public means of power thus gathers people to the universal, emergent public of the reign of God;
> - acts as the Spirit of deliverance from human distress and sin, and the Spirit of the restoration of both solidarity and the capacity for communal action;
> - acts as the Spirit of preservation in the midst of ongoing affliction in the most varied contexts of life;
> - transforms and renews people and orders, and opens people to God's creative action;
> - makes it possible to recognize evil spirits and lying spirits;
> - provides a concentration on God's presence in the midst of the impossibility of getting an overview of the world and of life . . .
> - persistently works toward the universal establishment of justice, mercy, and knowledge of God in strict reciprocal interconnections;
> - grants authority to the person who is publicly powerless, suffering, and despised;
> - extends beyond imperialistic monocultures and the condition of being tied to a particular situation and time, and makes possible the prophetic community of experience and of testimony of women and men, old and young persons, ruling and oppressed persons;
> - enlists the services of this finite and perishable community, and changes and renews it in order to make God's power of creation and of new creation manifest and effective through and for this community.[18]

The Holy Spirit has worked deliverance in our congregational community in all of these ways! Miraculously, we have remained a body in the face of fracturing forces from within and without. We have provided support and challenge for one another in our common call to faithful living in this time. We have engaged in more public outreach with the spoken witness

18. Welker, *God the Spirit,* pp. 220-21.

of the gospel and in tangibly hosting and sharing meals with those in poverty in our community. We pray for one another, especially for those in physical danger and those who have survived trauma and live with its effects. In the early days of the war in Iraq we contributed toward the health care of children in Iraq through denominational partner churches. Ministries of healing have grown in our congregation, and the capacity of people to pray with and for one another (out loud!), to speak God's word in love with one another, and to grow in accompanying one another along the walk of faith are growing and continuing to grow. I am given the energy to speak a freeing word and to support those who are freed to engage in these ministries. It is clearly the deliverance of the Spirit at work.

Struggle, Surrender, Spirit

The experience of struggle, surrender, and deliverance by the Spirit is an important ongoing process in the life of any Christian person. I am not suggesting a "theology of progress" by which someone is improved before God through repeated cycles of struggle, surrender, and deliverance/outpouring of the Spirit. The cross saves once and for all. However, in the course of our human lives we experience this salvation again and again. As Luther wrote regarding the third article of the Creed, in the Large Catechism, "Holiness has begun and is growing daily. . . . Now we are only halfway pure and holy. The Holy Spirit must continue to work in us through the Word, daily granting forgiveness until we attain to that life where there will be no more forgiveness."

Moreover, experiencing this process and reflecting upon it theologically will, I believe, contribute toward forming a pastor and his or her community for a theologically grounded and substantive ministry. To the degree that one publicly reflects upon this process, one invites this kind of theological reflection among others in the various forms of church in which one speaks. Recounting God's salvation and the gift of the new creation we have already received keeps the promise before us in the struggle of today, that we and those for whom we pray will again experience the grace of God in the concrete details and realities of our lives and of our churches' lives.

Formation and Re-Formation of a Pastor-Theologian and of the Church

Taking his cue from Barth's later writing, Douglas John Hall writes, "One does not become a serious theologian until one has experienced the freedom to pursue the promptings of the divine Spirit without always looking over one's shoulder to see whether 'the authorities' approve."[19] However, Hall notes that this kind of freedom comes only after one has served a long apprenticeship to a particular Christian tradition or traditions. So, my first proposal is that pastors consciously and conscientiously apprentice themselves to a tradition and seek to embody it in their context of ministry. From those who do so, the Spirit may free a few for original theological thought and work. For all the rest, the church will be well served simply from their conscious and conscientious and sustained reflection, and work out of a particular Christian tradition.

Luther said that theologians are made not just by reading and speculating, but by "living, dying and being damned."[20] My second proposal is that as pastors in the church we reflect publicly and theologically on our experiences of being formed and re-formed theologically in this way. In particular, I am asking that we develop a more robust, concrete, and pastoral pneumatology to describe the actual work of God in our local contexts. The frame of struggle, surrender, and Spirit helps me make a beginning in doing so. To be sure, describing concretely the work of the Spirit takes us into territory where many fear to tread, and we will undoubtedly have some spectacular failure-dives as we test our wings on this wind. However, I believe that the reality of the Spirit must be taught and named among us with much greater clarity and specificity so that God's people also can learn to see the true revelation of God and work of the Spirit in their lives and in our world.

A pastor is called by God and the people to lead them into the presence of God through the means God has given — of the word and sacraments, prayer and faith, hope and love — bearing witness to the grace of God in Christ Jesus. God calls pastors and has created the office of the ministry for the sake of the church, so in that sense a pastor exercising the office of ministry in the church is a creation of God. True ministry is exercised with an

19. Douglas John Hall, *Bound and Free: A Theologian's Journey* (Minneapolis: Fortress Press, 2005), p. 18.

20. D. Martin Luthers Werke: Kritische Gesamtausgabe, Abteilung Werke, 5.163.28.

awareness of the work of God in and among us, as in repeated cycles of struggle, surrender, and receiving the Spirit anew. Pastoral work with a theological basis is then a gift of the Spirit to the church; and we may delight, like Hopkins, whenever this one of God's created beings, a pastor among the people of God, exercises her ministry with a grounding in theological awareness formed and re-formed in her through daily maneuvers, like a falcon in flight — and in doing so is being what she is and doing what she was created to do.

The Formative Power of Significant Events

Robert C. Ballance

Why does one pastor preach, teach, and minister from an engaging theological foundation while another does the same from almost no foundation at all? Are there specific factors that generate a meaningful and challenging theological perspective? Is it possible, for instance, that a specific event — whether during the formative years or later — can be said to determine a pastor's engagement with the church's theological tradition? What sources might be investigated in search of meaningful answers and insights?

Biography and autobiography must serve as our primary resource for this study, including memoirs,[1] correspondence, specific theological writings, and biographical surveys of pastors who understand themselves to be theologians. In addition, significant events in the lives of pastor-theologians together with significant people who influenced their lives will be considered in relation to the formation of theological existence. We turn now to the significant events in the lives of six pastor-theologians: the apostle Paul, Origen, Reinhold Niebuhr, Harry Emerson Fosdick, Dorothy Day, and Frederick Buechner.

1. See G. Lee Ramsey Jr.'s discussion on the value of pastoral memoir in "Borrowing Inspiration: Pastoral Memoirs and the Narrative Imagination," *Congregations* 34 (Winter 2008): 15. For Ramsey the pastoral memoir can be a source that allows the reflective pastor to overhear the sounds of the gospel as it reverberates through the life of another minister. Ramsey's research and experience indicate that such overhearing sparks, clarifies, and challenges the reading pastor's own theological considerations and narrative imaginings.

The Apostle Paul

Though not considered a systematic theologian, Paul, during his missionary travels and church plantings, was forced to deal with issues and challenges generated by first-century Christians. Like Moses in the wilderness with the Israelites, Paul was forced into a leadership role that demanded a sound theological foundation. On the anvil of experience and often in the throes of considerable conflict, the Tarsus-born apostle fashioned a theology of great meaning and purpose centered in the ministry, crucifixion, and resurrection of Jesus Christ.[2] A man both at ease with the written and spoken word and filled with an intense energy that drove him to action, Paul unknowingly carved for himself a substantive place in human history and the drama of God's redemptive actions as the church's foundational theologian.

Luke's inclusion in Acts of some of Paul's significant experiences may provide useful insight. In Luke's account, the apostle was arrested by a tribune outside the Temple in Jerusalem and bound in chains. There he addressed the surrounding mob offering biographical information about himself: "I am a Jew, from Tarsus in Cilicia, a citizen of an important city" (Acts 21:39ff.). He spoke in Greek, but switched to Aramaic, which surprised his hearers. "[I was] brought up in this city [Jerusalem] at the feet of Gamaliel, educated strictly according to our ancestral law, being zealous for God, just as all of you are today" (Acts 22:3ff.). We also learn in his answers to questions from the tribune that Paul was a Roman citizen (Acts 22:25ff.). Hans Küng warns that the words Luke puts in Paul's mouth cannot be taken as seriously as words written directly by Paul.[3] We learn from the apostle himself that he was "circumcised on the eighth day, of the people of Israel, of the tribe of Benjamin, a Hebrew born of Hebrews; as to the law, a Pharisee . . ." (Phil. 3:5).

No one knows for certain how he came to be a Roman citizen. F. F. Bruce entertains the notion that Paul's father or grandfather, who were tentmakers, might have offered some service for the Roman cause, but that is not a fact anyone can support.[4] However that may be, to be a Roman citizen in Tarsus, a city of great intellectual resources, would have afforded Paul op-

2. Ramsey, "Borrowing Inspiration," p. 214.

3. Hans Küng, *Great Christian Thinkers* (New York: Continuum, 1994), p. 18.

4. F. F. Bruce, *Paul: Apostle of the Heart Set Free* (Grand Rapids: Eerdmans, 1980), p. 37.

portunities, protections, and freedoms he would not have enjoyed otherwise. Bruce, with these facts in hand, concludes "that Paul was born into a Jewish family which enjoyed citizen rights in a Greek-speaking city, Aramaic and not Greek was the language spoken in the home and perhaps also in the synagogue which they attended . . . ; [that] this family was strictly observant of the Jewish way of life and maintained its links with the home country. Paul would have been given little opportunity of imbibing the culture of Tarsus during his boyhood: indeed, his parents made sure of an orthodox upbringing for him by arranging for him to spend his formative years in Jerusalem."[5] Paul apparently grew up as a boy who was taught to value the life of the mind.

Other scholars, Friedrich Nietzsche in particular, create a less flattering vitae for the apostle. Nietzsche went so far as to make Paul the founder of Christianity,[6] while simultaneously charging him with being its chief "falsifier" and "dysangelist."[7] Hans Küng carefully refutes all of those claims, however, offering a much kinder assessment of Paul and his contributions to Christian theology:

> Only through Paul did the Christian mission to the Gentiles (which already existed before and alongside Paul) become a resounding success, in contrast to the Jewish-Hellenistic mission.
>
> Only through Paul did Christianity find a new language of original freshness, direct force, and passionate sensitivity.
>
> Only through Paul did the community of Palestinian and Hellenistic Jews become a community of Jews and Gentiles.
>
> Only though Paul did the small Jewish "sect" eventually develop into a "world religion" in which West and East become more closely bound together even than through Alexander the Great.
>
> So without Paul there would have been no Catholic church . . . , no Greek and Latin patristic theology . . . , no Hellenistic Christian culture,

5. Bruce, *Paul: Apostle of the Heart Set Free,* p. 43.

6. Hans Küng ably refutes Nietzsche's assertion in his *The Antichrist* that Paul is the founder of Christianity, but Küng argues even more ably that Nietzsche abuses Paul by referring to him in ways so unkind. For the full discussion, see Küng's *Great Christian Thinkers,* p. 17; see also p. 20.

7. Küng, *Great Christian Thinkers,* p. 17; see also Friedrich Nietzsche's "The Jewish Dysangelist" in *The Writings of St. Paul,* ed. Wayne A. Meeks (London/New York: Norton, 1972), pp. 291ff.

> and finally without Paul the change under Constantine would never have taken place. Indeed, later paradigm shifts in Christian theology associated with the names of Augustine, Luther, and Barth are also unthinkable without Paul.[8]

For these reasons, Küng offers this additional assessment of Paul as theologian: his theology is not about human beings generally, or the church, or even the history of salvation; rather, Paul's theology is centered on Jesus Christ himself, crucified and risen.[9] Finally, as Peter McEnhill and George Newlands note, Jesus Christ has divine status and thus occupies an "exalted position" in Paul's understanding of God's purposes. Jesus acts with God's authority, ushering in a radically new age:[10]

> But what anyone dares to boast . . . , I also dare to boast. . . . Are they Hebrews? So am I. Are they Israelites? So am I. Are they ministers of Christ? . . . I am a better one: with far greater labors, far more imprisonments, with countless floggings, and often near death. Five times I have received from the Jews the forty lashes minus one. Three times I was beaten with rods. Once I received a stoning. Three times I was shipwrecked; for a night and a day I was adrift at sea; on frequent journeys, in danger from rivers, danger from bandits, danger from my own people, danger from the Gentiles, danger in the city, danger in the wilderness, danger at sea, danger from false brothers and sisters; in toil and hardship, through many a sleepless night, hungry and thirsty, often without food, cold and naked. And, besides other things, I am under daily pressure because of my anxiety for the churches. (2 Cor. 11:21b-28)

Paul, already an intelligent, articulate, passionate individual, raised in a radically observant Jewish household, and a deeply serious Pharisee,[11] was jolted into his position as Christianity's first and longest-lasting theologian by way of one central event: the Damascus Road experience (Acts 9:1ff.). Without that experience, Paul would not have been the theologian of the new movement that he was. Without that experience, no one would know

8. Küng, *Great Christian Thinkers*, pp. 21-22.

9. Küng, *Great Christian Thinkers*, p. 22.

10. Peter McEnhill and George Newlands, *Fifty Key Christian Thinkers* (New York: Routledge, 2004), p. 220.

11. Küng, *Great Christian Thinkers*, p. 19.

his name, and Christianity, if it existed at all, would have moved forward in a very different direction. For Paul that single event is pivotal; his subsequent persecutions, imprisonments, pastoral experiences, and attempts to manage church conflict only serve to refine his understanding of purpose — that of preaching Jesus Christ crucified and him alone.

Origen

Much of what is known about Origen is known through several sources. In addition to Origen's own writings, we have Eusebius's *Ecclesiastical History* as well as the work of Origen's mentor, Pamphilus, in his *Apology for Origen.* The *Address to Origen,* composed by a supposed student of his, Gregory Thaumaturgus, is yet another. Some scholars find fault with Pierre Nautin's 1967 pivotal work, *Origèn. Sa vie et son oeuvre,* in which he subjects Eusebius's narrative to source-critical methods, whereas others consider it to be a reliable source.[12] The main source for our purposes, however, comes from a more recent work by Joseph W. Trigg titled *Origen,* which is one volume in a multivolume series titled *The Early Church Fathers,* edited by Carol Harrison.

Origen was born about A.D. 185 in Alexandria, an intellectual center, one in which there would have been an established enclave of well-educated, Greek-speaking Jews.[13] While Nautin questions the authenticity of the claim that Origen and his father had a close relationship, others are confident that Origen's father submitted him to a thorough and demanding study of Christian scripture.[14] Ample evidence exists to support the conclusion that Origen was a student of advanced intelligence, one who took what he learned seriously, and who folded into his life the demands of what he learned.

At age seventeen, his father lost his life in the persecutions ordered by Emperor Septimius Severus in his attempt to hinder the growth of the Christian movement.[15] His father's fate could well be part of the reason Origen developed into what Hal Koch describes "an almost fanatical Chris-

12. Joseph W. Trigg, *Origen* (New York: Routledge, 1998), p. 3.
13. Trigg, *Origen,* p. 3.
14. Trigg, *Origen,* p. 4.
15. Trigg, *Origen,* p. 4.

tian of the most exclusive variety."[16] One gets the feeling that from the time of his father's death and beyond, Origen desired martyrdom for himself, a desire that would later be fulfilled. As Trigg notes, even the demythologizing Nautin asserts that the father's untimely death generated a "tie of blood" that attached Origen to the church and its purpose the remainder of his life.[17]

While other Christian teachers fled the persecution (likely including his mentor Clement) Origen, courageous perhaps to a fault, was readily and publicly available to pagans desiring catechesis following their conversions and prior to baptism. He visited arrested Christians facing death in prison and walked with many to their executions, encouraging them and praying for them as they faced their final moments of life. This same Origen interpreted Matthew 19:12 as a command for self-castration, performing the procedure upon himself[18] and thus providing evidence for Koch's charge of fanaticism.

While Paul's theological center was the crucified and risen Christ, Origen's theological center was God, but not God understood anthropomorphically. Rather, with scripture as the foundation for his thought and conclusions, Origen believed God to be the pure primal living One.[19] His life and work produced a systematic theology covering God, Logos, Holy Spirit, spiritual being, redemption, soul, and apokatastasis.[20]

Full of wisdom and personal piety near the beginning of his fifth decade of life, Origen created a school at Caesarea with a massive library. Here he enjoyed two more decades of productive work, nurturing students who became theologians of note, even some who became saints and martyrs.[21]

While Origen's father was a passionate and educated Christian who saw to it that his son received the same, his father's martyrdom was surely the major formative event that shaped the rest of Origen's life and thought. Driven by this event, Origen's teaching and preaching, along with his determination and demanding passion, would produce a meaningful body of theological works. That determination and passion would push him to demand the same of all of his students, as evidenced in this brief portion from his letter to Gregory Thaumaturgus:

16. Cited in Trigg, *Origen,* p. 4.
17. Cited in Trigg, *Origen,* p. 5.
18. Trigg, *Origen,* p. 14.
19. Küng, *Great Christian Thinkers,* p. 50.
20. Küng, *Great Christian Thinkers,* pp. 50-51.
21. Küng, *Great Christian Thinkers,* p. 53.

> Greetings in God, my most estimable and venerable son Gregory, from Origen. As you know, an innate capacity for understanding can, with disciplined practice, achieve as far as possible what one may call its purpose, the thing for which the exercise is intended. Your natural ability can, therefore, make you an accomplished Roman lawyer or a Greek philosopher of one of the reputable schools. Nonetheless, I have desired that with all the power of your innate ability you would apply yourself, ultimately, to Christianity. I have, for this reason, prayed that you would accept effectively those things from the philosophy of the Greeks that can serve as a general education or introduction to Christianity and those things from geometry and astronomy that are useful for the interpretation of the Holy Scriptures. For just as servants of philosophers say concerning adjuncts to philosophy, we say this very thing about philosophy itself with regard to Christianity.[22]

Reinhold Niebuhr

Richard Fox opens his very fine biography of Niebuhr with an introduction that includes a scene from James Chapel at Union Theological Seminary, New York. On Sunday, February 3, 1952, Niebuhr, barely over an intense bout of flu (the same year he would suffer a stroke), stood behind the pulpit eager to unpack his chosen text from Matthew's Gospel: "For he makes the sun rise on the evil and on the good, and sends rain on the just and unjust." In the thirty-minute sermon that followed, he summarized what he saw as problematic for the Christian of his day: "When we say that we believe in God, we are inclined to mean that we have found a way to the ultimate source and end of life, and this gives us, against all the chances and changes of life, some special security and some special favor."[23] In that sermon, Niebuhr, as always, waxed prophetic — like Amos before God's people. Fox notes that for Niebuhr Christianity had nothing to do with protection, but was rather "a basic trust that put misfortune into perspective."[24]

Because of his position in time — between the Great Depression and the Cold War of the 1950s — Fox calls Niebuhr a "crisis theologian," one ea-

22. Origen, "Letter to Gregory," as cited in Trigg, *Origen*, pp. 210-11.

23. Richard Fox, *Reinhold Niebuhr: A Biography* (San Francisco: Harper & Row, 1985), p. ix.

24. Fox, *Reinhold Niebuhr*, p. x.

ger and prepared to address the harsh challenges of those several decades.[25] His father, Gustav Niebuhr, a strong man of determined spirit, instilled in the young Niebuhr an unshakable sense of self. Emigrating from Germany in 1881, Niebuhr's father was eighteen upon his arrival in America. Ordained in 1885, he became a minister of the German Evangelical Synod of North America.[26] Reinhold was "the polished apple of his father's eye: ebullient and disciplined, spontaneous yet cooperative"; he put every effort into being just like his father, so much so that all knew he would become a preacher.[27]

Born in 1892 in Wright City, Missouri, Niebuhr attended Elmhurst College near Chicago, a school for boys preparing to attend Eden Theological Seminary. Terribly bored by the lack of challenge at Elmhurst, he put forth little effort at Eden. He was drawn, however, to Professor Samuel Press, the first American-born professor at the seminary and the first to teach his classes in English. Press would also become Niebuhr's father figure when Niebuhr's father died suddenly in April 1913.[28]

The passing of time and his own maturity of thought drove Niebuhr to prove that belief in a personal God was rationally justified.[29] As to what specific events, experiences, or persons might have shaped his theology and enhanced his passion for such study, we are fortunate to have the following from Niebuhr's own pen:

> The first formative religious influence on my life was my father, who combined a vital personal piety with a complete freedom in his theological studies. He introduced his sons and daughter to the thought of Harnack without fully sharing the liberal convictions of that theologian. I attended the college and seminary of my denomination. The little college had no more than junior college status in my day, and I was not interested in any academic disciplines. The seminary was influential in my life primarily because of the creative effect upon me of the life of a very remarkable man, Dr. S. D. Press, who combined a childlike innocence with a rigorous scholarship in Biblical and systematic subjects. . . .
>
> After completing my studies at the denominational college and theological seminary, I completed my graduate training at the Divinity

25. Fox, *Reinhold Niebuhr,* p. xi.
26. Fox, *Reinhold Niebuhr,* p. 2.
27. Fox, *Reinhold Niebuhr,* p. 10.
28. Fox, *Reinhold Niebuhr,* p. 24.
29. Fox, *Reinhold Niebuhr,* p. 30.

> School of Yale University. . . . [There] professor Macintosh, the systematic theologian, opened the whole world of philosophical and theological learning to me, lent books to me out of his own library, and by his personal interest inspired a rare and timid student who had made his first contact with a great university. . . .
>
> Family needs . . . and my boredom with epistemology prompted me to foreswear graduate study and an academic career to which it pointed, and to accept a parish of my denomination in Detroit.[30]

The church Niebuhr served in Detroit thrived under his pastoral leadership, growing "from a handful [upon arrival] to over 800 souls."[31] Yet it was also in the context of his first pastorate that he found his youthful optimism undermined:

> [T]he social realities of a rapidly expanding industrial community, before the time of the organization of the workers, and under the leadership of a group of resourceful engineers who understood little about human relations, forced me to reconsider the liberal and highly moralistic creed which I had accepted as tantamount to the Christian faith.[32]

His reflections during his time in this particular parish gave way to a journal later published as *Leaves from the Notebook of a Tamed Cynic.* His first entry of 1920, written when Niebuhr was in his late thirties, reveals his ongoing struggle with the substance of what he had accepted as truth about the Christian faith earlier in life:

> I think since I have stopped worrying so much about the intellectual problems of religion and have begun to explore some of its ethical problems there is more of a thrill in preaching. The real meaning of the gospel is in conflict with most of the customs and attitudes of our day at so many places that there is adventure in the Christian message, even if you only play around with its ideas in a conventional world. I can't say I have done anything in my life to dramatize the conflict between the gospel

30. Reinhold Niebuhr, "Intellectual Autobiography," in *Reinhold Niebuhr: His Religious, Social, and Political Thought,* ed. Charles M. Kegley and Robert W. Bretall (New York: Macmillan, 1961), p. 4.

31. Niebuhr, "Intellectual Autobiography," p. 5.

32. Niebuhr, "Intellectual Autobiography," p. 5.

> and the world. But I find it increasingly interesting to set the two in juxtaposition at least in my mind and in the minds of others. And of course ideas may finally lead to action.[33]

His friend Sherwood Eddy convinced the faculty at Union Theological Seminary to invite Niebuhr to join them as associate professor of Christian Ethics in 1928. He was elected by only a one-vote majority.[34] Intimidated by their impressive credentials, he nevertheless accepted, writing ten years later that during the first decade in that position he began to study Augustine carefully, fully shocked at the thoughtful answers this forebear of Christian faith provided to so many of Niebuhr's intellectual struggles.

Unlike Paul and Origen, for whom there were specific events that might well have generated their energy and theological rigor, for Niebuhr there was a series of events and people who formed him as a theologian over a longer period of time: his father, his father's death when he was seventeen, Professor Press at Eden, his time as pastor at Bethel Church in Detroit, his reflections there that produced *Leaves from the Notebook of a Tamed Cynic,* and a host of experiences following his time at Bethel. Granted, Niebuhr names his father as the greatest influence, but the evidence is not convincing. This relationship would be central but it would not be all that would motivate him in his astounding theological formulation.

Harry Emerson Fosdick

Robert Moats Miller, in the opening paragraph of his biography of Harry Emerson Fosdick, says "the immediate purpose [of this first chapter] is to single out several central themes of Fosdick's adult life and to search for the roots of those themes in his childhood."[35] At the outset, Miller cites Fosdick's childhood remembrance of his mother, Amie Weaver Fosdick, a considerable influence upon his life: "She was a kind of divine judgment seat, where one faced the ultimate standards of character."[36] He continues:

33. Reinhold Niebuhr, *Leaves from the Notebook of a Tamed Cynic,* with a foreword by Martin E. Marty (Louisville: Westminster/John Knox Press, 1990), p. 27.

34. Fox, *Reinhold Niebuhr,* p. 106.

35. Robert Moats Miller, *Harry Emerson Fosdick: Preacher, Pastor, Prophet* (New York: Oxford University Press, 1985), p. 3.

36. Miller, *Harry Emerson Fosdick,* p. 22.

> In the most perilous temptation that I ever faced in my young manhood . . . what do you suppose it was that saved me? What saved me was nothing scientific, nothing unscientific, but something deeper — the imagined face of my mother rose in my mind with such dominant restraint that even yet, across nearly half a century, I can feel its power.[37]

Miller affirms the role of Fosdick's mother as a religious and moral force. However, Miller also notes that her methods at instilling her values into her oldest child left significant scars upon a then young Fosdick's sense of self, squelching his passion to experience more fully the cultural and aesthetic aspects of life. Meanwhile his father Frank, though not a lenient individual by any means, was likely the more benevolent force of the two parents. On the day the younger Fosdick left for college, turning in his key, the senior Fosdick gave it back, saying, "My boy, you keep the key, and you let it be a symbol to you as long as you live, that you can come home any time, from anywhere, and come in without knocking."[38]

While a meaningful and challenging Christian faith, active membership in a nearby Baptist church, and intellectual stimulation were a large part of the Fosdick family's daily life, at the same time crisis was no stranger to the Fosdick home. The birth of Ethel, his sister, in 1881 when Harry was three, and then her death from diphtheria just a few months later, coupled with young Harry's own near-death illness that same year, provided the family with little confidence for facing the future. The birth of the Fosdick twins, Raymond and Edith, just two years later, along with continual financial difficulties, forced the family to move from their modest home in Buffalo, New York, to a far more modest neighborhood in Westfield. Each move brought about a change in schools for Harry. The last move, however, put the family closer to both sets of parents, a source of strong emotional support in a time of desperate need as well as a source of significant influence upon his formation.

Soon it became evident that the birth of the twins, along with the frequent moving, was more than his mother, Amie Fosdick, could bear. A nervous breakdown confined her to bed in 1885 for an extended time. The three children were farmed out to nearby grandparents for a significant stay while Mrs. Fosdick was nursed back to a level of mental health that at least enabled her to function minimally.

37. Miller, *Harry Emerson Fosdick,* p. 22.
38. Miller, *Harry Emerson Fosdick,* p. 18.

Meanwhile Harry, frequently haunted by guilt that it was his fault his mother had suffered her breakdown, listened carefully to the preaching of Albert Tennant, the pastor of a small Baptist church in Westfield. The sermon on one particular Sunday focused on the call to "go ye therefore and teach all nations."[39] Feeling a sense of responsibility for his mother's illness at the age of seven, Harry made a decision on that day to be baptized, making his decision known to both church and family, as well as his conviction that he should become a Christian missionary.

Two significant events exerted powerful influence on Fosdick's life and thought. The first took place during his preparation for the ministry at Union Theological Seminary, New York. He called this event "the most hideous experience of my life."[40] Fosdick mused that he supposed he had earned a nervous breakdown. High strung and sensitive, he was emotionally and physically built for one. In one of his later sermons, Fosdick spoke of how young Tolstoi decided to kill himself; how Mark Twain, only thirty years old, put a loaded pistol to his head but failed to kill himself only for want of courage; how William James, in his youth, seriously contemplated suicide. "My congregation at Riverside did not recognize that those references were autobiographical," Fosdick wrote. "One dreadful day I reached the pit of utter despair, sure that all my hopes were vain and that I was finished. I have often wondered whether, if my father had not been there saying, 'Harry! Harry!' I would really have cut my throat with that razor."[41]

Shortly thereafter Fosdick entered the sanitarium in Elmira, New York, where he remained for four months, tutoring the son of his physician in Latin in return for his treatment. Following a trip to Europe upon his release from the hospital, he returned to Union against the advice of his fiancée. "I used to study a half hour, and then walk a half hour, and so inched along, but the fact that I could take up my work on any terms helped immensely. Gradually the clouds lifted as it became clear that I could carry on."[42] Fosdick later said that this event was one of the most significant factors in his preparation for the ministry. His own testimony to the power of this event to shape his theology, as well as his perspective on the pastoral ministry, deserves our hearing.

39. Miller, *Harry Emerson Fosdick,* p. 4.

40. Harry Emerson Fosdick, *The Living of These Days: An Autobiography* (New York: Harper & Brothers, 1956), p. 72.

41. Fosdick, *The Living of These Days,* p. 73.

42. Fosdick, *The Living of These Days,* p. 74.

> For the first time in my life, I faced, at my wits' end, a situation too much for me to handle. I went down into the depths where self-confidence becomes ludicrous. There the technique I had habitually replied upon — marshaling my wit and volition and going strenuously after what I wanted — petered completely out. The harder I struggled, the worse I was. It was what I did the struggling with that was sick. I, who had thought myself strong, found myself beaten, unable to cope not only with outward circumstances but even with myself. In that experience I learned some things about religion that theological seminaries do not teach. I learned to pray, not because I had adequately argued out prayer's rationality, but because I desperately needed help from a Power greater than my own. I learned that God, much more than a theological proposition, is an immediately available Resource; that just as around our bodies is a physical universe from which we draw all our physical energy, so around our spirits is a spiritual Presence in living communion with whom we can find sustaining strength.[43]

Turning to Fosdick's years in the pastorate, we see that a second significant event was to alter the substance of Fosdick's theological reflection. That event was World War I. A strong critic of Woodrow Wilson for his slowness to enter the war, Fosdick boldly preached about "Things Worth Fighting For."[44] For him, there was no tension between patriotism and New Testament Christianity.[45] Then in February of 1918, he headed to England and France on a troopship to begin a half year tour of duty for the Y.M.C.A. and the British Ministry of Information — a ministry essentially of encouragement to American soldiers and its allies. There can be no doubt that something significant happened in this time to change the direction of Fosdick's theological reflection and to embolden his proclamation of the gospel. Upon his return, though still not a pacifist, his public addresses and sermons were very different. By 1923 and for the remainder of his life, he wrote and preached against war. In 1939, the Fellowship of Reconciliation commissioned Fosdick and Allan Knight Chalmers to draft an "Affirmation of Christian Pacifist Faith," later signed by nineteen hundred clergy:

43. Fosdick, *The Living of These Days*, p. 75.
44. Fosdick, *The Living of These Days*, p. 76.
45. Fosdick, *The Living of These Days*, p. 77.

> We believe that God is the Father of all mankind, that his will as revealed in Jesus Christ is universal love, and that Christ's gospel involves the faith that evil can be overcome only with good.
>
> We believe that in the cross is revealed God's way of dealing with wrong-doers, and that to this way all Christians are called.
>
> We believe that war, which attempts to overcome evil with more evil, is a denial of the way of the cross.
>
> We believe that the church is called to the way of the cross.
>
> We believe that when the state in the prosecution of war seeks to compel the denial of the gospel, the church must resist at whatever the cost.
>
> We believe that God leads his church into new life through obedience of the individual believer in refusing war for Christ's sake.
>
> Therefore we proclaim to a world which is once again madly preparing for war that the gospel of God as revealed in Jesus Christ, which leaves us with no choice but to refuse to sanction or participate in war, contains also its hope of redemption. We affirm our faith that the mission of the church today is to witness with singleness of heart, at whatever cost, to the power of good to overcome evil, of love to conquer hate, of the cross to shatter the sword.[46]

Fosdick's theological reflections on this moment may be found in his 1939 Armistice Day sermon:

> Ah, war! I hate you most of all for this — that you lay your hands upon the loveliest of things in human life, that rightly used would make a heaven on earth, and you use them to make a hell on earth instead. You take our courage and far from letting it be a benediction to the world, you use it to bomb cities, and sack cathedrals, and slay men. You take our loyalty by which the earth might be redeemed, and you harness it to an enterprise that inevitably means the rape of women, and the daughters of children, and the starvation of whole populations. You take our religion, and to help your deadly work you rend our God into pieces, and make of him tribal deities before whom men pray, as old barbarians before our Lord had come, prayed to their idols as the gods of war. You

46. Fosdick's "Affirmation of Christian Pacifist Faith" cited in Miller, *Harry Emerson Fosdick*, p. 515.

> take our science . . . and you make of that an effective implement of hatred. . . . And now, if we let you, you will lay your hands upon one of the finest things in America — our sense of mission, our desire to be of use to the world — and you will employ that to hurl us into the bloody maelstrom of another European war that a generation from now, like the last, will be a record of blasted hopes and futile outcomes. . . .[47]

While other experiences and persons throughout his life would shape Harry Emerson Fosdick's theology and extraordinary ministry, his early illness, where he saw himself unmasked, and the time in France, where he saw the devastation of war up close, changed him profoundly. If he had been spared these formative experiences, his life and witness likely would have been far less influential in American church history than in fact they were.

Dorothy Day

Though not ordained a pastor, Dorothy Day's work and writings have been helpful to others in their attempts to develop a meaningful theology. For Day, the crucible of theological reflection is to be found in the difficulties and hardships of a life devoted to the struggle for justice. The significant event that recurred and continued to deepen her own theological reflection in times of hardship and difficulty was the event of being alone.

Day was born into a lower- to middle-class family in Brooklyn on November 8, 1897, the third of five children. Her father, a traveling sports writer in search of work, took his family to Oakland, California, soon after her birth. Their brief time there ended when the San Francisco earthquake abruptly disrupted the lives of all — a traumatic event in and of itself. To escape the trauma, the family immediately made its way to a new home in Chicago.[48]

Once there, and apparently with no parental encouragement, young Dorothy presented herself — by herself — for baptism in the Episcopal Church. Her venture into the church's faith would be brief, as she seemed to find little in its tradition that proved worthy of continuing interest. Rather, the poverty of Chicago made a lasting impression upon her young mind, so

47. Fosdick cited in Miller, *Harry Emerson Fosdick*, p. 518.

48. Robert Ellsberg, ed., *Dorothy Day: Selected Writings* (Maryknoll, NY: Orbis Books, 1997), p. xix.

much so that by the time she entered the University of Illinois in Urbana at age sixteen, the struggle for social justice was to be the struggle that marked her mind and her life. She began heaping all of her energy and passion upon the agenda of social and political radicals. An aspiring writer, she took a job with a Socialist daily. Robert Ellsberg offers a synopsis of how her passion began to take shape. "Finding lodging in an apartment on the Lower East Side, Dorothy immersed herself in the vibrant street life of the immigrant quarter, and set to work on her articles: interviews with Leon Trotsky and birth-control advocate Margaret Sanger, stories about strikes, picket lines, and evictions, all written in indignant, occasionally tabloid style."[49]

Two disparate and disturbing experiences in Day's early years merit mention. Her first job as a staff writer ended when *The Masses*, a journal committed to disturbing the conscience of middle-class America, came under government scrutiny and was forced to cease publication. No doubt this experience personalized and sharpened her struggle for justice. Later, while protesting in Washington on behalf of the suffragist agenda, Day was arrested and placed in solitary confinement, a truly terrifying experience. Disappointed at her lack of stamina during her incarceration, she was both embarrassed and shocked that she requested a Bible and then read it in a desperate search for comfort and meaning. The latter experience — alone in solitary confinement — increasingly was to define her driving passion for social justice. Here we also may begin to trace the pattern of disruption leading to devotion that would plot out the rest of her life.

During the harsh winter of 1917-18, while back in New York City, she would stay up all night listening to her new companion, Eugene O'Neill, and his monologues about the meaning of life. She would walk him home after he would drink himself into a stupor, put him to bed, and then at dawn slip into St. Joseph's Church in the Village. Alone in the sanctuary, she loved staring at the soft lights and watching those who came to worship as they knelt to pray. In that sanctuary she found an indescribable sense of peace.[50]

That peace was disrupted by pregnancy. Having fallen in love with a writer she met while working as a nurse intern in a Brooklyn hospital and fearing that he might leave her if he found out she was pregnant, she had an abortion — an extremely traumatic experience for her physically and psy-

49. Ellsberg, ed., *Dorothy Day: Selected Writings*, p. xix.
50. Ellsberg, ed., *Dorothy Day: Selected Writings*, p. xx.

chologically. For five years, she stumbled about — alone — weighed down by guilt and not knowing what to do with her life.

By the spring of 1924 she pulled herself together and was well enough to write an autobiographical novel, *The Eleventh Virgin,* which made her enough money to buy a small house on Staten Island. There she fell in love with a biologist from England named Forster Batterham and became pregnant again. Tamar Teresa, whom she considered a gift from God, was born in March of 1926. Immediately after the child's birth, Day thought of the Catholic Church and desired the child to be baptized. Batterham was furious and told Day if she had anything to do with the Catholic Church, then he would have nothing to do with her.

Sad to lose the man she loved, she chose the Church and in so choosing found herself alone once again. Her grief was almost unbearable. Though her faith made her confident she did the right thing, for five years she struggled alone to raise her child. Then in December of 1932, she met Peter Maurin and together they founded the Catholic Worker Movement for which she would become so very well known.

Day's own musings regarding significant events that shaped her theologically confirm our observations:

> It is difficult for me to dip back into the past, yet it is a job that must be done, and it hangs over my head like a cloud. St. Peter said that we must give a reason for the faith that is in us, and I am trying to give you those reasons. . . .
>
> While it is often true that horror for one's sins turns one to God, what I want to bring out in this book [her autobiography] is a succession of events that led me to His feet, glimpses of Him that I received through many years which made me feel the vital need of Him. I will try to trace for you the steps by which I came to accept the faith that I believe was always in my heart. . . .
>
> . . . But always the glimpses of God came most when I was alone.[51]

More than others included in this chapter, Day's theological formation, at least for the first half of her life, seems to have come more on the anvil of life's difficulties and hardships. She suffered significant emotional trauma because of the choices she made in human relationships, especially

51. Ellsberg, ed., *Dorothy Day: Selected Writings,* p. 6.

in her choice of men! Equally devastating to her, however, were her arrests and incarcerations for stands taken against governmental policies. She seemed to suffer great emotional trauma from those times as well. Yet she was most vulnerable to God's presence when she was forced to be alone. Difficult times proved to be among her most powerful experiences regarding theological formation and growth.

Frederick Buechner

Frederick Buechner has worn many hats: novelist, apologist, teacher, essayist, and preacher.[52] "I must remember what my ordination has meant," said Buechner to Doris Betts in a 1997 interview. After all, "it gave me my subject and my passion." Without his ordination, he notes: "I would have been a writer, but I would have been a writer of the same kinds of books everybody else writes."[53] For him, the process and event of ordination as a Presbyterian minister was an extremely formative event.

Buechner writes from a reflective place in his soul, often articulating poetically what others have been unable to articulate about matters of God and faith: "If God speaks to us at all other than through such official channels as the Bible and the church, then I think he speaks to us largely through what happens to us. " With that notion in mind, in the opening pages of his *Now and Then,* part two of his autobiography, he encourages his readers to "listen back over what has happened" to find meaning.[54]

In *Sacred Journey,* his autobiography that runs from childhood to the time he entered Union Theological Seminary, he remembers another formative event that holds intense meaning for him:

> Down below was the gravel drive, the garage with its doors flung wide open and the same blue haze thick inside it and drifting out into the crisp autumn day. I had the sense that my brother and I were looking down from a height many times greater than just the height of the second story of our house. In gray slacks and a maroon sweater, our father

52. Doris Betts, "Frederick Buechner: Doubt and Faith," in *Of Fiction and Faith: Twelve American Writers Talk about Their Vision and Work,* ed. W. Dale Brown (Grand Rapids: Eerdmans, 1997), p. 31.

53. Betts, "Frederick Buechner: Doubt and Faith," p. 31.

54. Frederick Buechner, *Now and Then* (New York: HarperCollins, 1983), p. 3.

> was lying in the driveway on his back. By now my mother and grandmother were with him, both in their nightgowns still, barefoot, their hair uncombed. Each had taken one of his legs and was working it up and down like the handle of a pump, but whatever it was supposed to accomplish, it accomplished nothing as far as we could see.[55]

Later in life, when he attempted to discern what he was called to be and do vocationally, he remembers with great affection an exact moment in time and an exact phrase from a theological mentor:

> For the first time in my life that year in New York, I started going to church regularly. . . . My reason for going, which was simply that on the same block where I lived there happened to be a church with a preacher I had heard of and that I had nothing all that much better to do with my lonely Sundays. The preacher was a man named George Buttrick, and Sunday after Sunday I went, and sermon after sermon I heard. It was not just his eloquence that kept me coming back, though he was wonderfully eloquent, literate, imaginative, never letting you guess what he was going to come out with next but twitching with surprises up there in the pulpit, his spectacles a-glitter in the lectern light. What drew me more was whatever it was that his sermons came from and whatever it was in me that they touched so deeply. And then there came one particular sermon with one particular phrase in it that does not even appear in a transcript of his words that somebody sent me twenty-five years later so I can only assume that he must have dreamed it up at the last minute and ad-libbed it — and on just such foolish, tenuous, holy threads as that, I suppose, hang the destinies of us all. Jesus Christ refused the crown that Satan offered him in the wilderness, Buttrick said, but he is king nonetheless because again and again he is crowned in the hearts of people who believe in him. And that coronation takes place, Buttrick said, "among confession, and tears, and great laughter."[56]

Thirteen novels, eleven works of nonfiction, three volumes of autobiography, many essays and sermons later, as well as two book-length critical studies about his life and writings, Buechner provides much fodder for en-

55. Frederick Buechner, *The Sacred Journey* (New York: Harper & Row, 1982), p. 40.
56. Buechner, *The Sacred Journey,* pp. 108-9.

abling a deeply personal kind of reflection on the meaning of faith and a theology of belief. Obviously, he places emphasis on events and the power of those specific events to shape and mold us theologically. In that regard, he is perhaps the most articulate of all the theologians included in this paper. Had he not experienced these several events, by his own eloquent confession and reflection, he would not be the theological meaning-maker he has been and remains, both for himself and others.

Overarching themes from the lives of these pastor-theologians have emerged. In the first place, all possessed tremendous passion, energy, and interest in things theological. In the second place, all possessed what Hans Küng calls "existential need,"[57] i.e., a drive to wrestle with, know, and understand the reason for God's redemptive drama. Finally though not exhaustively, all were turned by significant events and persons toward a personal wrestling with the God whose claim upon their lives became the claim of theological existence. Whether founding churches, instructing catechumens, struggling for social justice, or proclaiming the gospel in pulpit and print, each came to see the world through the lens of the God revealed in Jesus Christ.

In the case of Paul through his Damascus road experience, Origen in the martyrdom of his father, Reinhold Niebuhr in the juxtaposition of gospel and world, and Frederick Buechner through the influence of a great preacher, significant single events do appear to generate theological reflection. Henceforth one seeks to understand life's meaning and purpose from that event forward. Buechner in particular encourages us to look back constantly on our lives, experiences, and the people we encounter for clues concerning God's epiphanies to us. The minister-in-the-making will do well to live with eyes wide open to such meaning-making; indeed, even those of us who are seasoned pastor-theologians would do well to do the same.

57. Küng, *Great Christian Thinkers,* p. 140. Although Küng's comment has to do with Martin Luther, the very same existential need seems present in each pastor-theologian included in this paper.

The Call of a Lifetime

W. Rush Otey III

> *Unless those who are in the office of preacher find joy in him who sent them, they will have much trouble. Our Lord God had to ask Moses as many as six times. He also led me into the office in the same way. Had I known about it beforehand, he would have had to take more pains to get me in. Be that as it may, now that I have begun, I intend to perform the duties of the office with his help. On account of the exceedingly great and heavy cares and worries connected with it, I would not take the whole world to enter upon this work now. On the other hand, when I regard him who called me, I would not take the whole world not to have begun it. Nor do I wish to have another God.*
>
> Martin Luther[1]

The notion that God calls certain people to specific tasks or functions in the life of the church has both fascinated and confounded the casual observer. The history of the church is replete with call stories. Church examining bodies, pastor search committees, and many church members still expect ministers to relate their sense of God's call to the Christian ministry. This should

1. Luther's Works, vol. 54, "Table Talk" (Philadelphia: Fortress, 1983), pp. 12-13.

I am indebted to Wallace Alston for his cooperation in the authorship of this essay.

come as no surprise to anyone who reads the Bible. The Bible contains numerous accounts of calls extended by God to patriarchs and prophets, apostles and disciples. It recounts the imperatives and risks involved when Jesus calls people out of their previous lives and prior commitments, the most dramatic example being the blinding of Saul on the road to Damascus.

As important as these dramatic moments are in determining the subsequent direction of one's life, there is the larger mystery of the call that continues to engage a person throughout his or her life, one well known to those who discern it to be God's invitation to enter upon the vocation of pastor-theologian. Moreover, in both scripture and tradition the call of God also includes one's own death in the proclamation of the gospel of life.[2]

No doubt the call to ministry begins with a progression of events in a person's life. First, there is the question of whether to believe in God at all. Then there is a wrestling with the invitation or command of Jesus to "Deny yourself, take up your cross, and follow me." As many of my colleagues acknowledge in this volume, there is no accounting for the sense of call apart from the operation of the Holy Spirit through personal experiences, families, friends, mentors, education, griefs and joys, the Bible and the nurture of the church. In these ordinary ways, God claims particular people to be ministers of the Word and Sacraments.

Once this claim has been acknowledged, the prescribed course of study completed, and the call of a church extended and accepted, one is likely to discover that God's claim or call encompasses a lifetime and is, in fact, God's claim on the totality of a person's years and gifts, however few or many, however magnificent or paltry. For this reason, ministry is at heart not a profession but a confession, involving the surrender and offering of the whole life in service to God.

A profound understanding of the call of a lifetime is apparent in the life and witness of Dietrich Bonhoeffer. His reflections on a life lived in response to God's call have served as a touchstone for many pastors, providing significant insights into the perception, evaluation, reception, and, at times, the renewal of the call to ministry. Benjamin A. Reist, in his treatment of "the promise of Bonhoeffer," observed that Bonhoeffer's thought cannot be understood simply as a chapter in the history of ideas. Events provide the clues to Dietrich Bonhoeffer's theology. That is the case with everyone, of

2. See Virgil Thompson's chapter, "The Bible and Theological Formation: On Becoming a Theologian of the Cross," in this volume.

course, but with no one more poignantly than with Bonhoeffer. There is no understanding Bonhoeffer's sense of call apart from insight into the turbulent events of his time.[3]

According to Eberhard Bethge, his biographer and friend, the call of a lifetime came to Bonhoeffer in terms of two turning points in his life.

> The first [turning point] may have occurred about 1931-32 and might be formulated thus: Dietrich Bonhoeffer the theologian became a Christian. The second began in 1939: Dietrich Bonhoeffer the Christian became a contemporary, a man of his own particular time and place. . . . the steps he took each time to combine intellectual expertness [the theologian] with life-engagement [the Christian] and finally with unreserved presence [the contemporary] brought about immense changes in his way of living and writing. Each step by itself might have suffered to give content to a man's activity, but the two had to combine to chisel out his life's work, and both together make his name what it is for us now.[4]

We know very little about the first turning point because Bonhoeffer only infrequently mentioned it, but it is apparent that he underwent some form of conversion. He would not have used that word or described what took place in his life in that way. According to Bethge, we can only surmise from his writing that there was a growing certainty of his vocation and direction. In a letter written in the winter of 1935-36, which may have referred to a period of time in 1931 when he began his work as teacher and pastor, Bonhoeffer said,

> I hurled myself into my work in an unchristian and unhumble manner. . . . Then something else came along, something which has permanently changed my life and its direction. . . . I had often preached, I had seen a lot of the church, I had talked and written about it, but I had not yet become a Christian. (I know that until then I had been using the cause of Jesus Christ to my own advantage. . . .) The Bible, most particularly the Sermon on the Mount, has freed me from all this. Since then, everything has changed. . . . I now realized that the life of a servant of Je-

3. Benjamin A. Reist, *The Promise of Bonhoeffer* (Philadelphia: J. B. Lippincott Company, 1969), p. 37.

4. Eberhard Bethge, *Bonhoeffer in a World Come of Age* (Philadelphia: Fortress Press, 1968), pp. 78-79.

sus Christ must belong to the church, and step by step it became clearer to me to what extent this must be so.[5]

The interplay of pastor and theologian present in the call of God manifests itself in different ways. Karl Barth, for instance, went from the pastorate to an academic chair. The preacher had need of the systematician. To save the majesty of God from being cheapened in the pulpit he spoke of God's remoteness and inapproachability, and cautioned against confusing concretions. Bonhoeffer, in contrast, went from the academy to the pastorate. The theologian had need of the preacher. To preserve the majesty of God from being cheapened in the pulpit he concentrated on the proximity of a God who continued to intervene in the affairs of the world, and emphasized concretions as the actualization of grace.[6]

In the first turning point in 1931, the ecumenical movement provided for Bonhoeffer a safe place for his vocation. This stage of life brought him into a community of young pastors in Finkenwalde, where he led a disciplined life of worship, study, prayer, and relaxation.[7] It was during this period that he became involved with the Confessing Church, wrote *The Cost of Discipleship* and *Life Together,* and began his outspoken opposition to the National Socialist regime and its church policy. During these years, the course of his life was moving into a new dimension in response to a call to which he could only respond. It became clear to him that one could not be a Christian, much less a pastor-theologian, in a vacuum. He began to scrutinize his call in light of his growing conviction that he could not be a servant of Jesus Christ in isolation from the particular time and place to which God had assigned him. He now saw that the possibility of being Christian, at least for him, was inextricably involved with becoming a contemporary with his family, his friends, and fellow Germans. In a sermon in 1932, Bonhoeffer predicted that the blood of martyrs might once again be demanded, but "this blood, if we really have the courage and loyalty to shed it, will not be innocent, shining like that of the first witnesses of the faith. On our blood lies heavy guilt, the guilt of the unprofitable servant who is cast into outer darkness."[8] We return later to the phenomenon of the "guilty martyr."

5. Bethge, *Bonhoeffer in a World Come of Age,* p. 80.

6. Eberhard Bethge, *Dietrich Bonhoeffer* (New York: Harper & Row, 1970), p. 138.

7. See Cynthia Jarvis's chapter in this volume on mentoring for a fuller treatment of this time.

8. Cited in Eberhard Bethge, *Bonhoeffer in a World Come of Age,* p. 87.

This second turning point, which brought Bonhoeffer into a circle of conspirators dedicated to the elimination of the oppressor and the creation of a new Germany, was marked by the publication of *Letters and Papers from Prison* and the posthumous publication of his *Ethics*. This period of his life occasioned a new discernment of the call to discipleship that was distinct yet not different from that which he had known before. It was a call that would demand of him, not only the sacrifice of his ordination, but finally the sacrifice of his life. "It transported him from a relatively clear world where the choice was simply between confessing and denying, a Yes or a No, into an ambiguous world where expedients, tactics and camouflage, success and failure, all had to be carefully calculated."[9] Once he had followed God's call into the church and there he found his identity as a Christian. Now the call was into the world, where his destiny, humanly speaking, would be compromised by factors beyond his control.

In what follows I would like to reflect on Bonhoeffer's sense of call in an effort to understand the call that comes to many of us to accept the vocation of pastor-theologian. Bonhoeffer would not likely have approved of anything that smacked of a psychological evaluation of his Christian experience. He left little for us to work with when it comes to his sense of call. In order to say anything at all on the subject, we must read his theological work and prison letters in the light of the life he lived. We must read the lines he wrote during each of these two turning points, but we must also read between the lines if we are to understand his call of a lifetime in ways that assist us in discerning and interpreting our own.

The First Turning Point

If one reads *The Cost of Discipleship* and *Life Together* with a view to understanding Bonhoeffer's sense of call, it may be possible to venture certain inferences and conclusions.

First, Bonhoeffer experienced the call of God in Christ as a call that comes to a person both once for all and time and time again throughout one's life. "Call" is a word Bonhoeffer assigned to the claim and leading of the Spirit in and through the internal and external circumstances of one's life. It is that sense of the presence of God that assures one that one is not

9. Bethge, *Bonhoeffer in a World Come of Age*, pp. 88-89.

alone, that gives to one an intuition of Presence before whom one lives, and that infuses one's thinking and acting with the permission of a "may" and the summons of a "must."

Bonhoeffer's ecclesiology was based on gratitude. It is in thanksgiving for the little things that we perceive the leading of the Spirit. The little things are God's daily gifts by which we are both nurtured and drawn into daily obedience. Foremost of these daily providences is the fellowship of the church. "If we do not give thanks daily for the Christian fellowship in which we have been placed [which is Bonhoeffer's way of speaking of call] even where there is no great experience, no discoverable riches, but much weakness, small faith, and difficulty; if on the contrary, we only keep complaining to God that everything is so paltry and petty, so far from what we expected, then we hinder God from letting our fellowship grow according to the measure and riches which are there for us all in Jesus Christ."[10]

Bonhoeffer goes on to say that this applies particularly "to the complaints often heard from pastors and zealous members about their congregations. A pastor should not complain about his congregation. . . . A congregation has not been entrusted to him in order that he should become its accuser. . . . When a person becomes alienated from a Christian community in which he has been placed and begins to raise complaints about it, he had better examine himself first to see whether the trouble is not due to his wish dream that should be shattered by God; and if this be the case, let him thank God for leading [calling] him into this predicament."[11] The daily call of Christ to a life of gratitude in the community of the Spirit, we may assume, was the general pattern over which his understanding of the particular call to ministry was traced. The very daily-ness of this call implies a chronology that includes both once for all and time and again.

Second, the immediate response sought when God calls a person is not belief but obedience. "The response of the disciples is an act of obedience, not a confession of faith in Jesus. . . . Jesus summons men to follow him not as a teacher or a pattern of the good life, but as the Christ, the Son of God."[12]

The call of Christ does not provide one with a program or strategy for living a good life or for changing the world for the better. Its primary thrust

10. Bonhoeffer, *Life Together* (New York: Harper & Row, 1954), p. 29.

11. Bonhoeffer, *Life Together,* pp. 29-30.

12. Bonhoeffer, "The Call to Discipleship," *The Cost of Discipleship* (New York: Macmillan, 1961), p. 48.

is not to set before a person an abstract idea or a theoretical ideal for a person to hold or to attain. The call of Christ is a summons to an exclusive loyalty and devotion to the person of Jesus that takes the form of discipleship. An abstract doctrinal system that spells out the doctrine of justification by grace through faith, or a creed that defines the deity of Jesus Christ, might render the daily following of Jesus superfluous. It is the presence and activity of the living Christ, who calls people once for all and time and again to follow him from place to place, from historical context to historical context, that saves Christianity from detached speculation and defines it as obedient discipleship.

Third, Bonhoeffer's sense of call included the experience of being sent and placed. In his comment on Jesus' sending of the Twelve (Matt. 10:5-6), Bonhoeffer declares that those who are called to represent Jesus Christ are not free to choose their own places of service or to write their own job descriptions. Their work is to be what Bonhoeffer called "Christ-work," the implication being that they are absolutely dependent on Christ's own will and work for a description of their own. When Jesus says to the Twelve, "Go not . . . enter not . . . but go rather" in this passage, he makes it clear that the "choice of field for their labours does not depend on their own impulses or inclinations, but on where they are sent. This makes it quite clear that it is not their own work they are doing, but God's."[13]

Fourth, the call to follow Jesus involves suffering. Contemporary disciples are not above their Master. One who would represent Jesus in the contemporary world will, by definition, be rewarded with a cross. "When Christ calls a man, he bids him come and die."[14]

It is unlikely that Bonhoeffer anticipated how literally this would be true for him. That would become clearer in the second turning point of his life, as the call to be a representative of Jesus Christ was contextualized by the evils of Hitler's Germany. When in *The Cost of Discipleship* Bonhoeffer spoke of the cross, he was referring, first, to the cross which is laid on every Christian. "The first Christ-suffering which every man must experience is the call to abandon the attachments of this world. It is that dying of the old man which is the result of his encounter with Christ."[15] But there are other kinds of suffering which the Christian is not spared, namely, the suffering of temp-

13. Bonhoeffer, "The Work," *The Cost of Discipleship,* p. 184.

14. Bonhoeffer, "Discipleship and the Cross," *The Cost of Discipleship,* p. 79.

15. Bonhoeffer, "Discipleship and the Cross," p. 79.

tation, the suffering of bearing the sins of others, the suffering of shame and guilt. Suffering is "the badge of true discipleship."[16]

Fifth, according to Bonhoeffer the call of Christ is a summons to the "extraordinary," the unusual, that which is not a matter of course. What is the "extraordinary" of which Bonhoeffer speaks? "It is the life described in the beatitudes, the life of the followers of Jesus, the light which lights the world, the city set on a hill, the way of self-renunciation, of utter love, of absolute purity, truthfulness and meekness. It is unreserved love for our enemies, for the unloving and the unloved, love for our religious, political and personal adversaries. In every case it is the love which was fulfilled in the cross of Christ."[17]

The extraordinary is that which those who are called do. In doing the extraordinary, the disciples participate in the life and suffering of Jesus. Once again it is worthy of note that the full implication of the extraordinary in all of its risk and consequences was as yet unknown to Bonhoeffer, and would not be revealed until the call of his lifetime led him into the circle of conspirators, and even then not until the day of his death in Flossenburg.

Finally, the call of Christ is accompanied by the admonition, "Be not afraid." Those who are called to represent Jesus Christ are not to fear for their security, their standing, their reputation, their position, or any other consequence of the opposition they incur in preaching, teaching, and pastoral care. "The power which men enjoy for a brief space on earth is not without the cognizance and the will of God. If we fall into the hands of men, and meet suffering and death from their violence, we are none the less certain that everything comes from God. The same God that sees no sparrow fall from the ground without his knowledge and will, allows nothing to happen, except it be good and profitable for his children, and the cause for which they stand. We are in God's hands. Therefore, 'Fear not.'"[18]

Other insights into Bonhoeffer's sense of call may be gained from reading his theological reflections from this period of his life. The six mentioned here — the continuing call of God, the invitation to obedience, the experience of being sent and placed, the inevitability of suffering, the challenge of the extraordinary, and the promise of ultimate security — were chosen because of their peculiar relevance to the contemporary discernment

16. Bonhoeffer, "Discipleship and the Cross," p. 80.

17. Bonhoeffer, "The Enemy — the 'Extraordinary,'" *The Cost of Discipleship*, p. 137.

18. Bonhoeffer, "The Decision," *The Cost of Discipleship*, p. 195.

of God's call to ministry. It was in the second turning point, however, that Bonhoeffer's sense of call was contextualized and particularized, as Bonhoeffer the pastor-theologian discerned his call to be one of rethinking the content and implications of the Christian faith for a world come of age.

The Second Turning Point

In a poem written in July of 1944,[19] Bonhoeffer identifies four "stations on the way to freedom" that give definition to the call of a lifetime: discipline, action, suffering, and death. Each is a response to God in Christ and each offers a means of reflecting on the whole of one's life as servant and theologian. These four stations, which represent the continuing call of God, may also be significant to one seeking to discern the call to ministry today.

Discipline

> If you set out to seek freedom, then learn above all things to govern your soul and your senses, for fear that your passions and longings may lead you away from the path that you should follow. Chaste be your mind and your body, and both in subjection, obediently, steadfastly seeking the aim set before them; only through discipline may a person learn to be free.[20]

Even a cursory review of the history of the church reminds us that the transmission of the faith from one generation to another depends upon discipline. The word, of course, is related to the word "disciple" or "follower." To follow the way of Jesus is difficult and requires not impulsiveness but effort, discernment, and training. If this is required of every Christian, it is particularly incumbent upon those who are called to exercise leadership in the Christian community.

It is the quality and character of Bonhoeffer's disciplined life that is often forgotten by those who find in his prison letters no more than a starting point for secular or religionless Christianity. Bonhoeffer understood disci-

19. Bonhoeffer, "Stations on the Way to Freedom," in *Letters and Papers from Prison* (New York: SCM Press/Macmillan, 1967), pp. 194-95.

20. Bonhoeffer, "Stations on the Way to Freedom," pp. 194-95.

pline to be a prerequisite of discipleship. He cultivated a discipline of mind that wrought in him a constructive and outgoing personal bearing. This, in turn, readied him for the single-mindedness that the extraordinary situations in his latter years required of him.

Where did Bonhoeffer's discipline originate? In the first place, his was a disciplined family. No doubt, as Eberhard Bethge remarked, "The fullness of his forebears' lives set in Dietrich Bonhoeffer the standards of his own. . . . He grew up in a family that derived its real education, not from school, but from a deeply-rooted sense of being guardians of a great historical heritage and intellectual tradition."[21] It was in the structure of the family that Dietrich's discipline was born. Writing from prison to his fiancée, Maria von Wedemeyer, he spoke of the "astringency in the relationship between father and son" as "a sign of great strength and 'inner security.'"[22] Likewise Bethge describes Dietrich's mother as energetic and indefatigable. "In her youth, with a spirit of independence that was shocking at the time, she had fought for and obtained permission to take the qualifying examinations for women teachers. She gave lessons at home to her own children, chiefly the bigger ones, together with the children of some of her husband's professor friends, and at the year's end she was always able to enter her pupils successfully for the state examination, in which they did very well."[23] The sort of discipline of mind and liberal learning that is essential to a faith that seeks understanding may not always begin in the home. Yet if one examines the early years of many who have later been claimed for a theologically thoughtful ministry, such a beginning is often cited as significant to the discernment of the call of a lifetime.

Discipline marked Bonhoeffer's early years as a pastor. His pastoral schedule was organized and vigorous. In Barcelona in 1928, he visited the home of every child in the economically disadvantaged parish who attended Sunday school and youth groups. At Berlin-Wedding he often took the members of his confirmation class on weekend outings. Bonhoeffer's disciplined pastoral life stands in marked contrast to the practice of many contemporary pastors. The reason for this difference in perspective on the ministry may be located in Bonhoeffer's understanding of ministry as the

21. Bethge, *Dietrich Bonhoeffer,* p. 4. There are also significant insights into the Bonhoeffer family to be gained from Ruth Alice von Bismarck, Ulrich Itz, and Ulrich Kabitz, eds., *Love Letters from Cell 92: The Correspondence Between Dietrich Bonhoeffer and Maria von Wedemeyer, 1943-1945* (Nashville: Abingdon, 1995).

22. Bethge, *Dietrich Bonhoeffer,* p. 6.

23. Bethge, *Dietrich Bonhoeffer,* p. 7.

exercise of discipleship rather than the pursuit of a career. That said, there was a place for play in Bonhoeffer's rigor. Although he was usually at work shortly after 6 a.m. in Finkenwalde, he left evenings free for recreation or informal discussions with his students.

Finally, it should be said that Bonhoeffer's role in the conspiracy against Hitler would have been unthinkable apart from the exercise of discipline, a discipline of mind and heart, but even more, a discipline of faith in grace. Our own circumstances may never demand from us the dramatic witness that Bonhoeffer's time demanded of him, but his experience is nevertheless instructive of our own.

Bonhoeffer never tried to justify his involvement in the conspiracy against Hitler, nor did he feel that what he was doing was unequivocally right. In fact, in dealing with the life of Dietrich Bonhoeffer, we are confronted with one of the most ambiguous and confounding experiences in Christian ethical life, namely, that of the guilty martyr. What was involved in Bonhoeffer's complicity in the planned "coup d'état" was not simply a courageous stand against a terrible tyrant. What was involved for Bonhoeffer was the sacrifice of his commitment to the Christ of the Sermon on the Mount and to his conviction that pacifism rather than violence was the Christian calling. "Bonhoeffer's theology will always be of cardinal significance for those who must live through revolutionary times, not because he was a ruthless revolutionary, but because he could not stand aside while the world was dying. The risks that he willingly shared were the risks that always attend the hard collision of one way of ordering the life of man with another. Such concreteness is always marked by the almost unavoidable possibility of error, even of guilt."[24] Bonhoeffer knew that, if his actions were to be justified, it would be a matter of grace. His life was living testimony to the ambiguity present in every answer given to the ethical question put by his friend Paul Lehmann, "What am I, as a believer in Jesus Christ and as a member of his church, to do?"[25] Yet in the time of my own ministry, surely the prophetic voices that led the church in countless unknown and undocumented places to bear a costly, courageous witness in the struggle for civil rights and world peace could not have spoken so apart from a discipline of mind and heart, or more importantly, without a discipline of faith in grace.

In sum, discipline was a key element in Bonhoeffer's understanding of

24. Reist, *The Promise of Bonhoeffer,* p. 42.

25. Bonhoeffer, *Ethics in a Christian Context* (New York: Harper & Row, 1963), p. 25.

his call even before he associated himself with the conspirators, but discipline was never an end in itself. It pointed beyond itself to the hope of his calling. When the Finkenwalde seminarians were met with criticism for their forthright and emotional opposition to government intervention in church affairs, Bonhoeffer said, "I do not need to tell you that I agree with you that all indiscipline discredits the truth we proclaim. But the proper testimony to Christ lies not in the act of discipline, but in the assurance of hope for the future."[26] Discipline is an expression of the fullness and freedom of a life of discipleship to Jesus Christ.

Action

> Daring to do what is right, not what fancy may tell you, valiantly grasping occasions, not cravenly doubting — freedom comes only through deeds, not through thoughts taking wing. Faint not nor fear, but go out to the storm and the action, trusting in God whose commandment you faithfully follow; freedom, exultant, will welcome your spirit with joy.[27]

Dietrich Bonhoeffer believed that Christian faith encompasses the whole of a person's existence. Though he followed the discipline of prayer and often worked in solitude, he did not allow himself to become isolated from the pain and distress of the life of the world. For him there were always competing possibilities to be pursued, each within the vocation of a minister. There was the life of scholarship. There was the option of giving himself completely to traditional pastoral work within the boundaries of the church — administering the sacraments, praying for the sick and the needy, attending meetings — whether in London, Switzerland, Scandinavia, or Germany. There was the attraction of living and working in the United States, a professorship and continued ecumenical contacts. Finally, and most unlikely, there was political activity.

To understand why Bonhoeffer was drawn from ecclesial and professorial life into political activity, we begin with his experience in the United States. Reacting negatively to much of what he observed in the United States, he wrote in the summer of 1939 that "America [is] forty years behind Ger-

26. Bethge, *Dietrich Bonhoeffer*, p. 415.

27. Bonhoeffer, "Stations on the Way to Freedom," pp. 194-95.

many, twenty years behind Scotland. It seems that Germany is still the land of spiritual discoveries."[28] However, his American experiences undoubtedly moved him closer to more direct political involvement in Germany. He was introduced to Walter Rauschenbusch's social gospel and saw first-hand its relevance to life in the slums of New York. He attended the Abyssinian Baptist Church in Harlem and heard the preaching of Adam Clayton Powell. He witnessed the poverty of the Great Depression and pondered the impact of economic conditions on the human spirit. When surveying internal turmoil that finally led Bonhoeffer to return to Germany despite the urging of his friends, including Paul Lehmann, to remain, what is striking is his growing conviction that theology must do business both with the struggles of the church and the demeaning aspects of a complex world. The vocation of the pastor-theologian is to reflect theologically on what is taking place in the world as well as the church, and to act accordingly.

As had been the case in London, Bonhoeffer was confronted with the extent of his personal attachment to and his responsibility for the shaping of Germany's future. Distance enabled him to gain clarity about himself and his country that was to prove invaluable in the ensuing years of crisis. According to Bethge, only four prominent Protestant church officials in Germany were involved in the "active conspiracy" stage of the resistance. Again we must ask why Dietrich Bonhoeffer was one of these.

First, action for Bonhoeffer became increasingly tied to effectiveness. In a time of political confusion, Bonhoeffer, who had previously planned to travel to India in order to learn more of Gandhi, came to view pacifism as too ineffective and individualistic. Thoroughly theological in origin, this insight led Bonhoeffer to construct what he believed to be a realist ethic. He reasoned that one more pacifist would have had little effect on the events of the 1930s. But more central to his action in this regard was the strong communitarian emphasis in his theology. He rejected an *a priori* pacifism in favor of more direct, cooperative approaches to the severe challenges of his time.

In the end, Bonhoeffer acted against Hitler only when there appeared to be a reasonable prospect of success. He did not wish to give himself up to thoughtless and premature calculations. However, there was an element of "never say die" in Bonhoeffer. He was an avid reader of Cervantes's *Don Quixote,* and saw this knight errant as a possible model for making ethical decisions. He wrote to his brother in 1939: "I am quite sure that for the Church,

28. Bonhoeffer, *The Way to Freedom* (New York: Harper & Row, 1966), p. 233.

what matters supremely is that we hold out now, even if it means great sacrifices. The greatest sacrifices now are small compared with what we should lose by wrongly giving in. I do not know anything that is worth our wholehearted commitment today, unless it is this cause. The main point is, not how many are in it, but that there are at least some."[29]

Second, discipleship for Bonhoeffer began to require active opposition to the evil of his time. By 1938, when Bonhoeffer first began to meet with resistance leaders, he already had become disillusioned with the Confessing Church. The church had equivocated on its opposition to the Nuremberg Laws, which instituted a more ordered phase of Jewish persecution by creating a second class of "nationals" who were without full political rights and by forbidding so-called mixed marriages between "Aryans" and Jews. Furthermore, he found it intolerable that the Barmen Declaration had been so quickly abandoned by the church. "We are not vagabonds," he said, "who obey one government one day and another the next."[30] Within the Confessing Church much time was spent defining and debating the proper boundary between church and state, a longstanding controversy in Lutheranism. For Bonhoeffer this was a moot point, since there were the more pressing issues of totalitarian rule and the persecution of human beings which required immediate response. In an often quoted sentence, Bonhoeffer said, "Only he who cries out for the Jews may sing Gregorian chants."[31]

Bonhoeffer reminds us that a pastor is called to participate critically and prophetically in the ordering of the common life as a part of the call of a lifetime. The Barmen Declaration was the work of theologically astute pastors in the German church who were equipped to articulate the dangers faced by the church at that particular time. Pastors in our day who have attempted to bring social, political, and economic issues into the pulpit know that they do so effectively only insofar as they reflect on these issues from the vantage point of scripture and the theological tradition of the church. Martin Luther's "Here I stand," with which a prophetic preacher is often wont to identify, it must be remembered, was a theological stance, not merely that of an advocate for change.

Finally, William Kuhns suggested that Bonhoeffer's patriotism was also a key motivating factor for his returning to Germany and participating

29. Quoted by Eberhard Bethge in *Dietrich Bonhoeffer*, pp. 515-16.

30. Bethge, *Dietrich Bonhoeffer*, p. 435.

31. Bethge, *Dietrich Bonhoeffer*, p. 512.

in the effort to assassinate Hitler.[32] Like his military friends in the resistance, but for somewhat different reasons, Bonhoeffer believed Hitler could and would bring nothing but ruin upon Germany. Thus, sacrificing his pacifism to his sense of call, Bonhoeffer decided that his participation in the conspiracy was in the interest of peace. It was clear to him that there could be no peace for Germany as long as Hitler was in power, and the way to peace was "not just to bandage the victims under the wheel, but to put a spoke in the wheel itself."[33] He feared that the German people had failed to see that their zeal to serve the state could be employed for unjustified ends.

The contemporary Lutheran professor, Lisa Dahill, concludes that "despite his limits, [Bonhoeffer] inspires us with the unfolding of a joyful, mature, and spiritually free Christian life in one of the most brutal periods in human history. He gives us insight into particular tools helpful to us as well for discipleship within a public sphere increasingly — ominously — marked by greed, arrogance, deceit, cynicism, and xenophobia. And ultimately he points us beyond himself to the One who desires our joy, our maturity, our spiritual freedom."[34]

Bonhoeffer offers a model to a contemporary pastor for a theologically profound praxis that involves a wrestling with one's call in relation to the social order. This wrestling cannot be limited to one moment in time or to any one issue, but rather is the call of a lifetime.

Suffering

> A change has come indeed. Your hands, so strong and active, are bound in helplessness now you see your action ended; you sigh in relief, your cause committed to stronger hands; so you now may rest contented. Only for one blissful moment could you draw near to touch freedom; then, that it might be perfected in glory, you gave it to God.[35]

32. William Kuhns, *In Pursuit of Dietrich Bonhoeffer* (Garden City, NY: Doubleday, 1969), pp. 227-65.

33. Bonhoeffer, *No Rusty Swords* (Nashville: Abingdon, 1977), p. 225.

34. Lisa Dahill, "Bonhoeffer and the Resistance to Evil," *Journal of Lutheran Ethics*, August 2003. Available online at http://www.elca.org/jle/article.asp?k=35 (no pages given).

35. Bonhoeffer, "Stations on the Way to Freedom," pp. 194-95.

The call of a lifetime renders the pastor highly vulnerable and places the pastor at the intersection of life and death, both in the church and in the world. This should come as no surprise to anyone who reads the New Testament. The symbol of the Christian faith is not a crib or even an empty tomb, but a cross. The cross of Jesus Christ is at the center of the Christian life. His cross is our sign that to be a pastor-theologian with any degree of integrity is to engage willingly and decisively in the human dilemma. It is not only to acknowledge and reflect upon the presence of the ironic, the absurd, the ambiguous, and the tragic in human experience. It is so to be for the other that these contortions of life, when experienced by another, become one's own. Suffering is participation in the cross of Christ in the world.

For Bonhoeffer, the pastor, being representative of the vocation of all Christians, is called to enter unreservedly in the sufferings of ordinary persons. In the essay "After Ten Years," written at Christmas of 1942, he surmised that "the Christian is called to sympathy and action, not in the first place by his own sufferings, but by the sufferings of his brethren, for whose sake Christ suffered."[36] The suffering that Bonhoeffer experienced was seldom physical until his days of imprisonment and death. Income from his father's position allowed the family to have a summer home, dress in fine clothing, and receive a full education. Even in prison Bonhoeffer was comparatively well treated. He was allowed books, visits, and food packages, and there is little evidence to suspect that he was tortured. Bonhoeffer, who refused to be called a martyr, wrote in March of 1944 that "suffering must be something quite different, and have a quite different dimension, from what I have so far experienced."[37]

Until his execution the suffering that Bonhoeffer endured was primarily inner suffering, uncertainty, loneliness. In Finkenwalde he had been periodically besieged with "accidie, tristitia," a depression stemming from self-doubt and feelings of inadequacy. According to Bethge, this was a recurrent struggle for Bonhoeffer throughout his lifetime.[38]

Bonhoeffer suffered because of his sense of responsibility. At Finkenwalde he feared that he would not be a good teacher. In prison he feared that he had brought unjust hardship upon his family and fiancée. All this, coupled with his disappointment at the failure of the conspiracy and the dimin-

36. Bonhoeffer, *Letters and Papers from Prison*, p. 126.

37. Bonhoeffer, *Letters and Papers from Prison*, p. 126.

38. Bethge, *Dietrich Bonhoeffer*, p. 736.

ishing possibilities for personal satisfaction in marriage, taught Bonhoeffer something profound about suffering, namely, that it had many painful faces, and that it was universal to humankind. Bonhoeffer may not have suffered as painfully or as ignobly as did many of his contemporaries prior to his execution in Flossenburg, but his time would come, when on the gallows his call of a lifetime was granted its new beginning.

The pastor, if he or she is to be both theologian and pastor, must indeed relate empathetically and hopefully to the feelings and questions and ambiguities evoked by the life situations of the members of his or her congregation, and this can be, and often is, exhausting. But if one's understanding of the energy sufficient for the task is that help comes from the Lord and is therefore inexhaustible, there remains for one the capacity to reach out beyond a local congregation to the needs and incalculable sufferings of the larger world. As Bonhoeffer put it,

> The Church is the Church only when it exists for others. To make a start, it should give away all its property to those in need. The clergy must live solely on the free-will offerings of their congregations, or possibly engage in some secular calling. The Church must share in the secular problems of ordinary human life, not dominating, but helping and serving. . . . In particular, our own Church will have to take the field against the vices of *hubris,* power-worship, envy, and humbug, as the roots of all evil. It will have to speak of moderation, purity, trust, loyalty, constancy, patience, discipline, humility, contentment, and modesty. It must not underestimate the importance of human example (which has its origin in the humanity of Jesus and is so important in Paul's teaching); it is not abstract argument, but example, that gives this word emphasis and power.[39]

In a world in which the gulf between the comfortable and the poor is ever widening and all too obvious, suffering in Christ's name will continue to be that for which a Christian prays and that which the call of a lifetime invites the Christian to do.

39. Bonhoeffer, *Letters and Papers from Prison,* pp. 203-4.

Death

> Come now, thou greatest of feasts on the journey to freedom eternal; death, cast aside all the burdensome chains, and demolish the walls of our temporal body, the walls of our souls that are blinded, so that at last we may see that which here remains hidden. Freedom, how long we have sought thee in discipline, action, and suffering; dying, we now may behold thee revealed in the Lord.[40]

The call of a lifetime involves God's claim not only upon the length of our days, but on the end of our days as well. In a culture in which great effort is expended on the denial of death, the pastor-theologian is called to look death in the face and to name it for what it is.[41] Bonhoeffer's culture was similar in this regard. Nevertheless, even as a child, Bonhoeffer had been intrigued by death. The death of his older brother, Walter, who was killed in battle in World War I, left an indelible mark of sadness upon the twelve-year-old Dietrich, who sensed even then something of the mystery and intrusion of death.

In a circular letter to his Finkenwalde students at the beginning of World War II, Bonhoeffer spoke of "death from without" and "death from within." The latter seems to grow from the New Testament teaching about losing oneself in order to find oneself. "Our death is really the only way to the perfect love of God."[42] In "After Ten Years," Bonhoeffer wrote from prison: "It is we ourselves, and not outward circumstances, who make death what it can be, a death freely and voluntarily accepted."[43]

Bonhoeffer did not really come to terms with death until after he was imprisoned. He was yet a young man. He had told his American friends as he prepared to return to Germany that he did not return to die. He did not seek or relish death; rather death sought and found him. But when death became imminent, he faced it, saying, "at even and at morn God will befriend us."[44] He witnessed to this trust by his support of his fellow prisoners and guards and in his letters to his family and friends.

The pastor-theologian lives and must cope with death theologically

40. Bonhoeffer, "Stations on the Way to Freedom," pp. 194-95.

41. See "The Pastor-Theologian and Death," by Allen C. McSween Jr., in this volume.

42. Bonhoeffer, *Letters and Papers from Prison,* pp. 76-77 footnote.

43. Bonhoeffer, *Letters and Papers from Prison,* p. 17.

44. Bonhoeffer, *Letters and Papers from Prison,* p. 213.

day by day. Over the course of the call of a lifetime, countless hands are held for one last time, a multitude of services are performed before open graves, and the grief of those left behind is enclosed in the pastor's attempt to bear witness to and take hold of the eternal life to which we were called and for which we were made (1 Tim. 6:11). Early in his life as a theologian, Karl Barth wrote concerning the Word of God and the task of the ministry, "It is evident that [our congregants] do not need us to help them live, but seem rather to need us to help them die."[45]

Theological education would do well to evaluate the adequacy of the preparation currently being given to men and women preparing to be pastor-theologians. Few seminaries or divinity schools, except perhaps the Roman Catholic institutions, adequately prepare one with a theology of death and resurrection, and little or no attention is given to the manner in which the pastor may bear witness to the Christian hope before, during, and after the funeral or memorial service.[46] This is curious and lamentable when one considers the abundance of biblical and theological material available on these essential occasions of human life. While many pastors have been aided by psychological/clinical pastoral education approaches to death, the pastor whose calling is understood to be that of a theologian must be prepared to contextualize the time of death by throwing about its various moods and anxieties the testimony of the ages to the Christian hope.

In a brief but magnificent sermon for the funeral of his own ninety-three-year-old grandmother in 1936, Bonhoeffer proclaimed:

> Such a meaningful, wise life stands also under the limitations of death, which all humankind must bear. We too must eventually go, with all our ideals, our principles, and our work. It will be wise, therefore, to view our life from its limits, from its end; but much more to know of what lies beyond that limit, of the God who is from everlasting to everlasting, into whose hands we fall, whether we wish it or not, into whose hands she is now fallen. What else shall we say of this fulfilled and rich life? We call upon God, our refuge, to whom we can flee in all times of sorrow and trouble: Jesus Christ, in whom there is all truth, righteousness, all free-

45. Karl Barth, *The Word of God and the Word of Man,* trans. Douglas Horton (Gloucester, MA: Peter Smith, 1928), p. 188. See also the essay on pastoral care by Cynthia A. Jarvis in this volume.

46. See Allen McSween's chapter in this volume, "The Pastor-Theologian and Death."

> dom, and love. We call upon God who has overcome all hate, all lack of love, and all that disturbs our peace to accept us by his overwhelming love on the cross of Jesus Christ. We pray that what is here veiled and hidden under sin and death may be revealed in eternity, that in peace and clarity we may behold the eternal face of God in Jesus Christ.[47]

In death and dying the pastor-theologian is called both by the Head of the church and the church of which Christ is the Head to bear witness to "the communion of saints, the forgiveness of sins, the resurrection of the body, and life everlasting," none of which are self-generated or self-validating. They are promises of the gospel made to all creation by a good and gracious God. The contemporary pastor-theologian, like Bonhoeffer, seeks to be an honest witnesses to the truth, and, like Bonhoeffer, he or she stakes everything on the conviction that the gospel is true. The call of a lifetime is the invitation and permission to rejoice, in spite of and in the presence of death, in the fragmentariness of the creature and in the beauty, grace, freedom, and power of the Creator. The witness of Dietrich Bonhoeffer began with the determination to live and to explore what it meant to be with Christ; it ended by exhibiting to us what it means that Christ is with us. On February 23, 1944, he wrote the words with which I conclude.

> The important thing today is that we should be able to discern from the fragment of our life how the whole was arranged and planned, and what material it consists of. . . . I'm thinking, e.g., of the *Art of Fugue.* If our life is but the remotest reflection of such a fragment, if we accumulate, at least for a short time, a wealth of themes and weld them into a harmony in which the great counterpoint is maintained from start to finish, so that at last, when it breaks off abruptly, we can sing no more than the chorale, "I come before thy throne," we will not bemoan the fragmentariness of our life, but rather rejoice in it.[48]

47. *Dietrich Bonhoeffer's Christmas Sermons,* trans. Edwin Robertson (Grand Rapids: Zondervan, 2005), p. 123.

48. Bonhoeffer, *Letters and Papers from Prison,* p. 121. See also Robert O. Smith, "Bonhoeffer and Musical Metaphor," *Word and World* 26, no. 2 (Spring 2006): 195-206.

The Practice of a Pastor-Theologian

Loving God with the Mind and Thinking with the Heart: The Pastor-Theologian in the Pulpit

John M. Stapleton

Theology, in the most general sense of the word, is thinking about God. Christian theology is reflection on the scriptural witness to the revelation of God in Jesus Christ in the history, practice, and contemporary experience of the church.[1] Considering that each of these enterprises exists to illumine and to support the gospel of Jesus Christ, which it is the joy and calling of the minister to proclaim, the lack of intentional theological reflection in preaching today is astonishing and represents a major aspect of the current crisis in the church. We address the crisis here by asking why preachers should be concerned with the manner in which theology affects and judges the content of sermons. Why should faithfulness to the proclamation of the gospel require attention to theology *in* preaching?

These questions point to a related issue: What is the proper relationship between theology and preaching? One does not *preach* theology as such. If it is argued otherwise, one intensifies the question, asking precisely what

1. Cf. Emil Brunner, *The Christian Doctrine of God,* vol. 1, *Dogmatics,* trans. Olive Wyon (Philadelphia: Westminster Press, 1950), p. 90. For his own reasons Hendrikus Berkhof likes the phrase "the study of faith" (*Christian Faith,* trans. Sierd Woudstra [Grand Rapids: Eerdmans, 1979], p. 31). The phrase has its appeal, but *theology* as that which Brunner described as the "all-inclusive term" and Robert Jenson (*Systematic Theology,* vol. 1, *The Triune God* [New York: Oxford University Press, 1997], p. 3) refers to as the "continuing discourse" of the church "about her individuating and carrying communal purpose" rightly links us to the church's thought manifested in the disciplines we have named.

preaching theology would mean. Clarity about their close relationship evokes attention to a theology *of* preaching, exploring not only what makes preaching as such distinctive in Christian communication but, even more, returning theological substance to the preaching office.

Challenges to Theology *in* Preaching

There are ministers who take theology seriously not only in preaching but also in every aspect of the work to which they have been called.[2] Nevertheless a remarkable and curious resistance or even indifference among ministers regarding theology confronts the contemporary church. I think here of a colleague who describes his preaching as an extension of his work as a "therapist," by which he understands his overall work as a minister. He speaks with echoes from the last millennium when Harry Emerson Fosdick equated preaching with pastoral counseling *en masse.*[3] Another minister holds that sermons should inspire hearers to action involving issues of peace and justice, viewing theology as getting in the way of a message that clearly pronounces those imperatives or as being in some sense unnecessary to them. To others theology suggests an esoteric if not boring discipline unrelated to so-called real life that regularly challenges caring and dedicated ministers of the gospel. What, one broods with Hamlet, does theology really have to do with "the thousand natural shocks/That flesh is heir to" and that it is the duty and concern of the preacher to address?

Moreover, the manifold requirements of the parish minister, including not only counseling but tasks related to weddings, funerals, administration, education, business, and representation on church boards and agencies, seem to be more important than the theological work that is necessary before one steps into the pulpit. In fact, serious sermon preparation is often thought to intrude on the business of running the church. It is this plethora of activities that causes many of us to fill our sermons with no more than "trite moralisms, slick therapy, the cooing illustrations, and the futile exhor-

2. Albert Outler appropriately wrote, in "The Pastor as Theologian," in *The Pastor as Theologian,* ed. Earl E. Shelp and Ronald Sutherland (New York: The Pilgrim Press, 1988), p. 12: "And yet there are pastors . . . who speak of themselves as theologians, without discernible embarrassment or immodesty."

3. We hardly need to stress that Fosdick neither understood nor practiced pastoral care apart from serious attention to the minister's theological work.

tations that characterize much of what is being offered to not only the patient, but sometimes enthusiastic congregations today."[4]

In another unusual and intriguing perspective on theology, Will Campbell connected theological work with violence. According to him, all theological statements, all creeds are potentially dangerous. Jesus never insisted that to follow him one must know the nature of the Trinity or a plan of salvation or conviction of sin or consciousness of forgiveness. In fact, one need not hold any belief whatsoever! Jesus only talked of such things as a cup of cold water. "Ah," Campbell continued, "but we must build a global sprinkler system. . . . So enter creeds and theologies to contain, to systematize. Enter violence to protect and to propagate the creeds and theologies."[5] Such a perspective on theology implies that preachers who take seriously creeds, confessions, and doctrines have supported or even encouraged religious violence and persecution. Yet one could also contend that serious attention to theology and the history of doctrine may be the antidote for the uncritical religious fervor of our day.

Preachers holding those various perspectives regarding theology do not forswear references to God and Jesus Christ. But theology as a discipline, as a self-conscious, intentional activity of the preacher, seldom engages their attention or respect. Despite his pastoral dedication and caring, the minister for whom I worked as a young associate pastor summed it up, to my huge regret, in a remark to his church of over two thousand members: "It took me nineteen years as a parish minister to get over my seminary education." Obviously, the purpose of a seminary is *theological* education! That said, it is also the case that those involved in seminary education have sometimes themselves been haunted by thoughts that the study of dogmas, creeds, biblical exegesis, history, and heresies are unrelated to the tasks and challenges of the parish preacher today.

4. David Read, "What Pastors Can Teach Theologians," in Shelp and Sutherland, eds., *The Pastor as Theologian*, p. 90.

5. Will D. Campbell, "Values and Hazards of Theological Preaching," in Shelp and Sutherland, eds., *The Pastor as Theologian*, p. 84. The title of Campbell's essay here mentions "values" as well as "dangers" in theological preaching. I am unable to ascertain where for him the values may be found. He ends by quoting a friend who answers a question of belief with "Yeah. Uh huh." Campbell judges it here as one of the most profound affirmations of faith he ever heard and perhaps one of the greatest bits of theological preaching as well (p. 87). As we say later, one cannot escape theology, violence to the contrary. The question is whether one does theology by implication or by conscious effort and intention.

Theology *in* Preaching as Loving God with the Mind and Thinking with the Heart

When speaking of doing theology, Karl Barth often spoke of *obedience* to the gospel. I do not question that obedience has its place in theological thinking. Dedicated preachers will not ignore the challenge of obedience in their work. However, when the word is spoken in the context of clergy who resist theological reflection and study, it brings to mind something one must do rather than something one wants to do.[6] Obedience can and often does imply a certain resistance or hesitancy — attitudes, to be sure, one cannot escape in the service of the gospel. Or there is the word *commitment,* an attitude certainly not absent from the work of theology and not irrelevant in assessing a preacher's own faith in the gospel. Faith abides and surely includes obedience and commitment, but accuracy in describing theology *in* preaching involves a dimension beyond obedience and commitment, crucial as they may be. That dimension involves love for God and all others in God. I dare, therefore, to rise to the happy generalization that those who preach really do love God. *However, to disregard the role of theology* in *preaching can trvialize the preacher's love of God and love for those given into the preacher's loving care.*

We are echoing the Great Commandment here as professed by Jesus.[7] His command to love God with heart, mind, soul, and strength means that love of God governs one's total life and, for the preacher, directs one's thinking about God. I am reminded here of St. Augustine's understanding of Romans 5:5, wherein the Apostle rejoices that "God's love has been poured into our hearts through the Holy Spirit that has been given to us."[8] In addition I think of the author of 1 Peter 1:8, who writes: "Although you have not seen him, you love him; and even though you do not see him now, you believe in him and rejoice with an indescribable and glorious joy." The writer of 1 Peter knows of obedience and reverence, but

6. See "The Splendid Embarrassment" by Tom Currie in this volume.

7. Matt. 22:37-40; Mark 12:29-31; Luke 10:26-28.

8. I am grateful for this reference in Robert Louis Wilken, *The Spirit of Early Christian Thought* (New Haven and London: Yale University Press, 2003), pp. 288-89. Wilken concedes that the saint's interpretation of Romans 5 is "idiosyncratic" but still plausible. And St. Augustine is speaking in this connection of how our love of God relates to virtues. I am, admittedly, enlarging that love to include the virtue of theology. I dare to think the saint would approve!

"adds a dimension of relatedness that is distinctive, that of love on the part of the believer."[9]

If indeed love of God governs one's whole life, theology *in* preaching has to do with loving God with the mind and thinking with the heart. Loving with the mind means that love seizes theological thought and drives theological reflection. The classic guidance of St. Anselm with his definition of theology as *fides quaerens intellectum* — faith seeking understanding — does not signal the irrelevance of the mind's love for God but its profound expression.

Theology *in* preaching also includes the "heart," our typical way of speaking of the wellspring of emotions, feelings, and passions associated with love. The word used by Jonathan Edwards, early America's first great theologian, in this connection was *affections,* as indicated in his famous title of 1746: *A Treatise on Religious* Affections.[10] "True religion, in great part," he reminded us, "consists in holy affections." And he observed: "Our people do not so much need to have their heads stored as their hearts touched."[11] Quite obviously, however, he taught us that thought and affections work in tandem. To think with the heart does not mean to ignore or to restrain the affections but to bring them to language. Edwards himself resolved in his New Year's resolution of January 12 and 13, 1723, "never to allow any pleasure or grief, joy or sorrow, nor any affection at all, nor any degree of affection, nor any circumstance relating to it, but what helps religion."

The tradition of Edwards found expression later in the young Reinhold Niebuhr, who noted when he preached that people are not ordinarily moved from their lethargy by cool and critical analyses. An appeal to the emotions is necessary. But he cautioned against the assumption of the average revival preacher for whom it seemed "that nothing but an emotional commitment to Christ is needed to save the world from its sin and chaos. They seem never to realize how many of the miseries of mankind are due not to malice but to misdirected zeal and unbalanced virtue."[12] Even as the mind expresses love, the affections in turn welcome thought, ennobling and guiding a "madness" the young Niebuhr experienced in himself.[13]

9. Luke Timothy Johnson, *Living Jesus* (San Francisco: Harper, 1999), pp. 92-93.

10. Jonathan Edwards, *The Complete Works* (New York: Leavitt & Allen, 1855).

11. Edwards, *The Complete Works,* vol. 3, pp. 2, 335, 336.

12. Reinhold Niebuhr, *Leaves from the Notebook of a Tamed Cynic* (New York: Meridian Books, 1957), pp. 56, 71.

13. "Why is it," Niebuhr wrote, "that when I arise in the pulpit I . . . am sometimes

Theology *in* Preaching and the Sunday Sermon

Given the dynamic relationship of the loving mind and the thinking heart, we declare with Karl Barth that "the normal and central fact with which dogmatics has to do is, very simply, the Sunday sermon of yesterday and tomorrow, and so it will continue to be."[14] Another theologian holds that dogmatics is "preaching to the preachers."[15] Both of these statements assert that theology functions as a loving "watch dog," guarding and protecting the gospel of the church, which the preacher loves with the mind and out of which the preacher thinks with the heart. Robert Jenson further describes theology as "how to do something, and the thing to be done is to carry on a specified message," further describing theology as a second-order discourse, the first-order discourse being, "on the one hand, proclamation and, on the other hand, prayer and praise," with "theology as hermeneutic reflection *about* this believing discourse."[16]

The distinction between first- and second-order discourse, to which Jenson refers, is crucial and will concern us later in more detail. For the moment suffice it to say that while second-order discourse talks *about* first-order discourse, the latter involves either speaking *to* God, as in prayer or praise, or involves the word that comes *from* God, as in scripture and the Sunday sermon. The speaking that comes *from* God defines preaching in the classic Protestant understanding of it.[17] Therefore the adequacy of a preacher's theology constitutes the crucial issue and calls for an intentionality about study and rigorous thinking that support the preacher's first-order discourse.[18]

---

possessed by a madness which makes my utterances extravagant and dogmatic?" *Leaves from the Notebook of a Tamed Cynic,* p. 56.

14. Karl Barth, *Church Dogmatics* I/1: *The Doctrine of the Word of God,* ed. G. W. Bromiley and T. J. Torrance (Edinburgh: T. & T. Clark, 1960), p. 91. Cf. note 4.

15. Heinrich Ott, *Theology and Preaching,* trans. Harold Knight (Philadelphia: Westminster Press, 1961), p. 23.

16. Jenson, *The Triune God,* pp. 14, 18.

17. I am thinking here of the classic Protestant view of preaching as stated in the Second Helvetic Confession: *Praedicatio verbi Dei est verbum Dei,* that is, "preaching of the word of God *is* the word of God." An elaboration of this statement may be found in my article on "Resounding the Gospel," in *Theology Today,* January 2007.

18. Jenson remarks, "whenever a preacher says to me, 'I'm not a theologian,' I want to reply 'Of course you are — you're either a good one or a bad one'" (Jenson, *The Triune God,* p. 95). Cf. also Albert Outler, "The Pastor as Theologian," in Shelp and Sutherland, eds., *The Pastor as Theologian,* p. 12.

As a preacher prepares the Sunday sermon by intentionally employing mind and heart, the preacher's love of God and love for the people of God are being manifest. As a loving, thinking "watch dog," theology helps the preacher guard and protect the integrity of the speaking carried on in the first-order discourse. Such love as expressed in the love of one's mind and in the thought serving one's deepest affections can help the preacher get it "right,"[19] so to speak, or as right as one can get it, remembering Barth's description of theology "as trying to describe a bird in flight."[20] In the coming of Jesus Christ into the world the most wonderful thing has happened. A loving response to that happening requires critical thinking about the scriptures that tell of him, serious exploration of the doctrines that try to explain and give expression to those scriptures, and a testing and learning from those who have — long before we were — loved with their minds and thought with their hearts.

A congregation enters a sanctuary with questions, opinions, beliefs, experiences. The preacher who loves God with the mind and thinks with the heart will thoughtfully and lovingly ask, how, *theologically* speaking, shall this specific congregation be addressed? In Heinrich Ott's words, dogmatics "is concerned with the understanding of the whole, with systemization. . . . Preaching on the other hand is marked by its intent towards the *hic et nunc,* the here and now, its concern with a given pastoral situation. This trait is completely foreign to dogmatics."[21] Ott inspires a poetic paraphrase: a sermon is "the cry of its occasion." It moves "straight to the Word, straight to the transfixing object."[22] Paul Scherer rightly worried that preachers would neglect their theological work to do no more than "find out what people want, or think they must hear, and give it to them . . . where in a thousand

19. Likewise Barth: "Language about God here . . . means very simply instruction, teaching about what the Church up to date . . . has recognized and confessed as the *right* faith . . . with which proclamation today has to link up." *Doctrine of the Word of God,* p. 55. My italics.

20. Karl Barth, *The Word of God and the Word of Man,* trans. Douglas Horton (New York: Harper Torchbooks, 1967), pp. 282-83, 285. Karl Barth, *Evangelical Theology: An Introduction,* trans. Grover Foley (New York: Holt, Rinehart & Winston, 1963), p. 10.

21. Ott, *Theology and Preaching,* p. 40.

22. The paraphrase is of Wallace Stevens, who said, "The poem is the cry of its occasion." A poem "mov[es] straight to the word, to the transfixing object." Wallace Stevens, "An Ordinary Evening in New Haven," in *Poems by Wallace Stevens,* ed. Samuel French Morse (New York: Vintage Books, 1959), pp. 148, 147.

pulpits the Gospel is reduced to a plaintive warning, with a vague promise, held together with a bit of advice."[23]

The preacher's loving mind and thoughtful affections drive us to ask how, in an age swirling with questions pertaining to divinity, does the Christian faith understand and experience God?[24] The scripture of the Christian church dares to say that God is love (1 John) even as Jesus Christ gives shape and substance to that love. How is it that God's love and the work of Jesus save us? How do the listeners in a congregation understand their own need to be saved? In an age awash with religious talk or so-called spirituality, what is the salvation given in God's love that is the work of Jesus? How shall the preacher address the longing for salvation in a congregation if not from the profoundly theological perspective of faith in a loving God who raised Jesus from the dead?

The Scope of Theology *in* Preaching

In response to questions such as these, George Lindbeck offers the preacher an astounding[25] perspective of the scope of theology *in* preaching. In his book *The Nature of Doctrine,* Lindbeck sets out to develop new and better ways of understanding the nature and function of doctrine as well as the use of scripture. The task of theological interpretation, he declares, is "absorbing the universe into the biblical world."[26] This means that the preacher who loves God in mind and heart will self-consciously and intentionally — and this from the pulpit on Sunday morning — bring all of reality into a Christian understanding.

One approach to theology in preaching is propositional; that is, the

23. This is a summary of his challenge as stated in my article on "Scherer, Paul Ehrman," in *Concise Encyclopedia of Preaching,* ed. William Willimon and Richard Lischer (Louisville: Westminster/John Knox Press, 1995), pp. 426-27.

24. I admit a certain naïveté in this question, but the fact is that religion and so-called God talk are inextricably a part of the human condition in every age, to say nothing of understanding of God in the various religions.

25. For example, astounding to James Gustafson, *An Examined Faith* (Minneapolis: Fortress Press, 2002), p. 9. Cf. William Placher's response to Gustafson in *The Christian Century,* June 19, 2004. Lindbeck aligns himself with what he defines as "postliberal theology," helpfully discussed by Gary Dorrien in *The Christian Century,* July 4-11 and July 18-25, 2001.

26. George Lindbeck, *The Nature of Doctrine* (Philadelphia: Westminster Press, 1984).

preacher deals with theology as propositional statements about objective realities.[27] Certainly for the preacher, propositional statements regarding the Christian faith have "all of reality" in view. However, this approach does not embrace reality so much as impose or interject statements upon it. The statement "God is love," for example, is imposed, an understanding of its meaning assumed and human experience or questions about love ignored. The sermon thereby becomes a discourse wherein verbal correctness about God's love is required rather than a plumbing of the depths and mystery of human experience and the ensuing struggle to wring from language a meaningful and fresh expression of God's love.

A second approach to theology *in* preaching focuses upon "inner feelings, attitudes, or existential orientations . . . constituted by harmony or conflict in underlying feelings, attitudes, existential orientations, or practices."[28] Here one searches for what seem to be "universal structures of thought or experience."[29] One deals with theology or doctrine as expressive of "basic attitudes, feelings, or sentiments."[30] To continue the illustration, one attempts to define a universal and common experience of love. From this perspective the preacher directs efforts toward making the faith intelligible on the basis of a foundation outside the faith itself. One tries to identify "the modern questions that must be addressed, and then to translate the Gospel answers into a currently understandable conceptuality."[31]

The third approach centers upon how a given religion, in this case Christianity, has its own understanding of reality, its own language and rules by which faith is thought and practiced. It declares the normative and distinctive quality of the faith — somewhat akin to the cognitive or first approach without the requirement of a specific or propositional language. Believers do not find their stories in the Bible; rather they make the biblical story — the Christian story — their story. In this third approach, language

27. Lindbeck, *Doctrine,* p. 16. I am eschewing here Lindbeck's description of his theories as pre-liberal, liberal, postliberal — alternatively cognitive, experiential-expressive, cultural-linguistic. In my view those terms, important as they are in his argument, obscure the relevance of Lindbeck's conclusions for preaching; moreover, we can dare avoid taking into account the serious and quite important discussions which have followed on his work, as summarized in the *Century* articles cited in note 25 above.

28. Lindbeck, *Doctrine,* pp. 16-17.

29. Lindbeck, *Doctrine,* p. 130.

30. Lindbeck, *Doctrine,* p. 33.

31. Lindbeck, *Doctrine,* p. 132.

causes human experience. The preacher's work is shaped, molded, in fact constituted, by a word outside the self, a *verbum externum* and not, as in the second approach, by common, inner experiences.[32] The meaning of love may vary, but for the Christian believer only love shaped by the understanding of Jesus (*the Word* from outside the self) qualifies as Christian. For the preacher the third approach may be dialogical, confrontational, confessional, or evangelistic, depending upon the "cry" of a specific situation.[33] But in all instances Christian preaching involves "the offer and the act of sharing one's own *beloved* language — the language that speaks of Jesus Christ" with all who are interested.[34]

Lindbeck makes his proposal with the full knowledge that we may be trying to preach the gospel in what he calls a "dechristianized" world. He speculates that such dechristianization may reduce the Christians for whom his third way of doing theology governs their preaching into a small minority. He goes so far as to say that this third way may be untenable today in "mainstream" Christianity. The desire of the churches "to maintain membership and of theologians to make the faith credible, not least to themselves" will continue to favor Lindbeck's second approach.[35]

Despite his warning, the third way of doing theology *in* preaching offers the most plausible description of what is involved in the preacher's theological work. What we earlier spoke of as first-order discourse, signaling the preacher's love of God and the people of God, receives here its most appropriate theoretical grounding. More important, Lindbeck's observation that his third way of fulfilling the theological task may be inoperable in mainstream Christianity these days strikes me as too pessimistic. Never has the church or her preachers *not* faced the challenge of expressing faithfully and intelligibly the message of its sacred texts, its historic language, its doctrines.[36] The work of the preacher in every time of the church has precisely that intelligibility as its focus. And there are yet those servants of the Word who have in love and devotion left all to follow Jesus Christ, and those who will gladly respond to them (Luke 5:11; Mark 12:37).

32. Lindbeck, *Doctrine*, pp. 34, 117, 118, 135.

33. Cf. note 13.

34. Lindbeck, *Doctrine*, p. 61. Emphasis mine.

35. Lindbeck, *Doctrine*, pp. 133-34.

Theology *of* Preaching

Theology *in* preaching takes place when the preacher asks how theology might affect and judge the content of the sermon as the preacher seeks to proclaim the gospel. But an exploration of theology and preaching also calls for theological reflection about the phenomenon of preaching in relation to a theology *of* preaching.

The issue first confronted me when a member of a congregation I served spoke rather judgmentally to me, noting how my preaching differed from that of my predecessor. The layperson said, "He did not give us theological lectures from the pulpit. He *preached!*" Putting aside my pride, I acknowledged that the layperson's remark deserved a reflective response. What in fact *is* preaching? Was the judgment correct? Had I in fact been offering only theological lectures from the pulpit? And, if so, how were they unlike preaching?

The layperson's concern accords with the observations offered by the theologians whose reflections we have been sharing. To recall Robert Jenson's earlier description, theology is second-order discourse, and preaching is first-order. We noted that the one speaks *about* God while the other speaks the word of God. Jenson's comment agrees with the observation of Barth that theology — second-order discourse — though specifically related to the Sunday sermon, cannot as such "claim to be proclamation."[37]

How then may we properly define proclamation as distinguished from language *about* God? Ott viewed preaching as "the impulse of power which drives the thinker to his dogmatics . . . the inspiration which urges the theologian to think out to the true conclusion his dogmatic sequences of thought . . . the criterion by which the validity of doctrine is to be measured."[38] A theology *of* preaching is second-order discourse concerning how the "impulse of power" is given or how by God's grace the "inspiration" made manifest in preaching actually operates.

36. Consider the words of an author whose book was once widely used as a homiletics text: "At any rate, the student of preaching in our day should be aware that the work and message of the preacher have to face not only the judgment of an indifferent and unbelieving society outside the church, but also within the church the critical judgment of biblical scholars and theologians." Henry Grady Davis, *Design for Preaching* (Philadelphia: Muhlenberg Press, 1958).

37. Barth, *Doctrine of the Word of God,* p. 55. The remark communicates insistence and the requirement to explore the distinction.

38. Ott, *Theology and Preaching,* p. 27.

These descriptions must not obscure the fact that a "fluid" (Barth's word)[39] line exists between theology and preaching, an observation also made by Ott and others.[40] Aware of such a line, how may we yet describe preaching as first-order discourse?

Preaching as a Phenomenon

To answer the question, I turn to a work written during the time of the Cold War by a theologian named Roger Mehl. Despite the time that has elapsed since his work was first published, I continue to find his perspective one of the most helpful in assessing the distinction between theology and preaching. Mehl titled his small volume *La Rencontre d'Autrui: Remarques sur le Problème de la Communication,* which records lectures he gave at the Ecumenical Institute in Bossey, Switzerland.[41] The strength of his work for us here lies in his attempt to deal with the phenomenology of communication considered in tandem with the philosophical work of Husserl and his followers. Although the historical context has greatly changed since his lectures were given, Mehl's work continues to illumine the nature of Christian preaching as first-order discourse.

Mehl described levels of communication. A hierarchy is suggested by the word *level,* but each aspect of the phenomenon has its integrity. The first level involves the transmission of information in the manner of news in a newspaper or mass media as well as human conversation outside the media. Here the meaning or interpretation of such facts is minimal. To be sure, the choice of what facts to report reflects interpretive decisions on the part of the reporter. But the intention of the reporter, as Mehl described it, is simply to deal with the empirical facts. An example in this connection would be the small number of references to Jesus in early, extra-canonical writings, such as those written by Tacitus, the Roman historian,[42] and Josephus, the Jewish historian.[43]

39. Barth, *Doctrine of the Word of God,* pp. 55, 56.

40. Ott, *Theology and Preaching,* p. 25.

41. *La Rencontre d'Autrui: Remarques sur le Problème de la Communication* [The Encounter of the Other: Remarks on the Problem of Communication] (Neuchâtel: Delachaux and Niestlé, 1955.) The quotes given here in the text are in my translation and are found on pages 25-26.

42. Tacitus, *Annals* (c. 116), 15:39-43, where he describes Nero's persecution of the Christians in 64.

43. Josephus, *Antiquities of the Jews* (93), xviii, 3.3.

The second level of communication, Mehl said, has to do with the presentation of ideas, reflections, understandings — in Barth's word, *instruction*.[44] That level is often typified by the relationship between teacher and student. In Christian terms these matters include what the scripture tells us about Jesus as well as his own teaching in sayings and parables. Obviously, the second level further includes the doctrines and teachings of the church concerning him. Various theological perspectives and issues belong to the second level as well. The second level corresponds in our analysis here to theology.

Mehl continues with a description of yet a third level of communication which he calls proclamation *(predication)*. What distinguishes this third level from the second is that the proclaimer — the *predicateur* — does not "propose to demonstrate the truth or error of a system, or propose to analyze data, at least not in the first instance." Instead the *predicateurs* "voice the authority to which their existence is subordinate, and they testify that that authority is of value for their listeners." This authority gives "clarity" to a human situation that is "in process of being closed, of becoming inextricable or impossible." In *predication* one orients the message to "the discovery of an outcome," a future different from the past.

As regards the Reformation understanding that preaching of the word of God is indeed the word of God,[45] the theologian no less than the *predicateur* surely respects the authority to which we are subordinate and which has value for our existence. Moreover, a driving desire of theological work, certainly as conducted by one who loves God in mind and affection and shares that love with others, surely has to do with "the discovery of an outcome," where one seeks to evoke that same love in another. Concern for the truth of the faith, analysis of authoritative data within scripture and tradition, the desire for an outcome — all may show us the fluid line between proclamation and theology. It finally obtains, however, that theological reflection as written or spoken essentially exists in the second level of communication. It is discourse *about* God and the Christian faith. To use Barth's terms, proclamation is "its raw material and its practical goal, not its content or its task."[46]

Engaging the full force of this analysis necessitates our understanding that *predication* or *proclamation* may not always be limited to the Christian

44. Cf. note 20 above.

45. Cf. note 12 above.

46. Barth, *Doctrine of the Word of God*, p. 55.

faith. Again, we emphasize that Mehl spoke phenomenologically, although his analysis has important theological implications. As *phenomena,* all proclamations are similar! In that sense and that sense only, communism was a kind of "gospel." For in *predication,* wherever it occurs, one intends to give vision to a new future and a hope. For the Christian preacher it cannot be "communicated by an instruction [read for our purposes *theology*] but by a *proclamation* that announces in Jesus Christ an imminent coming, the imminence of a new time." Proclamation aims to "constitute a new group, class, party," in short, for the Christian preacher a *church,* to assure that the proclamation is perpetuated throughout time. The Christian preacher proclaims Jesus Christ and all that *that* means for future life: a living presence "who authenticates by his presence the action of his Spirit, the words I declare." A relationship of *faith* obtains between the Christ who is thereby preached and the hearers of the word. Their "spiritual destiny depends uniquely upon this faith."

Proclamation as a Happening

A theology *of* preaching now presses us to ask, how may a preacher give specific expression in preaching to the phenomenon of Christian proclamation? — referring always in this connection to Mehl's description of *predication.* Gerhard Ebeling's answer is decisive. "The Word," he wrote, "is not just a bearer of a certain content of meaning which can be isolated, but a happening which brings something to pass and moves towards what it has in view."[47] Theological work precisely involves content. Such content or a statement of meaning may, to use Ebeling's word, be "isolated" from life both by the one who is listening and by the one who is speaking or writing. Such isolation can be the result of second-order discourse *about* something. Despite the activity and work of a loving mind and a thinking heart, communication of content about something alone may not cause anything to happen. However, the Word of God as *proclaimed* aims to bring about a *fait accompli.* It manifests the preacher's *first-order* discourse and seeks above all to make something *happen* to the hearer and to break open his or her future.[48] The

47. Cf. Amos Wilder, *The Language of the Gospel* (New York: Harper & Row, 1964), p. 24. The quote is in Wilder's footnote.

48. Ebeling, also supported by Wilder, *The Language of the Gospel,* has much to say

nature of such discourse is further illumined with Flannery O'Connor's phrase "experienced meaning."[49] Or again by Northrop Frye's description of the *kerygma.* "Language in the *kerygmatic* mode," Frye wrote, "seems to be language that uses man rather than man uses language."[50]

For example, it is one thing to talk theologically *about* the forgiveness of God or salvation by Jesus Christ. It is another thing to effect forgiveness. In this regard John Calvin writes:

> Forgiveness of sins, then, is for us the first entry into the church and the Kingdom of God. Without it, there is no covenant or bond with God . . . that entrance into God's family is not open to us unless we first are cleansed of our filth by his goodness. . . . So carrying, as we do, the traces of sin around with us throughout life, unless we are sustained by the Lord's constant grace in forgiving our sins, we shall scarcely abide one moment in the church. But the Lord has called his children to eternal salvation. Therefore, they ought to ponder that there is pardon ever ready for their sins.[51]

Likewise L. Gregory Jones in his book *Embodying Forgiveness* notes that "the forgiving grace of Jesus Christ gives people a new perspective on their history of sin and evil . . . people are mistaken if they think of Christian forgiveness primarily as absolution from guilt; the purpose of forgiveness is the restoration of communion, the reconciliation of brokenness . . . a way of life to be lived in fidelity to God's kingdom."[52]

Both statements offer responsible and helpful theological understandings of forgiveness that bear upon the proclamation of the gospel. It is another matter entirely, however, for forgiveness to be preached in such a way as to have it actually occur or to have its meaning experienced in the act of

---

about the Word as involved in personal relations. It is a matter worth much attention but not entirely apropos to our concern here (pp. 23-24).

49. O'Connor's comment referred to the writing of fiction, but the phrase still applies because the experience is precisely what she was after in fiction, which for her was not untruth but an expression of truth. An interesting connection obtains here between her "use" of fiction and the outcome of a sermon. Flannery O'Connor, *Mystery and Manners* (New York: Farrar, Straus & Giroux), p. 96.

50. Northrop Frye, *Words with Power* (New York: Harcourt Brace Jovanovich, 1990), pp. 116, 118.

51. Calvin, *Institutes,* IV.1.20, 21.

52. L. Gregory Jones, *Embodying Forgiveness* (Grand Rapids: Eerdmans, 1995), pp. 4-5.

proclamation. The grace of God alone makes the gospel *happen* in human lives. Nevertheless the preacher who loves God with the mind and thinks God with the heart remains open to the working of such grace in both mind and heart.[53]

When the Word of God is proclaimed, theology *in* preaching and theology *of* preaching, theologian and preacher, happily become as one. In the mystery of God's grace, they may succeed as a preacher who:

Deals — One — imperial — Thunderbolt —
That scalps your naked soul —[54]

53. Cf. the possible forms of the sermon as mentioned in *Concise Encyclopedia of Preaching,* ed. William H. Willimon and Richard Lischer (Louisville: Westminster/John Knox Press).

54. Emily Dickinson, "He fumbles at your soul," in *The Poems of Emily Dickinson,* ed. Thomas H. Johnson (Cambridge, MA: Harvard University Press, 1983).

The Recovery of Theological Preaching

Wallace M. Alston Jr.

One of the great needs of the church in our time is the recovery of theological depth in preaching. The observation that will serve as a target for this essay is that theological preaching is in short supply in the contemporary American Protestant church. I cannot speak for the Roman Catholic and Orthodox churches in this country, but I have no reason to believe that the situation is materially different in these communions. Theological preaching has given way to popular homilies that are difficult to distinguish from the various secular forms of address with which the culture is well acquainted, such as storytelling, luncheon club speeches, late-night television monologues, group therapy discussions, newspaper editorials, moral exhortations, or parental advice on issues of etiquette and good manners. The apparent demise of preaching that is theologically serious is shocking and warrants critical analysis by those charged with the stewardship of the church.

Theological preaching is not one style of preaching among others. Hughes Oliphant Old, in his extraordinarily rich study of preaching as worship, identified five genres of preaching that have appeared and reappeared throughout the history of the Christian church: expository preaching, evangelistic preaching, catechetical preaching, festal preaching, and prophetic preaching.[1] Expository preaching is the systematic exploration of scripture

1. Hughes Oliphant Old, *The Reading and Preaching of the Scriptures,* vol. 1 (Grand Rapids: Eerdmans, 1998), p. 8.

done on a week-by-week basis, or even day-by-day, in the context of congregational worship. Evangelistic preaching announces that the time is fulfilled and the kingdom is at hand, and calls the hearer to repent and believe. Catechetical preaching attempts to explicate basic Christian teaching derived from scripture and summarized in the historic creeds and confessions of the church. Festal preaching seeks to explain the themes of various holy days on the liturgical calendar of the church. Prophetic preaching tries to discern God's word for a particular time and place that calls for the abolition or reform of some ecclesial or societal practice.[2] Sermons representing each genre, however, may or may not be theological sermons.

All preaching, of course, is theological in the general sense of the word. The reference to theological preaching in this essay has to do with preaching that is informed by the theological tradition of the Christian church. In this sense of the word, a sermon in any of Old's five categories may or may not be theological. An expository sermon may or may not be informed by the history of Christian thinking and believing. Much expository preaching is little more than imaginative storytelling with a bit of literary analysis thrown in to suggest erudition. An evangelistic sermon may represent the theological idiosyncrasies of the preacher with no reference whatsoever to the best thinking of the holy catholic church. A prophetic sermon may be well crafted and highly articulate, but reflect little more than a political party line. Theological preaching does not parrot the church's party line, but it does evidence that fact that the preacher is cognizant of and familiar with the history of Christian thinking and believing (or not!), and that he or she is aware of the intellectual and behavioral risks involved in the truth-claims of this tradition. Theological preaching, in this sense, is indeed rare in the contemporary American pulpit, a fact that preachers themselves may be unwilling to admit, but one that is frequently noted and discussed by members of their churches.

2. I have no quarrel with Old's typology; it is as good as any other, and many others have been suggested. I do find its boundaries between genres somewhat artificial. Insufficient note is taken of the manner in which the genres regularly morph into one another, blurring if not altogether erasing any discernible distinction. Expository preaching may exhibit an eschatological urgency that calls for decision. Prophetic preaching, when done with integrity, will issue from the exposition of a biblical text, and a festal sermon may combine any two or all five characteristics of the five genres.

The Rarity of Theological Preaching

It has not always been so. Until relatively recently, in fact, preaching from North American pulpits has reflected, albeit to varying degrees, theological depth and the homiletical skill to carry it into public discourse. American pulpits during the first two-thirds of the twentieth century were not only graced by the likes of Halford Luccock, Ernest Fremont Tittle, Ralph Sockman, Harry Emerson Fosdick, Henry Sloane Coffin, James McCracken, George A. Buttrick, James A. Jones, Edmund Steimle, Harold Bosley, James T. Cleland, Browne Barr, Warner Hall, Joseph Sizoo, David H. C. Read, Carlyle Marney, and Paul Scherer, but with countless others in churches small and large, who preached Sunday after Sunday sermons of theological depth and clarity. Why is it that today theological preaching is only rarely to be found? Contemporary Christian preaching is not necessarily bad. It is simply dull, often too dull for words, or too cute to serve as a vehicle for the gospel. Why is that so?

Many things might be said in answer to that question. One might cite the influence of the entertainment and communications industries, which have tempted the public at large to subordinate content to form and style in any evaluation of public address. One might also cite the narcissism of the preacher, the compulsion to be liked, even loved, by the congregation; in addition one might add the avoidance of conflict, the hunger for fame, and the fear of criticism. The four explanations I will venture, however, do not dwell on the influence of the secular culture or on the personality flaws of the preacher, but rather on the state of mind in the contemporary American church.

First, the emphasis on biblical preaching. I am aware that the reigning consensus among preachers that the sermon must be biblical is a reaction against preaching that is unrelated to the normative witness to revelation in scripture. Nevertheless, I would argue that the misunderstanding of what constitutes a biblical sermon is largely responsible for the scarcity of theological preaching in our time.

Biblical preaching is routinely equated uncritically with expository preaching, as if exposition were the only way that biblical preaching could be done. Expository preaching, to be sure, goes back to the synagogue long before Jesus, where the Law was read and interpreted on the Sabbath. Jesus was an expository preacher, though not exclusively so. Origen was an expository preacher, as were John Chrysostom, Bernard of Clairvaux, Bonaventure, and the Reformers, Ulrich Zwingli, John Calvin, and Martin Luther. The church has never lacked for expository preaching, but expository preaching is not the only way to preach from scripture. Instead of moving from text to sermon, a biblical sermon might legitimately move from doctrine to text, or from a life crisis to more than one text, or dialectically between sacrament and text.

The problem with many supposedly biblical sermons is that the preacher remains inside the text, as one might do when studying a Shakespearean play, wandering about the story-line, musing about who said what and why, making canonical connections here and there, without reflecting on the role and place of the text within a coherent theological vision of reality. Harry Emerson Fosdick noted that this kind of preaching assumes "that the congregation came to church that morning primarily concerned about the meaning of those ancient texts." Only the preacher, Fosdick continued, "proceeds still upon the idea that folk come to church desperately anxious to discover what happened to the Jebusites."[3] Biblical preaching is not the paraphrasing of Bible stories! Preaching is authentically biblical when it explores and proclaims the meaning of a text in the light of a coherent theological framework of creation, fall, redemption, and consummation, that holds life together and permits people to locate themselves, their church, and their world as a part of that vision of reality.

Second, loyalty to the lectionary. The lectionary has been highly esteemed in many parts of the church since the Middle Ages. By the eighth century, when the number of feast days requiring festal sermons increased, according to Hughes Old, the Venerable Bede constructed a cycle of sermons that covered about half the year. "When Charlemagne began to set the liturgical foundations of his Holy Roman Empire, he wanted to ensure that every parish church in western Europe had a sermon for every Sunday and every feast day of the year."[4] The responsibility of trying to construct a plan to facilitate Charlemagne's vision fell to Alcuin (735?-804), an English educator and disciple of Bede, who put forward a set of appointed scripture passages, not only for every feast day, but for each Sunday of the year. According to Old, much of the preaching of the Western Church from this point on was based on Alcuin's festal calendar. In the Reformation period, Lutherans gen-

3. Harry Emerson Fosdick, *The Living of These Days* (New York: Harper & Brothers, 1956), p. 92.

4. Old, *The Reading and Preaching of the Scriptures,* vol. 1, p. 16.

erally retained it, whereas Reformed communities abandoned it in favor of the "lectio continua."[5]

The long and honorable history of the lectionary in the life of the church notwithstanding, I would argue that lectionary preaching has had a deleterious effect on the quality of preaching in the contemporary American church. Few if any of the great preachers of the twentieth century have been lectionary preachers. The contemporary emphasis on the lectionary has encouraged the kind of biblical preaching mentioned above, posing for preachers, in addition to the exegetical issues inherent in the text, the mystery of why these particular texts were chosen and grouped together, by whom, and with what agenda. There is no data to support the claim that lectionary preaching has increased biblical literacy in those congregations where it is practiced. In fact, it might be convincingly argued that it has not done so, that, before lectionary preaching began to dominate contemporary homiletical strategy, biblical literacy was greater than it is today. If the intent of the lectionary is to protect a congregation from the pet passages and peeves of the preacher, there is little indication that it does more on that front than to cloak these homiletical failings in canonical guise.

There are at least two things that the lectionary does well: one is to marginalize the reforming possibilities of intellectual diversity by encouraging uniformity (not unity) throughout the church, and the other is to discourage the preacher from taking full theological responsibility for the exposition, explication, and application of the Word of God in the particular congregation to which he or she has been called. No ecclesial committee or governing body, regardless of how devout and wise its membership, has the right or the mandate to discern how the Word is to be rightly "divided" (2 Tim. 2:15 KJV) in a congregation in which they have no part. It is the task and the privilege of the pastor, functioning as a theologian for the church, to plan preaching so thoughtfully and carefully that the divine address will be perceived and received as particular to the time and place of his or her service.

Third, the loss of a coherent vision of reality in the church. Until relatively recently preachers could take it for granted that a unified framework or vision of reality was shared by members of their congregations. There was general agreement about human origins, human destiny, and that which makes life worth living between birth and death. The preacher could take for granted a general theistic consensus, supported by a pervasive natural theol-

5. Old, *The Reading and Preaching of the Scriptures,* vol. 1, p. 16.

ogy in the culture at large, a basic knowledge of the Bible, and devotion to Jesus Christ. Furthermore, the individual Christian had a sense, often vague and undefined, of his or her place within this metanarrative. This sense of identity not only secured the individual from the threat of feeling cosmically "out of place," isolated, abandoned, or lost, but it also provided the preacher a framework within which to explicate particular texts, passages, doctrines, and creeds. It also provided the individual with an organizing and integrating vision that could hold all particular expressions of that vision together, giving them clarity and coherence.

The fact that a coherent vision of reality can no longer be assumed calls for preaching that is both theologically serious and intellectually courageous. Notwithstanding the critics at the door who regularly remind the preacher of their preference for more entertaining and accessible sermons, congregants today do not leave their minds at home when they enter the church. More people are attending colleges, universities, and graduate schools of various sorts than at any time in the history of the country. On any given Sunday morning, church pews are occupied by men and women whose daily existence demands a high degree of thoughtfulness and discernment. They bring to the sermon critical faculties that were once considered to be unfaithful in a Christian worship service. Contemporary preaching, therefore, must have an apologetic edge if it is to come to grips with such things as doubt, disbelief, relativism, and the many competing "spiritual" alternatives. The absence of a transcendent narrative of plan and purpose calls for theological preaching that is able to set forth the Christian alternative to the vacuity of a secular point of view.

Fourth, the theological inadequacy of the preacher. Many ministers, especially those under the age of forty, have never been exposed to theological preaching on a regular basis. They did not grow up in churches where, Sunday after Sunday, preaching was done with theological seriousness; they were taught to preach in seminary by persons who had not preached sermons of this kind in a single congregation for a significant period of time. Furthermore, it is not clear that systematic theology and the history of doctrine are taught in seminaries and divinity schools today with a view toward theological preaching.[6] Theology is seldom taught in Protestant theological schools from a basic text, as Roman Catholics are schooled in Aquinas or as Presbyterians were once taken through Calvin. Students may graduate today

6. See my essay on theological education in Part I of this volume.

with the basic degree in divinity without ever having been exposed to a complete theological system, or without having read extensively in any single theologian's work. As a result, the language, conceptuality, and structure regularly employed by theology, as well as the issues attendant upon theological thinking, do not become a part of the working imagination of this one who now must regularly explicate the gospel in a gathered congregation.

Theology taught with a view toward theological preaching presupposes basic competence. John Leith, who is often quoted in this volume because of his unique influence in the formation and practice of pastor-theologians, set forth in outline a basic agenda for anyone who aspired to be a pastor-theologian. If, as Leith believed, to be a constructive theologian requires the mastery of certain texts, one would not be adequately equipped for the task if he or she had not had a survey course in the history of doctrine. One should possess the ability to write a theological commentary on the Apostles' Creed, the Nicene Creed, and the Chalcedonian Definition. One should be knowledgeable of the development of the doctrine of the Trinity, culminating in the work of the Three Cappadocians and Augustine of Hippo. One should have read the *Letters of Ignatius;* Justin's *Apology;* Athanasius on the *Incarnation of the Word;* Augustine's *The City of God* and *Confessions;* Anselm's *Proslogion;* Aquinas's *Summa Contra Gentiles,* ch. 1–25, or *Summa Theologiae,* Q. 1-4; Luther's writings of 1520 ("The Freedom of the Christian," "On Christian Liberty," and "The Babylonian Captivity of the Church"); Calvin's *Institutes of the Christian Religion;* Schleiermacher's *Christian Faith,* pp. 1-31; Jonathan Edwards's *Treatise Concerning Religious Affections;* and at least one of the following: Karl Barth, Emil Brunner, or Otto Weber. In addition, one should be able to explicate the following rubrics: we believe in order to understand; faith seeks intelligibility; and *Lex orandi, lex credendi.*[7]

This is an ideal if not an idealistic agenda, to be sure, but it does illustrate the intentionality of one teacher of preachers, and of the commitment of one theological institution, to take with utter seriousness the equipment of pastors for the theological task of preaching. It also may serve as a wake-up call for the church as regards what is not being done in theological education adequately to equip men and women to be theologians in and for the church. However that may be, it offers a measure of insight into why there is so little theological preaching in our time.

7. John Leith, "On Teaching Theology at Union Theological Seminary in Virginia," in *Pilgrimage of a Presbyterian,* ed. Charles E. Raynal (Louisville: Geneva Press, 2001), p. 187.

Preaching as a Theological Occasion

The decline of theological preaching is implicitly sanctioned by the distance at which the practice of ordination is allowed to live from the discipline of an ordered ecclesiology. Ordination, not only in sectarian religious groups but also in established religious traditions, is commonly understood as permission rather than commission. It has been treated as a form of licensing, whereby men and women are legitimated as religious entrepreneurs. The equation of ordination with permission, however, is a huge distortion of the church's ancient rite. The minister, and particularly the minister as preacher, is not a private entrepreneur. He or she belongs to a history, a series or order of ministry in the church and for the church, and to the church he or she is responsible for the congruence of what is said and done with the reigning consensus of the ordaining community.

Preachers who relate to the revelation of God in the history of Israel and in Jesus Christ as though they were first-order witnesses are not dealing honestly with the truth.[8] There is always something that stands in between immediate or subjective religious experience and the revelation itself, such as time, history, geography, and language, to name only a few of the more obvious. The theological occasion is created by the fact that preachers are not eyewitnesses of that to which they bear witness, nor can they prove that what they say about it is true. They were not present when the things of which they speak happened; they never met the persons whose stories they tell; they were not numbered among the prophets or apostles who wrote of what they had seen and heard. Preachers at best are second-order witnesses and preaching is the medium of their witness, which, humanly speaking, links the present to scripture, and scripture to revelation. "As scripture is the Word of God in time and history, and as such the presupposition of the church and its preaching, revelation is the eternal Word of God. Both together are the basis of Christian preaching."[9] It is this "linking," and particularly the all-too-human role played by the preacher in making it happen, that makes of preaching a theological occasion.

As for the human role, the church has made claims about the relation of preaching to the "Deus dixit" of revelation that are difficult to understand

8. See John Stapleton's essay on theology and preaching in this volume for a different perspective on first- and second-order discourse.

9. Karl Barth, *The Göttingen Dogmatics*, vol. 1 (Grand Rapids: Eerdmans, 1991), p. 36.

and even more difficult to accept. The Reformers often spoke of the Bible as the Word of God, though at their best they did not simply equate God's Word with Isaiah's words or Paul's words. When they referred to God as the author of scripture, they knew that God did not dictate the very words of the Bible. They were fully aware of the fact that the Bible contains human words taken captive by the Holy Spirit. The church has always had to reckon with the possibility that the Logos takes shape in human flesh. They understood the statement that scripture is the Word of God to be a strictly paradoxical statement.

When the Reformers spoke of preaching as the Word of God, they knew both what they were saying and the risks they were taking. The Second Helvetic Confession of 1566, for instance, stated that the preaching of the Word of God is the Word of God. "Wherefore when this Word of God is now preached in the church by preachers lawfully called, we believe that the very Word of God is proclaimed, and received by the faithful."[10] This claim raises issues that are beyond the scope of this essay. What is germane for us is the seriousness with which the church, and particularly older Protestantism, took preaching as the means by which the Spirit of God links the words of the preacher to revelation by way of scripture, such that the "Deus dixit" of revelation is heard as God's contemporary address. This is what makes of preaching a theological occasion.

The faithful preacher knows this all too well each time she enters the pulpit to preach. The preacher knows better than her critics how inadequate she is to speak her poor words that may in fact be so inhabited by the Spirit as to become for another the Word of revelation. The Word of God, which she has been ordained to proclaim, judges her first before any other, but that does not take from her the call and the command to enter the pulpit and to preach the sermon she has labored to prepare! First as a young naval officer, then as a student in theology, I was struck by the burden of preaching, as each Sunday morning the preacher in the Harvard Memorial Church knelt following the sermon to claim for himself the forgiveness of sins.

Where am I likely to hear God speak to me? Anything is possible: a long winter's walk on a snowy road, a brilliant piece of music beautifully sung, a great piece of literature, the love between parent and child, the words of the Dalai Lama. Each possibility must be weighed on a case-by-case basis in the light of scripture and revelation. With God, all things are possible. But

10. *The Second Helvetic Confession,* Chapter 1.

Karl Barth spoke for me when he answered that question for himself, "Yet first of all I must notice where I myself am deliberately and purposefully addressed as a baptized Christian who is set under God's Word. This place is *my own church*."[11]

Theology and Preaching

Christian theology is critical reflection on the revelation of God in the history of Israel, in the person and work of Jesus Christ, in nature and human experience, and wherever else it may appear in time and space. The Bible is and always has been the final authority and arbiter of Christian truth, providing theology with a body of literature and a language with which to work. The task of preaching, humanly speaking, is to bridge the present situation, the Bible, and revelation in ways that may prove to be serviceable to the Spirit's uttering of God's contemporary address.

The church discovered very early in its history, however, that guidance needed to be given concerning how a canon of scripture was to be constructed and how it was to be interpreted. The Rule of Faith ("Regula Fidei"), being the precursor not only of the catholic creeds but of the canon itself, amounted to a summary of belief about which the early Christian communities had achieved a general consensus.

Paul M. Blowers has persuasively argued that the Rule of Faith "served the primitive Christian hope of articulating and authenticating a world-encompassing story or meta-narrative of creation, incarnation, redemption, and consummation." In those crucial years prior to the Council of Nicaea (A.D. 351), Blowers goes on to say, "the Rule, being a narrative construction, set forth the basic 'dramatic' structure of a Christian vision of the world, posing as a hermeneutical frame of reference for the interpretation of Christian Scripture and Christian experience, and educing the first principles of Christian theological discourse and of a doctrinal substantiation of Christian faith."[12]

Irenaeus (A.D. 120-202) sought to represent the central Christian story as a story not only of Israel but of the entire cosmos. In his mind, what

11. Barth, *The Göttingen Dogmatics*, p. 35.

12. Paul M. Blowers, "The *Regula Fidei* and the Narrative Character of Early Christian Faith," *Pro Ecclesia*, 6, no. 2 (1997): 202.

counted for new converts to Christianity was not only that they be familiar with the essential narrative, but that they entertain that narrative as the story of their lives. "The Rule in effect offers the believer a place in the story by commending a way of life framed by the narrative of creation, redemption in Jesus Christ, and new life in the Spirit. It immediately sets the believer's contemporary faith and future hope into the context of the broader, transhistorical and trinitarian economy of salvation."[13] That is to say, the Rule of Faith was not only a matter of literacy. It was also, even primarily, a matter of identity, the presupposition of a distinctive way of life. It became the theological framework or vision of the whole within which the preachers of the early church proclaimed and explicated Christian truth.[14]

Numerous historians have tried to identify more than one "regula" operating in Christian communities during the first three centuries of the church's life, and so it might have been. It would come as no surprise to discover that rules of faith differed from community to community. But in the overall landscape of ante-Nicene Christianity, Blowers tells us, the various renditions of the Rule give the impression of harmony, not cacophony. "A maturing solidarity and self-understanding is discernible in this period, commensurate with a hard-earned balance of fixity and flexibility, conformity and freedom, unity and diversity. Such was not achievable solely by churches fixing upon a canon of sacred Scripture, or by the bishops' exercise of strong pastoral and magisterial oversight; to a great extent it was rendered possible by those churches finding consensus on a common rule of intelligibly Christian truth within a shared 'narrative world.'"[15]

There is something startlingly contemporary about the church's ante-Nicene experience. The painful lack of unity in the one, holy, catholic and apostolic church, exacerbated by the distressing divisions within and among

13. Blowers, "The *Regula Fidei,*" p. 214.

14. "The *good* which God does to us can only be experienced as the *truth* if we share in performing it (Jn 7:17; 8:31f.); we must 'do the truth in love' . . . not only in order to perceive the truth of the good but, equally, in order to embody it increasingly in the world, thus leading the ambiguities of world theater beyond themselves to a singleness of meaning that can come only from God. This is possible because it is already a reality for God and through God, because he has already taken the drama of existence which plays on the world stage and inserted it into his quite different 'play' which, nonetheless, he wishes to play on our stage. It is a case of the play within the play: our play 'plays' in his play" (Hans Urs von Balthasar, *Theo-Drama: Theological Dramatic Theory,* trans. Graham Harrison [San Francisco: Ignatius Press, 1988], vol. 1, p. 20).

15. Blowers, "The *Regula Fidei,*" p. 227.

the various communions, calls for the kind of "maturing solidarity and self-understanding" found by the ancient church when a general theological consensus was reached concerning the nature and scope of Christian truth. Fixity and flexibility, conformity and freedom, unity and diversity have never fared very well in a church that lived at a distance from that consensus. A community in which pluralism is practiced rather than merely tolerated cannot be coerced or manipulated by books or bishops, however holy and wise they may be. The "Regula Fidei" was authoritative in the early church because it preserved a particular story, this story rather than any other story, as the ground and canon of faith. It was the avenue, as it were, into the godhead to which the church had been granted the right of way. The current dilemma of the church should be read as a summons to contemporary pastor-theologians to recall what it is that enables the church to grow "by the proper functioning of individual parts to its full maturity in love,"[16] as Sunday after Sunday they seek to give incarnational shape to a Christian identity by the proclamation of the gospel.

Accents in Theological Preaching

Theological preaching aims at creating a theologically literate church. It is the antithesis of the mediocre, the mundane, the lowest common denominator. It unashamedly and unapologetically aims at creating and nourishing theologically literate men and women, who are able to articulate in simple outline what it means to be a member of the church of Jesus Christ, and to do so in a way that distinguishes the church from the Rotary Club, a political party, Alcoholics Anonymous, a labor union, or any other form of social organization. Theological preaching seeks to counter the vacuity of secular society by providing a unified vision of reality, funded by the faith and reflections of two thousand years of Christian thought and experience, thus enabling individuals, churches, and social orders to find a theologically intelligible place in it.

Many accents will be detected in sermons of theological depth. Some aspect of each of the following, I maintain, will seldom be lacking.[17]

16. Eph. 4:16, J. B. Phillips trans.

17. Several of the accents mentioned were suggested to me by Jaroslav Pelikan, both in personal conversation on the occasion of his visit to the Center of Theological Inquiry and in his June 1961 commencement address at Wittenberg University, titled "A Portrait of a Christian as a Young Intellectual."

First, a commitment to truth. Augustine said long ago that we must first love the truth if we are to know it. Christians have all too often not only failed to love the truth; they have feared it and opposed its publication. It is both ironic and tragic that the scientific revolution, which occurred in Western culture where the doctrines of God and creation had profoundly influenced the understanding of the world, setting nature free for exploration from the pagan gods of wind, fire, and water, found the church to be, more often than not, its enemy rather than its friend. Theological preaching reflects the assumption that there is no inherent conflict between faith and reason, that where conflict exists, either reason has been distorted or faith has been wrongly understood.

Theological preaching, when done with integrity, tells the truth both about the biblical text under consideration and the human situation to which the sermon is addressed. It evidences a wide-ranging reading agenda on the part of the preacher. It does not mask the preacher's doubt when understanding or belief is hard to come by, engaging without fear the questions raised by unbelief against the faith she seeks to proclaim. It honors and draws upon truth that comes from any source, especially the sciences. It employs insights and illustrations from literature and the arts, current events and ordinary human experience, as well as from Bible commentaries and books on theology. Theological preaching uses every source and manifestation of truth at its disposal in order to articulate a coherent theological framework or vision of reality in which people can find an intelligible place to live and die.

Congregations do not always find the honesty of theological preaching immediately attractive. It is not always unsettling, but it may be at times. Listening to sermons that require concentration on the part of the listener is not always entertaining or easy to do. In fact, it often takes time for people to become acclimated to the intellectual honesty of theological preaching. But once people have grown accustomed to preaching of biblical and theological depth, they usually find it difficult to be enticed ever again by actors and performers in the pulpit that bring to preaching anything less.

Second, a passion for being. Theological preaching takes for granted the essential goodness of God's creation. It reflects the conviction that by the power of the God who created "all things visible and invisible," all things have an essential goodness that is finally impervious to any destructive power. But it does not fail to take account of the conundrum caused by the upper hand apparently held by sin and evil in determining the details and destiny of created existence. From Sunday to Sunday, week in and week out, theological preaching seeks to help people navigate that narrow space between uncritical optimism on the one side and faithless pessimism on the other. Few people live for very long in despair. Reinhold Niebuhr taught us that misplaced optimism is the greater enemy of Christian faith. "The optimistic man trusts life because he believes in his nation, or in his culture, or in the goodness of his church, or in the goodness of pious men, or in the capacity of human reason for infinite growth, or in the ability of one particular class to build a civilization that will be free of the evils by which all previous civilizations have destroyed themselves."[18] Theological preaching seeks not only to affirm and to proclaim, but also to unmask the idols and to dethrone the false gods in which people regularly place their trust.

Theological preaching attempts to help people understand that the Christian faith is something quite other than uncritical optimism. "It is trust in God, in a good God who created a good world, though the world is not now good; in a good God, powerful and good enough finally to destroy the evil that men do and redeem them of their sins."[19] Its aim is to equip men and women to discern the goodness of creation beneath its corruptions, and to live confidently and passionately as an instrument of love, justice, mercy, and peace in the midst of the ambiguities of life.

Third, a profound respect for language. The Christian cause depends upon language, and without it the life of the church would be impossible. One could argue that the whole of human history is a history of words: the mysterious origin of words in signs and sounds; the application of words to circumstances and events; the distortion of words by superstition, pride, greed, or the will to power. We say of an argument, "It's only a matter of words," mere semantics, but there is nothing "mere" about words.

The human capacity for speech lies somewhere near the center of our human uniqueness. Both the grandeur and misery of humanity are bound up with the gift of language. In the beginning, "God *said*. . . ." God *spoke* to the prophets. In the fullness of time, "the *Word* became flesh." Yet, if the Bible is to be believed, temptation as well as revelation entered the world by way of language. The serpent *spoke* to Eve in the primordial garden; Satan *spoke* to Jesus in the wilderness of temptation. Theological preaching is pro-

18. Reinhold Niebuhr, "The Ultimate Trust," in *Beyond Tragedy* (New York: Charles Scribner's Sons, 1937), p. 115.

19. Niebuhr, "The Ultimate Trust," p. 131.

foundly aware of the power of language, of the good that language can do when properly used and of the horrors that language can cause when abused. To adapt a thought from a recent book review by Walter Brueggemann, "in a culture that wants to turn communication into techno-speak and to kill utterance with psychobabble," perhaps it is in the embrace of word *as* sacrament that we are most fully human, most fully enacting the image of God.[20]

Theological preaching assumes that the spoken word is still the primary point at which the eternal God makes contact with humankind, and still the point at which Satan finds us most vulnerable. One does not have to be a great theologian to preach with theological depth, but theological preaching does betray a profound respect for language. Theological preaching, by its thoughtful choice of words, confesses the faith that language is a divine gift, possessing the power to point the finger, after the manner of John the Baptist in Grunewald's Isenheim altarpiece, to the truth that sets people free. In the Middle Ages, a crystal-clear and highly polished glass bowl was one of the most familiar symbols for Mary, the mother of Jesus, for "the Logos seeks vessels such as this."[21] To make our talk about God into one such vessel is the task of theological preaching.

Finally, an enthusiasm for history. The Christian interpretation of life has never been content to rest its case with a commitment to truth, or a passion for being, or a reverence for language. The Christian faith has always looked ahead in an attempt to assess the human prospect and to anticipate how faithfully to cope with that which is yet to come. The Christian doctrine of God, in fact, is incomplete without the doctrine of the Holy Spirit, who is the Agent of the future.

At one point in a delightful little book, which consists of conversations between Robert Jenson and his eight-year-old granddaughter, Jenson defines the Holy Spirit as God's liveliness. "When we say someone is lively," Jenson explains, "we mean they are looking forward, that there are things that they are interested in. Being lively is being directed to the future. So God as the Spirit is God's own future that [God] is looking forward to."[22] Theological preaching strains forward toward the future with an enthusiasm that

20. In *The Christian Century* 124, no. 26 (December 25, 2007): 30.

21. Barth, *The Göttingen Dogmatics,* p. 274.

22. Robert Jenson, *Conversations with Poppi about God* (Grand Rapids: Brazos Press, 2006), pp. 41-42.

betrays the conviction that life is headed for fresh manifestations of God's liveliness in a future that belongs to none other than God. The tone of theological preaching is neither apprehensive nor fearful, but hope-filled and expectant, open to the unpredictable, and receptive to the graciousness anticipated in the as yet unknown. An enthusiasm for history as the scene of the Spirit's lively determination finally to render all things subject to the will and purposes of God is the liberating thrust of theological preaching that sets people free to live with serenity and poise, come what may.

In conclusion, let it be freely admitted that there are many ways to preach the gospel, many styles of preaching that are helpful, many types of preaching that evoke faith and commitment. But let it also be admitted that there is good reason to believe that the recovery of theological preaching is absolutely crucial for the renewal of the church in our time.

Pastor and Teacher: A Way Forward from the Old Congregational Order

James L. Haddix

If the current crisis in the church is in theology and not strategies for church growth or marketing techniques for religion, one might expect pastors to be particularly well placed to address the crisis.[1] By education, training, and the recognition of their office by congregations, pastors are the persons that Christian churchgoers naturally look to for guidance. Pastors are expected to preach and Christians must surely assume that pastors base their teaching on biblical knowledge and theological training. If there is a single person in most Christian congregations who is expected to know about theology and to communicate theological knowledge it is the pastor. If congregations are to be called to theological understanding and engagement, pastors *must be* theologians.[2] If congregations are to gain — or regain — a grasp of the im-

1. "The so-called 'crisis of the church' is neither organizational nor programmatic, but theological. The heart of the matter is the loss of the church's identity as a theological community, occasioned by the distance at which the church lives from the source and sources of its faith and life. Thus the renewal of the church begins, at least on the human level, with the recovery of those sources and practices that historically have enabled people to encounter and to be encountered by 'the grace of our Lord Jesus Christ, the love of God, and the communion of the Holy Spirit.' It begins, as well, with the recovery of the identity of the ordained minister or priest as theologian and scholar." Wallace Alston, in the Center of Theological Inquiry's Pastor-Theologian Program statement, "The Crisis in Theology and the Church."

2. Barth writes about the pastoral task of doing theology: "How much more so those

portance of the central teachings of the Christian tradition, pastors will be the first, and perhaps most important, embodiment and expression of those teachings.

Pastors as theologians speak and teach from and for the received faith and central traditions of the universal Christian church. The task of the pastor as theologian is to help build in his or her congregation a Christian culture formed by all that has, across the centuries, provided the unifying heart of the Christian faith. One cannot build such a culture without ecumenical care and sensitivity, or without dedicated study and continuing engagement with Christian theology. For this work one needs, as Isaiah confirms, the Lord God's own gift of "the tongue of the learned" that one should know "how to speak a word in season to him that is weary."[3] Valued in parts of the church, learned pastors are still sought by many Christian congregations. This theme will run throughout this chapter.

In spite of an emphasis on learning and special training, pastors do not necessarily or naturally think of themselves as theologians. To help form pastors with an eye toward this essential work it is useful to explore an office of the ordained ministry that, at one time, was closely associated with the role of pastor: the office of teacher. In some circles the pastor is still identified as "pastor and teacher." An exploration of what this teaching function (or office) entails can be an important and encouraging beginning for working pastors if they are to frame and practice their calling as theologians for the church.

---

who are specially commissioned by the community, whose service is preeminently concerned with speech. . . . It is always a suspicious phenomenon when leading churchmen . . . are heard to affirm, cheerfully and no doubt also a bit disdainfully, that theology is after all not their business. . . . [J]ust as bad is the fact that not a few preachers, after they have exchanged their student years for the routine of practical service, seem to think that they are allowed to leave theology behind them as the butterfly does its caterpillar existence. . . . This will not do at all. Christian witness must always be forged anew in the fire of the question of truth. Otherwise it can in no case and at no time be a witness that is substantial and responsible, and consequently trustworthy and forceful. Theology is no undertaking that can be blithely surrendered to others by anyone engaged in the ministry of God's Word. It is no hobby of some especially interested and gifted individuals. The community that is awake and conscious of its commission and task in the world will of necessity be a theologically interested community. This holds true in still greater measure for those members of the community who are specially commissioned." Karl Barth, *Evangelical Theology: An Introduction* (Grand Rapids: Eerdmans, 1963), pp. 40-41.

3. Isa. 50:4.

A Brief History of the Teacher's Office

First, we will consider the teaching office of historic American Congregationalism.[4] We will see something of the shape and responsibilities of that office before it disappeared, leaving a void in the life of local congregations.[5]

The teacher in the Congregational tradition was specially charged with teaching the Word, reading the scripture aloud with comment in services, and catechizing both child and adult members of the church. The teacher was educated and ordained specifically for this ministry.[6] In early colonial New England, the established Puritan (later, Congregational) order had five churchly offices: pastor, teacher, presiding elder, deacon, and widow. In these earliest Congregational churches the idea of prophesying was an acceptable part of worship. Prophecy was heard primarily from lay members. Soon prophesying in worship had to be approved by the clergy,[7] until eventually the practice died out. The office of widow, an office for older women that included prayer and visiting the sick, also disappeared in this period.[8]

What emerged was an order of church leadership with four offices:

4. Cambridge Platform of 1648, Chapter VI, 5: "The office of pastor and teacher appears to be distinct. The pastor's special work is to attend to exhortation, and therein to administer a Word of wisdom; the teacher is to attend to doctrine, and therein to administer a word of knowledge; and either of them to administer the seals of that covenant, unto the dispensation whereof they are alike called; as also to execute the censures, being but a kind of application of the word: the preaching of which, together with the application thereof, they are alike charged withal."

5. The title "teacher" was attached, most naturally, to the title "pastor," hence the current pastor and teacher. The tasks of teaching were also, but not uniformly, transferred to the pastoral office.

6. While this office was prominent in Reformed circles, it is interesting to note that in times past, Anglican clergy sometimes donned academic hoods when they ascended the pulpit to preach. So, at least conceptually in connection with learned ministry, specially prepared teachers of the church are not foreign to some liturgical churches. The Cambridge Platform of 1648 says that teachers are not only for "the schools," though "schools are . . . lawful, profitable, and necessary for . . . literature or learning," but pastors and teachers are "for the church, and the teacher [not just] for the schools."

7. A similar phenomenon is apparent in many contemporary Pentecostal churches where clergy test the word of prophecy from lay members against scripture before the word is allowed in worship. Reference to this practice is made in my article, "And the Word of the Lord Came to Jonah a Second Time: Pastoral Reflections on Mystical Convergences as They Affect Biblical Authority and the Mission of the United Church of Christ," *PRISM: A Theological Journal for the United Church of Christ* (Cleveland: United Church Press, 2006).

8. Some functions of the office would find their way into the later office of deaconess.

pastor, teacher, elder, and deacon. The latter two were lay offices. While in our time churches of the Congregational type often speak of the Diaconate as the church body most concerned with the spiritual welfare of the congregation, in earlier times the offices of elder and of deacon were seen as offices of service, not of spiritual welfare. The elder (presiding elder) was responsible for administrative tasks in the church, with particular charge for church meetings, church discipline, and services of ordination.[9] The deacons were responsible for financial matters in the church, particularly for the needs of the poor. Deacons also visited the members of the parish and saw to the maintenance of order in the community as well as in services of worship. The deacons, it was said, served at three tables: the table of the Lord, as they provided for the elements and served at the table for the Lord's Supper; the table of the poor, since they oversaw and distributed the voluntary gifts of the congregation dedicated to the relief of the needy (particularly members of the local church); and the table of the ministers, since they saw to the temporal needs of the clergy when such care was required.

While in time the work of ministry became focused in pastor and deacons (with administrative tasks taken up by officers like moderator, clerk, and treasurer), we will consider the ministerial offices during that brief but formative period when pastor and teacher were often — in fact, usually — occupied by two different persons. It was these clerical offices to which the Puritans looked for the spiritual welfare of the churches.

While prophecy by lay members in worship quickly declined, the ideal of the prophet (imitating Christ's own work as prophet, priest, and king) was increasingly identified with the offices of the pastor and of the teacher. Harvard College, Yale, Dartmouth, and others in turn were established as "prophets' schools," schools where clergy were trained to assume the offices of pastor and teacher. The "learned clergy" were God's prophets, the voice of Christ to the congregation, and a true source of the people's spiritual welfare. The pastor proclaimed the Word by preaching and exhortation;[10] the

9. This office, too, was soon eclipsed by increased ministerial authority, particularly in matters of church discipline that became contentious, even church dividing, by the time of the Great Awakening.

10. The pastor's freedom of the pulpit had nothing at all to do with "freedom of speech" (a later American political notion) but was based on the pastor's education in proclamation of scripture. Architecture was pressed into service. Pulpits in Puritan meetinghouses were centered on the long axis of the meetinghouse and raised high above the floor level. This represented the centrality and elevation of the Word in worship.

teacher instructed the people in the faith as it was disclosed in the Word. Both offices were tied to scripture. Scripture was seldom read without interpolation or commentary in worship services. It was the teacher's job to read and to comment.

While in our time the clerical office of a church often has a division between the minister of the Word and a minister of Christian education, reminiscent of the earlier division between pastor and teacher, the differences are greater than the similarities. In earlier times, there were no Sunday schools and certainly nothing like what contemporary Christians usually call "Christian education." The Christian education of children was the responsibility of heads of households or, more likely if both parents were present in the home, of both parents. Parents were charged with teaching the faith to their children and other dependents.[11] Education of the young in the Christian faith was a home project, and this meant teaching the children their catechism. The teacher of the church was charged with catechizing the parents so they could effectively teach their children. The teacher and pastor would visit the home to see how the parents were progressing with their catechetical task. "Catechesis was a vital part of Puritan spirituality and religious training. An understanding of and belief in fundamental Christian doctrines were considered necessary for salvation."[12] The teacher taught adults who, in turn, taught their children and other dependents. Doctrine was important for people of all ages and walks of life. The Westminster Catechism was often used in the churches, but the pastors and teachers of American congregations "continued to strive for [a catechism with] plainer, biblical language."[13] Toward this end, teachers of congregations often wrote catechisms for those they were called to teach.[14]

Cambridge-educated New England divine Thomas Shepard was well

11. If Separatist Susanna Wesley was at all typical of how English parents took responsibility for their children's education, the effectiveness and vigorousness of educational efforts by women in Puritan households cannot be discounted.

12. "The First Principles of the Oracles of God, 1648, by Thomas Shepard," in *Colonial and National Beginnings,* ed. Charles Hambrick-Stowe, The Living Theological Heritage of the United Church of Christ, vol. 3, Barbara Brown Zikmund, series editor (Cleveland: The Pilgrim Press, 1998), p. 37.

13. "The First Principles of the Oracles of God, 1648, by Thomas Shepard," p. 37.

14. Puritans of New England held to the Westminster Confession in all matters except church polity, where they differed from the Presbyterian way, substituting their own Cambridge (Massachusetts) "Platform of Church Discipline." Adaptations of the Westminster Catechism show their pattern of adapting the English forms to local usages.

known for the catechism he composed for adult believers. His catechism was used extensively in New England and in England during the time of Puritan dominance there. Some of his works remained in print for over a century after his death. His catechism was particularly

> designed for . . . training the heads of households for their catechetical task. The epigraph on the title page of the book quotes Hebrews 5:12: "For when for the time ye ought to be Teachers, ye have need that one teach you again, which be the first Principles of the Oracles of God."[15]

Teaching and the teaching office are thus linked to the saving work of sound doctrine.

The separate offices of teacher and pastor were also reflected in differences in attire. A Puritan pastor wore "a pastor's robe when discharging the pastor's office. This would include leading public worship, administering the sacraments . . . participating in ordinations and installations and so forth." The teacher (or, later the pastor when discharging the duties of a teacher) would wear the teacher's robe, "the academic robe of one's divinity training."[16] Both pastor and teacher wore the Geneva bands or "tabs" associated with both Reformed and Anglican clergy. Since lay teachers could also wear the teacher's robe, the Geneva tabs set the ordained teacher of a church apart visually from his lay teaching brethren. The tabs showed the "specifically ordained vocation of teachers" who, like pastors, were set apart by "the laying on of hands and the Ordination Prayer for the Holy Spirit."[17]

Between 1660 and 1730, there were significant institutional changes in Congregationalism. It was in this era that the office of presiding elder fell away (for reasons of polity but also of ecclesiology). In this era the office of teacher disappeared from most parishes as well, falling victim to lack of funds. Churches found it increasingly difficult to employ *two* spiritual leaders. In place of the separate offices of pastor and teacher, though the termi-

15. "The First Principles of the Oracles of God, 1648, by Thomas Shepard," p. 38.

16. W. Scott Axford, "Aspects of the Tradition: The Attire of the Pastor and Teacher," *Bulletin of the Congregational Library* 43 (Winter and Summer/Spring 1992): 4. Both quotes are from Axford, who also notes that when the offices of pastor and teacher were combined in the duties of a single person, it would have been more common for the pastor to wear the academic gown throughout the service, but if someone else were preaching, the pastor would have worn the pastor's robe.

17. Axford, "Aspects of the Tradition."

nology was not uniform, the "minister" emerged, usually retaining the dual titles of pastor *and* teacher. Surprisingly, the minister seldom exercised this dual role in the ways to which congregations had become accustomed.

An even more surprising development followed the loss of the office of teacher: in most congregations the reading of scripture in services simply ceased! Where scripture did continue to be read, it was usually read without the once-customary explanation or commentary. Prior to this time, American Puritans insisted that scripture be read with commentary by the teacher. Scripture read without comment was called "dumb reading" and was despised as a popish thing.[18] Von Rohr summarizes this odd chapter in New England religious history thus:

> The basis for this departure [from regular Bible reading] lay in the fact that traditionally interpolation in the Scripture reading had been the responsibility of the teacher, rather than the pastor. . . . So with the inability of numerous churches to maintain financially the teaching office, the reading itself was sometimes removed from the order of worship. In the early 1700s, however, churches began to return Scripture reading to the service and to present it in uncommented form. By 1726 Cotton Mather could even insist that to call this a "dumb reading," as Puritans long had done, would be "improper and indecent." Yet resistance continued to both developments. Some churches did not restore Bible reading until the 1760s, whereas the change to uncommented reading was not completed until the nineteenth century was about to begin.[19]

Catechesis also suffered with the disappearance of the teacher. Some pastors kept up home visits to encourage parents to catechize their children. But in the years following the American Revolution — with the disestablish-

18. As early as 1699, the (some may have said "upstart") Brattle Street Church in Cambridge, Massachusetts, returned to the older Anglican practice of reading scripture in services *without* commentary. This "innovation" was shocking and roundly condemned. How much more shocking it now seems that, with the teaching office, scripture reading also disappeared from most Sabbath services.

19. John von Rohr, *The Shaping of American Congregationalism* (Boston: The Pilgrim Press), p. 166. It is interesting that Cotton Mather's father Increase Mather had, about a quarter century before, during the controversy occasioned by the Brattle Street Church's move to "dumb reading," said that one chapter of scripture read with explanation instructs more than thirty chapters without comment.

ment of the Puritan order and the appearance of Sunday schools (separate, usually lay-led schools for children held on Sabbath days between the meetings of the church) — the catechetical work of the teacher was taken over by others. The responsibility for religious instruction by parents was gradually given over as well. While it remained a principle of Congregationalism that each church member, under the guidance of the church officers, had the "right" to teach the Christian faith,[20] one must observe that a *right* is sometimes rather different from an *obligation,* which before had been the rule.

Complex changes in American life and Congregational church life are beyond the scope of this paper. The old Congregational way was collapsing. This is most evident in changes in church government and discipline. As the lay office of presiding elder was eclipsed by clerical authority, just so clerical authority was increasingly challenged and often eclipsed by lay authority in matters of governance and, as time went on, even of doctrine. If Congregational church polity had been, in the ideal of its founders, a mixed government of monarchy (under the Head of the Church, Jesus Christ the King), aristocracy (with the church officers representing that level of authority), and democracy (with the people giving their free assent to the headship of Christ and the authority of the officers), the early decades of the 1700s saw dramatic change. New emphases on personal, individual conversion and confession ushered in an almost complete collapse of the old forms of church discipline. Common faith expressed in covenants and creeds were de-emphasized as greater emphasis was placed on the personal religious experiences of individual believers. Certainly a core of Christian doctrine remained (as the later Unitarian schism would demonstrate), but without the formal teaching offices and tools of earlier times, and with a new atmosphere of indifference — or hostility — toward pastoral teaching and authority. As Cooper writes of this era, "concord between pastor and people [often revealed only that both pastor and people] agreed to disregard church order."[21]

The loss of the teaching office in Congregational churches and the strange developments this occasioned in religious life and practice of congregations was only part of a sea change in religion and culture in colonial

20. *Manual of the Congregational Christian Churches,* revised by Oscar E. Maurer, D.D., ed. (Boston: The Pilgrim Press, 1947), p. 51.

21. James F. Cooper Jr., *Tenacious of Their Liberties: The Congregationalists in Colonial Massachusetts* (New York: Oxford University Press, 1999), p. 208.

New England. To suggest recapturing or returning to such an office (which in fact was only briefly practiced) is fruitless and, even if desirable, impossible. Still, there are things to be learned.

First, the terms "pastor" and "teacher" have remained joined in common usage in Congregational churches and their successors in the United Church of Christ. Just how fully the notion of "teacher" is comprehended by pastors is not clear. There have been occasions in the recent history of the United Church of Christ when the teaching role of the pastor was reemphasized.[22] Institutionally, little has been done to invest this teaching function with particular meaning, namely, what it might mean to teach doctrine or whether it needs to be taught. Nor have techniques been recommended such as the reintroduction of catechesis for adults or children. Even if ordained clergy may not have thought through the implications of their work as teachers, the title persists and with it the residue of an idea that pastors have a teaching role to perform.

The Pastor as Teacher Today

What might a pastor as teacher look like? What modest moves might a pastor make to function as a teacher in congregational life and ministerial practice? In what ways, beyond the private conversations in the pastor's study, might a pastor teach those entrusted to his or her ministry?

First, the pastor as teacher would be one who *delights in doctrine*, who, like Jaroslav Pelikan, has never had "fundamental doubts about the essential rightness of the Christian faith."[23] To be an effective teacher, surely a pastor must have as full a grasp as possible of "the underlying unity and continuity of what the New Testament calls 'the faith once delivered to the saints' (Jude 3)."[24] The teacher has a set curriculum (broad and deep to be sure) in the church's received faith. The teacher must know the need of the faithful to be taught again "the first Principles of the Oracles of God."

Failing an inbred love and almost gestational assurance and devotion to

22. The Rev. Reuben Sheares, of the United Church of Christ's Office of Church Life and Leadership, made this emphasis — the reinvestment of teaching as a pastoral duty — as recently as the 1980s.

23. Timothy George, "Delighted by Doctrine," *Christian History and Biography* 91 (Summer 2006): 43.

24. George, "Delighted by Doctrine," p. 44.

the received faith of the church, the pastor as teacher[25] must be aware of the very high calling to which he or she has submitted in accepting the yoke of ministry and by drawing a paycheck from a Christian church. If one takes money from Christ's church (one hates to be crass), one ought at least to offer back *bona fide* Christian teaching and not just one's own opinions and individual insights, however wonderful. In contemporary understanding a "prophetic" teacher, preacher, or bishop is one who possesses unique, even extra-biblical, insights or some new doctrine given her or him (apparently) directly by God. It may be instructive to compare this understanding of prophetic ministry with that of former times, when the "prophet," equipped by education in the Word and authorized by a congregation of Christians, expounded on the Word or shaped catechesis to form and inform the body of believers.[26]

Second, the pastor as teacher embodies *the teaching of the church.* Whether or not he or she intends it, the pastor as teacher embodies the teaching. Thus, people are set apart in ordination. There is a long recognition of special gifts, special piety, special education, and special responsibilities associated with the offices of pastor (and now by extension, teacher). This is well expressed in a memorable moment from the New England Unitarian-Trinitarian controversy. Trinitarian Congregationalists insisted it was essential for them to have the right to choose their own pastors, pastors who *embodied* their doctrinal stance, because "the pastor of a church, is a living creed, more efficacious than written documents."[27] This is why clergy

25. The writer realizes that he is writing from a Protestant and, more particularly, Reformed Protestant place. The teaching office resides differently in other ecclesiologies. In the Congregational tradition, the teaching office resides in the local congregation. This is fraught with difficulty, of course, and also charged with great possibility for the faithful.

26. While on the subject of money, it is appropriate to consider these reflections by Archbishop Wulfstan from the late Anglo-Saxon period (c. A.D. 1000). This is from his *Institutes of Polity.* He begins by quoting from the prophet Hosea: "Woe to those priests 'who devour and swallow up people's sins.' Those are they who will not or cannot, or dare not warn the people against sins and punish sins; but nevertheless want their monies for tithes and for all church dues; and neither lead them well with examples, or teach them well with preaching, or cure them well with penances, or intercede for them with prayer, but seize whatever they can grasp of men's possessions, just as voracious ravens do from a carcass wherever they can get to it." Francesca Tinti, "The Costs of Pastoral Care: Church Dues in Late Anglo-Saxon England," in *Pastoral Care in Late Anglo-Saxon England,* ed. F. Tinti, Anglo-Saxon Studies, 6 (Woodbridge, UK: The Boydell Press, 2005), p. 37.

27. "Unitarian Controversy and Disestablishment: Rights of Congregational Churches," in Hambrick-Stowe, ed., *Colonial and National Beginnings,* vol. 3, p. 202.

misconduct (a euphemism for "presumptuous sins") is so deeply troubling, and why clergy who are innocent of theology work such mischief (sins of omission[28]).

Third, while the Word is embodied in some important ways in the pastor-teacher by the work of the Holy Spirit and the assent of the church, in that embodiment the office of teacher is based in *knowledge of scripture.* It is the teacher's task to use the primary language of scripture to shape doctrines that, in turn, shape the spiritual and intellectual formation of the faithful. Shepard, in his "First Principles of the Oracles of God," was only one colonial American Puritan to fashion a catechism of plainer [than the Westminster Catechism] biblical language "suitable for their flocks."[29] The Bible is the ground of theology, and it was no coincidence that in colonial Puritan America the teacher had particular responsibility for reading and explaining it. Theology must, in David Hart's turn of phrase, have a biblical shape.[30]

The Language of Teaching

What language shall we borrow to teach the doctrines of the church? It is no small question. Two great contemporary teachers of the church, Robert Jenson and Eugene Peterson, pay constant and close attention to the language of the church and the language of teaching. Both Peterson and Jenson could wear the teacher's robe in Christian worship. Both are ordained and come to their work with pastoral care. Jenson insists that the language of the church must be "iconic" while Peterson, convinced that the language of scripture was not the "elevated" language of the English translation trajectory, has spent his recent years setting the English Bible in "American" (as he puts it) and drawing out the implications of such imme-

28. Though Roman Catholics do allow for a more militant ignorance — different from innocence or lack of knowledge — that may afflict some pastoral practitioners. Actually, the Romans call this "invincible ignorance." While strong it is nevertheless not necessarily to be applauded.

29. "The First Principles of the Oracles of God, 1648, by Thomas Shepard."

30. David B. Hart, "The Lively God of Robert Jenson," *First Things,* October 2005, pp. 28-34. Here, specifically, Hart is writing about Robert Jenson: "theologians of every stripe should praise him for enunciating a Trinitarian theology with whose biblical *shape* — that is to say, specifically, his reading of scripture as Trinitarian throughout — it is impossible to take issue." (Emphasis is original with Hart.)

diacy of speech for the spiritual life of churchgoing believers. Both would agree that the church has a unique message, and both would agree that language is not incidental or even natural for a worshiping community of Christians. As Jenson puts it,

> the Church has her own culture, as she has her own polity. And therefore the Church inevitably is her own linguistic community also, however hard we may, in misguided moments, fight against this. We can banish Latin or Jacobean English if we insist, but something else will quickly replace it as the special church-language; and at that juncture we had better be alert . . . lest we replace the good with the mediocre or worse.[31]

Eugene Peterson, one of the most compelling pastor-teachers of our times, would be among the first to banish Jacobean English, at least from parts of the church's life. Nevertheless he is acutely aware that the church "is her own linguistic community," a community formed spiritually by the Word. All his works of pastoral theology, which ring true to great numbers of pastors, include poetic references that qualify as "iconic" language.

Early on as a working pastor, Peterson came to see the importance of his role as the teacher of his people. At first, what he wanted to teach was prayer. Praying, he instinctively knew, was grounded in the Psalms. In order to give his parishioners the vigorous language of the biblical Psalms, he began his work as translator of scripture. Prayer, as well, has a biblical shape and, in the Psalms, conveys theological truth. The Reformers all turned to the Psalms for prayer, worship, and theological resource.

Peterson refers to the Bible studies he led as "immersion in Scripture" with "experiences of surprise and recognition." In this kind of study, "moments always seemed to occur when first one, then another [of his parishioners], would become capable of revealing herself, himself, cautiously edging out from behind the disguises and make-up by which we all attempt to make ourselves respectable and acceptable in the world."[32]

When Peterson found his people unmoved by a study of Galatians, he set to work translating Paul's letter into the kind of street talk that he believes

31. Robert Jenson, "Joining the Eternal Conversation: John's Prologue & the Language of Worship," a lecture at the summer 2000 conference of the Center for Catholic and Evangelical Theology, at St. John's Abbey in Collegeville, Minnesota.

32. Eugene Peterson, *Eat This Book: A Conversation in the Art of Spiritual Reading* (Grand Rapids: Eerdmans, 2006), p. 132.

the common Greek of Paul to have been. His efforts were received with new interest and excitement, encouraging him in his teaching-translating task of rendering the whole Bible "into American for the congregation beyond my congregation."[33] Peterson embodies and demonstrates what every pastor as teacher must know, that is, the fundamental importance of the Bible for Christian prayer, theology, and practice. His product — *The Message* — and whether his paraphrase/translation of scripture got it right, is not the central matter here. What is important is his sustained and focused effort as a teacher of the church to find a language to communicate Christian truth to his parishioners. Pastors as teachers should be prepared for this kind of work: prepared to find the fitting language of pedagogy while appreciating the balance needed in corporate worship for the "iconic" language that Jenson urges. Teaching requires the use of a language that can open hearts and minds in the present, speaking in and through the prevailing culture.[34] The language of worship is intended to help create the true and substantively different culture of the church itself, for the church is a culture within and, in many ways, over against the prevailing culture in which it is embedded.

Christians have, since the earliest days, insisted on the translatability of Scripture. This is to say that Holy Scripture can be translated from what are called "original" languages into the vernacular of any tongue. It is the visitation of the Holy Spirit at Pentecost that is the undeniable center of this Christian impulse, that all may hear the Christian *kerygma* in their own tongue. Christians have a mandate to address a given culture at a given time in the language of that culture and time. Almost no Christian would think of this as problematic, much less as illegitimate.

Lamin Sanneh has written one of the best explorations of the

33. Peterson, *Eat This Book*, pp. 135-36.

34. One surprising discovery in a backward glance to late Anglo-Saxon pastoral practice (tenth-eleventh centuries) is the rather widespread liturgical use of the vernacular. "The common characteristic of the instances where the vernacular is found in a liturgical context is that they are direct addresses by a priest to an individual (not necessarily a layman) in circumstances in which it is critical that he understands what is happening." Helen Gittos, "Is There Any Evidence for the Liturgy of Parish Churches in Late Anglo-Saxon England? The Red Book of Darley and the Status of Old English," in Francesca Tinti, ed., *Pastoral Care in Late Anglo-Saxon England* (Rochester, NY: Boydell Press, 2005), pp. 79-80. F. Tinti writes in this same volume (p. 15) that "the vernacular was not considered as just a poor substitute of Latin in liturgy. . . . Pastoral aims might have had a part in such a development." This pre-Reformation and widespread use of the vernacular is at least noteworthy for our present concerns.

translatability of Christian scripture and its implications. Because of the willingness of Christians to use the vernacular, the Christian impulse to spread scripture and, therefore, Christian teaching, has "created a worldwide pluralist movement distinguished by the forces of radical pluralism and social destigmatization, spread out on a massive arc at the center of which mission placed the 'true and living God' of the disciples."[35] Recognizing the vernacular as a worthy medium for the transmission of the (Christian) message, Sanneh notes, is the strength of Christianity. The weakness of this is the multiple local manifestations of that message. This is why, as the church engages the surrounding culture in the vernacular and in the language of the cultural moment, teachers of the church must also draw those who are locally and immediately addressed into a different ecclesial culture in which the language of the church is clearly of a different order. To teach the faith requires of Christian teachers serious attention to content, creative use of contemporary language, and an ability to use that language to communicate the received and inherited faith.

A Way Forward

Where might the historical model of the pastor and teacher of the old Congregational order be informative today?

It models the iconic language of worship that belonged to the pastor and the more accessible language of the catechism fashioned, as Shepard and others sought to do, into a simpler yet biblical language. It also gives us visible signs of each office. When presiding at the table or leading worship, the pastor's robe is worn; when teaching the Word or proclaiming it, the teacher's robe is more appropriate. This is not to suggest that the pastor-teacher should be changing robes for each distinct act, but it does help the pastor to think symbolically and clearly about which task is being performed at a given time.[36] So the worship service has both pastoral and teaching aspects about which one should be conscious and intentional. The iconic language that ties the congregation to the great congregation that spans time

35. Lamin Sanneh, *Translating the Message: The Missionary Impact on Culture* (Maryknoll, NY: Orbis Books, 1989), p. 234.

36. It may also provide some relief from the current ecclesiastical fashion show in which clergy adopt all kinds of interesting, if essentially meaningless, clerical garments that do no more than suit their taste.

and space must be present. This iconic language reminds us that the Christian church is a distinct culture and a peculiar linguistic community. Visitors should feel that they have come into a very strange, new place. Some of the language of worship should make them uncomfortable and not-at-home, introducing them to the iconic language of ancient and otherwise forgotten times. Yet there also should be teaching that is accessible, that speaks, as good teachers must, to people of the present moment. Worship participates in the ancient and the timeless; teaching is more local and immediate. The Christian pastor-teacher is responsible for both functions.

It is worth thinking again about the Puritan teacher of the church whose job was to read scripture in Sabbath worship and to comment on it, that is, to teach it. There may be good liturgical and practical reasons not to do this, nor is it mandatory to put the Bible into "American," or common street language.[37] Still, inertia need not rule. Scripture already seems mysterious beyond relevance to many even in church. A pastor as teacher might, with care, open scripture to the people and teach it to them in worship. The English translation used, then, becomes less important as the teacher explains the Word while the people encounter it. The teacher must be aware of the assumed superior knowledge of the clergy in such arcane things as scripture and doctrine;[38] but Christian congregations are interested in the Bible and hunger for the Word, sensing they should know more about it, but often feeling unable to tackle Bible study on their own. Conversely, individual believers may feel *too confident* in their own ability to know all there is to know about scripture — its "plain sense," which may not be so plain after all. In this case, the teacher must bring to bear the insights of the ancient tradition, of the church Fathers, and something of the depth and breadth of interpretation and encounter that has characterized Christian experience across time. Private study of scripture, from the church's own experience, is not always a good idea. The Reformers, while insisting that each believer should

37. One of the largest Protestant churches in the Bangor, Maine, region is Calvary Chapel — a strikingly young congregation (though there are older people, too) with its own Christian school — in which the King James Version of the Bible is used exclusively. Many of the youth of the congregation not only study this version and quote large portions of it by memory, but also wear it on their belts as "God sword" (a play, of course, on "God's Word").

38. One would wish to avoid the unhappy division between the clergy and people in the days of the crumbling old Congregational order, characterized by Samuel Stone as "a speaking aristocracy (the clergy) in the face of a silent democracy (the congregation)." Von Rohr, *The Shaping of American Congregationalism*, p. 99.

have the Word in his or her native tongue, nevertheless also intended that the individual be grounded in the gathered body of the Christ, the church, and in the broadly agreed-upon teaching of the ancient councils and creeds. The Bible requires a community of understanding and of interpretation. The teacher is an important person in that community. The pastor must know when to put on the teacher's robe and what to say when wearing it.

Should the pastor teach in worship? Certainly. Philip Schaff wrote that "next to the Word of God, which stands in unapproachable majesty far above all human creeds and confessions, fathers and reformers, popes and councils, there are no religious books of greater practical importance and influence than catechisms, hymn books, and liturgies."[39] The Trinity is the distinctive of Christian faith and practice. All worship, all liturgy, should reflect the Trinity and invite all Christian believers into the eternal relationship of which the doctrine of the Trinity speaks. We pray to the Father with the Son in their Spirit.[40] Trinitarian liturgies, with their prayers, hymns, and the catechisms of the church, like the patristic theological project itself, have scripture as the "gravitational force" at their center.[41] By lack of pastoral teaching in worship, by pastoral avoidance of the biblical shape of theology, the gravitational center of liturgy has been de-energized and the people set adrift. The pastor must be a teacher and, in all these ways, must teach the church.

In the old Congregational order, under pressure from a growing emphasis on individual religious experience, personal (even private) piety, and a restless laity, much of church life was given over to lay committees. This lessened the bitter contentiousness that had developed between clergy and congregations in the Great Awakening, but it also did much to undermine the authority of faith and the importance of Christian doctrine. These had been the particular reserve of pastors and teachers and not of the laity, though laypersons were not without their own theological opinions. Certain of the laity — many in fact — were willing to break covenant on the basis of their personal theological conscience.

> As church goers came to place even greater value upon privacy and personal piety, church covenants and mutual watchfulness became far less

39. Philip Schaff, "The New Liturgy," in *Reformed and Catholic: Selected Historical and Theological Writings of Philip Schaff*, ed. Charles Yrigoyen Jr. and George M. Bricker (Pittsburgh: Pickwick Press, 1979).

40. Robert Jenson, in conversation.

41. R. R. Reno, "The Return of the Fathers," *First Things*, November 2006, p. 17.

> relevant, which further helps explain why, in churches throughout [the Massachusetts Bay] colony, ministers suffered so much difficulty in managing their congregations.[42]

While individualism and personalized religion[43] are still lively issues, there does seem to be a renewal of interest in tradition and in the peculiar culture of the Christian church. While congregations themselves have contributed to the loss of the integrated worldview that once shaped the education and mental habits of modern people in the West, parts of the church are beginning to appreciate the importance of doctrine and of the Bible and trinitarian doctrine that inform Christian systematic theology, pastoral theology, spiritual practices, and political theory. Central to this project is the pastor as teacher.

The work of the teacher must be central in worship and in study, in prayer, and in conversation. It is a "collective, multigenerational project."[44] The pastor as teacher must teach adults who then join the pastor-teacher in teaching the faith to others. The teaching and catechizing of adults, with all this implies about personal, face-to-face instruction, is a critical piece of the church's life that is in need of restoration. In this way, the church shapes the faith of individuals. The Reformers were correct to conclude that the Bible was not for isolated, individual believers, but was most profitably engaged within the congregation as a community of faith and interpretation.[45]

42. Cooper, *Tenacious of Their Liberties,* p. 206.

43. One thinks immediately of "Sheilaism," the private faith of Sheila Larson, reported in the study by Robert Bellah et al., *Habits of the Heart* (New York: Harper & Row, 1985), p. 221.

44. Reno, "The Return of the Fathers," p. 15.

45. Calvin taught that "the Church precedes the individual and not the other way around as has become so popular in contemporary spirituality. It is into the Church that we are brought by baptism and it is in the context of the Church that we grow up into Christ by use of the means of grace. . . . The Lord alone knows who are his. But that in no way lessens our obligation to be part of the visible Church since God has willed that she be our mother. . . . The Christian joins in the prayers of the people of God on the Lord's Day and in daily services in the Church. But by himself he is not at home praying. He is out in the world engaging in obedient ethical activity. To be sure that ethical activity is nourished and supported by his life in the Church; but as Abraham Kuyper has reminded us . . . Calvin had a total view of the necessity of self-consciously penetrating the domain of politics, science and art as well as the domain of religion." Howard G. Hageman, in *Protestant Spiritual Traditions,* ed. Frank C. Senn (New York: Paulist Press, 1986).

The pastor as teacher must have, by virtue of calling and education, particular care for the language of the church. The teaching of the church is intended to create a Christian worldview that penetrates politics, science, and art. The pastor as teacher must remain lashed to the mast of the Word.[46] The pastor as teacher must teach adults in personal encounter, in class study, in confirmation classes, in catechism, and in worship. The pastor as teacher must equip others to teach the faith of the holy catholic church, for the sanctification of those who are taught. It is to this work that the church calls its pastors. It is for this work that the church sets them apart.

The question for us is not whether the pastor will be teacher of the church. The question is: What faith will the pastor teach?

46. Another image from Eugene H. Peterson, in his *The Contemplative Pastor* (Grand Rapids: Eerdmans, 1993).

On Not Offering Psychological Banalities as God's Word: A Reformed Perspective on Pastoral Care

Cynthia A. Jarvis

A Pastoral Context

For six weeks, I had driven daily to the bedside of a young member of my congregation who was doing battle with his inevitable death at a university hospital. He had celebrated his thirty-second birthday on New Year's Day and, two weeks later, his death day arrived. In the scant three months since his diagnosis, I had become a minister to his geographically scattered family as they gathered in shifts to keep vigil night and day. Their alleged minister had also been a husband and a stepfather until he had left them to take up with the Christian educator a few years earlier. Each member of the family had a story to tell of the struggle back to faith and the church, stories recounted amid the morphine-induced sleep of a son and brother who was determined not to go gently into that good night.

My congregant and his family were all medical professionals of one stripe or another themselves. Not surprisingly, they were surrounded by the best medical team rank could pull together, and they were supported, as well, by colleagues and former classmates wanting to be of help. Furthermore, this incredibly erudite young man not only monitored every pill dispensed and I.V. bag hung, but also took to instructing the new residents as they made their rounds, praising them or correcting them on their bedside manner as though he were the attending. There were also the promised visits of a pastoral counselor to whom I had referred him when his wife announced her departure from the marriage a few months before his diagnosis. "We made sure to tell the counselor that we would pay her for her visits," one sister assured me, "because we know her time is valuable." As far as I know, she made one visit before the unpredictable balance of his wakefulness and deep sleep made the trips not worth a paid professional's while.

The point is that my congregant's condition was addressed clinically from every angle. Had I embraced the pastoral self-definition imposed and rejected long ago in Clinical Pastoral Education or had I perfected the pastoral responses taught in my post-sixties seminary classroom, then awash with sensitive Rogerian prompts, I would have been one in a long line of technically trained (with the emphasis on technique) professionals on the team around his bed. My part would have been to translate what he called "the issues" — edema, bowel obstructions, fluctuating white blood cell counts, nausea — into "feeling statements" offered back with scant comment. The conversations could have been a CPE supervisor's verbatim heaven.

I was, instead, his minister. As I said to him one day after he had listed the particular medical issues for the day, I was not much good at dealing with anything on that list, but might be of some help with the "God issues." He nodded and said, in what was now labored speech, "That's a plan. That's a good plan." Having been raised in strictly Presbyterian territory, he chose to die as he had lived: thoughtfully and with no excess of emotion. "Avoidance" would have been the analysis of my training: make him deal with his feelings about death! My Reformed theological instincts told me otherwise.

In the end, the God issues were issues that only briefly made it onto a list, for his pain began to demand more and more morphine. So now I made my daily pilgrimage simply to listen for the "sighs too deep for words" — not only his, but those of his family — and to offer in response the images and language of scripture (the 91st Psalm, for instance, on the day when he said he was being pushed off the edge of a cliff), the substance of the church's confessions (when the only comfort to be had, body and soul, in life and in death, was belonging to God), and the familiar lines of the church's hymns suggested by the angst of the moment. ("I want to sing 'The strife is o'er, the battle done,'" I said on one particularly pain-filled night. "Not yet!" he retorted as he refused to give in to death.) And I was there to pray, no matter his state of wakefulness or deep sleep. Though one time, when I thought he was politely saying I had stayed a little too long by suggesting that we pray, I took his hand and, before I could invoke God's name, he began to pray, simply and eloquently, a prayer of thanksgiving for friends by his side and far away.

To borrow the subtitle of John Leith's *The Reformed Imperative,* I was there to say what the church says that no one else can say. I was there as one who had learned in thirty years of pastoral ministry that "It is evident that they do not need us to help them live, but seem rather to need us to help them *die* . . . the whole reason that they come to us, strange as it may seem, for wisdom, is because they know the whole network of their life is hung upon a thread like gossamer. They suddenly awake to a realization that they are walking upon a ridge between *time* and *eternity* that is narrower than a knife-edge."[1]

Robert Coles made the same point long ago in *Harvard Diary: Reflections on the Sacred and the Secular.* In an essay titled "Psychiatric Stations of the Cross," Coles tells of a medical school classmate in a teaching hospital in Boston who had been diagnosed with a cancer that would eventually take him. The man had "always been a rather quiet and thoughtful person — a stoic temperamentally. But he is also a deeply religious man."[2] This was my congregant precisely, whose reading material while undergoing an extreme form of chemotherapy was Dietrich Bonhoeffer's *Ethics.* "When I came to see him," Coles writes of this encounter with his friend, "he was angry, and quite ready to tell me why. A priest had just come by, and indicated a strong interest in how the doctor/patient was managing to 'cope.' My friend said he was doing 'fine' the way (he assumed) any of us had the right to say 'fine.' . . . For the visiting clergyman, however, such asserted poise and reticence were not to be accepted at face value. The priest persisted in asking questions which, in sum, amounted to a relentless kind of psychological inquiry. How was the patient 'feeling'? How was his 'spirit'? How was he 'managing' in view of the stress he had to 'confront'? Did he want to 'talk about' what was happening?"[3] Though the direct questioning of a patient likely would have been critiqued in CPE from the standpoint of methodology, I offer Coles's account simply as evidence that this characterization of clinical pastoral training, pastoral counseling, pastoral care and its resultant technique, poorly or properly practiced, once had wider warrant than my own individual recollections.

According to Coles, his friend "had wanted to talk with the priest

1. Karl Barth, *The Word of God and the Word of Man* (Gloucester, MA: Peter Smith, 1978), p. 188.

2. Robert Coles, *Harvard Diary: Reflections on the Sacred and the Secular* (New York: Crossroad, 1988), p. 10.

3. Coles, *Harvard Diary,* p. 10.

about God and His ways, about Christ's life and death, about the Gospel of Luke (a particular favorite), about Heaven and Hell — only to be approached repeatedly with psychological words and phrases."[4] The underlying and unexamined anthropology of one trained in the practical art of active listening, or in the more tangible categories of so-called pastoral psychology, denies the central theological claim we are ordained to represent. Namely, the one to whose side we are summoned as Christian clergy is one who, first and foremost, has been addressed by God in Jesus Christ. Either we come to bear witness to a word not our own or we might as well not come at all. "He comes here with a Roman collar," roared Coles's dying friend, "and offers me psychological banalities as God's word!"[5]

Within the confines of this brief paper, and with only a distant academic grasp on the subject, I want to explore the distinctive understanding of pastoral care and the cure of souls rooted in the rich theological heritage of the Reformed tradition, a perspective that was, for the most part, eschewed for many years in favor of the professionalization of the ministry and its captivity to a culture of technique.

A Historical Context

In the recently translated 1923 lectures of Karl Barth on *The Theology of the Reformed Confessions,* the *Confessio Tetrapolitana* (1530) is explicated by Barth in such a way that it seems a fit, if obscure, beginning for naming the unique perspective of Reformed theology on the practice of pastoral care. Noting the subtle but significant distinction between the *Augustana Confession* and the *Tetrapolitana* as regards the doctrine of justification, Barth points out that the *Augustana* asks, "How shall I be saved?" whereas the *Tetrapolitana* asks, "Who saves me?"[6] Clearly the first question could imply a technical answer, albeit theological, as God and the church are confessed to be the significant actors in pulling off the "how." But if later the crack in the door swings our way, then the move simply shifts the means of our self-help from the institution to the individual. The *Tetrapolitana's* question presumes

4. Coles, *Harvard Diary,* pp. 10-11.

5. Coles, *Harvard Diary,* p. 11.

6. Karl Barth, *The Theology of the Reformed Confessions* (Louisville: Westminster/ John Knox Press, 2002), p. 72.

the initiative of God alone toward us and therefore leads with the theological and scriptural claims of faith.

Both battling the medieval church's peddling of the means of grace, the Lutheran and Reformed confessions differ, according to Barth, in that, "If the *Augustana* warns against false trust, the *Tetrapolitana* warns against false gods. The direction in which the polemical interest of the Reformed confession is to be sought is plain: *It battles Catholicism as an attempt at self-help,* and it sees in this desire to help oneself an arrogance and presumption that do not lead to the goal but rather are an insult to God and thus make genuine help impossible. For God desires to help. But he helps as the one who alone helps. To believe means to affirm that God alone is our helper."[7]

"That God alone is our helper" returns us to the first question of the more familiar Heidelberg Catechism, a question that serves as the theological bedrock for pastoral care in the Reformed tradition: "What is your only comfort in life and in death?"[8] The comfort is in the hand of the God "who protects me so well that without the will of my Father in heaven not a hair can fall from my head." Bracketing the further question of God's agency in the bad things that happen to sinful people, we may trace the emphasis on God's comfort and God's initiative toward humankind in love from Heidelberg through the pastoral intent of the doctrine of predestination in the Second Helvetic Confession and (with a little less comfort) the Westminster Confession of Faith to the ringing affirmation in the Confession of 1967 that we are to accept ourselves and love others "knowing that no one has any ground on which to stand except God's grace." From the beginning, then, Reformed theology reframed the question to which a distinctly different understanding of pastoral care was the response. Pastoral care was not interested in personal psychology or the internal state of an individual soul, but in turning the individual or the community toward the God who alone is our helper.

In the second place, Reformed pastoral care led with the word written, proclaimed, and explicated in the context of the public and personal lives of those in need of help. Prior to the Reformed movement, late medieval culture, according to David Cornick, was "intensely visual and tactile rather than cerebral."[9] Pilgrimages to shrines, pieces of relics (which according to

7. Barth, *The Theology of the Reformed Confessions,* p. 72.

8. The Heidelberg Catechism, 4.001, *The Book of Confessions* (Louisville: The Office of the General Assembly, 2007).

9. David Cornick, "The Reformation Crisis in Pastoral Care," in *A History of Pastoral Care,* ed. G. R. Evans (London: Cassell, 2002), p. 224.

Peter Brown replaced the pilgrimage to Rome with God's tangible dwelling in a village church), the sacraments that ordered a believer's life from birth to death, and supremely the repeated sacrifice of the Eucharist characterized popular piety. In addition, the ritual of confession wherein "the penitent was guided through a check-list of the seven deadly sins, the Ten Commandments, the five senses, the seven works of mercy, the seven gifts of the Spirit, the seven sacraments and the eight beatitudes"[10] offered an answer to the question of *how* a person could be forgiven and, ultimately saved. This was the self-help that only the church could dispense.

"This landscape," says Cornick, "was to be irrevocably changed by the reformations. As 'justification by faith alone' laid waste the penitential system, the whole panoply of confession and works of satisfaction fell into disrepair, for they were no longer needed. . . . The guts of popular religion had been surgically removed."[11] In their place was the church's preaching and teaching of the Word, the sacraments of the Lord's Supper and baptism and an understanding of pastoral care that began to raise up a flock seeking to understand and inhabit the narrative of salvation as put forth in scripture.

Not surprisingly, preaching for the first Reformers and for Ulrich Zwingli in particular, was pastoral care. In all of his writing, he says little directly about pastoral care, but rather subsumes all into the work of the preacher: "Preaching was not a rarified academic activity, although in [Zwingli's] eyes it demanded the very best of scholarship. Applying the Word of God to the life of God's people, indeed of God's world, was at its heart a pastoral activity, just as it was for the Old Testament prophets in whose works he delights. It was all of a piece — public, prophetic, private, consoling, broken into the multiplicity of the minister's work, baptizing, administering the sacraments, visiting the sick, caring for the poor from the Church's resources, but above all teaching."[12] That Zwingli began his ministry at the Grossmünster in Zurich with a *lectio continua* and so a sermon series lasting twelve years suggests that, by way of his preaching and teaching, he longed for his congregation to hear in the narrative of God's saving history the address of the God who alone is their help. That was the supreme care a pastor could give a people.

In addition, such an understanding of pastoral care also imposed a

10. Cornick, "The Reformation Crisis in Pastoral Care," p. 227.
11. Cornick, "The Reformation Crisis in Pastoral Care," pp. 227-28.
12. Cornick, "The Reformation Crisis in Pastoral Care," p. 236.

pastoral responsibility for the holiness or ethical dimension of a congregation's response to the gospel. This involved not only the personal but also the public lives of Christian witnesses. Zwingli believed the minister's work was not to be exhausted by preaching, for he must

> "prevent the washed sheep falling to the excrement, that is, after the believers have come into a knowledge of their savior and have experienced the friendly grace of God, they should hereafter lead a blameless life so that they no longer walk in death." . . . Sheep need a shepherd when they are in danger. So they are to defend their sheep from idolatry and unrighteousness, and "attack and destroy all buildings which have raised themselves against the heavenly Word," and do "eternal battle with the powerful and the vices of this world."[13]

Pastoral care was more than a private affair between minister and congregant and even more public than between minister and congregation. The care for the well-being of the flock required a preacher to do battle with the powerful of the world, even unto death! Zwingli also implied that the minister would do well to be on guard for such abuses of power, and so for idolatry (giving people a god who is not God as though they were being of help: psychological banalities instead of God's Word) within the church and among fellow clergy. Following the Johannine image of the good shepherd, Zwingli's Sixty-Seven Theses of 1523 warn against the Christlessness of the so-called clergy who would lead the flock to enter a door (such as church doctrines and tradition) other than Christ.[14]

Though the brevity of this paper will allow for only a cursory treatment of John Calvin, we can discern, through his pastoral practice, the distinctively Reformed character of the care he gave to the souls entrusted to him. As Jean Daniel Benoit observed, the Genevan Reformer "was a theologian in order to be a better pastor,"[15] or as Cornick put it, "he was a theologian only in so far as theology supported and grew out of his pastoral work."[16] From his life, we can glean that he was well acquainted with the brief and broken nature of human existence: the death of a wife and child,

13. Cornick, "The Reformation Crisis in Pastoral Care," p. 235.

14. Barth, *The Theology of the Reformed Confessions,* p. 73.

15. John T. McNeill, *A History of the Cure of Souls* (New York: Harper & Brothers, 1951), p. 198.

16. Cornick, "The Reformation Crisis in Pastoral Care," p. 240.

the unsuccessful marriages of stepchildren, the ruthless critique of a community, these human difficulties were known to him personally.[17] Yet his own life's circumstances drew no mention from his pen except as they could be presumed to be the personal crucible out of which the urgency of his preaching, teaching, and pastoral care were wrought.

Two aspects of his pastoral practice warrant mention as we catalogue the development of a Reformed understanding of pastoral care. The written record of his care and advice to his congregants was in the form of letters. In these we see that his counsel is deeply rooted in scripture. "First, he writes in an atmosphere totally impregnated by the Bible," says Benoit, "and assumes an intimate knowledge of it on the part of the receivers of his letters. Secondly, he continually urges the reading of, and meditation on, the Scriptures. Thirdly, he dwells upon the doctrinal points of his biblical faith, writing with a certitude that leaves no place for doubt."[18] Behind the assumption that his correspondents are as intimate with the biblical text as he, there is an understanding of pastoral care that, once again, rests upon the spadework of scriptural preaching and teaching. Only with that foundation can the church provide the rich and deep soil in which the Christian life may take root. Thus counsel from out of scripture is at the heart of the Reformed practice of pastoral care, not as literal moral injunction, but as the metaphor and narrative over which human beings trace the troubles and trials of their common life, so as to trust God's leading and discern life's meaning and purpose.

In the second place, Calvin's understanding of the pastoral relationship between minister and member, a relationship still reckoning with the Roman system of confession and penance, also underlines the ethical dimension of a distinctively Reformed understanding of pastoral care. Calvin understood himself as a "spiritual director" in the sense that he was a physician of the soul, called in at times of crisis rather than as a permanent guide: "He expect[ed] his patient to recover and normally to control his own health."[19] The advice he gave was not the advice that was meant to lead toward perfectionism, but was "'advice that tends' to Christian living."[20] McNeill cites Hermann Strothmann in suggesting that Calvin's pastoral work with souls involved him in the process of moral transformation and re-

17. Cornick, "The Reformation Crisis in Pastoral Care," p. 240.

18. McNeill, *A History of the Cure of Souls,* p. 209.

19. McNeill, *A History of the Cure of Souls,* p. 200.

20. McNeill, *A History of the Cure of Souls,* p. 200.

newal.[21] Not the inner psychological workings of an individual's personal life, but the outward response of a forgiven Christian in the world was what engaged Calvin's pastoral practice and theological reflection. Hence he was less interested in "the retrospective of sin" and more taken by the "transformation of repentance."[22] This is why, when asked for spiritual direction, a Reformed minister will often suggest a night spent with the homeless or a day given to feeding the hungry rather than signing up for a prayer retreat or taking a labyrinthine walk.

No examination of the distinctive practice of pastoral care in the Reformed tradition would be complete without attention to the author of *The Reformed Pastor.* Richard Baxter's little treatise, written to his pastoral colleagues some 350 years ago, is still read today. According to Andrew Purvis (commenting from the perspective of today's Reformed pastor who believes a minister's job encompasses five days a week — or less if one is to be compensated in time off for attendance at evening meetings), Baxter's method of pastoral care "appears to be an exercise in compulsive overwork and a recipe for exhaustion."[23] Yet the most salient observation of Purvis in relation to this study is that we are given, in Baxter's writing, not "pastoral technique skillfully applied," but rather the application of "a spiritual and theological understanding of human beings to the work of pastoral ministry, which begins with the continuing conversion of the pastor and leads to the conversion of the parishioner."[24]

Theologically, Baxter was an admixture of Roman, Reformed, and especially Arminian influences,[25] believing that though salvation had been accomplished in Jesus Christ, the faith of the convert remains a condition and so a necessary aspect of imputed righteousness. Out of this, he developed a doctrine of continuous justification and a somewhat Pelagian spirit as regards moral effort[26] — both on the part of the pastor as well as the parishioner. From these theological premises, his pastoral work followed: continuous visitation! He is best known for his rigorous schedule of calling on families in his parish. He and his "faithful unwearied Assistant" personally called

21. McNeill, *A History of the Cure of Souls,* p. 198.

22. McNeill, *A History of the Cure of Souls,* p. 198.

23. Andrew Purvis, *Pastoral Theology in the Classical Tradition* (Louisville: Westminster/John Knox Press, 2001), p. 95.

24. Purvis, *Pastoral Theology,* p. 105.

25. Purvis, *Pastoral Theology,* p. 102.

26. Purvis, *Pastoral Theology,* p. 110.

upon eight hundred families numbering about four thousand people once a year while envying his colleagues in smaller parishes who could visit once a quarter! Yet it is the content of those visits that should both interest and instruct us in our present ecclesial malaise.

While he no doubt befriended and gave comfort to his people, his primary concern was that their faith would grow in understanding to the end that they would know themselves as persons who must stand before God. "Baxter reminds us that trying to bring comfort in the midst of life's tragedies but failing to address a person's life in and before God is no care at all."[27] He, therefore, became a teaching elder in the most demanding sense of that office, an office renamed in Reformed circles today to the detriment of our distinctive Reformed pastoral self-understanding. While many Reformed ministers may not share the theological perspective that propelled Baxter into his parishioners' homes, nevertheless we would do well to imitate the catechetical thrust of his calling.

In addition, Baxter's admonition concerning regular pastoral visitation was aimed not only at his colleagues' slothful practice of the same, but also at the church's understanding of the pastoral office.

> Little do they know that the minister is in the church, as the schoolmaster in his school, to teach and to take an account of every one in particular, and that all Christians, ordinarily, must be disciples or scholars in some such school. . . . They consider not, that all souls in the congregation are bound, for their own safety, to have personal recourse to him, for the resolving of their doubts, and for help against their sins, and for direction in duty, and for increase of knowledge and all saving grace; and that ministers are purposely settled in congregations to this end, to be still ready to advise and help the flock.[28]

As though he were writing of pastoral practice today, he notes that most church members commonly think a minister exists to preach, to administer the sacraments, and to visit them in sickness. In these times, the misconception is not always the fault of the minister, but often the result of a person's casual commitment to the community of faith. Yet even this

27. Purvis, *Pastoral Theology*, p. 110.

28. Richard Baxter, *The Reformed Pastor* (Edinburgh: The Banner of Truth Trust, 1974), p. 181.

Baxter traces to poor pastoral visitation. His own visitation resulted in a church so crowded on Sunday mornings that an addition had to be built to accommodate the well-over one thousand souls for whom worship became a habit. This should offer itself not as a technique to be added to church growth seminars, but a starting point for the *substantive* renewal of a theological tradition and a pastoral office marked, historically, by a faith that seeks understanding.

Baxter enjoins the regular visitation of families for instruction and care within a church whose ministers had apparently quit this discipline in favor of time misspent "in unnecessary discourse, business, journeys or recreations. It will let them see that they have no time to spare for such things; and thus, when they are engaged in so much pressing employment of so high a nature, it will be the best cure for all that idleness, and loss of time."[29] Even more to the point of the church's current woes, "It will be some benefit, that by this means we shall take off ourselves and our people from vain controversies, and from expending our care and zeal on the lesser matters of religion, which least tend to their spiritual edification[!]"[30]

Finally, underlying all that he would have ministers do, Baxter's most pressing concern is the faith of the minister. As Purvis notes, "Baxter's unambiguous conviction concerning the conversion and spiritual renewal of the pastor can hardly be overemphasized, for that emphasis is rarely found today in much pastoral theology literature. Today the focus is more likely to fall on the pastor's mental health,"[31] a focus recast presently in the church's uncritical embrace of cultural spirituality and the "how" of spiritual technique. Baxter speaks rather of the minister's own growth in understanding, emphasizing theology in the service of pastoral practice. Clearly the point of a pastor's biblical and theological study is the strengthening of faith, which in turn will strengthen the faith of the flock.

> O what sadder case can there be in the world, than for a man, who made it his very trade and calling to proclaim salvation, and to help others to heaven, yet after all to be himself shut out! Alas! that we should have so many books in our libraries which tell us the way to heaven; that we should spend so many years in reading these books,

29. Baxter, *The Reformed Pastor*, pp. 186-87.
30. Baxter, *The Reformed Pastor*, p. 187.
31. Purvis, *Pastoral Theology*, pp. 105-6.

> and studying the doctrine of eternal life, and after all this to miss it! . . . And all because we preached so many sermons of Christ, while we neglected him; of the Spirit, while we resisted him; of faith while we did not ourselves believe.[32]

From Baxter, we jump almost three centuries to Dietrich Bonhoeffer. The subject of the faith of the minister appears also in a series of lectures given at Finkenwalde, one of the seminaries of the Confessing Church, between 1935 and 1940. Bonhoeffer's own reflections on the understanding and practice of pastoral care were published under the title *Spiritual Care.* In an introduction to *Spiritual Care,* Jay Rochelle pointedly observes that "Unlike the traditional preachers' seminaries, in which only the practical aspects of ministry were taught in a technical-school setting, Bonhoeffer wrestled theologically with his students in order that they might confront the impact of the theology of the Word on pastoral work."[33]

Given this starting point and, I daresay, the socio-political context of doing theology at that time in history, Bonhoeffer directly dismisses the role of psychology in the training and practice of pastoral care. For the pastor, the parishioner is "a sinner whom God's mercy wants to encounter. That is the difference between spiritual care and psychotherapy, for which the method of investigation is all-important. Spiritual care puts no stock in such methods. There are no 'psychologically interesting cases' for spiritual care. . . . The pastor remains fundamentally pre-methodological and pre-psychological, in the best sense, naïve."[34]

Rather, the very delicate representation of law and gospel in the minister's encounter with the person estranged from or indifferent to God takes us on a different tack. Spiritual care begins with "bringing to speech" the point at which a person has become indifferent to God's Word. This is the grace of personal confession, which frees us from ourselves and for discipleship, taking up Calvin's interest in the transformation of forgiveness rather than the retrospective of sin. The counsel given includes counsel toward discipline and practice, scripture and prayer, forgiveness and then "the risk of a decision."[35] Though the pastor bears the other person's sin and struggle, the

32. Baxter, *The Reformed Pastor,* p. 72.
33. Dietrich Bonhoeffer, *Spiritual Care* (Philadelphia: Fortress Press, 1985), pp. 7-8.
34. Bonhoeffer, *Spiritual Care,* p. 36.
35. Bonhoeffer, *Spiritual Care,* p. 42.

other is set free for the possibility of obedience and of a renewed relationship with the God whose service is in the world.

To put this another way, for Bonhoeffer the office of Word and sacrament becomes personal address in spiritual care, "announcing that the search for God has been ended — in the Word which was effective in creation, now become incarnate in Jesus the Christ."[36] Yet this announcement, notes Jay Rochelle as he draws out the implications of Bonhoeffer's spiritual care for our day, takes place within the context of the community of faith, thereby differing both from psychological counseling and from pastoral counseling centers that function as a community service.[37] More significantly, spiritual care is not an end in itself, but "is aimed at freeing persons for service to God and world through their apprehension of the many dimensions of faith. It is aimed toward faith active in love."[38]

Perhaps the most powerful explication of the goal of spiritual care in the life of the individual, the church, and the world is to be found in the *Letters and Papers from Prison* where Bonhoeffer writes of *metanoia* on the day after the unsuccessful attempt on Hitler's life:

> I discovered later, and I'm still discovering right up to this moment, that it is only by living completely in this world that one learns to have faith. One must completely abandon any attempt to make something of oneself, whether it be a saint, or a converted sinner, or a churchman (a so-called priestly type!), a righteous man or an unrighteous one. By this-worldliness I mean living unreservedly in life's duties, problems, successes and failures, experiences and perplexities. In so doing we throw ourselves completely into the arms of God, taking seriously, not our own sufferings, but those of God in the world — watching with Christ in Gethsemane. That, I think, is faith; that is *metanoia.*[39]

When this is read through his earlier reflections on spiritual care, we can conclude that for Bonhoeffer, the goal of such care is a community thrown into the arms of God that lives for others and takes *God's* suffering in the world as their cue for action. At the end, Bonhoeffer clearly is speaking

36. Bonhoeffer, *Spiritual Care,* p. 23.

37. Bonhoeffer, *Spiritual Care,* p. 23.

38. Bonhoeffer, *Spiritual Care,* p. 23.

39. Dietrich Bonhoeffer, *Letters and Papers from Prison* (New York: Macmillan, 1972), pp. 369-70.

not only of nurturing such faith in those given into a pastor's care, but of the faith of the pastor.

Hence at the end of these lectures to his seminarians in Finkenwalde, Bonhoeffer acknowledges that those who have been called to exercise spiritual care also live in the greatest need of spiritual care themselves:

> Whoever takes the office seriously must cry out under the burden. One has to make visits, listen to and bear the needs and sorrows of many people, one has to carry on numerous conversations with those one accompanies on life's way and always with those who encroach on one's time. . . . One has to find the right word with the dying, at the graveside, for a wedding. One should — and here is the heaviest responsibility of all — preach out of genuine certitude in order that others are led to certitude. . . . The mission is huge and our skills are small.[40]

Here he counsels prayer, but he counsels more. For at the end of the day, the "greatest difficulty for the pastor stems from his theology. He knows all there is to be known about sin and forgiveness. He knows what the faith is and he talks about it so much that he winds up no longer living in faith but in thinking *about* faith."[41] One can but read what follows from the perspective of the end of Bonhoeffer's own life. Since Reformed ministers live so much in their heads, the danger is that faith becomes an abstract reflection upon a leap we have never taken personally.

Reaffirming that our mission is not to preach our experience but from scripture, he still insists that the gospel cannot be proclaimed with integrity when our own experience "lags so far behind the Word." The concern was not an idle one for a German pastor in the 1930s. No doubt Bonhoeffer had reason to believe that, when theology becomes an academic exercise, it can be easily used toward evil ends. If the minister is living at a remove from the risk of faith in the world, Satan is not and, according to Bonhoeffer, is a great theologian: "He keeps your understanding three steps removed from your body."[42]

The spiritual care he recommends for pastors in this situation is congruent with the care he has instructed them to give their flocks. Bonhoeffer's

40. Bonhoeffer, *Spiritual Care,* p. 67.
41. Bonhoeffer, *Spiritual Care,* pp. 67-68.
42. Bonhoeffer, *Spiritual Care,* p. 68.

final thoughts on the spiritual care of ministers will leave us only to offer some final reflections on the practice of pastoral care in our times:

> The only help is to call a person to the simplest things of Scripture, prayer, confession, and to concrete obedience in one definite matter. . . . The life of the pastor completes itself in reading, meditation, prayer and struggle. The means is the word of Scripture with which everything begins and to which everything returns. We read Scripture so that our hearts may be moved. It will lead us into prayer . . . which leads us into the world in which we must keep the faith. Where Scripture, prayer, and keeping the faith exist, temptation will always find its way in. Temptation is the sign that our hearing, prayer, and faith have touched down in reality.[43]

A Pastor's Context

What distinct hope do ministers have to offer those who seek our help because "they are walking upon a ridge between *time* and *eternity* that is narrower than a knife-edge"? What is it that we have to say in our postmodern, pluralistic, multicultural world that no one else can say? What may we reclaim from out of our theological tradition that will be of help to people that need our help in order to die that they may truly live?

In the first place, I think that we, who also are dying and are in need of help, will be given the help we need only as we do business, throughout our lives, with the substance of the faith for ourselves. As we have ceased wrestling with that substance, we have grown ashamed of the gospel in the sense that we are no longer able thoughtfully to articulate the complexity of the Christian claim in the midst of this pluralistic age. As we have allowed all the other demands of running an institution to crowd in, we have quit the discipline required to plumb the depths and dare the heights of scripture, and so cannot compellingly present the meaning of the biblical narrative for our day in the pulpit or the classroom or the hospital room. Once the door has been shut leading out of any formal theological education, too many of us try to make do on the little theology grudgingly read in the classroom. We have little to offer of help because we are running on empty!

43. Bonhoeffer, *Spiritual Care*, pp. 68-69.

As all of our Reformed forebears knew, pastoral care begins in the study leading to the pulpit, the font, the table, and only then to the home, the hospital, the office. In an oft-quoted sentence that has to do not only with preaching, but with the renewal of the practice of pastoral care, John Leith reminds us that, "The renewal of the church will come with the recovery of the sermon that is not moral advice or political rhetoric or personal therapy or entertainment but the means of God's grace to forgive and to sanctify, to heal and to fortify human hearts for the great crises and challenges of life."[44] We will only be able to preach such sermons as we renew our minds and our hearts through the disciplined study of scripture, a lively engagement with the substance of our theological tradition, and a seeking of the means of grace for the nurture and enlivening of our own faith. We need to reclaim the space and the time that has been given to "unnecessary discourse, business, journeys or recreation" for the sake of acquainting ourselves anew with the substance of God's grace to forgive and to sanctify, to heal and to fortify the human hearts given into our care.

In the second place, I believe pastoral care that offers the help people really need, which is to say introduces them to the God who is their only comfort, body and soul, in life and in death, rests on the nurture of a biblically literate congregation. Zwingli preached through the biblical narrative from his pulpit in Zurich. Calvin wrote letters to those under his care that were rich in biblical instruction. Richard Baxter organized his week around catechetical visits to parishioners who seemingly were as ignorant of scripture as most postmodern congregations. Bonhoeffer viewed all of life's duties, problems, successes and failures, experiences and perplexities as the occasion for minister and parishioner to throw themselves into the arms of the God made known through scripture.

We need to rethink how and where we tell the story of God's renovation of the world to the generation of our peers and, in turn, to their children and their children's children. What are the realistic means at hand that would allow us to sustain an adult's attention such that, at the end of a year or two or three, we could talk the same language, invoke the parables as stories that lend meaning to our own, offer the images of a psalm to name the rage or the sorrow or the deep joy that connects us with the depths of our human existence before God?

44. John H. Leith, *The Reformed Imperative: What the Church Has to Say That No One Else Can Say* (Philadelphia: Westminster Press, 1988), p. 23.

Finally, we need to wake to the urgency of our calling. What has been entrusted to us is the news that those who come to us "on the knife-edge" have been addressed by God in Jesus Christ. If we do not know the knife-edge ourselves, if we do not listen to our own crying out of the burden of the care we cannot give, then we will have missed the strange coincidence between those called out to speak of God's faithfulness and salvation and those left to wonder in the dark alone on Sunday night. We have been given to one another in Christ's church that we might together ask after our only comfort. "Those who do not ask," writes Karl Barth to theological students in Göttingen, "who do not ask very radically what is their one and only comfort in life and death, must be told to their faces that they also do not believe. Believers are not secure people. They are those who first know what questioning means. To be rid of the questioning is to be rid of revelation and not to be addressed by God, or to be addressed by him no longer."[45]

Therefore, at the prospect of the care I am to give, the word I am to speak, I am haunted by Graham Greene's whiskey priest who, on the way to jail, is asked by the policeman if he were hoping for a miracle. "No," he answers. "You believe in them, don't you?" "Yes," says the whiskey priest. "But not for me."[46] I am accompanied to the hospital bed by Georges Bernanos's country priest who cried out, "Oh miracle — thus to be able to give what we ourselves do not possess — sweet miracle of our empty hands! Hope which was shriveling in my heart flowered again in her; the spirit of prayer which I lost in me forever was given back to her by God. . . . Lord, I was stripped bare of all things as you alone can strip us bear, whose fearful care nothing escapes nor your terrible love!"[47] Finally, I am bowed down by the psalmist whose words were written on my heart by my colleague of many years, "I have told the glad news of deliverance in the congregation, lo I have not restrained my lips, as Thou alone knowest. . . . I have not concealed Thy steadfast love and Thy faithfulness from the great congregation. Do not thou O Lord withhold Thy mercy from me, let Thy steadfast love and Thy faithfulness ever preserve me" (Ps. 121:9-11).

45. Karl Barth, *Göttingen Dogmatics: Instruction in the Christian Religion,* vol. 1 (Grand Rapids: Eerdmans, 1990), p. 86.

46. Graham Greene, *The Power and the Glory* (New York: Bantam Books, 1967), p. 190.

47. Georges Bernanos, *The Diary of a Country Priest* (New York: Carroll & Graf, 2002), p. 180.

The Theological Significance of Administration in the Pastoral Ministry

Thomas W. Currie III

So teach us to number our days that we may get a heart of wisdom.

Psalm 90:12

The minister's task of administration has more to do with theology than one might think, and even more to do with that form of love that animates the body of Christ. To the extent that the task of administration is conceived simply in terms of managing the minister's time — that is, how to produce lessons, sermons, and talks, maintain the church's schedule, budget hours for counseling, hospital calling, visitation, and the work of various committees while still reserving time for one's own reading and renewal — to the extent that this is what is meant by "administration," the task, though not unimportant, is not very interesting or evangelically significant. The temptation, of course, is twofold: either the administrative task of the church is taken too seriously and tempts ministers to become such excellent managers of their time that they come to confuse managerial efficiency with faithfulness to the gospel; or, alternatively, the administrative task of the church is not taken seriously enough, and ministers are tempted to dismiss its demands as somehow beneath their best efforts when compared to preparation for proclaiming and teaching the Word, or engaging in pastoral care. This latter form of temptation is more romantic than the former but is equally as lethal.

The reason the administrative task of the church is of theological significance is that the work of ministry (and the time required for such work) is undertaken for the sake and in the name of Jesus Christ, whose kingdom is not one of confusion or disorder but of peace (1 Cor. 14:33). The grace that orders the love of God for sinners seeks some correspondence in our life together that will reflect and even magnify the peace that is ours in Jesus Christ. This means that the questions of administration, though often small, are rarely trivial, dealing as they do with the mission of the church and the relative priorities that mission lays out. Accordingly, the administrative task encompasses the working relations between redeemed sinners who are called to life in Christ, and the sometimes quite urgent matters that demand the minister's energy and attention, not to mention the equipping of those same fallen and redeemed saints for the work of ministry. As all disciples are daily compelled to do when looking at the "messiness" that constitutes so much of the church's life together, the minister has to ask the simple question, "What comes first?" and has always to keep in mind, "What is the end for which the ministry of the church is undertaken?"

What comes first? In 1933, Karl Barth wrote an essay titled, "The First Commandment as a Theological Axiom."[1] This essay, written against the background of the Nazi rise to power in Germany, asked the question as to what comes first in the church's life and witness. For Barth, the focus at that time was on "Natural Theology" and the temptation before the church to order its own life and work in terms laid down by another source of revelation than Jesus Christ, in this case, the Third Reich. The latter realm also possessed a "peace" and even an "order," and was, by all accounts, surpassingly efficient. In some ways, the question could have been described as merely administrative: Which order? Which peace? What comes first? Can we have both? Need we choose? Yet, such questions, though filled with administrative detail and practical concerns, were in fact deeply theological in nature. The questions underneath these questions asked, "Who is Lord?" and "What is the ordering of life together that is required in service to this Lord?"

Admittedly, church administration would hardly seem to raise such explosive issues today. But in truth, unless the minister is clear about "what comes first," her administrative work will assume a kind of neutral self-evidence that will accommodate a culture only too eager to number our days

1. Cf. Karl Barth, "Das Erste Gebot als Theologisches Axiom," in *Theologische Fragen und Antworten* (Zollikon: Evangelischer Verlag AG, 1957), pp. 127-43.

and determine the church's end. Management theory is well stocked with its own acolytes. Without a clear understanding of the church's mission and purpose, the administrative task will simply become yet another form of self-justification, another way of seeking to save our lives by becoming useful to this or that self-chosen end.

The administrative task of the minister involves the apportionment of time and work, and so the daily decision as to what is of first importance. Just as church budgets are best understood as theological documents, reflecting all too clearly the theological priorities of the congregation, so the minister's practice of administration reflects her own theological priorities. Therefore the question as to what comes first in the ministry of the church ought not, and indeed cannot, be avoided.

One might begin simply by asking what comes first each day. What comes first in the minister's own work?

Just as nothing reveals the wealth or impoverishment of our lives so much as the way in which we spend our leisure time, so nothing reveals the depth of one's theological convictions so much as the way in which one's day is ordered. Dietrich Bonhoeffer divided his meditation on the church's ministry[2] in the following way: Community, The Day with Others, The Day Alone, Ministry, and Confession and Communion. It is clear that he thought the administrative task of the pastor was for the sake of the church's life and ministry, but rather than describing that task in terms of management theory, he simply speaks of the "day" that God gives us to worship and work. As such, Bonhoeffer thinks first of the community for the sake of whose life together ministry is undertaken and whose ordering is not a function of the minister's own agenda, goals, or self-understanding. The ordering of this community, Bonhoeffer thinks, is Christological in its form and foundation. "I have community with others and I shall continue to have it only through Jesus Christ. The more genuine and the deeper our community becomes, the more will everything else between us recede, the more clearly and purely Jesus Christ and his work become the one and only thing that is vital between us."[3] In this sense, the administrative task of the church is something we receive, not something we contrive, an ordering into which we enter and work, not a system we put in place.

So how is that ordering expressed in the work of ministry, and how

2. Dietrich Bonhoeffer, *Life Together* (New York: Harper & Brothers, 1954).

3. Bonhoeffer, *Life Together,* pp. 25, 26.

does one go about entering it? The day begins. How does the minister's day begin? Given that the church lives in time, and we are invited to minister as human, time-bound servants, how do we begin? Where do we begin?

The minister's administrative work begins with the reading of scripture and prayer. This is not a pious admonition. It is simply the place where one begins if one is undertaking the task of ordering the day's work of Christian ministry. Beginning with the reading of scripture and prayer makes clear that the work of ministry is both impossible and vital, a gift and a task we enter into. This is not a new insight. Bonhoeffer himself reminded his seminary students at Finkenwalde that life in service to the Word always "begins with common worship at the beginning of the day."[4] It has only been fairly recently that ministry has been thought of in other terms, e.g., as a managerial task requiring the efficient use of time and the adroit negotiation of competing needs and agendas. "*Ora et Labora*" was the motto of the Benedictines, with *Ora* being understood as the most important form of *Labora*, and *Labora* being offered as the body's form of *Ora*. And though it may seem contrived, when ministers deliberately begin the day with the reading of scripture and prayer, they bear witness to the reality that they are a part of a long story whose plot and narrative center upon Another, whose claims take precedence over our agendas however full they may seem, and whose promise draws us into the work of Jesus Christ and his ministry. That is the story scripture tells and prayer confesses, the ordering and even peace that the minister acknowledges at the beginning. Anything else would be a contrivance.

So what kind of prayer? In twenty-five years of pastoral ministry, I never thought of myself as a great pray-er. In some ways, beginning in this way represented for me a great challenge. It was hard. I often felt stupid. My prayers did not seem worth answering or even attending to, and I often wondered whether God was as bored with them as I found them difficult to voice.[5] No matter. We are not called to be proficient at prayer but simply to persist in it, "to pray always and not lose heart" (Luke 18:1, and of

4. Bonhoeffer, *Life Together*, p. 42. "Common life under the Word begins with common worship at the beginning of the day. . . . The Scriptures, moreover, tell us that the first thought and the first word of the day belong to God."

5. In David James Duncan's novel, *The Brothers K* (New York: Bantam Books, 1996), p. 150, a book that has a great deal to do with prayer, he cites Tom Crawford as opining, "If I were God, I wouldn't answer my prayers either." This is a sentiment whose force I have often felt.

course, also v. 8b: "And yet, when the Son of Man comes, will he find faith on earth?").

The day begins and the work is organized by our asking. Petition is the heart of the minister's prayer — for the work of the church, for his work, for his family, marriage, children, for the needs of others, for the community, for near and distant neighbors, for her enemies, for her friends, for forgiveness, for joy, for the strength "not to lose heart," etc. — but just so, such asking bears witness to the grace and gratitude upon which all ministry is ventured. Yet such asking is hard, which is why it has so little to offer as a management technique. To ask is to admit one needs help. To ask is to confess that the way ahead is not clear, even that it is dark. To ask is to be put in the position of a supplicant, not a very dignified or responsible position to assume. Indeed, such a position, especially given the administrative expertise that is marketed both within and without the church today, is embarrassing. Yet just so does our embarrassment remind us of the impossible, not to say mysterious, miracle which is ministry. If the minister's administrative work does not begin with prayer, he or she might be tempted to think that ministry is possible, and from there, it is only a small jump to thinking that it is something that can be "managed" and even "achieved" by successful practitioners of this technique or that. It is true that ministry can benefit by the hard work of strategic planning and the real insights from the social sciences, but neither of these sources of wisdom can ever be allowed to define the work of ministry or its administrative tasks. Most ministry is messy and impossible, which is why its administrative work begins with asking for help, resisting any scheme that promises some easier way, especially a way of avoiding the mystery and the disciplines of the cross.

The day begins with prayer, but it proceeds with reading. If the administrative task of the minister begins, in some sense, in conversation with God, and to that extent, in the recognition that the ordering of ministry is an entering into Christ's work, then one continues that conversation with those who have and are reflecting on that work in the world. The first hour of the minister's day is to be given to reading. This reading may bear directly on the minister's work of sermon preparation or it may not. Or it may do so only indirectly. Here, however, the conversation is broad; and in truth, all roads, no matter how trivial or trashy, lead to the enriching of the minister's understanding of "what comes first." Reading is the kind of *Labora* that *Ora* intends. Unless the minister reads, daily, his ministry will be at risk of extending no wider or deeper than his own experience. Ministers are subject to all manner of sinful temptations, but being boring (i.e., self-absorbed) in the proclamation of the gospel is a sin against the Holy Spirit. Reading stretches the minister's imagination and enables her to enter into that great conversation God's people have conducted throughout history under the Spirit's guidance, a conversation that gives us words to describe the mystery and joy and gratitude that faith believes and is called upon to voice.

One need not read only works of piety or even works of piety at all. Nevertheless the minister should understand that if administration is for the sake of Christ's church, the most administratively effective work of reading will be in theology (broadly conceived) and biblical studies (again, broadly conceived), and in the works of imagination and creativity that enrich and reflect upon the church's calling to bear witness to the grace of God in Jesus Christ. Apart from prayer, the most significant administratively important work the minister can do is to study and read.

If the day begins quietly, it moves toward and even embraces the clamorous messiness of the church's life. It is not self-evident, much less biblically or theologically clear, how that messiness is to be brought into some sort of order. Perhaps, the Gospels offer some comfort at this point in their depiction of Jesus' ministry. Though there is a discernible pattern in their narratives, disconcertingly leading to the cross(!), their relating of Jesus' public ministry reveals Jesus in a variety of contexts in which his preaching, teaching, and doing works of healing are scattered among crowds of folk, individuals, children, family, opponents, and others who press various claims upon him with varying degrees of urgency. It is clear that his path is towards the cross; it is clear that he commits to work with disciples early on, and that teaching and preaching to them and to others and sharing table fellowship with them has a high priority for him; but it is not clear that his ministry is guided by any discernible administrative or managerial technique. He "went about doing good." His public ministry was largely peripatetic, though it did involve regular trips to Jerusalem. Luke tells us that he went to the synagogue on the Sabbath day "as was his habit" (Luke 4:16), a not insignificant clue to the ordering of his days.

Another aspect of his ministry seems to be his propensity to have time for others. The Jesus depicted in the Gospels is not the "quivering mass of availability" that Stanley Hauerwas scorns. He seems to be a person to whom those in need might dare to cry out, one who could be easily engaged in conversation, even interrupted, with some pressing appeal. He does not seem, in other words, to be too busy for such folk. Moreover, despite Bruce Barton's contention that Jesus' work of ministry evidenced remarkable business skills,[6] his preaching, his teaching, his healing miracles, his organizing and sending of the twelve, his visits to "un-kosher" places (e.g., Samaria, the Decapolis, etc.) seem less a matter of managerial genius than a way of exhibiting the strange world of the kingdom whose king would eventually rule from the cross. That is how he "organizes" things.

Perhaps a more helpful biblical guide here is Paul. Paul's letters are full of what might be called the minutiae of administrative work. Nearly all of his letters either respond to or set out how certain matters are to be ordered, whether it concerns eating meat offered to idols or when and how to celebrate communion or how Jewish and Gentile Christians are to live together. To be sure, these are often theological or ethical questions as well, but it would be a mistake not to see their administrative import. How often, for example, does Paul talk about taking up an offering for the saints in Jerusalem? How often does he relate his schedule to his readers, even exhorting them to receive Timothy or some other co-worker? How often does he deal with what we might call "people problems," i.e., "how we are to live together"? Nothing seems too small for Paul to consider as part of the life of Christ's people.

It is impossible to recommend a universally valid schedule for the administrative work of ministry. It all depends. Paul's congregations in Corinth and Philippi and Thessalonica, to name but three, had very different concerns, faced very different problems, and required different kinds of attention and administrative ordering. One might understand the administrative task of the minister better, I think, if one conceives of her work in terms of the rhythm of the church's life, paying attention to the ecclesiastical year and the ordering it brings, and paying even more attention to the rhythm of the church's week. Much of the administrative ordering of the minister's work flows from the centrality of worship on Sunday. The Lord's Day requires preparation. Accordingly, much time must be set aside *first* for the preparation of that day, not just in terms of music or bulletin information or even liturgy, though all of these are important, but especially in terms of sermon preparation and writing.

The Word proclaimed calls into being the life of the community, and that life requires attention and care. The body of Christ is not a vague or smoky thing, but a body whose members grow sick, die, suffer want, become

6. Cf. Bruce Barton, *The Man Nobody Knows* (Indianapolis: Bobbs-Merrill, 1925).

dislocated, grieve, etc. The "cure of souls" requires not just time but planned and designated time.

Every minister is also a teacher. Teaching too requires planning and preparation. Congregations need to see their pastors teaching regularly, in part to see them as interpreters of the Word (and therefore in some sense responsible for and to it) but also to be able to respond and even question and converse with them.

Eugene Peterson has argued that ministers should concentrate on preaching and teaching, leaving all other matters (e.g., the budget and stewardship matters) in the hands of the session or church council.[7] That strikes me as more than a little romantic, and perhaps even a bit docetic. The administrative task of the pastor extends, I believe, to knowing what the giving patterns in his congregation are like, what financial needs and challenges the congregation faces, and what resources and people can be called upon to help the community meet those needs and challenges. That means meetings and time. This is not the most important thing, but it is far from being the least important. It is hard and often energy draining and time consuming. Still, unless this work is embraced by the minister, his own ministry will become entirely too "spiritual" and not nearly as intimate as it needs to be. Life is in the minutiae, in the details, as is much of ministry.

But a more important reason for embracing the administrative challenge here and elsewhere is that the pastor's administrative work is for the sake of the church's mission to the world. It is not, finally, to enable the pastor to produce "great sermons" or to be able to offer significant pastoral care. Rather it is to enable the church to respond faithfully to God's invitation to participate in God's love for the world. The church does that most effectively when it does preach, teach, baptize, and eat the gospel of Jesus Christ, but it does all of this "for the life of the world." Therefore the church can do none of this insulated from those whose hunger and suffering and hurt bring us closer to Jesus than is comfortable. Shaping the disciplines attendant upon those who would seek to love the world for Jesus' sake — that too is the goal of administration.

There are so many other things that should be mentioned, things that, like life, tumble through the door: marriages, funerals, counseling, various crises. How does one organize all of that? I do not know, nor do I trust peo-

7. Cf. for example, Eugene Peterson, *Under the Unpredictable Plant* (Grand Rapids: Eerdmans, 1992), pp. 38-41.

ple who think they do. One simply navigates through all of that, sustained by the faith of the church and the energy that is given for that day. And this is not to mention the importance of time with family or one's self or the benefits of getting away for a while and looking at another piece of creation, or maintaining one's own sanity and Sabbath.

I would offer two final (though preliminary) thoughts about administration. The first is that though ministry can be, as I have argued, quite messy work, it is not slovenly or merely casual. Ministers can rarely control their days. This, in fact, is part of the joy of ministry. But the variety of tasks and people that engage the minister do not warrant a lack of preparation or planning, or an indifference to the schedules of other people, or a casual commitment to the day's work. A great deal of ministry, more than most ministers would like to admit, is about showing up and showing up on time. Messiness is not the same thing as slovenliness or laziness or self-absorption. Ministry can be very messy and quite resistant to our efforts to order it, but it is never slothful or self-centered. Indeed, the administrative task is the hard way ministry takes seriously its servant-character. The administrative task is rooted in the economy of God and therefore is an inherently generous and even courteous work. It is performed for the sake of others.

Which leads to the second and final point. There are few moments in ministry that afford a sense of completion. That is to say, at the end of the day, the minister's work is never done, never finished. Those who are so committed to the administrative task of the church that they must impose an order on each day that would leave the work done without remainder have an undeveloped eschatological perspective. The work of the minister is by its very nature unfinished and will ever be. The minister is not the one who consummates all things. A small matter, but useful in thinking about the administrative task.

Formed by a Lifetime of Theological Reflection and Study

Allen C. McSween Jr.

> *[T]he tasks of a pastor in preaching and teaching call for a wise mind, skilled in the use of language and metaphor, capable of imaging the situations of others different than herself or himself, able to engage in self-criticism and in holding more than one idea together at once, interested in the lives and situations of others, fascinated by the world itself, capable of learned and generous tolerance as well as fierce and passionate defense of important ideas. Pastors owe it to their congregations, as a moral obligation of their vocations, to be persons of study.*[1]

No collection of essays on the formation and work of the pastor-theologian would be complete without giving thought to the vocational commitment to a lifetime of serious theological reflection and study. In the formation of ones who view their ministry in explicitly theological terms, a host of influences come into play as is clear from the essays in the formation section of this volume. Not the least of these influences are certain apparently innate gifts for language, intellectual curiosity, and empathy that often manifest themselves at an early age. The use and development of these social and in-

1. Gordon W. Lathrop, *The Pastor: A Spirituality* (Minneapolis: Fortress Press, 2006), pp. 100-101.

tellectual gifts are as much a matter of Christian stewardship and mutual encouragement as any of the other gifts of life in creation.

At the first meeting of the team that produced this volume, each of us was encouraged to identify the major factors that have gone into our own theological formation. In almost every case the role of mentors, family, and friends was predominant. In this volume Cynthia Jarvis has explored well the role of mentors and theological masters in the formation of the pastor-theologian.

In my own case it was an apparently random remark made by a professor in seminary to the effect that I had "some promise as a theologian," that gave me the confidence to throw myself into theological study. As Frederick Buechner noted, "On such foolish, tenuous, holy threads . . . hang the destinies of us all."[2] It was a course in the theology of Reinhold Niebuhr the following semester that became my "intellectual conversion experience." Not only did theology become incredibly exciting, but so did politics and history and philosophy. The importance of mentors, pastors, teachers, and friends cannot be overstated in the formation of those who continue to pursue theological study in and for the life of the church long after they have graduated from seminary.

There are, however, strong cultural tides running against those who view ministry in explicitly theological terms. There is a daunting amount of anti-intellectualism in the church and in American culture in general.[3] To a significant degree that has always been the case, but in recent years there has been a particularly strong resurgence of anti-intellectualism, both from the "Religious Right" and from the "Religious Left." If some on the Right see no need for serious scholarship on the part of the pastor (especially the pastor-entrepreneur!), others on the Left see it as a distraction or cop-out from engagement with the pressing issues of the day.

A significant part of the project represented by this volume is an attempt to swim against the cultural tide that makes pastors feel guilty if they take time away from the "management of the church" to engage in serious reading, theological study, and writing. Sometimes the pressure comes from a congregation that expects its pastor to operate as its CEO or from mem-

2. Frederick Buechner, *The Sacred Journey* (San Francisco: Harper & Row, 1982), p. 109.

3. See, for example, Richard Hofstadter, *Anti-intellectualism in American Life*, and Mark Noll, *The Scandal of the Evangelical Mind*.

bers who view themselves essentially as consumers of the religious services of the church. Other times it comes from ones who do not want to be pressed to examine their lives and their moral choices in terms of who God is and what God promises and commands. But more often, I suspect, the pressure is internal — a nagging, culturally induced feeling that "non-productive" work like theological reflection is not what we are paid to do, especially if the congregation we serve is not flourishing numerically like the megachurch down the block.

Those who define their ministries as pastor-theologians face significant obstacles and resistance in the American church culture. But when has that not been the case? In this chapter I will argue that ministers who share a concern for theologically well-informed ministry need to do at least two things: (1) make their own scholarship a clear priority in their actual practice of ministry, and (2) find colleagues who share a similar vocational commitment for mutual support and encouragement.

The Priority of the Pastor's Scholarship

Clearly there are pressures from congregations to define ministry in organizational or therapeutic terms. But ministers of the gospel have an obligation to push back. One does not meekly have to accept the role assigned by those with a limited understanding of the church and its ministry. Those who value scholarship in the pastorate owe it not only to themselves and their congregations, but to their colleagues and those who will follow after them, to make clear the priority and value of sustained theological engagement. Several decades ago Joseph Sittler offered advice to ministers that still rings every bit as true today:

> It is, I think, not true that the parish demands of its minister to become simply an executive officer of multiple activities. The congregation is likely to accept, support, and be profoundly molded by the understanding of Office and calling which is projected by the minister's actual behavior. It will come to assess as central what the pastor, in the actual performance of ministry and use of time, makes central. And when this tightening and clarification of the minister's conception of the Office discloses, in the reflective depth and ordering skill of the sermon, where his or her heart and mind are centered, the parish will

honor this pastoral obedience to "take them more seriously than they take themselves."[4]

Ministers need to demonstrate in the way they order their time and focus their efforts the priority they give to ongoing theological scholarship. As Tom Currie makes clear in this volume, how ministers structure their day is a theological witness, not just a matter of "time management" and church administration.[5]

The same is true for what ministers call the room in which they do the majority of their work at the church. There is a subtle but significant difference in referring to it as the "pastor's *study*" and not the "pastor's office." The arrangement and organization of the pastor's study can itself be a theologically conscious act. The space devoted to the pastor's study and the way in which the room is arranged can demonstrate the priority a pastor gives to theological study and reflection. A few pastors may have the luxury of having a study separate from the office in which the pastor engages in counseling or conducts small meetings. Most of us, however, must combine the administrative functions with those of theological reflection. But that in itself can be a helpful witness to the congregation and a continual reminder to the pastor that even the most mundane administrative tasks of the pastorate are rooted in and surrounded by the accumulated wisdom of the "great cloud of witnesses" on the shelves of their study.

At a minimum in organizing a study a pastor will want ample bookshelves with books arranged according to subject, a desk at which he or she can work comfortably, a computer station or laptop, an ample supply of notepads and pens, and an adequate filing system for sermons preached, classes taught, articles collected, resources for worship, etc. It is helpful to have within easy reach the essential tools for writing sermons and planning worship — Bibles, hymnals, books of prayer, and basic reference works, including the polity of one's denomination.

4. Joseph Sittler, "The Maceration of the Minister," from *Grace Notes and Other Fragments* (Philadelphia: Fortress Press, 1981), reprinted by the Office of Theology and Worship, PC(USA), *The Shape of Pastoral Ministry,* Occasional Paper No. 13, 2000, p. 12.

5. See the essay in this volume by Tom Currie. "In many ways, the administrative task is simply the way the minister makes evident what is of first importance in her work. Just as church budgets are best understood as theological documents, reflecting, sometimes all too clearly in their details, the theological priorities of the congregation, so the minister's practice of administration reflects her own theological priorities."

Different ministers have different organizational styles and needs, but it is important to develop a style that minimizes time wasted in looking for needed resources. The same can be said for the organization of the files on one's computer. The less time that is wasted in looking for information, the more time will be available for the work of ministry and theological reflection. A number of pastors have a complete set of files for each Sunday in the three-year cycle of the common lectionary, so that whenever one comes across an idea in one's reading or an article in the news that relates to one of the lectionary texts, it can be filed in that folder for easy retrieval. Additional folders arranged by topics are helpful for keeping track of articles and ideas that will find their way into sermons and classes.

Of far greater significance than the organization of a study is what a pastor who is committed to a career of substantive theological reflection chooses to study and how.[6] In planning one's theological study it is important to think a number of years ahead. Instead of merely reading the latest "must read" book, over a period of time a pastor can deliberately be immersed in the theological classics that have enriched the faith and life of the church across the centuries. A new pastor would be well advised to develop a plan for reading with care and seeking to gain a working knowledge of at least one of the early Fathers (e.g., Augustine, Irenaeus, the Cappadocians), one of the major Reformers (e.g., Luther, Calvin, Wesley), and one modern theologian (e.g., Barth, Bonhoeffer, Tillich, the Niebuhrs, Moltmann). Spend a year or more with each theologian chosen, then cycle back to that theologian after reading some of the others.

I have also found it to be a helpful theological discipline to read a systematic theology every couple of years in order to keep in mind the whole scope of the biblical drama and how the various heads of doctrine form a coherent whole.[7] For those in a confessional tradition a regular reading of the confession or confessions of the church can serve a similar function.

Another helpful discipline is to read biographies of pastor-theologians. There are a number of outstanding volumes that will repay careful study not only in terms of one's theological understanding, but also in terms of minis-

6. See also the essay in this volume by Kristine Suna-Koro, "Reading as *Habitus:* On the Formative Preactice of Reading Theology Today."

7. Useful volumes for the pastor-theologian include Daniel Migliore, *Faith Seeking Understanding;* Shirley Guthrie, *Christian Doctrine,* rev. ed. John Leith, *Basic Christian Doctrine;* Robert W. Jenson, *Systematic Theology* (2 vols.); Gabriel Fackre, *The Christian Story;* and Hendrikus Berkhof, *Christian Faith: An Introduction to the Study of Faith.*

try in general and preaching in particular.[8] Some of the best biographies for the pastor-theologian include Peter Brown's classic study of Augustine, Eberhard Busch's insightful volume on Barth, Eberhard Bethge's moving study of the life and witness of Dietrich Bonhoeffer, and Richard Lischer's book on Martin Luther King Jr. entitled *The Preacher King.* There are also a number of autobiographies worthy of attention, by Harry Emerson Fosdick, C. S. Lewis, William Sloane Coffin Jr., Howard Thurman, and Jürgen Moltmann, as well as classics such as Reinhold Niebuhr's *Leaves from the Notebook of a Tamed Cynic* (a book I read every year for the first five years I was in ministry and still return to from time to time), and Richard Lischer's candid and engaging pastoral memoir *Open Secrets.*

I am not the best one to encourage the pastor's reading of novels. My attention span lends itself better to short stories and poetry, or at least to short novels like Marilyn Robinson's beautiful *Gilead.* Others are considerably better read than I am in contemporary literature. But reading more than works of theology is vital to the calling of the pastor-theologian. Great literature expands one's understanding of the human predicament. It broadens one's compassion. It opens new horizons of understanding, and vastly enriches the imagination. The pastor is called by the church to engage in a "priestly" reading, not merely for his or her own delight, but for a whole congregation of God's people. People often ask their pastor, "What are you reading?" A good pastor-theologian needs to have a helpful and worthy answer. People take seriously thoughtful recommendations and will respond with recommendations of their own, thus creating a community of readers in the congregation and opportunities for rich conversations.

A word of encouragement also needs to be offered for reading or, if possible, for listening to sermons by masters of the craft. Read or listen not only for content and organization, but for the sheer beauty of the language of masters of the craft like Harry Emerson Fosdick, Paul Scherer, Edmund Steimle, and George Buttrick. Closer to our time I would especially recommend the theologically profound sermons of Fleming Rutledge and the

8. One summer I preached a series of sermons on the life and witness of theologians who have played a major role in shaping contemporary theology. The sermons were built around passages of scripture that were central in the person's life and theology. The series included sermons on Luther ("Here I Stand"), Calvin ("The Man God Mastered"), Barth ("Troubadour of God's Grace"), Bonhoeffer ("Martyr/Witness for Christ"), Reinhold Niebuhr ("A Life of Grief and Grace"), and Frederick Buechner ("The Sacred Journey of Life").

gracefully written sermons of Barbara Brown Taylor.[9] The purpose of reading the sermons of others is not to imitate their style and certainly not to plagiarize their content, but to enrich one's own style and love of language in service to the gospel.

For busy pastors who must spend considerable time in their cars, a wealth of books-on-tape and CDs are available from local libraries, and a wide-ranging series of lectures by outstanding professors are available from "The Teaching Company." In addition, a number of seminaries make tapes or CDs of lectures available. Those with iPods or MP3 players may download lectures from a number of divinity schools and seminaries as well as sermons from church websites. The amount of information available electronically is increasing exponentially. The challenge, as always, is to focus on what is truly significant.

Not only is *what* the pastor-theologian reads important. *How* the material is read can be equally important. If the pastor-theologian reads more for *formation* than for information, reading less and reading more slowly is likely to serve better the long-term formation of the pastor-theologian than a hasty reading of books hot off the press. The American system of theological education in general and the information explosion in particular push one to attempt to read as much as possible. The pastor-theologian would be wise to resist the temptation. Read and ruminate on fewer books of greater significance over a longer period of time. Mark them, enter into dialogue with them, digest their wisdom, so as to be nourished for a lifetime of ministry fed by the sustaining traditions of the church ecumenical.

Colleagues for Mutual Encouragement

As important as wide-ranging reading is in the formation of a pastor-theologian, it is equally important to find conversation partners for mutual support and encouragement in ongoing theological reflection and growth. Those who view themselves as pastor-theologians may well expe-

9. Fleming Rutledge's books of sermons include *The Bible and "The New York Times"; Help My Unbelief; The Denial of Death; The Seven Last Words;* and *Not Ashamed of the Gospel.* Though she does not currently serve as a pastor, her sermons reflect the preaching of a remarkably profound pastor-theologian. Books of sermons by Barbara Brown Taylor include *The Preaching Life; Home by Another Way; Gospel Medicine; Mixed Blessings; God in Pain;* and others.

rience a sense of loneliness in going against the stream of American church culture. Yet with a little searching in almost every community one can find colleagues who share a similar concern for a theologically thoughtful ministry.

In my case the role of friends and colleagues has been crucial. I might not have sustained an interest in theology apart from the encouragement of a group of friends who graduated from Union Theological Seminary in Virginia around the same time I did.[10] Three years after graduation from seminary we began meeting for a week each summer to share papers we had written and to engage in theological reflection in the context of lasting friendships. Each year different ones of us would be assigned to produce a biblical study, a theological study, reflections on a cultural or social issue, a study of an issue in the church, or insights from a contemporary novel. We covenanted to read substantive theological works and to share papers we had written. The mutual encouragement of the group was a vital factor in the theological development of all of us, and it continues to bear fruit in the life of the church.[11]

Given the challenges of our first pastorates and the pressures for "relevance" in the late sixties and early seventies, it is doubtful whether all of us in the group would have continued to pursue the vocation of pastor-theologians apart from our mutual encouragement. I say all this to encourage the reader as strongly as I can to form or participate in colleague groups for mutual study and support. Personally, I have never been a fan of ministerial fellowships, but in almost every community there are pastors who share a common passion for the faith of the church. If they happen to belong to widely different theological traditions, all the better.

The Pastor-Theologian Program of the Center of Theological Inquiry (in which all the authors in this volume were privileged to participate) under the leadership of Wallace Alston developed a remarkably helpful model

10. See the paper in this volume by Wallace Alston on the importance of seminary education in the formation of pastor-theologians. One of the important aspects of seminary education that too often goes overlooked is the network of friendships that can have such important and lasting effects on the shape of one's ministry. Why some seminaries seem to do a better job than others in forming pastors who are collegial in their style of ministry is a matter that merits further attention.

11. Out of a joint meeting of the group mentioned above and a similar group of graduates of Columbia Theological Seminary came the impetus for a *Journal for Preachers,* one of the most useful publications for pastor-theologians.

for the ecumenical engagement of substantive texts and issues in regional groups of about fifteen participants. During the first nine years of the program, the regional groups met three times a year for three years along with two resource theologians to share in the process of reflecting on the work of the participants. In addition there was an annual conference that drew together the participants in the regional groups for four days of high-level presentations relating to the theme for the year. With very few exceptions, those who participated in the program found it to be one of the most renewing, theologically invigorating experiences of their ministries.

The factors that made the program so rewarding are easy to identify: the opportunity to engage in substantive theological discussions with people who take the theological vocation seriously, disciplined by the common reading of significant texts, in an ecumenical context, with members of the academy who see themselves not as experts in the field but as colleagues in a collaborative theological endeavor.[12] (It must also be confessed that meeting in lovely places and sharing good food and drink made it an even more rewarding experience!)

A number of different denominations have their own version of the pastor-theologian program, and various seminaries offer somewhat similar programs of study. A part of the legacy of John Leith is the Fund for Reformed Theology which he established. Colleague groups spend a year reading from a syllabus developed originally by Dr. Leith and gather for part of a week at a number of different seminary campuses. Again papers are shared, hospitality is enjoyed, and friendships are deepened.

For a number of years the Presbyterian Church (U.S.A.) through its Office of Theology and Worship has offered pastor-theologian seminars that follow a similar pattern. Pastors are invited to gather for a time of theological reflection built around common readings, study of scripture, and worship. Other denominations have similar programs. Whether such programs will continue in a time of financial retrenchment is unclear but doubtful, putting even more importance on ministers taking responsibility for their own continued theological development.

Another helpful model for theological study and mutual encouragement is found in the groups that covenant to meet together at least annually

12. At the final meeting of this research project team it was noted with some amazement that in our years of working together the divisive "hot button" issues troubling all our denominations had never dominated our discussions or become a point of contention.

to share reflections on lectionary texts in the company of a biblical or theological scholar. Again, what makes such groups fruitful for ministry is the commitment to common reading, study, and reflection on scripture and classic theological texts in the company of colleagues and friends.

The life of the church would be greatly enriched if such collegial groups for theological formation could be formed in seminary or at least very early in a pastor's career. For the better part of five years I was involved in a program developed by the Office of Theology and Worship of the Presbyterian Church (U.S.A.) with funding from the Lilly Endowment titled "Excellence from the Start." The program linked groups of seven or eight new pastors with two seasoned mentors. The purpose of the program was to inculcate and develop the habits of theological reflection from the beginning of one's ministry. Each participant covenanted to engage in daily prayer, readings of scripture and the confessions of the PC(USA), reading of assigned books, and the production of a paper to be shared with the group at each gathering. The assigned groups met five times in addition to an orientation meeting in Louisville and a final national meeting, at Flathead Lake, Montana, with Eugene Peterson. The biennial three-day meetings were structured around worship, the sharing of papers growing out of pastoral reflections in light of assigned readings, and fellowship, especially around shared meals. Sharing in the program was one of the most rewarding experiences of my career. I am convinced that as many as five of the participants in the group with which I worked might well have left the pastoral ministry had it not been for the support and encouragement of the group and the program in general. I cannot encourage too strongly anyone who wishes to pursue ministry as a pastor-theologian in our day to find or create a group willing to commit to common prayer, scripture reading, study, and theological reflection over a course of years.

Pastors are not academic theologians for whom scholarship is an end in itself. The study in which pastor-theologians engage is not for the sake of intellectual mastery alone. One of the finest pastor-theologians of our time, Eugene Peterson, rightly insists that "Pastoral work gathers expertise not by acquiring new knowledge but by assimilating old wisdom, not by reading the latest books but by digesting the oldest ones."[13] Peterson in particular makes a case for the formation of pastor-theologians by the slow reading of

13. Eugene Peterson, *Five Smooth Stones for Pastoral Work* (Grand Rapids: Eerdmans, 1992), p. 10.

proven classics over one's whole career.[14] Ministers who read merely for sermon illustrations, as at times we all must confess we do, may sound erudite, but most congregations quickly discover otherwise. Pastor-theologians do not engage in scholarship and study merely to impress a congregation, but to delve more deeply into the thick wisdom of the Christian tradition at its best. In his tremendously helpful little book, *Letters to New Pastors,* Michael Jinkins of Austin Presbyterian Theological Seminary writes,

> The best habits of reading are like the best habits of prayer. We read and pray not for people to be "impressed" with our piety or our trendiness, but because reading and praying are good in themselves, and are sources of communion and joy and nourishment.[15]

Attending to the proven wisdom of the past is not a retreat into the past. It is a way into the future with enough confidence and courage not to be taken in by "every shifting wind of doctrine" that blows through academia, or the bookshelves of Barnes and Noble. An anchoring in the wisdom of the past can save one from the anxiety of thinking that the challenges before us are the most daunting the church has ever faced. Even a cursory reading in Augustine or Irenaeus, not to mention Barth and Bonhoeffer, will quickly make clear what anxious nonsense that is. Michael Jinkins goes on to say,

> The voices of Basil, Chrysostom, Gregory, Julian of Norwich, Martin Luther, John Calvin, and many, many others give me perspective. They remind me that the church is far larger and grander and deeper and more extensive than my meager individual experience of God.

Christian scholarship, Jinkins insists, "is meant to function as the long-term memory bank of the church."[16] What a great phrase that is — *"the long-term memory bank of the church"!* Pastor-theologians who devote serious study to reading the acknowledged theological masters[17] and to the history of doctrine have a vital role to play in keeping alive the "long-term memory" of the

14. See Eugene Peterson, *Take and Read: Spiritual Reading, Annotated List* (Grand Rapids: Eerdmans, 1996).

15. Michael Jinkins, *Letters to New Pastors* (Grand Rapids: Eerdmans, 2006), p. 103.

16. Jinkins, *Letters to New Pastors,* p. 64.

17. See the paper on theological masters by Cynthia Jarvis in this volume.

church, apart from which the church inevitably drifts into faddishness and triviality.

It has been suggested that the great heresy of our time is not atheism, but superficiality — although a superficial atheism is clearly making a comeback on the best-seller lists. If that is true, we have no one to blame but ourselves. In our ordination to ministry the church set us "under orders" to preserve the "long-term memory of the church." Humanly speaking, the well-being of the church depends on our cherishing and passing on the best that has been "believed, taught, and confessed"[18] by faithful Christians over the centuries so that it may continue to deepen and invigorate the life of the church today.

In my tradition it once was common to refer to the minister as the "teaching elder." I fear that much has been lost in relinquishing the designation of the minister as "teaching elder." The title made clear the central importance of teaching in the work of the ordained ministry. But even if the term has fallen into disuse, pastor-theologians can help reclaim the designation of teaching elder by the demonstrated priority they give to teaching. There is no better way for a pastor to stay theologically sharp than by teaching courses that introduce a congregation to the best resources across the centuries for understanding scripture and one's theological tradition. In a time when biblical and theological illiteracy are increasing almost exponentially, the teaching function is very near the heart of the church's ministry. The pastor-theologian is the congregation's teacher-in-residence. Fulfilling that role faithfully and well requires a lifetime of disciplined study.

One of the most important purposes of the pastor's study is not to become studious. It is to enliven one's theological imagination. Imagination is crucial in the work of the pastor-theologian, who has nothing to say apart from symbols and images, metaphors and mystery. The essential work of the pastor-theologian is to hold together the visible and the invisible, the actual life of the world and the anticipated Reign of Christ. That cannot be done apart from a lively, well-formed imagination. Eugene Peterson insists that

> For Christians, whose largest investment is in the invisible, the imagination is indispensable, for it is only by means of the imagination that we can see reality whole, in context. . . . A major and too-little-remarked

18. Jaroslav Pelikan, *The Christian Tradition,* vol. 1, *The Emergence of the Catholic Tradition* (Chicago: University of Chicago Press, 1971), p. 3.

> evil in our time is the systematic degradation of the imagination. . . . When it (the imagination) is healthy and energetic, it ushers us into adoration and wonder, into the mysteries of God. . . . Right now, one of the essential Christian ministries in our ruined world is the recovery and exercise of the imagination.[19]

"Is it time," Peterson asks, "to get aggressive, time for the Christian community to recognize, honor, and commission its pastors as Masters of the Imagination, joining our poets, singers, and storytellers as partners in evangelical witness?"[20] Theological imagination is not a flight from reality. It is a deeper immersion in the realities of grace, best perceived and communicated poetically by the sanctified imagination.

Lest all this emphasis on study sound overly serious and daunting, it is important for the pastor that study not become a burdensome duty but be and remain a source of delight.[21] Ministers of the gospel are given the rare privilege of getting to "think about everything, all the time."[22] By its nature pastoral ministry involves intellectual curiosity. The study of that which delights, whether it be the poetry of W. H. Auden, learning a new language, taking art lessons, learning to cast a fly rod, or simply taking long walks in the woods with an eye to seeing what is really there, serves to keep the pastor spiritually and intellectually fresh and interesting.

Eugene Peterson, who has devoted his whole career to encouraging a theologically thoughtful ministry, issues a challenge to us all in the name of the church. Peterson imagines the church saying to its clergy at the time of ordination,

> We need help in keeping our beliefs sharp and accurate and intact. . . . We want you to help us: be our pastor, a minister of word and sacrament, in the middle of the world's life. . . . One more thing: we are going

19. Eugene Peterson, *Under the Unpredictable Plant* (Grand Rapids: Eerdmans, 1992), pp. 169, 171.

20. Peterson, *Under the Unpredictable Plant,* pp. 169-71. See also Walter Brueggemann, *Finally Comes the Poet: Daring Speech for Proclamation* (Minneapolis: Fortress Press, 1989).

21. See the paper by Tom Currie in this volume.

22. A woman said to her pastor after a sermon that touched on the nature of the gospel, events in the news, and more, "You preachers are the luckiest people I know. Unlike doctors who focus on medicine and healing, or lawyers who focus on legal matters, you get to think about *everything, all the time!*"

> to ordain you to this ministry and we want your vow that you will stick to it. . . . There may be times when we come to you as a committee or delegation and demand that you tell us something else than what we are telling you now. Promise right now that you won't give in to what we demand of you. You are not the minister of our changing desires, or our time-conditioned understanding of our needs, or our secularized hopes for something better. With these vows of ordination we are lashing you fast to the mast of word and sacrament so that you will be unable to respond to the siren voices. There are a lot of other things going on in this wrecked world and we are going to be doing at least some of them, but if we don't know the basic terms with which we are working, the foundational realities with which we are dealing — God, kingdom, gospel — we are going to end up living futile, fantasy lives. Your task is to keep telling the basic story, representing the presence of the Spirit, insisting on the priority of God, speaking the biblical words of command and promise and invitation.[23]

That is the work to which we are called by God and for which we are ordained by the church. Engage in it joyfully as the living God continues to call, equip, form, and reform us as pastor-theologians in and for the life of the Church universal.

23. Eugene Peterson, *Working the Angles: The Shape of Pastoral Integrity* (Grand Rapids: Eerdmans, 1987), p. 25.

The Pastor as Theologian of the Sacraments: Baptism

V. Bruce Rigdon

His name was Misha, the Russian nickname for Michael. An engineer, he was the son of highly placed bureaucrats in the Communist Party of the Soviet Union and was himself a rising member of the Party. During the summer of 1981, we worked together on a project that became a two-hour NBC documentary on the life of the Russian Orthodox Church in the USSR. The last NBC project to be done on film, the production involved a very large Soviet crew, two British technicians, an American director, and me. Misha was the head of the Soviet crew, and my role was that of a consultant and, in the end, the narrator of the film.

The first few days of the project were something of a nightmare, due in large measure to the frequent and explosive conflicts between the American director and the Soviet crewmembers. At times it felt as if the project had become a war, an endless series of confrontations in which the honor of the USA was pitted against that of the USSR. Misha and I discovered that by publicly shouting dramatically at one another in the midst of these eruptions we could satisfy the honor of each side and then retire quietly behind the scenes to figure out how to resolve each issue as it arose. Eventually everyone saw the humor in our public performances and settled down to try to make the best film that we could.

It took weeks of long hours and very hard work, but the day came when all of the film was "in the can." That last night there was a wonderful party. Each of us had our own reasons for celebrating the conclusion of the filming, and celebrate we did, with singing and dancing, and lots of elaborate toasts.

I was close to exhaustion and was eager to get to my room for some sleep before our early departure for Moscow's Sheremetyevo Airport. As I was leaving the dining room, Misha approached me and asked if I would go with him in order to sign the papers which would permit the film to pass through Soviet customs the next morning. I agreed, and we went to his room where a large stack of forms awaited us. I signed everything as quickly as I could and gathered up my copies so that I could get to my room and some sleep.

"Wait," Misha said. "There is something that I want to tell you before you go. I want to thank you for showing me something of my own history and culture as a Russian, something for which I had no appreciation. You know, Bruce, that I am a product of Soviet education. I believed that only the very old, only those who were stupid or poorly educated or superstitious could be religious. I could not imagine that conversations with such people would in any way be useful or even interesting. But in these last weeks I have seen in the churches some of the most beautiful art and heard some of the most wonderful and moving music of my whole life. I have actually had conversations with some of the priests and I found what we discussed and the priests themselves genuinely interesting. I understand, as never before, what an enormously important role the Orthodox Church has had in shaping what it means to be Russian and how beautiful our icons and church music are. Without your coming I might never have had this opportunity. So I thank you."

I thought that no foreign visitor to any country had ever been given a better gift or compliment than this, so I expressed my appreciation and headed once again toward the door. "There is something else," Misha said with a sense of urgency in his voice. I stopped and turned to look at him.

"When I was a baby my babushka (grandmother) came to live with us. Because my mother and father both worked, babushka took care of me. One day she took me to a priest whose church was some distance from our home. I was baptized by that priest, and when my father learned what had happened he was furious. He told babushka that if she ever told anyone that I had been baptized, or if she ever took me to church again, she would have to leave our family and our house and we would act as if she were dead. . . . He went to the priest and told him that if my name ever appeared on anything indicating that I had been baptized my father would use his influence to see that the priest was removed from his church and not permitted to be a priest anywhere else. After that, we never spoke of what had happened until after babushka had died. My mother eventually told me the story, and once or twice after I joined Komsomol (the Soviet youth organization) my father would tease me about being the only baptized member of that organization."

The story did not surprise me. I had heard similar stories many times and I had learned a very healthy respect for the faith and determination of the babushkas of the Russian Orthodox Church. What came next, however, did take me completely by surprise.

"I know, Bruce, that you are well educated and that you are a Christian, even some sort of a priest. So I want to ask you — you understand that I do not care personally, I am only curious — I want to ask you, do you think that anything happened to me because I was baptized?"

No question that I could recall from my ordination examination was more challenging than this. One thing was clear. If I told Misha that his baptism had been merely symbolic, meaning by that that nothing really happened, I could return to my room and get what was left of a night's sleep. As it was, we spent quite a long time talking about the subject in which Misha had insisted that he had little interest.

In the ensuing years I saw Misha several times during visits to Moscow. I never mentioned our conversation about baptism. He never failed to bring it up and to return to the answer I had given him. As the 1988 celebration of the millennium of the birth of Christianity in Kiev (i.e., the baptism of Prince Vladimir of Kiev) approached I met Misha for lunch. When he turned to the subject of baptism there was a smile on his face. "You remember," he said, "that you told me that if I ever decided to come to the church, I would be received as a son returning home, as someone who was already a part of the family? You told me that that was what had happened to me in my baptism." I did recall that as one of the themes in several of our discussions. "Well," he said, "you were right. I have been going to the liturgy for several months and the priest has told me that I will be received into the church, but that my baptism need not be repeated."

Some years later, Misha, by now a choir director in one of Moscow's churches, asked my help in gaining admission to a course of theological studies as a step toward ordination to the priesthood. Today my friend Misha, now Father Michael, serves as a priest in a Moscow church not so far from the one in which he was baptized many years ago.

I have told this story often, and I always ask those who hear it how they would have answered the question about whether or not anything happened to them in their baptisms. One way to approach that question is to ask how many people in a congregation know the date of their baptisms. When I have done that very few hands have been raised and people's faces showed some surprise at the question itself. The vast majority of us know nothing about our baptism, beginning with the date on which it took place. The exceptions are usually those who were baptized as children or adults. For those of us who do know the date, I suppose the next logical question is whether or not we celebrate this important event in our lives. When was the last time you participated in a celebration of someone's baptismal anniversary?

Does this seem an odd question? Think about it. We remember the important events in our lives and in the history of our families and communities. It is one of the things that keeps us human, shapes our identity, and gives us a profound sense of belonging. Imagine what it would be like if we forgot to celebrate our children's birthdays. What would a marriage without anniversaries be like, as evidenced by all of the jokes about forgotten anniversary dates? Could one imagine life in America without Fourth of July parades and festivities? Or what would the church year be without Christmas and Easter? Year after year, season after season, we relive these special days because they are important and they allow us to express who (and whose) we are.

If this line of thought is relevant, there is no other conclusion except that something is very wrong with the way most of us understand and practice baptism. No matter what we may tell our children about how important we believe baptism is, our behavior gives us away. It denies that our baptism has any lasting significance at all. Like marriages without anniversaries, or summers without Fourth of July picnics or Thanksgivings without feasts, baptism turns out to be merely a theological idea or abstraction, and perhaps not a very good one at that. Looked at in this light, it would appear that we live in something approaching a crisis, a crisis of both meaning and practice. Could it be that we have lived for so long in such a baptismal crisis that it has come to seem normal and therefore acceptable?

This has not always been so. In the early centuries of the history of the church we discover a quite different understanding and practice of baptism. From the beginning, baptism was the means by which new Christians were received into the fellowship of the church, entered into the death and resurrection of Christ, and received the promised gift of the Holy Spirit. Eventually all of this required a period of preparation, often quite lengthy, under the supervision of the bishop and specially chosen instructors or catechists. The theological and practical focus of baptism was the resurrection of Christ from the dead. Apart from that, baptism made little or no sense. Inevitably, therefore, baptism became profoundly connected with the church's celebration of Easter, or Pascha, as it was called in Greek. Indeed, one could say that the church created Easter for the purpose of baptism and that baptism gave the Easter celebration its shape and content. While each Sunday was celebrated as a little Easter, the church eventually established an annual celebration that quickly became the feast of feasts. Whether conscious of it or not, the church was engaged in a process of transforming the world's perception and experience of time, and the universal acceptance of Easter as the greatest of feasts was a major step in that direction, one that would eventually become part and parcel of the calendar of the Empire after the Constantinian settlement in the fourth century.

This feast was preceded by the longest fasting period in the church year. It led to an intensive series of services concentrated in Holy Week which marked the arrest, trial, scourging, and crucifixion of Christ. All of this served as a sort of school for the candidates, the catechumens, preparing for baptism. In many places the final period, Holy Week, or that part which came to be designated as the Triduum, the final three days, was a period when the candidates lived with the bishop and received the final instruction in their training for life as part of the Christian community.

The ancient tradition was that the vigil service leading to the celebration of the resurrection began late on Saturday night. It was preceded by the baptism of all of the candidates. They were baptized into Christ so that they could participate fully with the community in the feast of the resurrection, thus receiving Holy Communion for the first time. And, also for the first time, they would not have to leave the service when the deacon called out, "The Doors, The Doors," the sign that the first part of the service had ended, and all who were not yet baptized were to depart. To this day in the Orthodox Church the first part of the Sunday liturgy, the part of the service in which the Bible is processed into the service and the scriptures are read, is referred to as the Liturgy of the Catechumens, while the second part, previously reserved only for those who had been baptized, was designated as the Liturgy of the Eucharist.

Imagine the impact that this would have had not only upon those who were to be baptized, but upon the entire community. For one thing, for a rather long time everyone had the same baptismal anniversary and it was linked concretely with the celebration of the resurrection. Not only did this involve welcoming the newly baptized, but it also marked the remembering and renewing of their own baptisms for everyone else. And since Easter ended the long Lenten fast, at the conclusion of the service everyone returned to their homes for the best meal of the year. They broke the fast and celebrated the resurrection by feasting on all of the things they had not tasted during the long, dark days leading up to Easter. For a time, remembering your baptism and celebrating the resurrection by having a wonderful party were one and the same. And all of this was framed in the context of the congregation processing three times around the church at midnight in order to hear and respond to the dramatic announcement, "Christ is risen!" "He is risen indeed!" Until Pentecost this replaces the normal greeting whenever and wherever people meet one another. In the words of the Easter hymn, "Christ is risen from the dead, trampling down death by death, and upon those in the tomb, bestowing life."

It is a good thing, I think, that many churches are once again keeping the vigil in connection with celebrating Easter. That has opened once again the possibility of making direct connections between baptism and the resurrection of the Lord. For, you see, from what we have just observed, it would not be incorrect to say that one of the major reasons for establishing the feast of Easter in the first place was to baptize and welcome new Christians.

In the congregation in which I grew up I never saw anyone, infant or adult, baptized at Easter. Nor for that matter had I ever experienced the congregation celebrating Holy Communion on Easter Sunday. Indeed, Holy Communion always took place on Maundy Thursday evening as a remembrance of "the Last Supper," the occasion of the final gathering of the disciples to observe the Passover Feast, the night of Jesus' agony in the Garden of Gethsemane and his arrest by the Roman soldiers. I remember the service as somber and sad. No wonder the congregation could not imagine "celebrating" Holy Communion on Easter Sunday or, for that matter, why they were quite satisfied that they only had to "observe" it four times a year.

No wonder I was taken by surprise to discover these ancient connections and their implications for both the theology of baptism and its impact upon the whole Christian community.

It would be instructive at this point to look at what was actually done in these ancient baptismal services. That would not be very difficult, since we have some ancient texts and sources from this period in the life of the church. The services, however, were neither brief nor simple, and so for our purposes I would rather tell you a story about my own impressions taken from a service very close to the service that these documents have preserved.

I mean no disrespect in saying that Eastern Orthodox liturgical life is something like my grandmother's attic, which I loved to explore when I was a child. Everything has been kept, carefully preserved for the most part. As a result many of the services, rites, and customs derive from very ancient sources and have provided us with a remarkable continuity of tradition and traditions.

The story that I want to tell you took place on the island of Crete many years ago, when I was given permission by a remarkable bishop to serve as godfather to an infant recently born to a good friend of mine who was a member of the Greek Orthodox Church. I recall that on the night before he was baptized his mother and I were engaged in a theological conversation. As she rocked her son to sleep, Dora (I will call her) looked at me and said, "I have never understood why in the West you chose to create the doctrine of original sin. Why was it necessary? It misses the point altogether. Look at this beautiful little one. How can anyone call him a sinner? It is not at all obvious to me that he is so sinful that tomorrow we must baptize him lest he go to hell as divine punishment for sin. But what is obvious to me is that someday, whether sooner, God forbid, or later, this beautiful little one will die. I cannot believe that God who loves us created human beings to die. That is why we will baptize him tomorrow. It is so that I can tell him over and over again that he has nothing to fear from death because he is already dead and lives through Christ the life that death can never destroy. Because he is baptized, he will be free from everything that will threaten to separate him from the love of God in Christ." In Dora, St. Augustine had a worthy theological opponent!

The next morning a group of friends and relatives gathered outside the little house in the village. As godfather I carried the baby as we made a procession to the little church where the baptism was to take place. At the time it did not occur to me that these were the first steps in a lifelong journey of the baby in my arms and that I was privileged to be there at the very beginning. When we arrived at the church our little company stood outside the steps into the church and faced West where the sun sets and from which the darkness settles over the earth. Together we renounced sin, darkness, and the demonic and, as if to emphasize the seriousness of this act, many in our company spit rather loudly on the ground. We then turned to the East where the sun rises and from which the light comes and reaffirmed our commitment to Jesus Christ, the savior and light of the world. Baptism begins, therefore, with exorcisms and renunciations, indicating that a conversion is taking place. This conversion will involve a lifelong struggle against evil in order to manifest the reign of God to whom the world and everything in it belongs. The content of this is revealed in the Nicene Creed which was sung at this moment in the baptismal liturgy.

At this point the doors to the porch of the church were opened and the procession made its way inside. In this instance there was no elaborate baptismal font or baptistery. Instead an ordinary aluminum tub had been filled with water and would serve the purpose of the baptism. What took place next involved beautiful prayers sung antiphonally as the Orthodox service of baptism continued. Since this is not an essay on liturgics but the story of a baptism, I will simply recount my memory and impressions of what occurred next. The priest, having blessed the water and oil to be used in the service, made the sign of the cross with the oil three times over the water as everyone sang Alleluia three times. This blessing of the water recalled Christ's own baptism in the Jordan River through which all water was made holy, as the Orthodox feast of the Epiphany recalls. My godson's elaborate baptismal dress was removed and the priest took him in his arms and anointed him with oil, making the sign of the cross on his forehead, his chest, his ears, his hands, and his feet.

At that moment I heard his name for the first time as the priest chanted "The servant of God, Dimitri, is anointed with the oil of gladness in the name of the Father and of the Son and of the Holy Spirit." Following this the priest plunged Dimitri into the water until he was completely submerged. This occurred three times as the priest continued to chant, "The servant of God, Dimitri, is baptized in the name of the Father, Amen; and of the Son, Amen; and of the Holy Spirit, Amen."

By this time the newly baptized Dimitri was screaming his head off. Having his access to air cut off three times, he was literally yelling for his life. I was standing beside his grandmother, and amidst all of this noise I commented to her that at home we would have done almost anything to ensure that the infant would not cry. I intended this merely as a casual observation of no special significance. Dimitri's grandmother, however, reacted energetically. "If he didn't cry, we would pinch him until he did," she insisted. "Why would you do that?" I asked with disbelief. "When he was born we waited outside to hear his cry," she said. "We knew then that he had come through the trauma of birth. He was alive! It is the same with baptism, his second birth. If he didn't cry we would be very worried that something was terribly wrong! Do you understand?" she asked. And somehow I did understand that I had just been given a glimpse of a new dimension of the meaning of baptism. In fact I learned a great deal that day just by watching what was happening and later reflecting on it. At least four things were apparent in this experience of baptism as practiced in the Orthodox tradition.

The first is that baptism signifies washing, being cleansed of sin. The water covers every part of the body of the person being baptized. The second is that baptism involves entering into the death of Christ in order to receive the gift of his resurrected life. Dimitri had just demonstrated how existentially real that experience was as he screamed and gasped for breath.

The third is that Dimitri had received a new identity; he had been given his Christian name. In his case his parents did not disclose his name until it was heard in the baptism itself. They had instead called him "dear one" or "little one" or some other expression of their affection, but not his Christian or given name. And they had chosen his name from among the list of male saints who were commemorated by the church on the date of his baptism. That is why from that time on Dimitri would celebrate his Nameday in somewhat the same way that we celebrate birthdays. But his would be a celebration of his baptismal anniversary, a day for gifts, parties, congratulations, and the possibility of a blessing from his priest. By comparison, his natural birthday would take second place to his Nameday. Dimitri's parents would make sure that as he grew up he would know about the saint in whose honor he was named, and one of the gifts that he received from his parents that day was an icon of St. Dimitri to be hung on the wall near his crib.

The fourth is that Dimitri became a part of a new family. Just as his natural birth had introduced him into a biological family whose name he bore, so now his "second birth" made him a part of the Christian family, the church universal, and from that family he had also received a name. "This is the child of God, Dimitri," the priest had said as if he were introducing a new member of the family. And the priest had said this not only to us but to all of the saints represented in the icons of this little church. That, after all, is what his church understands about the catholic church: that it transcends time and space and includes the faithful of all generations.

Still in the priest's arms, Dimitri was now chrismated. I was struck by the fact that this part of the service was referred to as confirmation. Like most Christians descended from the Latin tradition of Christianity, my experience of confirmation was that at a particular age a young person who had been baptized as an infant now made a public profession of faith and took personal responsibility for the promises made in his or her behalf by parents and/or sponsors at the time of baptism. What one did was to "confirm" these promises by assuming responsibility for them.

Imagine my surprise to discover something so different among our Orthodox friends. Dimitri's confirmation had nothing to do with promises made by anyone. Instead it had to do with the gift of the Holy Spirit who confirms what the church has sought to do in the sacrament of baptism. Dimitri was again anointed with Holy Chrism, oil which is blessed and sent to each congregation by its bishop. The chrism was used to make the sign of the cross on his brow, his eyes, his nostrils, his lips, his ears, his hands, and his feet. While anointing Dimitri the priest chanted, "The seal of the gift of the Holy Spirit. Amen."

Baptism is then the gracious work of God from beginning to end. It is not in the first instance the faith of believers or their promises that constitute the effectiveness of baptism. It is a gift to which we spend the rest of our lives responding, whether faithfully or badly. Nor could one view baptism as some sort of hocus pocus in which if all of the words were intoned correctly it would have the effect of producing grace. The church depends upon the Holy Spirit to confirm what it has sought to be and do in relation to this and other sacraments.

To our previous list, therefore, we now add the gift of the Holy Spirit given in the life of the one who is baptized to confirm God's promise to the church and to journey with the baptized throughout life. Perhaps the oil had a calming effect on Dimitri. In any case, he had stopped crying and now was dressed in a beautiful white baptismal garment as the priest continued to chant, "The Servant of God, Dimitri, is clothed with the robe of righteousness in the name of the Father, Son, and Holy Spirit."

While I held Dimitri, the priest sprinkled him with water while chanting a special prayer during which he cut Dimitri's hair in the shape of a cross, the sign that the new life that begins now will be a life of offering, sacrifice, and service, a life constantly transformed into liturgy, that is, the work of Christ in the world. In other words, Dimitri now has a vocation, a vocation to be a disciple of Christ and to embody Christ's ministry.

As I held Dimitri in my arms, the priest led us in a procession around the baptismal font three times while everyone sang, "As many as have been baptized in Christ have put on Jesus Christ our Lord, Alleluia. Alleluia. Alleluia."

Our whole company now entered the sanctuary, and the Liturgy of St.

John Chrysostom began with the chanted announcement, "Blessed is the Kingdom of the Father and of the Son and of the Holy Spirit. Amen." The service was long and beautiful and we stood throughout. Prayers were offered, lessons read. Processions brought the scriptures in and later the gifts of bread and wine. *Liturgy* is derived from the Greek word for service. Worship is thus the service the church offers in behalf of the world. It is "the work" of the people of God. Likewise, *Eucharist* is a form of the Greek word for "thank you." We had now processed into the Kingdom to offer the world in all its brokenness and alienation to God, to celebrate God's love and transforming power, to offer our thanks to God and to bless God in order to be healed and nourished for our return to the world which God loves. And now the little one who had been baptized and confirmed (chrismated) received as the fulfillment of this his first Holy Communion.

As I held him, the priest placed a spoon in Dimitri's mouth that contained consecrated wine and particles of bread. From that time on Dimitri along with other infants would be the first to receive communion at every liturgy in which he was present. Until the age of eight he would receive freely. After that he would be taught the importance of fasting and other forms of preparation for participation in this mystery.

One of the things that is striking about this description is that from the beginning in the East, baptism, confirmation, and communion or Eucharist occurred in conjunction with one another. For the early catechumens all three took place on Easter night. But until now wherever baptism is celebrated in Eastern Orthodox churches it always involves confirmation and the Eucharist. Baptism, of course, can take place only once in a Christian's life, but it is recalled and made present as Christians in that tradition are anointed in the vigil before every major feast and on other appropriate occasions, and whenever they receive the sacrament of Holy Communion. Baptism is thus the initiation or entrance into the Christian community which is confirmed in the receiving of the Holy Spirit and leads directly to participation in the Lord's Supper. These are the forms in which the community experiences what it means to enter into the death of Christ and to receive the new life of his resurrection. The end of it all is to enter into Easter or paschal joy and to see the world and our lives not as something autonomous and opaque but rather as transparent to God who gives us everything as a means of communion with himself.

This, it seems to me, is much more difficult to understand or experience in many of our Western traditions for one simple reason: the separation of baptism, confirmation, and Eucharist from one another and the isolation of all of them from our Easter or Paschal celebration. My friend Dora would say that when she listens to us she has the impression that for us the fundamental human issue is sin and forgiveness, which may explain our tendency to view so many things from a juridical perspective. For Orthodoxy, she would insist, the fundamental human issue is not sin and guilt, but life and death. Though not mutually exclusive, these two perspectives tend to interpret the relationship between Good Friday and Easter Sunday very differently, both intellectually and experientially.

How did this separation of the three "sacraments" occur in the West? It would appear that the answer revolves around the function and authority of the bishop as it evolved in the Latin church. There it was decided, rather early, that while priests could baptize and celebrate the Eucharist, only bishops could confirm. The consequences are obvious. Since bishops could not be in attendance at all baptisms, confirmation would have to be postponed. A baptized child or adult living in an obscure and distant village might therefore have to wait for years before an episcopal visitation. Hence there came into being a pattern of baptism given soon after birth, while confirmation became a sort of rite of passage into adolescence or adulthood. Since, therefore, newly baptized children could not be given communion, a custom developed to arrange for "first Holy Communion" around the age of eight. In light of this practice theologians did what they always do, namely, they developed theological rationales or explanations for each of these events as separate and distinct and no longer related one to another.

While this does not explain everything, it at least supplies some of the clues that may help us to understand our own baptismal crisis. The answer is not simply to return to ancient custom because it is ancient, but rather to discover in the early and formative experiences of the church a theology and practice that may have a great deal to teach us and may offer us perspectives for dealing with our own contemporary problems. As Jaroslav Pelikan put it so well, "Tradition is the living faith of the dead; traditionalism is the dead faith of the living."

But what I have described as a crisis of baptism in our churches is not simply the result of internal developments within the churches but perhaps most of all because of the demise of Christendom and the evolution of secularism as the basis of so much of our political, cultural, and social life.

I am reminded of the profound disagreement that erupted in the post–World War II years between two of the most renowned Reformed theologians of the twentieth century, Karl Barth and Emil Brunner. On the issue of baptism Barth somewhat surprisingly assumed a traditionally Anabaptist position. He opposed the baptism of infants, one of the hallmarks of centuries of Christendom and its theological and political assumptions. That is, baptism had functioned as a mark of citizenship. I once heard Barth quoted as saying, "We can no longer baptize blond, blue-eyed baby boys who grow up to put on jackboots and murder Jews." Barth's point, in any case, was that being a Christian in a society that could no longer claim to be Christian involved such radical and perhaps risky commitments that it could only be undertaken as a decision by someone capable of sizing up the odds. Given Barth's experience in the Confessing Church in Germany, perhaps this stance is not so surprising after all.

If Barth's position gave enormous significance to the importance of existential human decision, Brunner insisted that what was at stake in the disagreement was the Reformation understanding of justification by faith through grace alone. In other words, this was no trivial matter. One of Brunner's students described his teacher's position by saying, "If we didn't already have infant baptism, we would have to invent it."

As a pastor I understood this to mean that when baptizing an infant I could quite honestly point out to the congregation that this little one had done absolutely nothing to deserve or qualify for God's grace or for membership in the church as the Body of Christ. He or she had made no decisions, had confessed to no faith or belief system, and had not made any moral or ethical commitments. Baptism was therefore in the first instance the free gift of God's amazing grace, a mystery, if you will, something that defies explanation or human reason. (Misha would have understood that very well.) And the point is that this is true of everyone who is baptized, however wise or stupid, young or old we may be. We spend the rest of our days responding consciously or unconsciously, faithfully or unfaithfully, to the grace and love of God which we did not earn and in that sense do not deserve. The infant is the concrete embodiment of this truth, as well as the reminder that the church community has an enormous responsibility to help all of us to understand and respond to the gift and calling that belongs to this mystery we call baptism.

What Barth and Brunner could agree on, however, was that in a post-Christian world the church must take baptism and its consequences and responsibilities with a far greater seriousness than has been the case for a very long time. This has both theological and practical implications.

For those who take this seriously, it involves something of a journey, a long one, which will require both time and hard work. No easy gimmicks or quick-fix programs will suffice. This must be undertaken by pastors, church leaders, and congregations together. It is multifaceted and complex, since theology and practice are so bound up in each other.

One might begin, I suppose, with a question about who should be baptized. In the days of Christendom the answer was obviously almost everyone. That was still reflected in the phone calls and requests that I received regularly as a pastor asking if someone's child could be "christened." Sometimes the caller would just ask if the baby could be "done." Or I think of the well-meaning grandmothers in the congregation who would ask for a private family baptism for a grandchild to be performed in the living room or the backyard, weather permitting. The anxiety in the grandmothers' voices often grew out of the fact that the parents of their grandchildren had not darkened the door of a church since their wedding, years before, and had no intention of raising their child as part of a church family in the distant city where they lived.

The governing body (the Session) of the Presbyterian congregation I served struggled with this question for a long time and finally developed a set of criteria by which decisions about whom to baptize could be made. Essentially the criteria focused on the necessity for parents and or sponsors to accept the responsibility to see that the child would be raised as part of this or another church family. The process made the Session more aware of the fact that these were the same criteria that should be applied to all who come seeking baptism. This gave clergy and congregational leaders a basis for saying no to families or individuals who exhibited no desire or intention to participate in the life and mission of the church. While I found this useful as a way of establishing the congregation's seriousness about its responsibility for nurturing its members, Misha's story always reminded me of how fallible human judgments are, even when made for the best of reasons.

The intention of this essay is to suggest that if a congregation sets out on this journey to seek the renewal of baptism, that congregation may be led to all sorts of theological insights and opportunities to reshape its practices. I know this to be true from my own experience.

To illustrate this, over a period of fifteen years our congregation experienced many such changes. The recognition that baptism marks entrance into the church led to the conclusion that when the family gathers to be fed in the Lord's Supper all who are baptized should be welcomed and fed, since baptism is about having a place at the family table. This meant not only that children were encouraged to participate, but that we gave communion to infants at the time of their baptism through the use of a spoon. More controversial in the beginning was the decision to baptize only on those occasions when the congregation celebrated the Lord's Supper, so as to demonstrate the interconnectedness of these two sacraments. The real issue, it became apparent, was whether or not we could achieve this without making the service last longer than sixty minutes!

Teaching the congregation about the meaning of baptism is important. We suggested that everyone should find out as much as possible about their own baptism, and we began to celebrate the anniversaries of our children's baptisms in Sunday school. Classes to prepare parents for the baptism of their children and classes for adults preparing for baptism included suggestions for ways to remember and celebrate this event in their lives. Infants received a white baptismal candle at their baptism that was to be lighted each year at the time for celebrating this event in their lives.

The messages that we send our children really matter. One young woman in our congregation remembered her anger and confusion at the time of her confirmation. She was thirteen, hardly an ideal time for making lifelong decisions. As she prepared for her appearance before the congregation she heard very conflicting things from her pastor and her teachers. One said that confirmation was the act of becoming a member of the church; another that it was preparation to receive Holy Communion for the first time. Still another emphasized that she was preparing to take responsibility for the promises that her parents had made in her behalf when she was baptized. Since she had been raised in a family that told her that she had become a member of the church in her baptism and since she had taken communion as a child in her previous congregation, she found her confirmation class became something of a nightmare, especially when some of her friends told her that none of this really mattered if she had not had a personal conversion experience.

As our Session began to understand this confusion and the mixed messages it sent to our young people, the decision was made to reshape and reclaim this event. It became a time for young people to study and talk about the church and the life of faith. They could then decide whether at that time in their lives they were ready to accept new responsibilities for the ministry and mission of the church. If they did so, they understood that they would be given new assignments in the congregation, including such things as reading lessons in worship, ushering, and assisting with the offering. It also meant that the church would assist them to make it possible to participate in work camps, service opportunities, and youth conferences. The church nominating committee also included the names of these young people as possible candidates for election or appointment to the councils and committees of the congregation.

Eventually our Session also decided to incorporate anointing with oil as part of the act of baptism and Holy Communion. Though John Calvin had rejected the use of oil or chrism, he had insisted on the importance of the "epiclesis," the prayer asking the Holy Spirit to descend upon the gathered community and to bring us into the presence of Christ. This occurs in both baptism and the Lord's Supper. Thus we had brought together once again baptism, confirmation, and the celebration of Holy Communion as it had been centuries ago. The reason for doing so was not antiquarian, but trinitarian. And in doing so we found that in sick rooms and hospitals we had reopened the possibility of anointing as part of the church's ministry of healing.

All of this might be viewed, however, as having little more significance than moving the furniture around. And that might well be true if such events in our journey did not bring us closer to seeing, understanding, and entering into the profound joy of Easter (Pascha). When all of our committees have finished their work, when all of our missions have been accomplished, what does any of it mean if we do not enter into this joy which only God can give?

For that reason our congregation worked very hard to reshape the journey through Holy Week to Easter. We attempted to make the services more transparent to the death of Christ and our own fears of death. We made of Easter morning a celebration of God's victory over death itself, as the first announcement was sung outdoors in our columbarium early in the morning. Easter became a time for baptisms, for celebrating the Eucharist, and for proclaiming the greatest mystery of all, Christ's resurrection from the dead and his victory over our last enemy, death itself. The shape of that event did in turn begin to change the ways in which we experienced life itself, its joys and sorrows, its fasts and feasts, its births and deaths. As a congregation we came to know and experience the great joy of the church across the ages as we, too, exchanged the paschal greeting, "Christ is Risen!" "He is Risen indeed!"

The Pastor as Theologian of the Sacraments: Holy Communion

V. Bruce Rigdon

I love the old Hebrew storytellers. They were so wise. For them life was of a piece, no little boxes marked sacred or profane, holy or mundane, spiritual or secular. All of life was a gift of God to be lived in God's presence. In their wisdom they knew much more than is at first apparent in the amazingly simple but profound stories they tell.

For example, if one had asked them what it is above everything else that makes us all human, the answer is quite obvious. They would not have suggested with Descartes that it is thought or consciousness. "I think, therefore I am." Nor would they have chosen any of the other complex modern theories about what it means to be human. For them the answer is both simple and apparent. "I hunger, therefore I am." Human beings are created hungry. We must eat or we die. We ingest matter; we eat the world in order to transform it into life, into our own flesh and blood.

The author of the first chapter of Genesis is quite earthy and very graphic about this. In the first conversation with human beings God talks about two things, sex and food. Human beings are to be fruitful; we are to multiply and fill the earth with our own kind. And we are to eat the earth itself. "Behold, I have given you every herb bearing seed and every tree bearing fruit . . . and to you it shall be for food" (Gen. 1:29). Humans are hungry beings whose life depends upon satisfying our hunger.

But you might insist, this is true of every form of animal life, from the amoeba to the elephant. Why would the Hebrew storyteller make of that the most basic meaning of what it is to be human? To the storyteller it is clear that God alone has created life and is the sole source of life. All vitality comes from God. Everything that has life receives it from God and it is derived from some form of consuming matter. It is true that human beings share that characteristic with all other life forms.

But human beings are unique among God's creatures. Like the amoeba and the elephant we hunger for matter, and like them we are capable of transforming matter into energy. Energy is life. But God, according to the storyteller, has given humans the additional capacity or gift to transform energy into spirit. What does that mean? It means that human beings can transform energy into creativity. In that respect we are just a little like God the creator. We are made in God's image, so to speak. When we create and use language, when we sing and dance, when we discover the secrets of God's creation, when we write poetry or design cities, when we transform the world around us, we express this amazing gift. We are culture-creating beings.

There is something wonderful and mysterious about this gift, precisely because it makes us a little like God. The storyteller knows this to be true when he describes human beings as those who can create words and "name" things. From his perspective, to name something or someone is an awesome thing because it involves recognizing the essence and purpose of the one who is so named. And this in turn involves seeing the one named in relation to God and God's creation. It is as if one sees things through God's eyes. In the Genesis account, the storyteller has God bring all of the animals to Adam so that he can name them.

Humans hunger for three things, the stories tell us. First, we hunger for food. This is so obvious that at first glance it appears to require no further comment. If we do not eat we will finally die. In the Presbyterian tradition in which I was raised there was little or no emphasis upon fasting. In the Eastern Orthodox community which I have come to know, fasting is an essential part of the Christian life. Once while visiting in Russia I asked a babushka, a grandmother, why it was that the community kept to a strict fast especially during Lent. She looked very surprised by my question. After a brief pause she replied with some astonishment, "We fast to get hungry, of course. If I invite you to my dinner party, how do you get ready? By snacking all day? We have to prepare by making room in our bellies, in our souls and in our hearts. We have to be hungry to eat the Pascha (Easter) feast and receive the joy of the Lord's resurrection."

Second, we human beings are hungry for each other, for fellowship with one another. My mother was my best teacher on this point. Many years after my father's death, my mother and I were having a conversation about what had been most difficult for her as a widow. "If you ever become a real pastor (as opposed to a faculty member in a theological school)," my mother said with a grin on her face, "don't mess with the potluck suppers." Behind the humor was a serious and painful point. Like so many women of her generation, my mother was born into a multigenerational family that gathered each day around the dining room table. After her marriage she prepared the meals for our small family to eat together each day. With my father's death for the first time in her life my mother sat alone at the table day after day. Of all of the problems that widowhood brought, none was more difficult or painful than having to sit and eat alone at the family table. I remembered her advice years later when I served a congregation that had what seemed to me an extraordinary number of potluck suppers. I understood that more than one hunger was being satisfied at those tables. And this in turn brought new understanding as to why it was in the earliest days of the life of the church that they continuously broke bread together.

Underlying these desires, however, is the third and deepest of all human hungers, the hunger for God. Without God, human beings have no way to know who we are or whose we are. Knowledge of self and knowledge of God were inextricably bound up in one another.

For the Hebrew storyteller, that is to say, for the author of Genesis, the whole creation is God's gift to humankind. It is a gift of God's very self and hence it is a revelation, a theophany, a mystery. God is present in and takes delight in all that God has made. God blesses everything and offers it to Adam and Eve. The creation is God's love made food, and God's intention is that eating is to be an act of communion. Eating and drinking in the Garden are not to be symbols of something else, of some deeper meaning, of something "spiritual." Food is the gift of God's life-giving love which sustains humankind and which is the cause of joy, delight, and deep satisfaction.

God blesses everything in creation and calls it good. Because creation is God-bearing and is the means of fellowship and communion with God, human beings find the joy-filled meaning of our lives in blessing God, in offering thanks and praise to the one who has blessed us so richly. "Taste and see how good the Lord is." Knowing God's goodness, human beings discover that they are called to be priests. That is, we are called to offer thanks and praise in behalf of all creation. We are called to bless God as we offer to God the whole creation and receive it back as gift. Human beings were to live in total dependence upon God as source and blessing. None of this is either spiritual or supernatural. Such distinctions do not exist for the Hebrew storyteller. All of this is the most natural thing in the world. It is the way that God made it. It is all about real hungers and real food and real communion.

This sense that eating is intended to be communion is not limited to the Jewish and Christian traditions. It is in fact to be found in every culture on earth. And the reason is that this is how all human beings are made. Even the "fast food" culture that is taking the world by storm cannot completely block it out. Fast food assumes that eating should be quick, easy, and cheap, allowing its customers to get on with the more important things that life offers. But even in a McDonald's culture, we still know that on those increasingly rare occasions when we can gather our families and our friends around our tables something very special can happen. It really matters that someone has taken time and made the effort to prepare a good meal. It really matters that the house is filled with the aromas of special dishes. It really matters what is said and shared at the table during the meal. Around this table relationships are renewed, strangers may become friends, and special events are remembered and celebrated. When these things happen, we are truly fed and we leave the table deeply satisfied.

Think about the number of times you have had that experience, especially when you have discovered it in a culture other than your own. I recall a long car trip many years ago with fellow seminary students as we made our way to Selma, Alabama. It is the first time in my own life when I can remember viewing state police as possible threats to my well-being. Looking back at that event I can still see Brown Memorial Chapel. I can recall angry crowds, blaring bullhorns, and growling police dogs. I still feel my emotions responding to powerful preaching, and to the astonishing courage of the demonstrators with whom I stood. But most of all I remember the kindness of the black woman who welcomed us into her home in the housing project behind Brown Memorial. No matter what the time of day or night we returned to her little house, she would gather us around her table and talk with us. And she would feed us with the things that she had made for us. In an amazing way what the demonstration outside was all about became a lived reality at her table. As we broke bread together at her table, as we talked about our hopes and our fears, we became the beloved community, black and white together, and the foretaste of that reality calmed our fears and sent us back to the demonstrations outside.

Or I recall a cold, wintry Sunday in the Soviet Union during the Cold

War when I spent the day with a Ukrainian bishop visiting the Orthodox parishes in his diocese. At each of the village churches the snowy path to the entrance to the church had been strewn with flowers and in the doorway stood a very elderly couple holding bread and salt, the ancient symbols of welcome and hospitality. No one seems to remember when that custom among Slavic peoples began, but everyone seems certain that it predates the coming of Christianity more than a thousand years ago. Each of the churches had prepared a feast in honor of this visit. The tables groaned with food and drink. And in each place I was treated as an honored guest. It did not escape the notice of any of us that I was an American and in that sense I was not only a stranger. I was a representative of an enemy state with which the USSR was engaged in a war of nerves that could at any point explode in nuclear disaster. But I was also a Christian, a brother in Christ. All day long around those tables in village after village we ate and drank together and prayed for the day when our peoples could live together without fear of one another. The ancient traditions of hospitality had allowed a stranger to be welcomed as a friend.

In yet another circumstance I remember taking friends to the Holy Land. After days of intense visits and conversations they finally had a little time to shop for souvenirs and gifts in a bazaar. I watched with some amusement at what happened next. My friends were very eager in the short time available to complete their purchasing. They did not understand that in Arab culture politeness required that transactions should occur among friends. "Becoming friends" required that food or drink should be offered and received. Consequently the shopkeepers were offering their prospective customers cups of very black, very hot, very sweet Turkish coffee. Many of the shoppers did not like Turkish coffee and were simply eager to pay their bills. Looking on I knew that I was watching a collision of cultures, and I realized that the next time I owed it to "the shoppers" to tell them about the traditions of hospitality in the culture of their hosts.

I cite these stories to underscore the fact that what the Hebrew storytellers knew is so deeply inscribed in human nature and experience that it is virtually universal. Though it takes many forms it is fundamental to all cultures. Human beings know instinctively, if not rationally, that there is more to eating and drinking than simply maintaining bodily functions. It is that "something more" that we seek to find, share, and celebrate.

Perhaps this helps to account for the fact that so many of the stories found in the Bible center around food. The Hebrew storyteller describes the

Fall, for example, in relation to food. Everything in the Garden is blessed by God and therefore bears God's presence, everything, that is, except for one tree. The tree of the knowledge of good and evil has not been so blessed. It alone does not convey God's presence and therefore its fruit is not a source of energy or life. On the contrary, to eat of the fruit of this tree is to bring about one's death.

I confess that the story of Adam and Eve's disobedience was an enormous problem for me even as a small child. I was afraid to talk about my difficulties with the story because everyone else seemed to treat it as if it were self-evident. Adam and Eve had disobeyed God's commandment that they should not eat of the fruit of that tree, and so it followed logically that they should undergo a severe punishment.

I understood that. When I did something that I should not do my mother would say that she was going to tell my father when he got home from work. I soon learned that this meant my father would administer an appropriate punishment. If my disobedience had been serious enough to merit it I would receive a spanking. I found that more humiliating than painful, but I always knew that when it was bedtime my father would come to tuck me in and in the process would talk with me about what I had done. He would make sure that I knew that I was not to do it again and would then assure me that he loved me and forgave me for what I had done. On the basis of that experience what I really wanted to understand was, what was God's problem? If my father, a mere mortal, could forgive me and give me a good-night hug and kiss, why could God not do at least that much? Much later Anselm of Canterbury gave me the classical answer of Latin theology in his justifiably famous treatise, "Why God Became Man" (Cur Deus Homo). God could not ignore and forgive this sinful disobedience, because to do so without an appropriate act of satisfaction would have compromised divine justice. If God had done that, God would no longer have been God, hence the necessity of the sacrifice, the atonement of a God-man. In simpler terms, I wanted to know why it was that when God came looking for Adam and Eve and found them hiding among the trees he couldn't have reprimanded them, told them to mend their ways, and then assured them that he still loved them like a father.

Much later I learned that there had been others in the history of the church, many of them Greek-speaking theologians like Athanasius of Alexandria (see *On the Incarnation*), who read the story from a quite different perspective. The tree was for them the presence of death in the Garden, since it was not blessed and therefore did not convey or impart life. It was like the nothingness, the non-existence out of which God had called the creation in the beginning. Eating of the fruit of that tree brought death itself into the whole creation. God could, from this perspective, have enfolded Adam and Eve into his embrace and forgiven them for their disobedience, but it would have done no good because they were already dying. And with them the whole creation had now become subject to death. God's problem was not simply the tension between love and justice in the face of human sin, it was the fact that the creation God loved and had called good was now in the grip of death. This required much more than making satisfaction and granting forgiveness. It meant that God would have to overcome death itself in order to save the entire creation. This put many things in perspective. It did not eliminate the central role of the law in both the Jewish and Christian traditions or the juridical images and concepts so characteristic of much of Latin theology, but it placed them in a far broader context.

The original sin that transpired in the story of the Garden was that human beings began to treat the world as if it were an end in itself. God had made everything to be transparent to Godself, sources of endless life, love, and blessing for humankind. But now the world became opaque to human eyes. When treated as an end in itself the world lost its value. Instead of being the source of life and the means of communion with God and neighbor it became a place of joylessness, violence, and death. The natural dependence of humankind upon God was replaced by the illusion of autonomy. The consequence, of course, was that Adam and Eve were driven from the Garden to earn their own bread by the sweat of hard labor. Ultimately they would die and return to the dust from which they had been created. Food became an end in itself. To control the food supply was an expression of power. But humankind now ate death. Food continued to be necessary even for this fallen life, but it no longer fully satisfied the deepest of human hungers.

Human beings had failed to respond to God's love with our love. We had chosen to live in the world without God. In so doing we lost our vocation, our identity as priests in this cosmic Eucharist. But the gospel is that God did not leave humankind in the darkness of exile, but came to us as light in our darkness. God spoke to us and reached out to us through judges, prophets, priests, and kings. God promised not only to come to us, not only to save us, but also to complete what God had set out to do in creation itself. And so God became one of us in the person of Jesus the Christ.

The theme of food continues as central to both the Old and New Testament scriptures. If the Fall takes place around eating, so too Israel's deliverance from slavery in Egypt imprints itself generation after generation through the repetition of the Passover Meal. Among Jews and Christians food is to be blessed, and in that act God is to be blessed as the giver of all good things. It is surely no surprise that in both communities the ultimate image of God's final victory over sin and death is a messianic banquet to which God's people will come from East and West, from North and South to sit together and to feast at God's holy table.

In creating their portraits of Jesus of Nazareth, the gospel writers give a great deal of attention to stories about eating and drinking. Jesus' first miracle takes place at a wedding feast in Cana of Galilee when he turns water into wine — the best wine — so that the guests may rejoice and celebrate. Jesus eats and drinks with his disciples, but most prominent in his ministry is the frequency with which he challenges the prevailing customs, rules, and laws with regard to eating and food. Put succinctly, Jesus is constantly eating and drinking with the wrong people in the wrong places at the wrong times. One might well make the case that Jesus was crucified in large measure for his table manners. He refused to observe the prevailing distinctions between those who are clean and those who are dirty, impure, and unacceptable. Lepers, publicans, tax collectors, women, sinners of every sort find a place at his table or he at theirs. His reported miracles involve the feeding of thousands of hungry people for whom he has compassion. Again and again he tells parables and stories about farmers, fields, vineyards, dinner parties, banquets, and feasts. In his Father's realm, he teaches, all are invited to the banquet, all will be fed, and all will be welcomed as God's children.

On the night he was betrayed, the gospels tell us, he sat at table with his disciples to observe the Feast of the Passover. It is the prelude to the story of his arrest, trial, and crucifixion. In that meal, as all Christians know, he blesses God and identifies himself with the breaking of bread and with the sharing of the cup of wine. At the heart of his community — those who follow him until this very day — is this act of thanksgiving. In it we celebrate his presence through the Holy Spirit, his resurrection and victory over sin and death, and his promises about God's faithfulness and love.

In this feast, food and drink once again become transparent to the goodness of God in Jesus Christ and we receive new life through communion with our Creator. In this meal we are united in fellowship with one another and with the whole communion of saints, and we have a foretaste of what it will be like when God completes the work of redeeming a fallen creation. By God's grace, we have a special place in God's continuing work. As forgiven sinners we stand as the Body of Christ before God to offer up ourselves and this broken world that God loves. We beg God's continuing mercy and compassion for all God's children. We offer everything to God in the context of our praise and thanksgiving for God's presence with us in Christ. And we receive the world back from God as a blessing and a task to be lived out. In Christ we have received once again our vocation to bless God and to be a blessing in and to the world. Whether the issues have to do with justice, mercy, peace, ecology, beauty, suffering, or death, we are called to seek what it means to love God with all our hearts, our neighbors as ourselves, and creation as God's gift.

The tragedy in all of this, of course, is that the gift of the Eucharist as an embodiment of the unity Christ has given to us has become the most divisive element in the entire history of the Christian church. For that reason alone it has lost the possibility of transparency to the unity of all humankind as God's gracious gift. Indeed, the fact that Christians cannot gather at this table because the church has become deeply divided is the scandal that obscures both the message of the gospel and the church's understanding of its mission in the world.

The reason I have learned to appreciate the Hebrew storyteller's simplicity and directness is that all of my life I have been caught between two seemingly contradictory notions of what Christianity and the mission of the church are about. On the one hand are those for whom Christianity is a deeply spiritual matter, a sort of inner retreat from the mundane world, a place where spirituality is to be cultivated. That, of course, is especially true today when so many people have abandoned the churches and all forms of organized religion, but describe themselves as deeply spiritual persons. On the other hand are those for whom Christianity is a profoundly worldly reality, one that needs constantly to be made more relevant to its particular context. If changing the heart is the object of the one, changing the world, that is, improving the world, is the concern of the other. But as a wise teacher once taught me, whether you spiritualize your religion or secularize your faith, the real world of daily life, the world of eating and drinking, of working and loving, is left empty and largely untouched. This is especially acute if one recognizes that the Christian faith is not in the first instance a series of ideas to be held in the mind and defended against attack, but rather a life to be lived, a way of life to be embraced.

Suppose that the Eucharist, the Lord's Supper, is not simply a rite or a ceremony, not simply a sacrament in some technical theological sense or an audiovisual aid. Suppose instead that it is the very heart and soul, so to speak, of what it means to be a Christian and of what the mission of the church is truly about. Suppose that it is not about setting bread and wine apart for a sacred use (one might add water and oil to a longer sacramental list) but rather discovering again and again that because this bread and wine are holy, all food and drink come as God's holy gifts to give us life, to make our life into communion and to bring us into God's presence. Suppose that because this table is holy, all tables have that hidden (mysterious) possibility.

Suppose that sacraments are not religious events with cause-and-effect sequences technically defined, ecclesiastically controlled, and recognized by conformity to carefully constructed formulae. Suppose rather that these are moments that are built into every human life: birth, hunger, illness, love, work, and death. If such a thing is possible, then the Greek New Testament's word, "mysterion," is closer to the truth than its Latin translation, "sacramentum." The latter means sign, to signify or symbolize. It has led to endless debates that have advocated an enormous gulf between symbol and reality. How is Christ present in this sacrament? Is the mode of his presence real or only symbolic? Given the way that the creator has wired us, made us creatures who only know what we know through symbols, beginning with language, all reality is symbolic and all symbols worthy of the title are real. The church is called to live these universal human events in a particular way that is in light of the gospel, so that by the grace that God alone may give these mysteries transform the life of the world. "Mystery" is a better word, because they are events in which God comes to us through the work of the Spirit. We do not control them or dispense them; rather we ask and trust God to fulfill the promises we have been given. Nor do we understand them, for they are far deeper than reason can fathom. We can only describe what we experience and witness to what the Word of God reveals. Our teachings are just that, what the church learns about the mystery of God through the experience of its life of prayer and worship and engagement with the world. The mystery, of course, is God, the one who comes to us and makes everything new.

Our mission, therefore, is neither to spiritualize nor secularize the good news of what it means to be a joyful people who live in hope. It is so to live out the grace hidden in the world that we ourselves may be transformed, and the world that seeks to live as if God were dead might discover the true joy of being God's sons and daughters.

If this be true, we have a very long journey ahead of us. For many reasons most Christians would not describe participating in Holy Communion as a joyful event, a little Easter, to which they long to come each week. Many Protestant communities celebrate this sacrament as few as four times a year. And many Orthodox and Roman Catholics who attend liturgy or the mass each week commune only once or twice annually. Moreover, it is not typical that worshipers recognize that a eucharistic life is one in which all people must have food and drink, shelter and work, and all Christians must practice hospitality in the broadest sense of that word. Nor do most Christians understand what it means that we stand before God in behalf of the world and its people, seeking justice, mercy, and peace, which in turn becomes the meaning of the work we do beyond the church community.

This suggests to me that our notions of the sacramental dimensions of life have to be deepened. That will only happen when the boundaries around what we have spoken of as sacraments are broken open and the shape of our everyday lives is fundamentally transformed. Our "instincts" sense the need we have for this as evidenced by the fact that though we do not celebrate the Eucharist at weddings or funerals, for example, we go to some other place to eat and drink and to try to capture the meaning of the event. This transformation will involve every level of our lives — personal, social, political, and material. It will require the special gifts of artists, ethicists, musicians, politicians, pastors, theologians, and of course storytellers.

In the course of this journey or pilgrimage we will certainly discover that some of us are literally starving for want of food and others are not yet hungry enough for the other blessings that come from communion with God and our neighbors. But if we pay attention to the Hebrew storyteller and most especially to Jesus, we may come to understand the mysterious truth that "we are what we eat."

The Role of the Pastor-Theologian in the Evangelization of the Church: A Wesleyan/Methodist Way Forward

Kenneth H. Carter Jr.

> The so-called "crisis of the church" is neither organizational nor programmatic, but theological. The heart of the matter is the loss of the church's identity as a theological community, occasioned by the distance at which the church lives from the sources of its faith and life.
>
> Thus the renewal of the church begins, at least on the human level, with the recovery of those sources and practices which historically have enabled people to encounter and to be encountered by "the grace of our Lord Jesus Christ, the love of God, and the communion of the Holy Spirit." It begins, as well, with the recovery of the identity of the ordained minister or priest as theologian and scholar.[1]

The mainline Protestant church in North America is in the midst of crisis. The symptoms are decline of active membership, inability to retain our youth, weakening of institutions that have shaped the vocational lives of prior generations, and lack of clarity about the pressing issues of our time. These symptoms are clearly visible, and yet the underlying causes of our

1. Wallace Alston, from the grant proposal to the Lilly Foundation, Inc., for funding for the Pastor-Theologian Program.

present condition are not often diagnosed. That condition has something to do, surely, with "the sources of [the church's] faith and life" and "the distance at which the church lives from them."

The diagnosis of this condition seems to me to be worthy of attention for pastor-theologians who understand the renewal of the church to be a theological and not merely practical endeavor. By extension, a deep appreciation for the tradition alongside an awareness of the present cultural reality is the precise context for the work of the pastor-theologian as evangelist within the congregation. Over thousands of years of history, God's people held to core traditions while also adapting them to varying circumstances: wilderness, promised land, monarchy, exile. These core traditions have been the sources of faith and life for Israel. Christians in twenty-first-century North America find themselves in need of the same skills: the capacity to reflect theologically and the willingness to diagnose the culture both internally and externally.

A number of intellectuals within and outside the church would diagnose the culture today in relation to the shift from modernity to postmodernity. And as most postmodern reflection is quick to note, this is more than a debate within academic departments. The artistic, popular, and ecclesial cultures are all shaped by postmodernism. The modernist division of sacred and secular has given way to the postmodern desire for wholeness and unity; imagination has attained a priority over rationality in theological reflection; confidence in progress and science has come into question; and human sin and evil are taken more seriously.[2]

I have become convinced of the importance of the church's evangelization in a postmodern culture, and the role of the pastor-theologian *as evangelist* sent to those already sitting in the pews. As Karl Barth noted in his discussion of evangelization, "The concern of evangelization is precisely to sound out the Gospel on this shifting frontier between true and merely nominal Christians."[3] The cultural shift across twenty-five years of serving as a pastor has occasioned in me a renewed interest in drawing closer and drinking more deeply from the wisdom of the Christian tradition for the

2. I am aware of the debate concerning postmodernism: whether it is an issue that merits attention, whether it is a movement that should be embraced by Christians or avoided, etc. Setting aside these issues, the role of the evangelist is inhabited in a different culture/climate from one or two generations ago. To see this in practice, compare C. S. Lewis, *Mere Christianity,* with N. T. Wright, *Simply Christian.*

3. Karl Barth, *Church Dogmatics* IV.3 (Edinburgh: T. & T. Clark, 1962), p. 873.

sake of those who "being 'Christians' before they know what is at issue or have made any resolve or expressed any desire to be such, are just as much strangers to the Gospel, or have only the same hearsay knowledge, as if they belonged to [the nations] to whom the disciples are sent."[4]

I would suggest we begin, in the first place, as ministers who work at being self-consciously theological in our practice of ministry. From out of my own tradition, this leads me to begin with grace as the *content* of evangelism. In the second place, the theological underpinnings of worship become the *primary context* for the evangelization of Christians otherwise unaware of the sources of the church's faith and life. At most, we have nominal Christians for an hour on a Sunday morning. The theological integrity of that hour is critical for the postmodern Christian who has come (consciously or not) to a place where faith seeks understanding. In the third place, the primary source of the church's faith and life is scripture. Therefore I have come to see scripture as the *primary curriculum* for evangelization and the teaching of scripture the means of recovering the church's identity as a theological community. Finally, I will offer a modest constructive proposal for the renewal of the church through evangelization.

The Wesleyan/Methodist Way of Graced Practice: The *Content* of Evangelism

Four theological emphases in Methodism have given content to my understanding of grace and have guided my own practice of evangelization.

In the first place, John Wesley's theology was shaped by his understanding of the *imago Dei,* which is his primary way of describing the process of salvation in our lives. This is how Methodists talk about those sources and practices that historically have enabled people to encounter and be encountered by God's grace. A contemporary theologian in the Wesleyan tradition, Geoffrey Wainwright, speaks of our capacity to commune with God by employing the biblical and theological concept of the *imago Dei.* Originally, we were made for a lively relationship with God. Thus two of Wainwright's favorite theological statements are taken from the first Westminster Confession: "What is the chief end of man? Man's chief end is to glorify God and to enjoy him forever." The

4. Barth, *Church Dogmatics* IV.3, p. 872.

second is taken from Saint Augustine: "Thou hast made us for Thyself, and our hearts are restless until they find their rest in Thee."[5]

When I live out of this theological beginning place as a pastor-theologian, I begin with the belief that those who seem content to remain nominal Christians or who take their clues for life's meaning from the culture are missing the fullness of life with God for which they were made. No matter how busy and challenging their lives are, they cannot fulfill their humanity apart from the experience of God's presence and a response to God's claim on their lives. That said, if the pastor-theologian does not proclaim the gospel in a compelling way, and through this proclamation raise the question of life's meaning and purpose substantively for those who have wandered through the church's doors, then likely no other voice in a postmodern culture will!

In the second place, having begun with the *imago Dei,* Wesley dealt with the distortion of that image (sin), which he identified as the condition of the heart curved in on itself. We are drawn toward God primarily through God's initiative (revelation), yet we resist God. We are apt to ignore our vocation (communion with God, growth in the image of God) precisely because we think we love the gods of our surmise more than the God who comes to us in the scandalous particularity of Jesus Christ. Given the distance we live from the sources of the church's faith and life, we can do so without conscience. Yet the distance of the church from its own sources of faith and life is but a symptom of the distance we each live from God's claim on our lives. We exchange the truth of God for a lie.[6] As Wainwright puts this, we ignore reality, which is a life lived "towards God." The people who come to worship God, Sunday after Sunday, come more often than not to worship a distorted image of God. I believe one of the chief responsibilities of a pastor-theologian in a time when most Christians know little of scripture and less of the substance of the church's theological affirmations is to be a theologian who can name the distortion from out of the sources of the church's faith and life and then proclaim the truth of the God who has come to us in Jesus Christ.

Moreover, a pastor-theologian cannot be a credible critic of the human condition or an evangelist set apart to enable people to encounter God's grace without a self-conscious theological anthropology. For instance,

5. *Doxology: The Praise of God in Worship, Doctrine and Life* (New York: Oxford University Press, 1980), pp. 16-17. See also Geoffrey Wainwright, "Towards God," *Union Seminary Quarterly Review,* Supplementary Issue (1981): 13.

6. Rom. 1:25.

Wainwright's emphasis on humanity understood as the image of God, whose vocation is communion with God, does not imply that he has an exalted view of human nature. The relationship between God and persons is understood as divine gift, due to the "character of God, his intention for humanity, his action to achieve his purpose." Methodist theology at its best has held together a *pessimism of nature* and an *optimism of grace,* and this has influenced my own practice as a pastor-theologian: I am not naïve about the human condition, but neither do I limit the possibility of God's intervention in a life or situation.

As a pastor I recognize this paradox not only in my congregation but also in my own personal life — that I am drawn to God, and yet I also resist God. The culture tempts us all to exchange the substance of the gospel for the convenient and comfortable lies. If from the Wesleyan theological perspective the image of God within communicates a capacity for God, then the reality of sin includes the many ways I invent to keep God at a distance, not only from my life but from the lives of the people I serve. This internal struggle is at the heart of a Wesleyan understanding of human nature.

In the third place, because Wesley held an essentially catholic view of sin as a malignant disease rather than an obliteration of the *imago Dei* in fallen human nature, he replaced the doctrine of election with a notion of "prevenient grace."[7] The presence of the "imago Dei" in each person draws the individual toward God. This movement is an act of prevenient grace.

The reality of prevenient grace has also shaped my theological understanding of pastoral practice. From the baptism of infants to an awareness that God is at work in the lives of individuals and groups prior to and apart from our knowledge or perception, I am aware of God's initiative with human lives. Wesley writes about the possibility of our participation in the means of grace prior to faith. He advised the early Methodists to "preach faith until you have it, and then preach faith because you have it."[8] In other words, concerning the relationship between pastoral practice and God's prevenient grace, practice is often prior to doctrine: we live into a new way of believing!

7. A helpful discussion can be found in Albert Outler, *Evangelism and Theology in the Wesleyan Spirit* (Nashville: Discipleship Resources, 1996), pp. 96ff. Outler more than any other figure is responsible for the advocacy of John Wesley as an ecumenical theologian meriting serious engagement in the twentieth century. See also the wonderfully titled "Predestination Calmly Considered," in *John Wesley,* ed. Albert Outler (New York: Oxford University Press, 1964), p. 17.

8. Outler, ed., *John Wesley,* p. 17.

Here a theology of God's prevenient grace begins to blend with an attention to practices. In the fourth place, Wesley's orientation — what he would call "practical divinity" — has influenced my own practices as a pastor-theologian. I think often of Wesley's journal entry where he insisted that: "The Lord's Supper was ordained by God to be a means of preventing, justifying or sanctifying grace . . . [thus] no fitness is required at the time of communicating, but a sense of our state, a sense of utter sinfulness and helplessness."[9]

For Wesley, salvation was a process by which men and women come to a deeper and more profound understanding and experience of grace. I live in the hope that, as a pastor-theologian, the sources and practices recovered for the sake of reclaiming the church as a theological community have aided persons in congregations on the journey that Eugene Peterson has wonderfully named "a long obedience in the same direction."[10] For Wesley they and we are partakers of the means of grace: "By means of grace, I understand outward signs, words or actions, ordained of God, and appointed for this end, to be the ordinary channels whereby He might convey to men [and women], preventing, justifying or sanctifying grace."[11]

There is nothing new here! These outward signs, words, or actions still, after two millennia, include prayer, individual and corporate; searching the scriptures; and receiving the sacraments. These means were, for Wesley, "my waiting in the way God has ordained, and expecting that He will meet me there, because he has promised to do so."[12] I once heard Ernest Campbell describe this pastorally as the call to "energize the usual rather than schedule the unusual."

These means (the common, ordinary practices within congregations) are at the heart of the vocation of the pastor-theologian. In prayer we commune with God, a primary dimension of what it means to be created in God's image. We commune with God as a means God has given us to com-

9. Reuben P. Job, *A Wesleyan Spiritual Reader* (Nashville: Abingdon Press, 1997), p. 112.

10. Eugene Peterson, *A Long Obedience in the Same Direction* (Downers Grove, IL: InterVarsity Press, 1980).

11. *The Bicentennial Edition of The Works of John Wesley,* vol. 1 (Nashville: Abingdon, 1984), p. 381.

12. *The Bicentennial Edition of The Works of John Wesley,* vol. 1, p. 391. For those seeking to grasp this in a Reformed framework, see Craig Dykstra, *Growing in the Life of Faith* (Louisville: Geneva, 1999), especially his reflection on the "Larger Catechism," p. 42.

municate with God (this is the priestly work of pastoral ministry), and even, at times, to communicate on behalf of God (the prophetic). In the reading of scripture we are encountered by the Word of God that is both human and divine. In receiving the Lord's Supper we acknowledge the material creation (bread, wine) as blessed by God and as a sacrament, as an "outward and visible sign of an inward and spiritual grace." The means of grace also shape us ecclesially, or as Craig Dykstra observes, "communities do not just engage in practices; in a sense, they are practices."[13] *The primary work of the evangelist is to communicate the internal logic and theological meaning of these practices.*

I have begun to sketch the link between a theology of grace, and the means of grace or practices that are the ordinary channels whereby God sanctifies human life and draws persons into communion with God. Craig Dykstra and Dorothy Bass have defined practices as "things Christian people do together over time in response to and in the light of God's active presence for the life of the world."[14] I believe that pastors and the congregations they serve are shaped by Christian practices. The core Christian practice, of course, is worship.

"Lost in Wonder, Love and Praise": Worship as the Context for Evangelization

Given that people dwelling in a postmodern culture enter a sanctuary with the expectation of worshiping the God they have cobbled together from the culture rather than the God revealed in the life, death, and resurrection of Jesus Christ, how does the worship of God become a self-conscious occasion for the pastor-theologian to engage in the evangelization of the nominal Christian? How are the lives of postmodern Christians formed and re-formed by the worship of the living God?

In his book *Worship as Theology,* Don E. Saliers speaks of the church's worship as "an intentionally gathered community in mutual dialogue with God's self-communication."[15] Yet what the nominal Christian believes

13. Craig Dykstra, "Reconceiving Practice in Theological Inquiry and Education," *Virtues and Practices in the Christian Tradition,* ed. Nancey Murphy, Brad Kallenberg, and Mark Nation (Harrisburg, PA: Trinity Press International, 1997), p. 173.

14. *Practicing Our Faith,* ed. Dorothy Bass (San Francisco: Jossey-Bass, 1997), p. 5.

15. Don E. Saliers, *Worship as Theology: Foretaste of Glory Divine* (Nashville: Abingdon Press, 1994), p. 26.

about the God whom the church praises, what the heart turned in on itself knows about the God whom the church beseeches, what the restless soul understands of the God who communicates through Word and sacrament must be assumed to be minimal. "If understood fully," Saliers goes on, "liturgy is doing God's will and work in the world while providing human beings with a time and a place for recalling who God is and who we are before God. . . . Worship that focuses primarily on self-expression fails to be worship in Spirit and in truth."[16]

Therefore the first word to be said about worship as evangelization is that it must be worship that resists the subjectivity of a culture turned in on itself as well as individual hearts turned in on themselves. Reverence and not relevance is the point. This is not to say that worship makes no connection with people's real lives. Quite the contrary! People enter the sanctuary with a restlessness, but it is a restlessness that they cannot name or a restlessness that has been misnamed by the media or the marketplace, by a culture of self-help or of superficial spiritualities. When the church's liturgy is ordered in such a way as to turn the lives of those gathered toward the "Maker of heaven and earth and of all things seen and unseen" through acts of praise, confession, proclamation, sacraments, and prayer, then the church's refusal to play to the heart turned in on itself responds to the actual need of the restless heart for God. As Saliers puts it, "Our pathos, the reality of human life, our daily struggle to make sense of longing, hopes, fears, joys, provides an experiential link. . . . liturgical celebration is that place of convergence where our lives are brought together about the book, the font, and the table of the Lord in which the grace of God becomes audible, visible, palpable, kinetic."[17]

In the second place, those who enter the sanctuary of a community of faith that is self-consciously theological in their worship of God will find themselves in a counter-community. That community, in Walter Brueggemann's words, "sings about and treasures a new world, a new social possibility in which swords will become plowshares, spears will turn to pruning hooks (Micah 4:3), in which you shall not plant and another eat (Isa. 65:21-22), in which everyone shall be content and none shall be afraid (Lev. 26:5-6).

16. Saliers, *Worship as Theology,* p. 27.

17. Saliers, *Worship as Theology,* p. 28.

18. Walter Brueggemann, *Israel's Praise: Doxology Against Idolatry and Ideology* (Philadelphia: Fortress Press, 1988), p. 153.

Israel's best doxology is not self-congratulation nor is it resignation. It is hope kept sharp by pain still present. It is praise kept honest by candid abrasiveness. It is celebration kept open for subversiveness."[18] That is to say, in the midst of praise, confession, proclamation, the sacraments and prayer, a nominal Christian may be initiated into the radical claims of discipleship that lead a person to begin to live as though God's grace has already trumped Herod's decrees.

In the third place, from out of a world obsessed with accumulation and achievement, the weary and heavy-laden enter the sanctuary as those who have forgotten or never known the inextricable connection between grace and gratitude. Though they were made to glorify God and enjoy God forever, most postmodern Christians are rarely given the opportunity to express thanks. As essayist Barbara Grizzuti Harrison put it, "I am not happy when I do not go regularly to church, and not (I think) because I am oppressed by the consciousness of wrongdoing, but because I am weightier, having missed the opportunity to meditate, express adoration, contrition, thanks and supplication in loving and dignified communion with others."[19] Or as Scottish theologian and preacher John Baillie noted at the conclusion of his Gifford Lectures, "Many of our own contemporaries in the Western lands who believe themselves to have wholly surrendered all their former ancestral Christian convictions, are nevertheless left with some impulse or feeling of gratitude for the blessings they have enjoyed, though they are now without any means of making this articulate."[20] So he recounts that Katherine Mansfield exclaimed upon seeing the Alps, "If only one could make some small grasshoppery sound of praise to some one, of thanks to some one — but to whom?"[21] The service of worship that seeks to recover the sources and practices that have enabled people to encounter and be encountered by the grace of God through praise, confession, proclamation, the sacraments, and prayer becomes the occasion for nominal Christians not only to name the One we were made to glorify forever but also to practice the scales of rejoicing so that their weightier selves are lifted.

Finally, though not exhaustively, participation in a community of praise, confession, proclamation, sacraments, and prayer is often the means

19. Barbara Grizzuti Harrison, *Italian Days* (New York: Ticknor & Fields, 1989), p. 332.

20. John Baillie, *The Sense of the Presence of God* (London: Oxford University Press, 1962), p. 249.

21. Baillie, *The Sense of the Presence of God*, p. 249.

by which the *imago Dei* is restored in a person whose sin has kept that person at more than an arm's length from God and from neighbor. Yet it matters immensely, as Saliers put it, "that the church's language about God . . . be grammatically appropriate to its true object." Theology, he goes on to say, is "the grammar of what is known when God is appropriately acknowledged, praised, invoked and supplicated." That is to say, when in worship we properly name God as the one who forgives sin, the reality of forgiveness is sometimes, by grace, understood and by faith received.

Reinhold Niebuhr tells of a woman in his congregation in Detroit who came to him some months after he had spoken about forgiveness. She reported that the service "had brought about a reconciliation between her mother and sister after the two had been in a feud for five years. I accepted the news," reports Niebuhr, "with more outward than inward composure. There is redemptive power in the message! I could go on the new courage that came out of that little victory for many a month."[22]

The worship of God is a practice, perhaps *the* practice, where the role of the pastor-theologian is most visible and critical. Doctrine and life, grace and human nature, the Word and the world — these realities come together in an hour of worship.

"Teaching Them to Obey Everything I Have Commanded You": Scripture as the Curriculum for Evangelization

The pastor-theologian as evangelist also is one who shapes the lives of the congregation he or she serves as the story of scripture is taught and told. "I believe," says Caleb in the midst of narrating the story of his family's life lived East of Eden in John Steinbeck's novel of the same name, "that there is one story in the world, and only one. . . . Humans are caught — in their lives, in their thoughts, in their hungers and ambitions, in their avarice and cruelty, and in their kindness and generosity too"[23] — in a net of one story. That story is what the church calls scripture and, according to Robert Jenson, "The church reads her Scripture as a single plotted succession of events, stretching from creation to consummation, plotted around Exodus and Res-

22. Reinhold Niebuhr, *Leaves from the Notebook of a Tamed Cynic* (1929; Louisville: Westminster/John Knox Press, 1990), p. 27.

23. John Steinbeck, *East of Eden* (New York: Penguin Books, 1992), p. 413.

urrection."[24] "Give me a used Bible," says Caleb's friend Samuel a bit earlier in the novel, "and I will, I think, be able to tell you about a [person] by the places that are edged with the dirt of seeking fingers. Liza," he adds, "wears a Bible down evenly."[25]

Likely those in the pews of our congregations have worn a Bible down not at all. As we noted at the beginning, nominal Christians are just as much strangers to the gospel, or have only the same hearsay knowledge, as if they belonged to the nations to whom the disciples are sent. Whether one uses *Disciple* developed by the United Methodists or *Kerygma* or the Bethel Bible Series or *A Year with the Bible* or no curriculum other than the voices of those who have sought meaning in these pages throughout the ages, there is no more important curriculum for the evangelization of the postmodern, nominal Christian than what has been available to the church since the beginning: the Bible. One can blog the Bible for the congregation, offer weekly Bible studies during the day and in the evenings, invite nearby academics in to teach on Sunday mornings, or hold periodic seminars on scripture, but again there can be nothing more critical for the evangelization of the people of God than a steady, substantive engagement with the Old and New Testaments.

In particular I have found the Gospel of Matthew to be, in the words of Paul Minear, "The Teacher's Gospel."[26] Wesley, in preparing the standard doctrines for the early Methodist churches in the years 1740-1760, left his *Explanatory Notes on the New Testament* and a collection of *Forty-Four Sermons,* of which thirteen are taken from the Sermon on the Mount (Matt. 5–7). A recurring theme in these sermons is the importance of what Wesley calls the "inward righteousness" in relation to external works. In them Wesley was working out the internal logic of the work of God's spirit in the Methodist movement. That he drew so deeply from Matthew's Gospel was not accidental, for this was also Matthew's purpose in providing guidance for his own community.

Minear reads the five discourses of Matthew as manuals for teachers of would-be apprentices or novices or interns in Christian discipleship. Understood in this way, they have instructed me in the evangelization of my own congregation. In the first place, the Sermon on the Mount (Matt. 5–7) gives

24. From a talk at the first pastor-theologian conference in Princeton, New Jersey, in June 1998.

25. Steinbeck, *East of Eden,* p. 267.

26. Paul Minear, *Matthew: The Teacher's Gospel* (New York: The Pilgrim Press, 1982).

nominal Christians a glimpse of the kingdom that has come near in Jesus and begins to give postmodern Christians an imagination for the counter-community the church only haltingly manages to be. Here would-be disciples are not eased into the radical demands of discipleship but confronted with them. Given the postmodern mindset that we identified earlier (a desire for wholeness and unity; the priority of integrity over rationality in theological reflection; the questioning of human confidence in progress and science; and the seriousness with which human sin and evil are taken), Jesus' first discourse addresses and engages this mindset in such a way that the radical call to obedience both convicts and compels the people I have been privileged to serve.

Jesus' second discourse (9:35–11:1) has been, for me, the next step in the evangelization of nominal Christians. Here I find that it helps to hear Jesus' sending of the disciples "to the lost sheep of the house of Israel" (Matt. 10:6) as the seminarians of the Confessing Church in Finkenwalde heard Dietrich Bonhoeffer's lectures on Matthew as the storm gathered in Germany. "They are charged," says Bonhoeffer of the disciples and to fellow pastors living already under the threat of National Socialism, "to proclaim the advent of the kingdom of heaven,"[27] the kingdom that has come near in Jesus, the kingdom that has been given content in his first discourse. Yet that content involves the love of the enemy and expects prayers to be said for the persecutor; it demands Jesus' followers not resist an evildoer but turn the other cheek. If the church is to be a beachhead of God's kingdom in the world, then the vulnerability of those who are being made into disciples by God's grace begins to come into focus. The nominal Christian, as if for the first time, confronts the cost of true discipleship. Here Bonhoeffer's words sharpen the edge of Jesus' words for our time: "The messengers of Jesus will be hated to the end of time. They will be blamed for all the divisions which rend cities and homes. Jesus and his disciples will be condemned on all sides for undermining family life, and for leading the nation astray; they will be called crazy fanatics and disturbers of the peace."[28] As we see through the lens of Germany in the 1930s, we begin to see what discipleship means in our own time and nation.

In the third discourse (13:1-52), the parables invite disciples who are

27. Dietrich Bonhoeffer, *The Cost of Discipleship* (New York: Simon & Schuster, 1995), p. 207.

28. Bonhoeffer, *The Cost of Discipleship*, p. 215.

being created by God's grace to a new level of insight. Now that they have been given an imagination for the kingdom that has come close in Jesus and have been sent into the world as witnesses to God's kingdom, now according to Minear the disciples' "eyes and ears were blessed with understandings of divine secrets that had been denied other [read: nominal] believers."[29] Now we begin to dig deep into scripture and together discover the riches of his grace in these stories that invite us to wrestle with the complexities of discipleship in a world where weeds and wheat are together sown.

The fourth discourse (18:1–19:2) returns us to the ordering of our own congregation and invites reflection on how we live with one another in light of the kingdom that has come close in Jesus. For all the understanding that has been given to the faith of the disciple in the discipline of reading scripture, so much remains for us to be and do. Issues within the community of faith — issues of authority and order; of seeking the lost and those who have gone astray rather than settling down in the herd; speaking the truth in love to those who have fallen short; forgiving one another as those who have been much forgiven: here we return to consider how disciples continue to discipline their life together.

Then in the shadow of the cross we study the final discourse (24:1–26:1) and find that we have more questions than answers! How are we to read the signs of the times? What have we learned about bearing the fruit of righteousness? As we wait and work for the kingdom to come, will we be watchful and productive servants or will we, for all of our study and discipline, find the door to the banquet shut in our face? What shall we do with the talents we have been given by grace? And finally, until he comes again, will we live as those who seek his face in the hungry, the thirsty, the stranger, the naked, the sick, the prisoner?

Yet it is the end of Matthew's Gospel that places the mantle of evangelization upon me as a pastor-theologian: "Go therefore and make disciples of all nations, baptizing them in the name of the Father and of the Son and of the Holy Spirit, and teaching them to obey everything that I have commanded you. And remember, I am with you always, to the end of the age" (28:16-20).

Disciples are made, not born, someone has said. The Christian life is therefore always a process, a journey. The call gets us started. To keep going we need disciplines. The disciplines make the connection between what we

29. Minear, *Matthew: The Teacher's Gospel,* p. 15.

hear from God in the worship and the teaching of the church and how we respond to what we have heard day by day. For some there will be no connection. "Not everyone who says to me, Lord, Lord, will enter the kingdom" (7:21). But for many in the congregation I serve, with the help of God, the discipline that is the study of Scripture has sent them out into the world changed. They read the newspaper, raise their children, welcome the stranger, tend the least of these, and do all that they do as though they have been called to be characters in the ongoing narrative of God's unfolding purposes in human history. "Everyone who hears these words of mine and puts them into practice," Jesus says, "is like a wise man who builds his house on the rock" (7:24). While the Reformed Christian would say this is a matter of election, the Wesleyan would say that it is a matter of God's prevenient grace.

As a pastor-theologian committed to the recovery of those sources and practices that historically have enabled people to encounter and to be encountered by "the grace of our Lord Jesus Christ, the love of God, and the communion of the Holy Spirit," I have sought to evangelize my people by means of the ancient practices of the church and ground them in the sources that will strengthen them for the living of these days. Go and make disciples, Jesus says, of all nations; go to the "ethne," the gentiles. Go not just to the lost sheep of the house of Israel (15:24). Go into all the world, even if it is simply the world that walks through the church door on Sunday morning or on Wednesday night. I am sending you into the world, Jesus says, not to conform to the world, but to shape the world into the image of Christ. Go and make disciples of all nations, baptizing them in the name of the Father, the Son, and the Holy Spirit.

The Pastor-Theologian as Evangelist: A Modest Constructive Proposal

At the heart of this paper are convictions that I have struggled with for some time. Since my own ordination, American Christianity has become increasingly anti-intellectual and so more interested in the practical effects and the visible results of a mission that is less and less understood by persons in the pew. This is not accidental, for the dominant philosophy in American culture is utilitarian and economic, the marketplace having invaded the temple long ago. That said, there is great intellectual capital, to borrow the metaphor from the last sentence, in our theological schools and in the rich traditions that have shaped the mainline churches. The role of the evangelist is to recover those sources and practices that historically have enabled people to encounter and to be encountered by "the grace of our Lord Jesus Christ, the love of God, and the communion of the Holy Spirit." As Scott Jones has noted, "the goal of human life is to allow God's grace to shape us into the kind of mature human beings God intends us to be."[30] Whatever our perception of the role of evangelist, pastor-theologians join the questions of those who are seeking God in sermons, in Bible studies, at gravesides, in counseling settings, in leadership amidst conflict, in public statements. They do not always provide answers, but they help those being mentored to commence the search.

The recovery of the role of the evangelist, in congregations large and small, will be the fulfillment of the great commission as it is directed to the faith of nominal Christians in this generation and in generations to come. I am convinced that the renewal of the church is dependent upon the recovery of a substantive ministry of evangelization. I trust that such a recovery will be yet another gift of God's grace. At times, more often than I would have imagined, this is the pastoral life. And this wholeness toward which we journey with restless hearts is nothing less than the recovery of the image of God — our original orientation — within ourselves and among the people God has given us to serve.

30. Scott Jones, *United Methodist Doctrine: The Extreme Center* (Nashville: Abingdon Press, 2002), p. 214.

The Pastoral Prayer as a Theological Occasion

Scott Hoezee

Pastors do well to pay attention to their words. That is true across the course of a worship service, but such mindfulness becomes particularly vital when it comes to the offering of public prayers, particularly the pastoral prayer. Not every church tradition has the practice of formalized spoken prayers. Some traditions scatter shorter, extemporaneous prayers throughout the service. Other traditions use only pre-written and prescribed prayers established for them by various books of order and other such liturgical resources. But in many Protestant traditions there has been a long practice of the pastor leading the congregation in a prayer that was composed for that particular day and worship service. Sometimes these prayers are completely written out in advance, sometimes they combine pre-written material with extemporaneous material, and sometimes they are completely extemporaneous.

The following essay will apply most particularly to pastors who minister in churches in which they have a free hand in the composing and offering of public prayers. It should be clear at the outset that these reflections apply not only to those who write out their prayers in advance but also to those who are looking for some theological guideposts by which to discipline prayers that are extemporaneous in nature. The goal of this essay is to foster greater theological thoughtfulness. Pastors need to remember that prayers offered in public have a shaping effect on the entire prayer life of the congregation. Over time congregations are formed and shaped by a given preacher — his ways of praying become the congregation's way of praying; her theological emphases become key points of reflection for the members of the congregation. Clearly, then, this is an area worthy of sustained reflection.

To foster such reflection this essay will begin with a brief consideration of how prayer may be a neglected area of thought. Next we will ponder the overall place of prayer in public worship and broach a number of theological issues regarding public, pastoral prayers. Then in the balance of the essay we will turn to three sources from which pastors can draw inspiration in the composing of pastoral prayers: the example of Christ as Intercessor, the book of Psalms, and the tradition of the church through the ages. Each of these sources can encourage pastors to compose and utter prayers that are properly broad in scope, prayers that will address not only local needs and concerns but also prayers that will evince a breadth of global concerns and theological perspective. The goal is not to encourage prayers that are eloquent, poetic, or particularly artful. Rather, the goal is to encourage prayers that help the entire congregation think their way into God's perspective on the world even as those same prayers reflect the huge variety of needs and experiences represented both in the wider world and within the congregation at any given moment.

"Just" Praying

For most people, the pastoral prayer offered by the pastor on Sunday morning is the longest, most focused prayer they will hear all week. Across church history, the weight and significance of such prayers was recognized by the fact that some church communions mandated that the only prayers offered in public worship would be formalized, pre-established prayers that bore the imprimatur of the official church. Prayers were prescribed in both their scope and content as well as in language that had been refined and studied by liturgical committees and others within the church's hierarchy.

For certain segments of the Protestant Reformation, eschewing formalized prayer books put daylight between themselves and the Roman Catholic Church. To this day, many denominations have no history with *The Book of Common Prayer* or other guides that lay out rubrics for public worship and praying. This essay is not the place to debate the relative merits or drawbacks of this liturgical change. However, this essay does contend that the church has rightly recognized the weightiness and import of prayers offered in public worship. Publishing pre-written and set prayers is one way to recognize that weightiness, but it is not the only way. Pastors can acknowledge the vital nature of prayer through the careful preparation of prayers they compose and offer. Indeed, the theological responsibility of the pastor for the offering of thoughtful public prayers is *more* daunting in those places that do *not* rely on prayers already bearing the stamp of church approval.

Recent decades have witnessed great foment in many areas related to public worship. The worldwide ecumenical movement gained momentum across the latter third of the twentieth century and helped many, especially Protestant, denominations recover certain liturgical treasures that had been abandoned in the Reformation. The success of both the charismatic/Neo-Pentecostal movement and the "front door evangelism" movement, spearheaded especially by the Willow Creek Church, shook up people's perceptions of what worship was or should be. The result was an avalanche of thought regarding the nature of preaching, church music, and the very structure and purpose of the Sunday-morning service. But in the heat of those so-called "worship wars," one area that did not receive attention was the nature and place of prayer in public worship.

To some observers, public prayers have fallen on hard times in recent years. Some prayers seem premised on the theological idea that God is not so much the Sovereign of the universe whom we approach with reverence and holy seriousness as our close friend who can be addressed as one preacher began his prayers: "Hey, God, some of us gathered here were thinking we'd like to chat with you for a bit." Whether or not a given pastor goes to that extreme of informality, some worship leaders have grown accustomed to tossing off prayers with little or no forethought. In recent years many liturgical scholars have lamented the trend of using the word "just" as a thoughtless filler in public prayers. "Lord, we just want to thank you for just being so awesome and so we just pray our praise to you." Why, many have asked, would we trivialize our prayers by throwing in a trite-sounding adverb like "just"? If a person wants to eat "*just* a little smidgen of that cheesecake," the presence of "just" is the foil to eating a lot of cheesecake. If you receive a gift that was not what you were hoping to get, you may say, "Well, I guess I will *just* have to make the best of it." Again, the qualifier "just" indicates a less-than-optimal situation.

When it comes to the offering of public prayers, pastors never "just" pray to God off the cuff. Public prayer always informs the prayers of the people the rest of the week. What God hears from his people six days out of seven will stem from what people pick up from their pastors on Sundays.

Pastor-theologians owe it to God to ensure the prayers God hears will be capacious and thoughtful in ways that are fitting for a God who is grand, sovereign, and compassionate.

Praying in Public

What is the point of offering public prayers in worship? Liturgical scholar Gordon Lathrop notes, prayer is hardly the sole provenance of the clergy and certainly is not restricted to formal liturgical occasions.[1] As a line from a traditional hymn once put it, to those who deride prayer as being useless, the Christian's response is "As I breathe, I pray." In traditional Christian spirituality, prayers of praise, rejoicing, confession, and petition are a daily reality. In fact, on any given week the number of prayers uttered by believers outside of the church sanctuary dwarf the comparatively few prayers uttered in the context of formal services of worship. As liturgical practices go, then, prayer is more portable than most other elements of public worship. For most people, a Sunday worship service is probably the only time all week when they will hear a sermon, give an offering, sing a hymn, listen to a choir, partake of the sacrament, or receive a benediction. But that same service will typically *not* be the only occasion all week when people will hear a prayer or engage in prayer themselves. This is one liturgical activity that is ongoing, well after the postlude has been played and the congregation has gone home.

Given the ubiquity of prayer as a standard piece of daily Christian piety, one could wonder about the place of prayer in public worship. Is there a distinction to be drawn between the nature and practice of public prayer vis-à-vis all other prayer outside of worship? Is there any kind of important — if not vital — connection between the prayers offered in public and the welter of other prayers offered by the people the other six days of the week? Any pastor who leads in public prayer would do well to reflect on such questions.

It is obvious that Christian worship cannot be held without prayer. The dialogic nature of worship demands that in addition to singing, a significant part of the human side of communicating with God will very naturally be in the form of prayer. However, all of these reflections traffic in larger

1. Gordon W. Lathrop, *The Pastor: A Spirituality* (Minneapolis: Fortress Press, 2006), pp. 108-12.

theological issues. Listening to a given pastor's prayers over a longer period of time provides answers to questions such as: Is it right to ask God for healing? Is it right to chalk up someone's successful spinal surgery to God's work? How does providence operate (and how much can we attribute to the direct work of God)? What do we make of unanswered prayers and are we able to parse the questions that naturally arise in people's hearts when we observe different outcomes for similar prayers?

That is to say, if a pastor, on behalf of the entire congregation, prays that God heal the cancer of both Marv and Louise only to have Marv eventually die and Louise make a full recovery, how does one deal with this prayerfully in worship? Did God actively choose to take Marv to his heavenly home but to keep Louise on earth a bit longer? Or did God respond only to the prayers about Louise but defer any action where Marv was concerned such that the disease took its natural course?

Every congregation has a Marv and a Louise. Given the mysteries that attend prayer and the difficulty in parsing whether or not a given prayer was really answered or not, should pastors dare to pray no more than generic petitions along the lines of "O Sovereign God, you know the needs that exist across the face of this congregation. In all situations, your will be done, whatever that will may be"? Do we set people up for a crisis of faith — or at least for the asking of acutely painful questions — by getting specific about every Marv and Louise out there?

A robust theology of prayer and providence would insist that we ask God for intervention in every case even if we know full well that in many instances we will be praying for the healing of people who will die or who will be disappointed or who will in some other way fail to receive what the pastor (and the congregation) prays for. Hard questions arise where praying is concerned, but believing in a providential God who invites prayer means the church keeps on praying anyway. The alternative to such bold and specific praying would be to conclude that we live in a universe fraught with randomness. Therefore pastors must hedge their prayers in ways that will prevent members of the congregation from trying to draw neat lines between a given outcome and the direct working of the Almighty. But we cannot ignore the human propensity to pray for very specific things. When a child is desperately ill, her mother does not typically offer up only broad-ranging prayers that seek the well-being of all sick children in all places. No, the mother prays for little Jill and makes no bones about the fact that she wants *this* child to receive a divine touch. Pastors whose theology prevents them from daring to be specific in their public prayers cut against the congregation's natural tendency to be very specific in the prayers they typically offer all week long.

This paper is not the place to plumb the prolix depths of theodicy, providence, and petitionary prayer. It may be enough at this point to remind pastor-theologians that when a given pastor engages in public prayers, he wears his theological heart on his sleeve. To see a pastor's heart exposed in the act of praying is a profoundly good and moving experience for any congregation.

There are other headwaters to be navigated here as well. Pastor-theologians who lead in public prayer need to be ever vigilant to make sure that prayer remains prayer, which means an utterance that is directed solely to God. Some years ago I attended a worship service at Princeton Theological Seminary as part of a summer continuing education event. I sat with a man who had once been a Reformed pastor but who later became a priest in the Episcopal Church. At that evening's worship service one of the liturgists offered a "prayer" that referenced God only in passing. For the most part the prayer was a political lecture clearly designed to instruct those of us in the pews on how we were to think about war and peace, economic policies, and similar issues. As we exited Miller Chapel, my colleague was apoplectic and sputtered, "That is why we need the *Book of Common Prayer* — to prevent a lecture like that from being passed off as a prayer to God!"

He was correct. The intended audience had been those of us in the pews. Such a pseudo-prayer is akin to a certain pastor who would, week after week, essentially begin his prayer by saying, "O God, no doubt you have read this morning's *New York Times*. . . ." There can be no doubt that prayers to God shape those who listen and are led in prayer. There can also be no doubt that the thoughtful pastor-theologian should compose and offer prayers that properly broaden the praying horizons of those in the pews.

But prayers that are sermons in disguise; prayers that are lectures incognito; prayers that smuggle in a rebuke to certain members of the congregation — all such quasi- or pseudo-prayers do more harm than good to all concerned. There is a place to ponder the implications of the gospel, to speak with a prophetic voice, to name the sins that are common to all, or to suggest possible ways to live out the gospel. That place is a sermon derived from a carefully exegeted portion of scripture. A prayer is addressed to God, and since in prayer no pastor or other worship leader can ever presume to know fully the mind of God on any and all subjects, prayers ask for clarity and wisdom where important social issues are concerned. Prayers do not presume to tell worshipers how to think. They encompass the concerns of the day and the headlines in the newspaper but do so in the proper prayerful modes of confession and petition offered by frail human beings who can pray out of one posture: utter humility.

Praying with the Lord

So often in the Gospels we are told that Jesus withdrew to lonely places in order to pray. Almost as often, the disciples search Jesus out on the apparent assumption that he and all of them had better things to do than pray. Eventually they locate Jesus and upbraid him with some version of the question, "What are you doing here? We've been looking all over for you!" The point is that the disciples again and again encountered Jesus in prayer. While they were doing other things, Jesus was praying. This happens every week when Christians gather for worship: worshipers approach a Savior who has been in ceaseless prayer. On Sundays the congregation does not encounter a Jesus who has been sitting around all week waiting for people to show up for Sunday worship. Instead believers find a Lord who has been in constant prayer. Therefore, whatever prayers the pastor offers on the congregation's behalf in the course of a worship service must be seen not as stand-alone or isolated incidents of prayer but rather as prayers that join in the ceaseless prayers being offered by Christ on behalf of the church and the whole world.

Eugene Peterson often points out that so much of the Christian life exists in the midst of what in the Greek language is known as the middle voice. In Greek as in English, there is an active voice and a passive voice for verbs. But there is also a middle voice reserved for verbs whose action began in the past and continues into the future. We can only jump into this already-moving stream of activity. We do not initiate the action (as in the active voice), nor do we passively receive some action (as in the passive voice). Instead we join ourselves to what is already going on — what was happening before we arrived and what will continue after we depart again.[2]

Christians serve not only a risen Savior but a praying Savior, an interceding Savior, one who sits at the right hand of God to plead our cause. From his vantage point as the cosmic Lord of lords and King of kings, Jesus' prayers range as broadly as the universe over which he rules as Sovereign.

2. Eugene H. Peterson, *The Contemplative Pastor: Returning to the Art of Spiritual Direction* (Carol Stream, IL: Word Publishing, 1989), pp. 110-11.

Nothing escapes the divine gaze. Of course, no congregational prayer could ever duplicate the full scope of dominical prayer. No one pastor can see widely, broadly, or deeply enough to come anywhere near a full-scale imitation of divine intercession. However, pastors can and must do what they can to model for the congregation something of this broader perspective. Karl Barth is reported to have said that Christians must hold the Bible in one hand and the daily newspaper in the other. The same can and must be said about pastors and public prayers. Pastoral and congregational prayers whose scope of concern never widens beyond the sanctuary walls do not mirror an interceding Savior whose eye is on the sparrow. In a world such as this one, that sparrow most assuredly includes victims of genocide in Darfur, victims of sexual, racial, and religio-ethnic discrimination, victims of domestic abuse and violence, victims of war and terrorism, the invisible people who are homeless, poor, and just generally marginalized from the mainstream of contemporary society.

Pastors who want to pray in imitation of the Lord Jesus allow their thoughts in prayer to range broadly both across the face of the earth as well as across the variety of experiences represented within the sanctuary itself on any given Sunday morning. While the discerning pastor must think his or her way into the lives of the people in the pews, this must go well beyond praying for the sick whose names are in the bulletin. The thoughtful, theologically informed pastor imagines his or her way into situations with which he or she may or may not have much personal experience. Nevertheless the pastor suspects these situations describe any number of people. So prayers are offered for the lonely and for those whose marriage is flat if not crumbling. Prayers are offered for the exuberant as well as for the depressed, for those dealing with failures in a career as well as for those trying to find thoughtful ways to deal with career successes. Prayers are offered for seniors who look back on a working life they fear in their heart of hearts did not make much of difference to anybody. Prayers are offered for those in abusive relationships as well as for those haunted by memories of abuses long past.

The idea is to stock the theological imagination with the whole panoply of human experience and seek to bring it to speech before God. Pastors must be constantly aware that they are *leading* the congregation in prayer. But if the people are to follow that lead and enter into the prayer along with the pastor, they need to sense some real traction between the prayer and the life to which they will return when the service is concluded (and the life that, in reality, they brought with them when they entered the sanctuary).

What may be needed is a recovery of the uniqueness of the pastoral vocation, a significant portion of which should be the ability critically to stand against certain prevailing attitudes as proffered by society. That is to say, as they ponder what to pray about on behalf of the congregation, pastors need not just to reflect theologically on the obvious needs that people have (the unemployed need jobs, the sick need healing, we all desire protection from terrorist attacks) but also to discern other needs that may not be so obvious. All of this is to say that well-formed prayers reveal needs people may not otherwise sense. When we pray "Your will be done, your kingdom come," among other things such a petition means that we are praying our way into God's world. Theologically formed pastors help the entire congregation do this when they name concerns that reveal God's way of looking at our world and so invite the congregation into cruciform, kingdom-shaped lives.

Barbara Brown Taylor once remarked that no one would be surprised if a pastor called up a member who had just lost his job and offered to come over and pray with him. When someone is in crisis, we expect a pastor to stand alongside of this person, praying for strength, for guidance, and for the opening up of new employment opportunities. But how taken aback (if not piqued) the average churchgoer might be if, upon hearing that a certain person had just received a major promotion at work, the pastor called this person to say, "I just heard about your new job status and was wondering if I could come over to pray with you about this. I'm concerned that this success could introduce some real spiritual temptations in your life and also make it that much more difficult for you to engage in kingdom work. So I'd like to pray with you for strength in the face of this new success." The sheer fact that this would be a striking (if not offensive) thing to say illustrates that pastors often fail to think theologically about the real lives of their people. We too are co-opted into secular ways of viewing the lives people lead Monday-Saturday rather than praying with the Lord on their behalf.

The Psalms: Trumpets, Ashes, and Tears

A key part of pastoral practice in the offering of public prayers in worship may come through a pastor's familiarity with the Hebrew Psalter, which is properly the prayer book of the church. If pastors take their cues from the Psalter, then it will soon become clear that the prayers of the people in worship will need to reflect the whole range of human emotion, including the all-important but oft-neglected category of lament. As John Witvliet has noted, when we take the prayers of the Psalter as a starting point for our own corporate prayer today in the church, we will see four key ingredients to a robust congregational prayer life:

> First, there is a startling diversity of affect and experience in the life of prayer. Religious experience in the Judeo-Christian tradition is as multiform as life itself. Second, the life of faith involves *movement* from lament to praise and back again that evidences the magnetic pull of tenacious faith, on the one hand, and a candid grappling with the problems of this world, on the other. Third, these varied religious affections *counterbalance* each other this side of the eschaton. Lament and praise are incomplete without the other, lest praise, particularly general or descriptive praise, be misunderstood as smug satisfaction or lament be understood as a denial or refusal of grace. Fourth, at some deep level, these diverse expressions *cohere.* Praise and lament do not tear each other apart. However anguished the tension between Psalm 88 and 150, they coexist in the Hebrew Psalter and in the life of prayer.[3]

For some years many have been influenced by the model of prayer that philosopher Nicholas Wolterstorff once offered: namely, the model of Trumpets, Ashes, and Tears. In every gathering of God's people for worship, inevitably there will be those who enter the sanctuary on an emotional and spiritual high, blowing the trumpets of praise to God because of the wonderful things that have happened to them in the week gone by. Others slouch into the sanctuary (or at least they are inwardly slouched even if they walk with a spring in their step), weighed down with guilt, bearing upon their hearts the ashes of repentance for some sin they fear even God may not be able to forgive. Still others come with hearts (if not eyes) brimming with tears of lament and sadness. Wolterstorff claims each condition can reflect an experience of God in the wider world:

> [I]f liturgy is to be authentic, we must also genuinely experience the world as gift and glorious work of God and feel the joy of gratitude; otherwise the songs of praise are mere sounds. We must genuinely experi-

3. John D. Witvliet, *Worship Seeking Understanding: Windows into Christian Practice* (Grand Rapids: Baker Books, 2003), p. 40.

> ence the world as disobedient to God and feel the regret of repentance; otherwise the gestures of repentance are mere gestures. And we must genuinely experience the world as the suffering of God and feel the agony of lament; otherwise the words of intercession are mere words. Authentic experience and life in the world is a condition of authentic liturgy. If the condition is not satisfied, God finds our words and songs and gestures deficient, sometimes even nauseous. . . . In the liturgy, while "holding in remembrance" what we have experienced of God, we give voice to our response. For that we need trumpets and ashes and tears.[4]

Each of these distinct experiences of God in the world — and the corresponding worshipers who have had more than one kind of experience in the days gone by — needs to have a place in the prayer life of the congregation. Each person, whatever his or her lot in life at that particular moment, must know that this season in his or her own life may properly be brought to speech before God. Congregational prayer signals this truth to these people. These are pastorally crucial moments. Particularly those who are in a season of lament, grief, doubt, or guilt-riddled uncertainty need to know their worship of God does not require them to don a mask internally or externally and "Put on a happy faith" (to quote a particularly dreadful, but commonplace, slogan often seen on church signs along with the ever-popular "We're Too Blessed to Be Depressed!").

Of Wolterstorff's three categories, however, the congregants most marginalized are those who come to worship with (and sometimes in) tears. Trumpets typically are given plenty of air-time in worship, particularly in the more exuberant forms of contemporary worship services. There trumpets blare along with steel guitars, drum sets, and "praise teams" whose glowing facial expressions send a kind of liturgical semaphore to the rest of the congregation that *this* is how they are supposed to be feeling, too. As a friend of mine once asked, "Why is it that no church ever has a lament team?" What are we conveying to the wider congregation by not leading worship with any emotion other than upbeat joy and happiness?

Like the psalms, public prayers in worship need to be as wide in scope as possible. Claus Westermann claimed "we can only describe and understand the psalms as originating from worship when worship is seen as the

4. Nicholas Wolterstorff, "Trumpets, Ashes, and Tears," *The Reformed Journal*, February 1986.

unifying center of [Israel's] common life. Prayer in public worship would lose its force without these experiences outside the sanctuary; such prayer is only given life by the movement inwards from outside and back again into daily life."[5]

Prayer in the History of the Church

In recent years, liturgical studies have increasingly turned to the past, to the deepest recesses of the Christian tradition for guidance in a variety of liturgical areas, including public prayers. Some believe that the past may hold the key to the formation of thoughtful prayers in the church today. This is what liturgical scholar Robert Webber has called "the ancient future" of the church.[6] Contrary to certain more contemporary practices of public prayer in worship, traditional prayers followed certain conventions that ensured the kind of wide-ranging petitions and thanksgivings for which this essay has been arguing.

As noted above, in some evangelical circles formalized, pre-set prayers are viewed as too stuffy, too ritualized to fit a contemporary idiom that emphasizes informality in worship settings. There everyone should feel as free and as qualified to participate in worship as formally trained clergy. One of the most recent trends in preaching has been "the roundtable pulpit" in which the entire congregation — or at least key segments of the congregation — are invited to become part of the sermon-writing process. Only such grassroots input into sermons, some now claim, can ensure authenticity for the preached Word. It goes without saying that if the laity is involved in the production of sermons, those same lay people will want a free hand in the uttering of public prayers as well.

In considering the practice of the pastor-theologian in the offering of public prayers, we cannot pretend that this democratizing element is unimportant, nor can we assume it will fade away anytime soon. What remains, then, is to help those who offer public prayers to recognize the value of learning certain ancient prayer patterns. Even if those ancient prayers are not uttered in any formalized way, the sensibilities embedded within them

5. Quoted in Witvliet, *Worship Seeking Understanding,* p. 59.

6. Cf. Robert E. Webber, *Ancient-Future Faith: Rethinking Evangelicalism for a Postmodern World* (Grand Rapids: Baker Academic, 1999).

may well leave behind a good residue, helping pastors form prayers that are more thoughtful than would be the case were there no guiding principles and patterns to be observed.

This applies equally to those who wish to preserve a measure of extemporaneous public praying. Even informal prayers will be enhanced when they are delivered by people who are well schooled in the tradition of Christian prayers. Skilled jazz musicians who improvise well improvise out of a knowledge and mastery of music. Similarly prayers in public worship — those that are written out formally in advance, those that are extemporaneously delivered, and those that are some combination of the two — will be enhanced through a greater awareness of ancient prayers: their rhythms, their core content, and the stereoscopic vision they often achieved in balancing the concerns of earth from the vantage point of heaven.

Liturgical scholar John Witvliet has suggested we need prayers that have a wide-angle vision, prayers that are, in his words, "spacious/comprehensive in scope and that unite and stereoscopically integrate creation/redemption, Word/Spirit, already/not yet."[7] The best of the ancient Christian tradition had a biblically based capacity to encompass a full-blown trinitarian view of God that not only addressed God in the fullness of triune divine identity as Father, Son, and Holy Spirit but also was able to take account of the full range of the works of this triune God.

If pastor-theologians discipline themselves in the pattern of ancient collects and other traditional prayer patterns (and there are now many resources that catalogue ancient prayers), their prayers will praise God for not just local wonders and intramural answers to prayers but for wonders that are as far-ranging as the cosmos God made and still maintains.[8] Disciplined praying will pray for people close to home and far away, for people who are familiar as well as for people who are about as foreign and different as can be imagined. Prayers modeled on ancient traditions will always feel incomplete if praises and petitions never go farther than the walls of the sanctuary or the confines of the nation in which the worshipers happen to find themselves. Ancient prayers remind us that it is not enough to pray for occupations that are familiar to us. We must pray for vocations and forms of com-

7. John D. Witvliet, "Embodying the Wisdom of Ancient Liturgical Patterns: Some Old-Fashioned Rudimentary Euchology for the Contemporary Church" (unpublished paper, 2007).

8. Cf. for instance, *The Worship Sourcebook* (Grand Rapids: Baker Books, 2004).

merce, agriculture, and crafts that may or may not be vital to the community offering the prayers but that are vital to other communities around the world. Ancient prayers remind us that we never pray in isolation. Rather, we join our voices to a chorus of witnesses, both living and dead, who ceaselessly praise God for all God is and has done and who just as ceaselessly cry to God for every conceivable need under heaven.

A person need not recite ancient prayers or exemplars of prayer from sourcebooks or the Book of Common Prayer to let these ancient patterns settle into one's consciousness and liturgical sensibilities. Learning the conventions of capacious praying to the triune God in ways that accord with that same God's being and works are a little like learning the conventions of storytelling. Every parent and grandparent knows that good stories begin "Once upon a time" and proceed forward to sketch certain characters, both the good and the bad, who face certain challenges, both the scary and the mundane, and who proceed through those challenges to some kind of "happily ever after" resolution. Most people intuitively know from having heard good stories as children themselves that stories need a beginning, a middle, an end, and a plot that is capable of moving among these temporal elements in ways that attract and hold the listener's attention.

Learning patterns of prayer is similar to absorbing — and then integrating into one's own being — just these standard elements, movements, and sensibilities. Pastor-theologians who have been well formed by having heard such prayers for many years should allow these patterns to inform every prayer they offer, whether a written prayer or one delivered extemporaneously. Those who did not have the benefit of exposure to such prayers should be encouraged to study and repeat ancient prayers and liturgies.

Finally, some liturgical scholars have developed sets of exercises designed to steep pastors and other worship leaders in the patterns of ancient collects. Pastors are encouraged to listen to their own prayers or to read transcripts of their spoken prayers, bringing their actual prayers alongside the best of the Christian tradition. In this way they come to appreciate what is already fine about their own praying while they critique the prayers of the church today by way of the prayers in scripture and in the liturgies of the church throughout the ages.

Conclusion

C. S. Lewis once wrote that when you add them all up, each person's prayers across the course of life would represent also that person's autobiography. Lewis was right. Our pains, our hidden fears, our joys, the things that make us cry, the problems that vex us the most, the very way we view the world: all are on display in our prayers.[9]

Pastors need not expose the full range of their hearts in public worship or through the prayers offered there. Still, the bottom line of their theology, what they think about God, creation, and their relation, what they hope, what they grieve and lament as well as what they celebrate and sing: all this comes through sooner or later in how they pray before the people of God. Public prayer is a privilege and a pastoral task that only a fool would take lightly. Wise pastors allow their prayers to be formed by a thoughtfully constructed apprehension of life in this world before the face of a sovereign God, by the concerns of the flesh-and-blood human beings seated before them, by the language of the Psalms, by the wisdom of the Christian tradition, and above all by the perspective — dim though we may apprehend it at any given moment — of a triune God whose grandeur and elegant work span the universe and beyond. Every thoughtful pastor-theologian should tremble with awe and feel something of the weighty responsibility that is the high and holy privilege of saying to God's people, "Let us pray."

9. Cf. C. S. Lewis, *Reflections on the Psalms* (Orlando, FL: Harvest Books, 1964).

The Pastor-Theologian and Death

Allen C. McSween Jr.

This discussion on the formation and work of the pastor-theologian grows out of a concern to address the crisis in the church and its ministry posed by the loss of sustained theological reflection on the practice of ministry in and for the life of the church. There is no shortage of substantive theological work produced in academic settings and no shortage of reflections on pastoral ministry from psychological and administrative perspectives, yet there does seem to be a serious lack of attention given to the actual work of ministry in light of the best theological resources of the church ecumenical across the centuries. It is out of a concern that all aspects of pastoral ministry be viewed as occasions for significant theological witness and reflection that this volume is offered.

Before we address the specific issue of the pastor-theologian and death, we must seek to clarify the term "pastor-theologian," and, in particular, the significance of the hyphen between the terms. The understanding reflected in these essays is that *pastor*-theologians engage in their work as *pastors* in terms of a deliberate effort to relate pastoral practice to the best that has been believed, proclaimed, and embodied in the traditions of the church catholic. Doing so does not necessarily make them better pastors than those who define their ministry in more relational or therapeutic terms, but it does anchor pastoral practice in the established wisdom of the church, apart from which pastoral ministry can too easily become captive to that which is merely popular at the moment.

Furthermore, pastor-*theologians* engage in serious theological reflection, but the location and context for their work as *theologians* is that of a particular community of faith that gathers for worship, celebrates the sacraments, engages in ministries of justice and compassion, and buries its dead. Attending to the concreteness and particularity of the congregation as the context for theological reflection is what distinguishes the work of the pastor-theologian from that of the academic theologian.

The particular aspect of the work of the pastor-theologian addressed in this paper is that which finds public expression in the funeral service, especially the funeral sermon. Placing emphasis on the funeral sermon is not meant to denigrate other aspects of the church's pastoral ministry at the time of death. The pastor obviously plays a vital role in marshalling and orchestrating the resources of the Christian community as it ministers to those who grieve. But in the work of comforting the bereaved the pastor-theologian has a distinctive role to play and a unique word to proclaim in the face of death that is and always will be "of first importance" (1 Cor. 15:1).

The Prerequisite of Kindness

The late John Leith, who formed and challenged the vocational identity as pastor-theologians of a number of the authors in this volume, emphasized the importance of a ministry on the occasion of death that is theologically well grounded.

> The funeral is a critical moment in the life of any Christian congregation. Death breaks community and threatens faith and life with meaninglessness. It also, at least frequently, leaves a painful void in the depths of the personal existence of those who are bereaved. Hence on the occasion of death the church is challenged to confess the faith and to assert the reality of its communal existence.[1]

Leith went on to insist that good taste, kindness, and pastoral sensitivity are necessary prerequisites for the church's ministry at death. Such a suggestion may sound trite, as Leith himself acknowledged, but such matters

1. John H. Leith, "The Message of Christian Faith on the Occasion of the Burial of the Dead," *Journal for Preachers,* Lent 1983, p. 20.

should never be taken lightly. Every pastor knows of people who have been grievously wounded by an insensitive remark at a time of grief or by a pastor's inappropriate use of the funeral as an occasion for emotional or theological manipulation. "In my own experience," says Leith, "death and the burial of the dead is a time in which kindness should take precedence over our own ideas or preferences."[2]

That is not to say that the pastor-theologian should merely accede to the wishes of the family of the deceased whatever they may be. There are times when one must say a clear and gracious No to requests that would not be appropriate for a service of witness to the resurrection. Yet even in saying No, the pastor-theologian has opportunity to say Yes in good conscience to things he or she would not necessarily have suggested but which can appropriately be used in a service of remembrance and witness to the resurrection. The planning of a funeral service should never be the occasion for an arrogant display of the pastor's authority. Kindness and pastoral sensitivity are necessary prerequisites for effective ministry at the time of death.

The Funeral Service

The form and order of the funeral service will vary according to one's denomination or context in ministry. Liturgical churches have the advantage of clearly defined services for the burial of the dead. Adherence to the stated liturgy can save the pastor from at least some of the pressures for improvisation present in the trends and issues we shall discuss later in this paper. Pastors in non-liturgical churches would do well to introduce and utilize the best resources from more liturgical traditions. Over a period of time congregations can be taught to appreciate the gift of well-formed liturgies that provide theological grounding amid the crises of life. As has often been noted, the more intense the emotion present in a service, or the more threatening the crisis which the service seeks to address, the more important it is to give that emotion form and voice in well-ordered liturgy. Liturgies shaped by centuries of pastoral and theological reflection can speak out of the depths without falling into bathos or sentimentality.

Here, however, pastor-theologians in the mainline North American context face the challenge posed by a culture that is largely disdainful of lit-

2. Leith, "The Message of Christian Faith," p. 21.

urgy, afraid of authentic emotion, contemptuous of the wisdom of the past, and lacking in the spiritual, emotional, and intellectual resources to face death realistically. Virtually all the current trends in funeral or memorial services point to the fact that pastor-theologians will need a clear understanding of what they are seeking to accomplish in the service and why, as well as the courage of their convictions.

In a wide-ranging essay on "Death and Politics," Joseph Bottum explores the intriguing proposition that "*The fundamental pattern for any community is a congregation at a funeral*" (emphasis his). Bottum argues that the loss of rituals dealing with death have profound and disturbing social and political consequences.

> A culture that closes down its public forms for the expression of mourning's irrationality — a society that eliminates rituals and ceremonies with at least a claimed origin in the most emotionally meaningful portions of its history — has forgotten the hazards that those rituals and ceremonies once channeled and controlled. . . . The inexplicability of mortality can, under the pressure of grief, issue in astonishingly destructive hunts for someone to blame. Grieving people are dangerous people.[3]

In my own tradition (Presbyterian) there is no required liturgy for the funeral service. In fact, at times there has been an antipathy toward anything other than the most austere funeral service. The first *Westminster Directory for the Publique Worship of God* (1645), under the influence of Puritanism specified, "When any person departeth this life, let the dead body, upon the day of burial, be decently attended from the house to the place appointed for public burial, and there immediately interred, without any ceremony." Furthermore, the Westminster divines insisted that "praying, reading, and singing both in going to, and at the grave, have been grossly abused, are no way beneficial to the dead, and have proved many ways hurtful to the living, therefore let all such things be laid aside."[4] No one I know would go that far anymore — nor should they. But given the fact that funeral services and sermons in particular have been "grossly abused" to exhort or threaten congregations in inappropriate ways, it is understandable that some people are

3. Joseph Bottum, "Death and Politics, *First Things,* June/July 2007, pp. 18, 19, 27.

4. Quoted in Stanley Hall, "Renewing the Rites of Death," *Insights: A Journal of the Faculty of Austin Seminary,* Fall 1994, p. 49.

leery of funerals in general. A long history of abuses legitimates their concern. A pastor's first responsibility in the crisis of grief is to do no harm.

The Limitations of Eulogy

If at times funerals have been an occasion for emotional exploitation, more often they have been used merely to eulogize the deceased. Instead of offering a thoughtful wrestling with the meaning of a particular person's life under God in light of the stark reality of death, funerals have been used to extol, sometimes in a less than honest way, the supposed virtues of the deceased. In many churches spoken eulogies have fallen out of favor, but in an increasing number of cases they are being replaced by video eulogies with even less connection to the faith and scriptures of the church. More about that trend later in this paper.

Over against the misuse of eulogies, the Roman Catholic "General Introduction to the Order of Christian Funerals" wisely instructs,

> A brief homily based on the readings is always given after the gospel reading at the funeral liturgy . . . but there is never to be a eulogy. Attentive to the grief of those present, the homilist should dwell on God's compassionate love and on the paschal mystery of the Lord, as proclaimed in the Scripture readings. . . . Through the homily members of the family and community should receive consolation and strength to face the death of one of their members with a hope nourished by the saving word of God.[5]

The Supreme Court Justice Antonin Scalia expressed well the significance of a funeral service that does not eulogize the deceased in a letter written to James Goodloe after the memorial service he had conducted for the former Supreme Court Justice Lewis Powell. Scalia writes in part,

> In my aging years, I have attended so many funerals of prominent people that I consider myself a connoisseur of the genre. . . . I am surprised at how often eulogy is the centerpiece of the service, rather than (as it was in

5. General Introduction to the Order of Christian Funerals, n. 27, from "Preaching a Funeral," Thomas J. Scirghi, *Homiletic and Pastoral Review,* February 2000.

your church) the Resurrection of Christ, and the eternal life that follows from that. I am told that, in Roman Catholic canon law, encomiums at funeral masses are not permitted — though if that is the rule, I have never seen it observed except in the breach. I have always thought there is much to be said for such a prohibition, not only because it spares from embarrassment or dissembling those of us about whom little good can truthfully be said, but also because, even when the deceased was an admirable person — indeed, especially when the deceased was an admirable person — praise for his virtues can cause us to forget that we are praying for, and giving thanks for, God's inexplicable mercy to a sinner. . . .

Perhaps the clergy who conduct relatively secular services are moved by a desire not to offend the nonbelievers in attendance — whose numbers tend to increase in proportion to the prominence of the deceased. What a great mistake. Weddings and funerals (but especially funerals) are the principal occasions left in modern America when you can preach the Good News not just to the faithful, but to those who have never really heard it.[6]

That has been my experience as well. The essential task of the pastor-theologian at the funeral is not to eulogize the deceased but to bear witness to the faith of the Christian community — that in the resurrection of the crucified Jesus the living God is triumphant over death and will raise to life eternal all who are in Christ. The death that destroys us cannot separate the believer from the eternal love of the triune God. The pastor-theologian rehearses for the gathered community the promise of the resurrection, not in general, but for a particular life lived amid all the ambiguities of human life in a fallen world. The funeral sermon proclaims the promises of God — God's eternal Yes to life, to love, to hope in the face of Death's great No.

It is important to note that in the funeral service the pastor-theologian is not merely seeking to offer comfort. He or she is engaging Death, "the last enemy," in a combat that, although essentially verbal, is nonetheless real. In that combat the pastor-theologian has a unique witness to offer which no one else in the culture can provide. Over against Death's claim to have the last word in the life of everyone who ever lived, the Christian faith declares that the true and final word belongs, not to the death that destroys us, but to

6. Letter from Justice Antonin Scalia to the Rev. Dr. James C. Goodloe, September 1, 1998. A copy of the letter was given to me by Dr. Goodloe.

the living God who has named and known us and from whose love nothing in life or death can separate us.

Death as "Appointed End" and "Last Enemy"

In order to delve more deeply into the unique ministry of the pastor-theologian at the occasion of death, it is important to distinguish between death as a biological event that comes to all that lives and Death as a spiritual power that seeks to negate the meaningfulness of life and the preciousness of love.[7] There is no single theology of death in scripture. Death is viewed both as the appointed end to human life and as "the last enemy," the spiritual power that seeks to rob life of its meaning and value. Both aspects must be taken into account.

Physical death is the universal human condition. It is the assured ending of life which when acknowledged honestly can make the passing of life more precious and the living of life more meaningful. Death serves as the stark reminder that we are vulnerable, radically dependent creatures who cannot secure our own being. Pastor-theologians owe it to their congregations to name death honestly and not bury it under euphemisms like "passed away." It is not morbid — it is an act of grace to remind people regularly of the fact of our mortality.[8] Thomas Oden sums up the reciprocal relationship between death and life succinctly. "Those who take life seriously take death seriously. Those who take death seriously take life seriously. Where death is avoided, life is avoided. Only one who has accepted the reality of death is prepared to accept life."[9]

In a profound and moving essay on a theology of death, written while he himself was dying of cancer, Alan Lewis of Austin Presbyterian Seminary distinguishes three aspects of the biblical understanding of death. He names them Consent, Confrontation, and Conquest. Lewis sets God's Confrontation and Conquest of death in the resurrection of Jesus Christ in the context of our Consent to the limits of our mortality in God's good creation. Before

7. In this paper I will capitalize Death when I am speaking of Death as a spiritual power and use the lower case for death as a biological fact.

8. It is said that Alexander the Great would have a servant wake him each morning with the words, "*memento mori*" ("Remember, you must die").

9. Thomas C. Oden, *Life in the Spirit: Systematic Theology,* vol. 3 (San Francisco: HarperCollins, 1994), p. 379.

death is experienced as curse or enemy, it first must be acknowledged as part of the finite creation which God declares good. Lewis writes,

> Perishability, which God has both given and indwelt, enhances rather than distracts from the loveliness of life; just as real flowers transcend the beauty of indestructible but artificial substitutes, precisely because they are so precarious and frail, teetering on the verge of dissolution. And along with beauty, fragility brings trust, thanksgiving, and wonder. Coming from dust and returning to it, we are summoned to value our dependence on Another, to accept our limitations and restrictions, to throw off the heavy burden of sole responsibility for our existence and entrust it back to its transcendent source. Likewise, our knowledge that it will not last forever, adds immeasurably to our gratitude for life, however short.[10]

Lewis goes on to insist that "the pastoral challenge is to help the dying give their own consent" to the boundaries of death, "freely and without rancor." Understood as the gracious limit to life in creation and embraced in faith, death for the believer can be experienced as the final chapter, an open door, the offering back to God the gift of life received. When the appointed limits to life are embraced in faith, the dying and the pastor may together rediscover trust and wonder, thankfulness and peacefulness, in acknowledging that they are finite creatures and that that is very good. Even when death comes tragically and prematurely, it is possible in retrospect to judge the abbreviated life not by its extension but by its quality and content; and to be grateful from the vantage-point of its last chapter for every page and word of the preceding human story, however short.[11]

Death can be understood biologically as a natural event that comes to all that lives and thus can be accepted as a given part of mortal life in creation. There are deaths that while sad are in no way tragic. When my father

10. Alan Lewis, "The Theology of Death and the Care of the Dying: Affirmations, Attitudes and Actions," *Insights: A Journal of the Faculty of Austin Seminary,* Fall 1994, p. 10. This excellent essay deserves to be considerably better known than it is.

11. Lewis, "The Theology of Death," p. 11. See also *This Incomplete One: Words Occasioned by the Death of a Young Person,* ed. Michael D. Bush (Grand Rapids: Eerdmans, 2006), for a very helpful collection of sermons given by outstanding pastor-theologians on the death of a child or young person. Included are Karl Barth's sermon on the death of his son Matthias and William Sloane Coffin's classic sermon, "Alex's Death."

died of dementia, none of us in the family would have wished him to suffer a day longer. When death finally came, it came more as an awaited friend than a dreaded enemy. It was the expected and not feared end of a long, full life lived intensely in service to God and love for others.

But the fact that the ordained limit of death can be accepted in faith does not make Death less of "a spiritual enemy," against which God contends and over which he triumphs. Lewis goes on to speak forcefully of "how implacable is God's own resistance to the demonic enemies of life."

> Confrontation is the *divine* response to death. Forget the spinelessness of "gentle Jesus, meek and mild"; jettison the shibboleth that makes "reconciliation" God's wimpish posture toward everything. Between the cross and resurrection we see confirmed once and for all and without ambiguity God's absolute *refusal* to be gentle with the aggressor, the divine determination *never* to make peace with death or to be reconciled to its destructiveness. God's passion for life has as its obverse an infinitely passionate anger — against the disfigurement of beauty, the disruption of harmony, the spoliation of the body, the rupturing of good life. Surely it is *God's* instincts, first and foremost, that Dylan Thomas captured with his quivering "rage, rage against the dying of the light."[12]

Under the power of Sin, death is not merely the appointed limit to life. Death is the demonic power that seeks to say No! to the promises and purposes of God; to say, most of all, a final and decisive No to love! In the funeral sermon the pastor-theologian is not calling the congregation to make its own separate peace with Death, but to confront Death with that "Word above all earthly powers."[13]

In a very helpful article on preaching at funerals, Tom Long sums up the purpose of the funeral sermon this way.

> When all is said and done, we do not preach at funerals primarily to provide comfort — though solace and support are, thank God, often given through the sermons. And we are not there to explain why all this happened — though the hunger for meaning in the face of meaninglessness, thank God, is often addressed in what we say. What is more, we are not

12. Lewis, "The Theology of Death," p. 12.
13. Martin Luther, "A Mighty Fortress Is Our God."

there to supply spiritual solemnity to an already somber situation. What we *are* there to do is unmask a lie.[14]

Death understood as a spiritual power proclaims the great lie that love is futile and ultimately absurd. Death says in effect, "Love anyone who is under my power, and sooner or later I will tear your beloved from you and leave you heart-broken. Love, if you dare, but you'll be sorry. Those who love much, suffer much."[15] In a world where Death wins every time in the life of everyone who ever lived, we all must ask in one way or another, "Is the pain of love really worth it?" We answer with our lives if not with our minds.

The pastor-theologian is called to probe deeply the profound relationship between death and love so as to do battle with the "Prince of Darkness grim."[16] The more we love life and the more we love those with whom we share the precious gift of life, the more painfully we grieve our separation in death. Death can be a matter of indifference only to those for whom life and love have ceased to matter deeply. Jürgen Moltmann is right; if death is "experienced as the destruction of a beloved life, then love rises up in rebellion against death and does not ask just about the meaning of this particular death; it calls death itself into question. Love wants to live, not die, to endure, not pass away. The life of love is 'eternal life'; so as long as we love we shall never accept death."[17]

Love is never "resigned to the shutting away of loving hearts in the hard ground."[18] And neither is God — not if we take our cues from the New Testament. The resurrection of Jesus from the dead is God's own refusal to be resigned to the shutting away of love in the darkness of death. God does not allow the beloved Son to be lost in death's dominion. God meets death head on and triumphs over it. "For as by a man came death, by

14. Thomas G. Long, "Telling the Truth about Death and Life: Preaching at Funerals," *Journal for Preachers,* Easter 1997, pp. 4-5.

15. The most powerful and poignant expression of this truth is found in Augustine's *Confessions,* Book Four, chapters 5-9, where Augustine speaks of the emptiness and bitterness that followed the death of his beloved friend.

16. Martin Luther, "A Mighty Fortress Is Our God."

17. Jürgen Moltmann, "Is There Life After Death?" in *The End of the World and the Ends of God,* ed. John Polkinghorne and Michael Welker (Harrisburg, PA: Trinity Press International, 2000), p. 239.

18. Edna St. Vincent Millay, "Dirge without Music," from *Buck in the Snow and Other Poems* (New York: Harper & Brothers, 1928).

a man has come also the resurrection of the dead. For as in Adam all die, so in Christ shall all be made alive" (1 Cor. 15:21-22). In the death and resurrection of Jesus God engages Death in mortal combat. "He must reign until he has put all his enemies under his feet. The last enemy to be destroyed is death" (1 Cor. 15:25-26; see also Psalm 110 — the most quoted psalm in the New Testament).

Preparing for Battle with the "Last Enemy"

As the living God engaged Death in battle, so the pastor-theologian in the funeral sermon engages "Death's lies in pitched battle."[19] But how is the pastor-theologian formed for such combat? What basic training is necessary? I would suggest that the pastor-theologian is best formed by an ongoing immersion in the biblical witness to the resurrection of the body, by wide reading in the best resources of the Christian tradition, and by years of reflecting on the nature of Christian hope. Formation does not happen quickly, but it can happen in those open to its disciplines. A pastor-theologian might well commit to reading at least one serious treatment of eschatology each year.[20] Preaching an extended series of sermons or teaching a course on the resurrection of the body would force the pastor-theologian to deal with the biblical witness and with the actual questions and concerns of the congregation. It would also lay the groundwork for the congregation's ability to participate more meaningfully in services of witness to the resurrection over time. Even small things, such as memorizing the great passages of scripture that articulate Christian hope, can play a large role in the formation of pastor-theologians who are called upon to proclaim and help embody that hope on the occasion of death.

In a remarkably helpful essay, "Is There Life After Death?," Jürgen Moltmann names and addresses the specific questions people most often ask in the face of death. The questions he identifies can serve well as an agenda for ongoing pastoral-theological reflection and formation. The questions include: What remains of our lives when we die? What awaits us? What lasts?

19. Tom Long, "Telling the Truth about Death and Life," p. 5.

20. Some suggested resources would include the previously cited *The End of the World and the Ends of God*, the works of Jürgen Moltmann, and N. T. Wright's massive *The Resurrection of the Son of God.*

Where are the dead? Moltmann also addresses issues of Death and Love, Death and Sin, the nature of the soul, and the relationship between the living and the dead.[21] Sustained reflection on those questions and issues over the years can serve to form pastor-theologians who are able to articulate the faith of the church on the occasion of death and in light of the real questions grieving people ask. Most congregations would eagerly engage in an extended study of such questions with their pastor.

Thus far in this paper we have dealt primarily with the *theological* side of the work of the pastor-theologian in the face of death. I would argue that in our time it is the most important side to be addressed. But there is also the *pastoral* side of the funeral service and sermon. It must not be forgotten that in the funeral or memorial service we are remembering and giving thanks to God for a particular life lived among us. The funeral service and sermon must not remain at the level of theological generalities. They must lift up a unique life in thanksgiving to God.

For all the problems with eulogies as previous stated, the pastor-theologian must deal with the concrete particularities of the life of the deceased in an honest and recognizable way. That life, however unfinished and incomplete it may have been, was a gift of God for which we give thanks. We do not counter Death's great lie with our own little lies about the deceased, as if somehow Death itself could be buried under a thick resumé of good deeds. But we do tell the truth in love about a part of a person's life, a person known and loved by the gathered community of faith. We lift up to God the narrative thread of grace woven in and through the tapestry of the life of the deceased. Often we do so through stories and remembrances. Time spent by the pastor-theologian with the family of the deceased in which they are encouraged to tell stories, to laugh and cry together, can be deeply precious. As the life of the deceased was God's gift to us, so in the funeral service and especially in the funeral prayer we can offer back that life to God with thanksgiving.

There is also what could be called an educational component to the funeral service and sermon. The word "educational" may sound overly didactic, but in every service the pastor-theologian is seeking to educate people in the Christian understanding of life, death, and destiny. Over time people can be given a vocabulary of faith and a grammar of hope. As the Christian community gathers in worship on the occasion of death, it bears witness to what

21. Moltmann, "Is There Life After Death?" pp. 238-55.

it most surely believes. The use of a creed of the church or a common affirmation of faith is an appropriate way to rehearse the faith of the church universal in the face of death. Will Willimon reminds us that,

> In a death-denying culture where death is looked upon as a bizarre intrusion and the resurrection is regarded as naive fantasy, a pastor might see every funeral as a time for proclaiming with evangelistic and missionary zeal, the radically honest and hopeful Christian word at the time of death among modern people who are infatuated with youth and who delude themselves into thinking that they have a natural right to immortality on their own terms.[22]

I would question whether "evangelistic and missionary zeal" is the appropriate tone for a funeral service, but Willimon is right in regard to the teachable moment provided by the funeral, and not just for the congregation of believers. Included in every funeral service will be some who no longer or never did believe, as well as some who long to believe again.[23] At least for a few moments the pastor-theologian has their attention. It is an opportunity to speak a gracious word of truth to the cultured despisers and the untamed cynics among us in a way they will not likely hear anywhere else. The opportunity to proclaim the resurrection of the body to ones who are infatuated with youth or who think only in terms of some form of natural immortality of the soul should not be squandered with pious platitudes. Because of the time pressure under which ministers must plan the funeral service and sermon, it is imperative that the pastor-theologian give serious, sustained attention as to how to communicate the Christian hope to contemporary people well before the occasion arises.

Trends and Issues

We move now to consider some trends in funerals that affect the work of the pastor-theologian. Funeral customs vary from region to region across the

22. William H. Willimon, *Worship as Pastoral Care* (Nashville: Abingdon, 1979), p. 111.

23. Recently, after a memorial service I conducted, a man from out of state told me how pleased he was that his two college-aged daughters had attended. "They don't have much use for the church," he said. "I'm glad that at least for once they heard the gospel."

United States, and certainly vary from culture to culture. The minister must be sensitive to regional traditions, while nevertheless seeking to shape the customs and expectations of funeral services over time.

The vast majority of the funerals I conduct are held in the sanctuary of the church. That is not the case in many other communities. To some degree it reflects the ethos of this particular community (Bible-belt South), but it also reflects the traditions and expectations of a congregation that have been carefully developed over the years. Yet even in Greenville, South Carolina, funeral customs are changing in ways that pose serious challenges to the pastor-theologian. In a study of the history of funeral customs and contemporary trends, Tom Long notes how swiftly and dramatically "a significant segment of North American Christians have over the last fifty years abandoned centuries of funeral traditions in favor of an entirely new pattern of memorializing the dead."[24]

The emerging pattern for funerals is still quite fluid. Indeed, as Long notes, the new funeral "rituals" (if indeed they can be called rituals) are marked by variations, improvisations, and personal customizations. While there is a great variety of emerging customs, there is consensus around certain elements which include: "1) a memorial service in which the emphasis is on remembering the deceased, often in very personal ways and often without the body or ashes being present; 2) a brief, simple, highly personalized, and sometimes improvised service, often involving a number of speakers other than or without clergy; 3) a focus on the life and life-style of the deceased complete with mementoes of that life-style; 4) a celebration of life marked more by joy than solemnity; 5) a private service of committal prior to the memorial service; and 6) an increasing preference for cremation (now approximately 30% nationwide and over 50% in many western states."[25]

Three additional trends in contemporary funerals merit consideration — the trend toward designer funerals that reflect the life-style of the deceased more than the life of the Christian community, the replacement of the sermon by a video tribute to the deceased, and memorial services in which no body or representation of the body is present and which seek to be almost unfailingly upbeat, a celebration of a life, not a confrontation with the reality of Death.

24. Thomas G. Long, "Whatever Happened to the Funeral?" *The Cresset: A Journal of Literature, the Arts, and Public Affairs,* Lent 2005, p. 12.

25. Long, "Whatever Happened to the Funeral?" p. 12.

In an article in the *New York Times,* John Leland describes the trend toward designer funerals orchestrated with the help of funeral concierge services. Leland says,

> As members of the baby boom generation plan their final services for their parents or themselves, they bring new consumer expectations and fewer attachments to church, traditions, or organ music — forcing funeral directors to be more like party planners, and inviting some party planners to test the farewell waters.[26]

Many funeral homes now offer elaborate videos of the life of the deceased. A number of funeral homes in my community have kiosks in which people can record memories and condolences that can then be inserted into a video tribute to the deceased. While video tributes may serve as well as spoken tributes or eulogies to remind the gathered community of the particular life of the deceased, they do not serve well to communicate the faith of the Christian community, which comes not from what is seen but from what is heard. Pastor-theologians can expect increased pressure to substitute videos for the funeral sermon. The better funeral homes get at producing slick, upbeat video eulogies, the greater will be the pressure to eliminate the funeral sermon altogether . . . and then at least some, if not all, of the scripture readings . . . and then the body itself . . . and, of course, the clergy.

We have already moved a long way toward eliminating the body and any visible reminder of the reality of death. For good reasons most churches require that the casket remain closed. The reaction against an overemphasis on the body (including the embalmer's art) was theologically warranted. But the less the body or symbol of the body is present in the service, the greater is the danger of a disparagement of created bodily, physical life — a significant concern for pastor-theologians in a time of resurgent gnosticism throughout our culture.

The essayist Thomas Lynch has written helpfully on the significance of the body from his perspective as a funeral home director. Lynch insists that, "We deal with death by dealing with the dead, not just the idea but also the sad and actual fact of the matter — the dead body."[27] And yet Mark Duffey

26. John Leland, "It's My Funeral and I'll Serve Ice Cream if I Want To," *The New York Times,* nytimes.com, 2006.

27. Thomas Lynch, "Good Grief: An Undertaker's Reflections," *Christian Century,* July 26, 2003, p. 21.

of Houston, who claims to have developed the first nationwide funeral concierge service, speaks for many of his generation when he says bluntly, the "body's a downer, especially for boomers. If the body doesn't have to be there, it frees us to do what we want. They may want to have it [the funeral] in a country club or bar or their favorite restaurant. That's where consumers want to go."[28]

The contrast between the perspectives of Lynch and Duffey makes clear one of the major challenges to the pastor-theologian and to the church. For those who believe in the incarnation of the Son of God and in the resurrection of the *body*, the body is not a "downer." It is the ensouled material reality created by God and redeemed from death for eternal communion with the living God. In the final resurrection of the body we are given a new embodiment appropriate for life in God's new creation. How we deal with bodies is at the heart of Christian morality. Thus, pastor-theologians who conduct a significant number of services involving cremation must give serious thought as to how appropriately to honor the body when no body is present.

Recently, an elderly woman in the church I serve died. A Presbyterian pastor in town, who was a relative of the deceased, was present at her home when she died. The hospice attendant asked if she wished to help prepare the body. She said that she would. The pastor described what a moving experience it was as they washed the body together. As they washed the feet of the deceased, the hospice attendant invited the pastor to imagine the places the woman's feet had taken her on her many travels. As they washed her midsection, she invited the pastor to think of the children and grandchildren she had held on her lap. As they washed her arms, she invited her to remember those whom the deceased had held in her arms. As they lovingly prepared the body for cremation, they remembered and rehearsed the life of the deceased in a way that truly honored the body. Few of us could or would do it that way, but all of us are challenged to find appropriate ways to honor the body of the deceased, especially when cremation is the option chosen.

The Christian hope is not a disembodied hope that seeks to deny the reality and sting of death. The Christian faith is ruthlessly honest about the power and threat of death, and so must pastor-theologians be. There is nothing within us that naturally escapes death. "God alone has immortality" (1 Tim. 6:16). Excessively upbeat funerals at a club or restaurant are merely another form of our persistent denial of death. Viewing the bereaved as con-

28. Lynch, "Good Grief," p. 21.

sumers reveals the widespread assumption in our culture that we are autonomous individuals called and claimed and answerable to no one but ourselves. All these things the pastor-theologian must challenge in the name of the living God, the Creator and Redeemer of bodies made for eternal communion. Ministers do not wish to be thought gloomy and somber, but someone in our society has to challenge the lie of Death, not with cheers and warm remembrances, but with the proclaimed reality of God's victory over Death, "the last enemy," in the bodily resurrection of Jesus and ours in him.

It is clear that in the years ahead those who view their vocational identity as pastor-theologians will have to develop the skills of a juggler, balancing the expectations of families that the service focus on the individuality of the deceased with the imperative of the church that the service focus on the Author and Finisher of our salvation. Well-thought-out, well-crafted funeral services and sermons that "hold the Bible in one hand and the clipped obituary in the other"[29] can go a long way toward helping maintain a proper balance. Doing so with theological integrity will be one of the greatest contributions the pastor-theologian can offer the whole church of the risen, crucified Christ.

29. Charles Hoffacker, *A Matter of Life and Death: Preaching at Funerals* (Cambridge, MA: Cowley, 2002), p. 13.

The Splendid Embarrassment: Theology's Home and the Practice of Ministry

Thomas W. Currie III

> *It is a great thing to presuppose that Jesus Christ is the Logos. It is an even greater and more daring thing to presuppose that the same Logos still speaks today through the Word of his witnesses.*
>
> Karl Barth[1]

> *When a man, any one of us, obeys this imperative and looks up to him, to Jesus Christ, a momentous change takes place in him. . . . Such a person experiences joy in the midst of his sorrows and sufferings, much as he still may sigh and grumble. Not a cheap and superficial joy that passes, but deep-seated, lasting joy. We may as well admit it: he has got something to laugh at, and he just cannot help laughing, even though he does not feel like it. His laughter is not bad, but good, not a mockery, but an open and relaxing laughter, not a diplomatic gesture as has recently become so fashionable in politics, but honest and sincere laughter, coming from the bottom of man's*

1. *The Göttingen Dogmatics: Instruction in the Christian Religion,* vol. 1, ed. Hannelotte Reiffen, trans. Geoffrey Bromiley (Grand Rapids: Eerdmans, 1991), p. 269.

An earlier version of this essay constituted a chapter in my book *The Joy of Ministry* (Louisville: Westminster/John Knox Press, 2007). This revision appears here with the publisher's permission.

> *heart. Such light and joy and laughter are ours when we look up to him, to Jesus Christ. He is the one who makes us radiant. We ourselves cannot put on bright faces. But neither can we prevent them from shining. Looking up to him, our faces shine.*
>
> Karl Barth, "Look Up to Him," a sermon preached in Basel Prison on Ascension Day, 1956, on Psalm 34:5[2]

One of the consequences of the Fall, Charles Williams has suggested, is the suspicion surrounding the phrase, "the joy of obedience." This seemingly oxymoronic joining together of terms baffles a culture that thinks the pursuit of happiness is a self-evident good, a right that must always bristle at any external claim on its obedience. In his book, *The Forgiveness of Sins,* Williams argues that the right ordering of our salvation accomplished in Christ is the right ordering of our life within "the body." In order to see the effect of sin in our world, Williams proposes that we simply reverse the terms of Ephesians 4:15 ("But speaking the truth in love, we must grow up in every way into him who is the head, into Christ, from whom the whole body, joined and knit together . . ." NRSV) to read: ". . . that we may grow away from him in all things . . . the whole body disjoined and decompacted. . . ."[3] The body splits, breaks apart, the knee bone no longer connected to the thigh bone, until all that is left is a valley of dry bones, with each bone bleached and alone in splendid isolation, a description, Williams thinks, of much of the way modern culture (and the contemporary church) feels.

What Williams sees very clearly is the corporal or communal nature of redemption and the "spiritual" or otherwise disembodied nature of damnation, or what is sometimes called freedom. He also sees that the forgiveness of sins in the person of Jesus Christ is a healing accomplished by his joyful obedience. Only in a fallen world are obedience and joy split apart, just as service to Another in such a world must seem ever implausible as perfect freedom. The effect of sin is schismatic here too, tearing things apart that belong together. Williams notes, for example, how the word *chastity* has for us mostly negative connotations, indicating some form of heroic self-restraint or even

2. In Karl Barth, *Deliverance to the Captives* (New York: Harper & Brothers, 1961), p. 47.

3. Charles Williams, *The Forgiveness of Sins* (Grand Rapids: Eerdmans, 1942), pp. 22-23.

quest for purity. But in fact, chastity is "the obedience to and the relation with the adorable central body,"[4] the glory even of that Divine Word in whom "all things hold together" (Col. 1:17 NRSV). In this respect, chastity and courtesy are twins, the one being the love of the soul for God and the other, the love of the soul for its created companions. Only our fallenness makes chastity an achievement and courtesy a matter of etiquette. Williams can even say that "[c]hastity is courtesy towards God; courtesy is chastity toward men."[5]

Can ministry really take the form of "joyful obedience"? No one who has ever practiced ministry for very long can maintain that it is particularly glamorous work. The depiction of congregations "without spot or wrinkle" is rightly called "ecclesiastical pornography" by Eugene Peterson, who knows that pastors themselves are tempted to pose as centerfolds of successful churches.[6] Peterson notes that scripture itself does not glamorize Israel, whose history is characterized less by success than it is by defeat and heartbreak, faithlessness and loss. He continues:

> A bare sixty or seventy years after Pentecost we have an account of seven churches that shows about the same quality of holiness and depth of virtue found in any ordinary parish in America today. In two thousand years of practice we haven't gotten any better. You would think we would have, but we haven't. Every time we open up a church door and take a careful, scrutinizing look inside we find them there again — sinners. Also Christ. Christ in the preaching, Christ in the sacraments, but inconveniently and embarrassingly mixed into this congregation of sinners.[7]

We find this mixture embarrassing because in a fallen world we too have become schismatics, tearing the grace of Christ apart from Christ's own body. We do this in a number of ways, the most obvious one being to spiritualize the faith, making it a journey of self-discovery. This is an old Gnostic trick but it never seems to wear itself out, and it has the advantage of protecting us from the gospel's embarrassing fleshliness while reassuring us that we are spiritually intact. Indeed, William Willimon suspects that is why most people go to seminary, namely, to become more spiritual or even Christian.

4. Williams, *The Forgiveness of Sins*, p. 24.

5. Williams, *The Forgiveness of Sins*, pp. 24-26.

6. Eugene Peterson, *Under the Unpredictable Plant* (Grand Rapids: Eerdmans, 1992), p. 22.

7. Peterson, *Under the Unpredictable Plant*, p. 24.

This is the only way, they think, that joy and obedience can be held together. Accordingly, training for ministry must become an individual if not private matter of spiritual growth and self-discovery. And as a result, actual encounters with the church inevitably become more or less rude awakenings whose dispiriting shocks and disappointing failures steadily undermine any joy in ministry. Ecclesial realities can be hard on individuals questing for some deeper spirituality. In reflecting on his own inclinations, Willimon writes,

> You see, I'm not a "community person" by natural inclination. Tell me I have some charismatic flair for leadership. Praise me for the art of my preaching or the empathy of my pastoral care, just let me share myself and pour out my feelings, urge me to become a spiritual virtuoso, but please do not yoke me to the Body, do not marry me to that unruly Bride, do not force me to find what I do and therefore who I am among those who gather at my so very mundane congregation.
>
> Let me do freelance ministry, give me a degree and tell me I'm special, encourage me to tack up a shingle, allow me to have some exotic spiritual *gnosis* that makes me holy, but do not hold me accountable to the church. I love Jesus, and I want to serve Him. But He married beneath His station. For me the real scandal of ministry, the ultimate stumbling block, the thing I avoid and fear the most, is the church. Like many of you, I set out to serve God and ended up caught among those whom God served. My problem, my difficulty with the Spirit, is that it wants to tie me to the church.[8]

That is the strange thing about the Holy Spirit, and what distinguishes it from other spirits: the Holy Spirit animates the body, gathers dry bones to create a muscular-skeletal form, and having covered it with flesh and given it voice, this Holy Spirit enables the body to offer articulate praise. The image may well be Ezekiel's but it has deep resonance with the resurrection narratives that depict Jesus as being raised from the dead in bodily form by the power of the Holy Spirit. That same Spirit is able also to give life to the scattered and often broken bones of the church's mortal body (Rom. 8:11). To walk by the Spirit is to inhabit this animated body, something that does not come naturally to any of us. Willimon is right to notice the awkwardness of

8. William Willimon, "The Spiritual Formation of the Pastor: Call and Community," in *The Pastor's Guide to Personal Spiritual Formation* (Kansas City: Beacon Hill Press, 2005), p. 25.

ministry that is so tied to the body. But such awkwardness is itself a sign that Christ's ministry insists relentlessly on being a gift and not a possession. Indeed, such awkwardness is itself a clue to the way joyful obedience begins to teach us what a gift looks like.

For if ministry is best thought of as inescapably connected to the body, then its joys will always be the embodied ones that nourish life together and celebrate its flourishing. Such joys will be the joys of the font, of being baptized into the body of Christ and discerning our true location in him, indeed, finding our identity in these cleansing waters. Such joys will also be the joys of the table, of coming with others to eat the food that sustains life and ministry in Christ, sharing with them in the undeserved grace that is the lavish gift of this feast. And the joys of the table will be narrated by the joys of the word, of the story that we are also invited to eat, the story that makes sense of all our eating and drinking.[9] This word brings with it the joys of listening — a rare gift in our time — but also the joys of speaking, of daring to proclaim this word to the community that this word has created.

Such joy is neither glamorous nor all that marketable in a consumer culture. It takes time. It requires collaboration with others. It is difficult to program. It is often quiet, though not always. More often it is hidden, like seed that has fallen into the ground doing its work invisibly and in depth. Still, Willimon is not entirely correct when he implies that we are simply stuck with such a gift or with the awkward contraption called "the body of Christ." The church's life is not a concession to our weakness, much less an onerous burden every Christian is called to bear. Calvin was wrong about that.[10] Rather, despite the barrenness of much of its life, and to its regular and utter astonishment, the church persistently discovers joy in the unlikeliest of places, its own body possessing a splendor that is inextinguishable and most surprising to itself.

We Protestants have long criticized any theology of glory that would make of the church an idol, but our modesty and self-restraint in this respect have often blinded us to the real splendor of the church. In rejecting a theology of glory we have come to trust our commitment to humility more than God's extravagant self-giving, and so have missed the splendor of the fellowship that

9. See V. Bruce Rigdon's essay in this volume on Holy Communion.

10. John Calvin, *Institutes of the Christian Religion,* IV.1.2, ed. John T. McNeill, trans. Ford Lewis Battles (Philadelphia: Westminster Press, 1960), p. 1012. In speaking of the church, Calvin writes: "Shut up as we are in the prison house of our flesh, we have not yet attained angelic rank. God, therefore, in his wonderful providence accommodating himself to our capacity, has prescribed a way for us, though still far off, to draw near to him."

both participates in the triune life of God and in the humanity that is ours in Jesus Christ. Faithful reflection on ministry surely begins then not with our virtuous self-restraint but with God's inconceivable largesse in Jesus Christ. He is the feast that makes joyful obedience something mercifully un-ironic. In "him all things hold together" (Col. 1:17). Of course, schismatics are ever ready to be tragic figures, especially religious ones. But Christ's joyful obedience will have none of that. His body tells the truth and refuses to take seriously our ironic poses of tragic isolation. It is the happy task of the ministry of the church to proclaim to ourselves and to the world that "we are not our own,"[11] and never have been, but that we belong to One who, in the midst of the hard realities that threaten to separate us from each other and from God, has made space for us within his own body. In just this way, his joy overflows and becomes true also for us. Ministry in the church begins here, in the joy of Christ's own body. It cannot be found anywhere else. Here too, Jesus shows the way.

Bodies, however, are extended in space and have location. That is why talk about ministry in the body must begin with talk about particular places.

The biblical story is relentlessly particular: Ur, Hebron, Canaan, Jerusalem, Shechem, Samaria, Goshen, Sinai, Jericho, Bethlehem, Nazareth, Capernaum, Galilee, Golgotha, Damascus, Philippi, Fair Havens, Rome. It is impossible to tell the story of Israel and the church, of Jesus and his disciples, without talking about particular places. Most Bibles have within their covers maps, sometimes showing ancient Israel or Jerusalem or perhaps the journeys of Paul. Why? Is it to show, in some graphic form, that this story really happened, that it can in some sense be located? Perhaps. But also these maps suggest that the truth the gospel is seeking to tell us is not a disembodied idea or concept but a truth that is wrapped up with particular places and their history, with a particular people, Israel and the church, indeed with a particular person, Jesus Christ. This story, like a family history, cannot be told without rehearsing and remembering places: where and when and who. The implication is that to know the truth of this story and to be able to tell it is to be drawn into this family history, to inhabit its body and remember its journey and share in its hope.

11. The phrase, of course, is originally from Paul (1 Cor. 6:19) but is powerfully voiced by John Calvin in his description of the Christian life. "We are not our own: let not our reason nor our will, therefore, sway our plans and deeds. We are not our own: let us therefore not set it as our goal to seek what is expedient for us according to the flesh. We are not our own: in so far as we can, let us therefore forget ourselves and all that is ours. Conversely, we are God's. . . ." *Institutes of the Christian Religion,* III.7.1, p. 690.

Undertaking ministry is to become well acquainted with this family and with the particular places where its life takes shape. That might seem a strange way of thinking about Christian ministry, as if it had something to do with genealogy or even geography. Surely one must begin elsewhere, with biblical study, for example, or pastoral care or even theology. Yet all of these important disciplines are taught for the sake of the body, that is, for the sake of the body's own witness to the joyfully disturbing presence of Christ in the world. And even that is not an intellectual or mental concept. Nor is it a reality that one can embrace without risk. Rather, it is a gift, whose surprising grace is often unwanted, even as it assumes terribly concrete form. The body of Christ always has an address. Like any good mystery, ministry begins with a place.

Brenham, Texas, is a town between Houston and Austin, located just west of the Brazos River in the rolling hills of Washington County. For many years a farming community principally peopled by German Lutherans and Polish Catholics, Brenham is best known today as the thriving home of Blue Bell Ice Cream. In 1976, armed with a Ph.D. in theology from the University of Edinburgh, I was called to serve as pastor of the ninety-four-member Brenham Presbyterian Church. My plans were to pastor for a while, get a taste of ministry, and then move on to the real work of teaching in a seminary or university setting. Brenham would be a stop along the way of my career, perhaps even a stepping-stone to something better.

I spent nearly thirteen years as pastor of this congregation. During that time my wife gave birth to two of our three children, all of whom were baptized in the Brenham Presbyterian Church, and all of whom grew up in a community of baseball, ice cream, Maifests, and Vacation Bible School. Lest one think such a setting for ministry was idyllic or insulated from the tensions of late twentieth-century America, it should be noted that during that time a young mother and her eleven-year-old son, both members of the church, were abducted from the parking lot after worship one August Sunday and murdered by someone who had recently been released from prison; issues of race, never far from the surface in many small towns and rural areas of Texas, surfaced here as well; the religious yearning to "get saved" by means of revivals and soul-winning crusades, so much a part of American piety (especially in small towns in the South), also impinged on this congregation's life and forced it to make some hard decisions. And in addition there were the grievous losses any community of faith might regularly encounter: a housefire and loss of a married couple's lives, a severely retarded young man succumbing to cancer, a brilliant young electrical engineer dying of the same disease before he was thirty years old, the loss of jobs and other economic dislocations familiar to small-town America, and on and on. Such losses are really indescribable, which is why talking about ministry often takes on an artificial tone, rather like old veterans recalling past battles.

In this context theories of ministry are of little use; the language of word and sacrament are more apt. They at least refer to a mysterious reality that is able to encompass loss and even death, all the while narrating a life together made possible by a faithfulness quite beyond us, yet a faithfulness that is able in the face of death itself to teach us words of thanksgiving and praise.

The thread that runs through all true narratives of ministry is the thread not of achievement or even of self-discovery but of the often belated and even rueful recognition that the kingdom of God has drawn near. Ministers are so often the last to know. But then disciples, according to scripture, have always been slow learners. Perhaps there is no other way. In any case, career counseling, even college and seminary courses, often fail to realize this and so do little to prepare pastors for such astonishing epiphanies. Perhaps there is little that can be done. Miracles are elusive things to manage. But to the extent that the whole educational process aims at cultivating leadership skills and developing professional competencies, it seems almost designed to insulate students from such life-shattering gifts.[12] That is why so many ministerial students are tempted to envision a "career" in ministry (as I did), and why their embarrassing stumbles are often the first indication that they have finally begun to find another path, one that leads in a quite different direction and traces a mysteriously unfamiliar landscape.

In his autobiography, *Unfinished Agenda,* Lesslie Newbigin writes of going out to India for the first time as a missionary and, fairly early on, having an accident in which one of his legs was badly broken. He had not even arrived at his first posting in Kanchipuram when he found himself at the mercy of hospital orderlies, surgeries, the care of others. When he most wanted to be active, he had to be helped by those whom he thought he was to lead. In reflecting on this period of enforced inactivity, Newbigin writes that "a new missionary has to accept a kind of drastic diminishment. To learn the language and culture of another people he must become a child."[13]

Such a drastic diminishment is the way ministers are introduced to the

12. See Wallace Alston's essay in this volume on theological education.

13. Lesslie Newbigin, *Unfinished Agenda* (Grand Rapids: Eerdmans, 1985), p. 46.

geography of the Kingdom. Though such a reduction may seem embarrassing, and indeed is so, it is the way ministry is learned and set apart for joy. To be sure, such learning is hard and requires asking help from others, always a humiliating prospect for high-achieving leaders, though it is the regular position of a child, or for that matter, one who prays.

In the second year of his ministry at a Lutheran church in Evansville, Indiana, Walter Wangerin discovered that his organist, a woman named Joselyn Fields, was dying of cancer. Wangerin made a point to visit her through hospitalizations, surgeries, days of recovery, and finally days of dying. He writes that at first, "I didn't know what to say, nor did I understand what I had the *right* to say. I wore out the Psalms; Psalms [I thought] were safe. I prayed often that the Lord's will be done, scared to tell either him or Joselyn what the Lord's will ought to be, and scared of his will anyway."[14]

One day, after she was recovering from a difficult surgery, Wangerin sought to cheer up his parishioner by describing the beautiful day outside, the things he planned to do that day, and even the wonderful day when Joselyn would be back in church playing the organ. Joselyn listened and then turned toward him and pointed a finger at his face, and said, "Shut up."[15] Shut up. Slow to learn, Wangerin heeded his organist's words and shut up.[16] "I entered her room at noon, saying nothing. I sat beside her through the afternoon, saying nothing . . . ; but with the evening came the Holy Spirit. For the words I finally said were not my own. . . . I turned to my Joselyn. I opened my mouth and spoke as a Pastor. I spoke, too, as a human. More than that, I spoke as a man to a woman. I said, 'I love you.'" And with her dying bones, Joselyn hugged her pastor and said, "I love you, too." Wangerin concludes: "And that was all we said. But that . . . was the power from on high, cloaking both of us in astonished simplicity, even as Jesus said it would. . . . And she died. And I did not grieve."[17]

It would be easy to dismiss this "splendid embarrassment" as simply a kind of passive-aggressive jujitsu that firmly establishes the pastor as the most humble servant of all, and therefore according to this scheme, the true master of all. But the diminishment of which Newbigin speaks and to which Wangerin's testimony bears witness is not the self-restraint of a modesty that

14. Walter Wangerin Jr., *Ragman and Other Cries of Faith* (San Francisco: Harper & Row, 1984), pp. 62-63.

15. Wangerin, *Ragman and Other Cries of Faith,* p. 63.

16. See Cynthia Jarvis's essay in this volume on pastoral care.

17. Wangerin, *Ragman and Other Cries of Faith,* pp. 63-64.

disguises a real arrogance. Rather, it is the dislocation that accompanies the ecclesial and embodied nature of Christian ministry, a dislocation that recognizes one has been pressed into the service of another narrative, assuming an office, even a status that it is precisely not a personal quest for self-discovery but an undertaking which the church requires to be done. The dislocation comes from our being trained to think that what is interesting about ministry is us, that is, our spirituality or gifts or even sense of call when, in fact, what is truly interesting about ministry is none of those things (hence, the dislocation and diminishment). Rather, it is the gospel itself, the strange gospel that requires certain roles to be filled in order to get itself heard. Such a gospel is absolutely shameless in its filling of these roles.

As pastor in Brenham, I served several years on the local public housing board. Our primary task dealt more with programs for senior citizens who would come to a community center than it did with housing. On this board there was a true cross-section of the community. One of my colleagues was an African American woman whose husband, a funeral director, was one of the leading citizens in the community. As it happened, he died while I was serving on the board with his wife, so I decided to attend the funeral, which was to be held at one of the black Baptist churches. The service was scheduled for 2:00 p.m. I arrived at about 1:55 and the church was overflowing with friends and family members. No matter, I was content to stand in the back foyer, hoping really to be invisible and just pay my own quiet respects. However, before the service began, a woman in a white robe came up to me from behind and motioned for me to follow her, which I did. "Where are we going?" I asked. "We want you to sit down front with the other clergy. You are a minister, right?" I answered that I was but that I was more than content to stand in the foyer by myself. "Oh no," she replied, "we want you to speak." "But I barely knew Mr. Harris," I said. "I am a friend of his wife." "No matter," this emissary replied, "you are a minister and you are to sit with the others, and when it is your time to speak, you can simply preach the gospel. That is what we need to hear today."

How little was her expectation that I was there to speak about my journey of faith; and how much was her expectation that I was to bear witness, with the whole church, to the living Lord who refuses to let death have the last word.[18] That was the question: Could I do that? How embarrassing, I thought, to be brought up front "to sit with the clergy." How eager I was to

18. See Allen McSween's essay in this volume on the pastor-theologian and death.

flee from such an outmoded privilege and make clear my own humble status! Yet, what a gift it was simply to take up the role the church had assigned and, like a donkey that the Lord might have need of, be given the task of bearing this particular Word into this community's midst. So there, in the face of death, I bore witness to him who will let nothing separate us from his love. Such a splendid embarrassment is precisely the way the joy of ministry becomes the joy of serving as a minister of the gospel of Jesus Christ.

"Man's" Chief End: The Freedom of the Minister

In his book, *After Virtue,* Alasdair MacIntyre argues that modernity has produced certain recognizable characters, who embody its prevailing ethos and perpetuate its moral fictions. These characters are, according to MacIntyre, "the aesthete, the therapist, the manager, and the bureaucratic expert."[19] A common feature of all these types of modernity, MacIntyre argues, is that none of them is particularly interested in ends but rather they focus their energies on means. They are all concerned with technique, with measurable effectiveness in terms of some particular task or goal. The reason moral discourse is so difficult if not impossible with these characters is that none of them are characterized by any professed "chief end." Unless one is clear about what human beings are made for, MacIntyre wants to argue, moral discourse becomes impossible and moral choice finally indistinguishable from "I like this rather than that."

MacIntyre ends his book wondering if what is needed is a new St. Benedict, that is, a new rule for life together in the community. Regardless of what one might think of that possibility, MacIntyre's book masterfully rehearses what happens to a culture that is unable to speak anymore of "man's chief end." And though his purpose is not to speak of ministry *per se,* his book points implicitly to the danger of the church's ministry being assimilated to one or more of the characters of modern life. It is startlingly easy, in our day, not to talk about ends.

One of the reasons theology matters so in the parish is that it forces ministers to think about ends. "What is man's chief end?" the Westminster Shorter Catechism asks. "Man's chief end is to glorify God and enjoy Him forever," the answer responds. Though the language is archaic and some

19. Alasdair MacIntyre, *After Virtue* (Notre Dame: University of Notre Dame Press, 1984), p. 73.

would say sexist, one ridicules the content of this answer at great peril. Lesslie Newbigin has written eloquently about what happens in a culture that no longer thinks humanity has this or any particular end. He wonders if "it is possible to believe that concern for minorities, for the poor, for the disabled is important if the fact is that human life is the result of the success of the strong in eliminating the weak."[20] If humanity has no end in the praise of God, then other ends will do. The twentieth century was disastrously full of a number of candidates.

Interestingly, the Shorter Catechism's answer does not say that our chief end is to discover our inner selves or even to gain salvation. Ministry becomes a joy precisely for that reason. Our salvation, strange to relate, and our spiritual journeys are not as important as our culture — and as we ourselves — often think they are. In a culture that is reluctant to talk about humanity's end in God, salvation of self not surprisingly becomes the primary, if often unstated, chief end of human life. We live in a culture that has made an idol of its own salvation, whether religious, political, economic, or cultural. Its particular hell is that it cannot forget self. That is why for all its obsession with salvation, its pursuit is finally joyless.

To hear that our chief end in life is to rejoice in what God has done and is doing in Jesus Christ is to hear a counter-cultural message. It is to be set free from obsession with our own salvation. Indeed, it is to acknowledge the wonderful gift that in Jesus Christ the matter of our salvation has been taken care of ("It is through the cross that joy enters the world"),[21] and we are set free for doxological lives of joy — to see our neighbor (and his or her needs), to rejoice in creation, and to give thanks to God. It was precisely this point that Osip Mandelstam, Russia's greatest poet of the twentieth century and a Jew, identified as being the source of joy for Christians, namely, that because Jesus Christ has redeemed the world, we do not have to pretend that that is our job. We are instead free to "enjoy the world."[22]

The church's ministry has the high calling of delivering this message and reminding the church and the world of this gift, of the glorious freedom

20. Lesslie Newbigin, *The Gospel in a Pluralist Society* (Grand Rapids: Eerdmans, 1989), p. 17.

21. The phrase is from the liturgy of the Orthodox Church's resurrection vigil. Cf. Alexander Schmemann, *For the Life of the World* (Crestwood, NY: St. Vladimir's Seminary Press, 1973), p. 55.

22. Clarence Brown, "Introduction" to Nadezhda Mandelstam's *Hope Against Hope*, trans. Max Hayward (New York: The Modern Library, 1999), p. xxii.

that is ours in Jesus Christ "to not be anxious about our life" (Matt. 6:25) as if our salvation were the point of this story. God's victory in Jesus Christ is the point of this story, and God has made us to participate in that victory, to rejoice in it, glorifying and enjoying God forever. Worshiping idols is exceedingly boring work, especially idols of our own salvation. Rejoicing in the glory of God, however, never fades or grows tiresome. "His greatness is unsearchable" (Ps. 145:3 NRSV).

The splendid embarrassment of ministry is quite simply the joy of unfolding this message. There is nothing more intellectually challenging, psychologically demanding, physically exhausting, and theologically satisfying than ministry. It is hard. It is full of disappointments and griefs and even failures. It takes courage. And hope. And often simple, stupid persistence. It is relentlessly embarrassing in the incommensurability of our gifts to the task set before us. Who would want to walk in Jeremiah's shoes or Paul's or even a small-town pastor's for very long? Who would even pretend to speak the Word of God?

Yet who would love her own emptiness more than God's abundance? Who would prefer the moral righteousness of his own embarrassment and, like a sulking elder brother, refuse the invitation to the joy of the banquet? Who would miss out on the splendor of standing alongside Jeremiah or Paul or some small-town pastor who finds herself having to say a very painful, if utterly evangelical, word to a congregation in that town? What if such joy is what we were made for, indeed, what all creation is made for — that is, to participate in the joy of God's own life? To be sure, as Jeremiah or Paul or that small-town pastor might well remind us, the church's ministry cannot be undertaken without groans, but such groaning cannot be given more weight than it deserves. In the end, to enter upon the church's ministry is to know this splendid embarrassment, this joyful passion[23] that is ministry. It is a venture the church risks, confident in the God who is familiar enough with tears to wipe them away from every eye, the God who in Jesus Christ puts an end to all mourning and crying and pain. This God's glory "does not allow itself to be diminished" or "to be disturbed in its gladness and its expression of gladness" or even "to be checked in the overflowing of its fullness." The God of Jesus Christ "is eternal joy."[24]

23. Cf. Eberhard Busch's introduction to the theology of Karl Barth, titled *The Great Passion*, ed. Darrell L. Guder and Judith J. Guder, trans. G. W. Bromiley (Grand Rapids: Eerdmans, 2004). I have been helped throughout by Busch's insights.

24. Karl Barth, *Church Dogmatics*, II/1, ed. G. W. Bromiley and T. F. Torrance (Edinburgh: T. & T. Clark, 1964), p. 648.

Contributors

Wallace M. Alston Jr. served as pastor of First Presbyterian Church, Wadesboro, North Carolina; First Presbyterian Church, Auburn, Alabama; First Presbyterian Church, Durham, North Carolina; Nassau Presbyterian Church, Princeton, New Jersey; and retired as Director of the Center of Theological Inquiry, Princeton, New Jersey.

Robert C. Ballance served as pastor of First Baptist Church, Spruce Pine, North Carolina; Highland Park Baptist Church, Austin, Texas; and is currently pastor of Heritage Baptist Church, Cartersville, Georgia.

Kenneth H. Carter Jr. served as pastor of the Smithtown Charge, East Bend, North Carolina; associate pastor, Christ United Methodist Church, Greensboro, North Carolina; pastor, St. Timothy's United Methodist Church, Greensboro, North Carolina; pastor, Mt. Tabor United Methodist Church, Winston-Salem, North Carolina; and is currently pastor of the Providence United Methodist Church, Charlotte, North Carolina.

Brant S. Copeland served as pastor of Altavista Presbyterian Church, Altavista, Virginia, and is currently pastor of the First Presbyterian Church, Tallahassee, Florida.

Richard R. Crocker served as pastor of Presbyterian churches in Ripley, Tennessee, and Montclair, New Jersey; Dean of College Life, Elizabethtown College; College Chaplain, Bates College; College Chaplain and currently Dean of the Tucker Foundation, Dartmouth College, Hanover, New Hampshire.

Thomas W. Currie III served as pastor of Brenham Presbyterian Church, Brenham, Texas; First Presbyterian Church, Kerrville, Texas; and is currently Dean of Union-PSCE at Charlotte, North Carolina.

James L. Haddix served as pastor of the Congregational Church, Temple, New Hampshire, and is currently pastor of All Souls Church (Congregational, United Church of Christ), Bangor, Maine, and adjunct professor of Old Testament at Bangor Theological Seminary, Bangor, Maine.

Scott Hoezee served as pastor of the Second Christian Reformed Church, Fremont, Michigan; Calvin Christian Reformed Church, Grand Rapids, Michigan; and is currently Director of the Center for Excellence in Preaching, Calvin Theological Seminary, Grand Rapids, Michigan.

Cynthia A. Jarvis served as associate pastor of the Westminster Presbyterian Church, Wooster, Ohio; assistant professor of ministry and director of field education, McCormick Theological Seminary, Chicago, Illinois; associate pastor, Nassau Presbyterian Church, Princeton, New Jersey; and is currently pastor of The Presbyterian Church of Chestnut Hill, Philadelphia, Pennsylvania.

Albert H. Keller served as a member of the Faculté de Théologie, Université Libre du Congo, Africa; campus pastor, University of Charleston, Charleston, South Carolina; professor of bioethics and the medical humanities, College of Medicine, Medical University of South Carolina; and is currently pastor of the Circular Congregational Church, Charleston, South Carolina.

Rebecca Kuiken served as pastor of the Stone Church Presbyterian Church, San Jose, California; interim associate pastor, Lafayette-Orinda Presbyterian Church, Lafayette, California; First Presbyterian Church, Oakland, California; Director of Communications, San Francisco Theological Seminary, San Anselmo, California; a consultant, Leading Edge Associates, San Jose, California; and is currently Director of the Interfaith Council on Race, Religion, Economic and Social Justice (South Bay), San Jose, California.

Allen C. McSween Jr. served as pastor of the Meadowthorpe Presbyterian Church, Lexington, Kentucky; Trinity Presbyterian Church, Laurinburg,

North Carolina; The Presbyterian Church of Bowling Green, Bowling Green, Kentucky; and is currently pastor of the Fourth Presbyterian Church, Greenville, South Carolina.

W. Rush Otey III served as Chaplain, Davidson College, Davidson, North Carolina; assistant pastor, Davidson College Presbyterian Church; Director, Uniting Campus Ministry, Louisiana State University, Baton Rouge, Louisiana; pastor, St. Andrews Presbyterian Church, Tucker, Georgia; First Presbyterian Church, Pensacola, Florida; and is currently pastor of the Selwyn Avenue Presbyterian Church, Charlotte, North Carolina.

V. Bruce Rigdon served as pastor of the Lumen Christi Presbyterian Church, Lisle, Illinois; professor of church history, McCormick Theological Seminary, Chicago, Illinois; pastor, Grosse Pointe Presbyterian Church, Grosse Pointe, Michigan; professor and president, Ecumenical Theological Seminary, Chicago; and in retirement serves as pastor, Siasconset Union Chapel, a summer chapel in Nantucket, Massachusetts.

John M. Stapleton served as pastor of the First United Methodist Church, Easley, South Carolina; Trinity United Methodist Church, North Myrtle Beach, South Carolina; Washington Street United Methodist Church, Columbia, South Carolina, where he also taught preaching at Lutheran Theological Seminary; and is currently theologian-in-residence at St. John's United Methodist Church, Aiken, South Carolina.

Kristine Suna-Koro served as pastor of the Latvian Evangelical Lutheran Church Abroad in Great Britain and Germany; pastor, St. John's Latvian Lutheran Church, Philadelphia, Pennsylvania; vicar of the Eastern Division of the Latvian Evangelical Lutheran Church in America; and is currently in the Ph.D. program in liturgical theology at Emory University, Atlanta, Georgia.

V. F. (Bud) Thompson served as pastor of the Bethany Lutheran Church, Dutton, Montana; Our Savior Lutheran Church, Pinehurst, Idaho; Bethlehem Lutheran Church, Spokane, Washington; and is currently teaching New Testament at Gonzaga University, Spokane, Washington.

Anita R. Warner is pastor of the Advent Lutheran Church, Morgan Hill, California.